Pornography
ON TRIAL

Pornography
ON TRIAL

*A Handbook with
Cases, Laws, and Documents*

Thomas C. Mackey

A B C ⬤ C L I O

Santa Barbara, California • Denver, Colorado • Oxford, England

Library of Congress Cataloging-in-Publication Data
Mackey, Thomas C., 1956–
  Pornography on trial : a handbook with cases, laws, and documents / Thomas C. Mackey.
      p.   cm.
Includes bibliographical references and index.
   ISBN 1-57607-275-4 (hardcover ; acid-free paper)
   1. Pornography—Law and legislation—United States—Cases.   2. Obscenity (Law)—United States—Cases.   I. Title.
KF9444.A7 M33   2002
345.73'0274—dc21   2002011718

07060504030201 10987654321

ABC-CLIO, Inc.
130 Cremona Drive, P.O. Box 1911
Santa Barbara, California 93116-1911

This book is printed on acid-free paper.
Manufactured in the United States of America

Contents

Series Foreword

The volumes in the *On Trial* series explore the many ways in which the U.S. legal and political system has approached a wide range of complex and divisive legal issues over time—and in the process defined the current state of the law and politics on these issues. The intent is to give students and other general readers a framework for understanding how the law in all its various forms—constitutional, statutory, judicial, political, and customary—has shaped and reshaped the world in which we live today.

At the core of each volume in the series is a common proposition: that in certain key areas of American public life, we as a people and a nation are "on trial" as we struggle to cope with the contradictions, conflicts, and disparities within our society, politics, and culture. Who should decide if and when a woman can have an abortion? What rights, if any, should those with a different sexual orientation be able to claim under the Constitution? Is voting a basic right of citizenship, and if so, under what rules should we organize this right—especially when the application of any organizing rules inevitably results in excluding some citizens from the polls? And what about the many inconsistencies and conflicts associated with racial tensions in the country? These are just some of the complex and controversial issues that we as a people and a nation are struggling to answer—and must answer if we are to achieve an orderly and stable society. For the answers we find to these disputes shape the essence of who we are—as a people, a community, and a political system.

The concept of being "on trial" also has a second meaning fundamental to this series: the process of litigating important issues in a court of law. Litigation is an essential part of how we settle our differences and make choices as we struggle with the problems that confront us as a people and a nation. In the 1830s, Alexis de Tocqueville in his book *Democracy in America* noted, "There is hardly a political question in the United States which does not sooner or later turn into a judicial one" (De Tocqueville, 270). This insight is as true today as it was in the 1830s. In *The Litigious Society* Jethro K. Lieberman notes: "To express amazement at American litigiousness is akin to professing astonishment at learning that the roots of most Americans lie in other lands. We have been a litigious nation as we have been an immigrant one. Indeed, the two are related" (Lieberman 1983, 13). Arriving in the United States with different backgrounds, customs, and lifestyle preferences, we inevitably clashed as our contrasting visions of life in America—its culture, society, and politics—collided. And it was to the courts and the law that we turned as a neutral forum for peaceably working out these differences. For, in the United States at least, it is the courthouse that provides the anvil on which our personal, societal, and political problems are hammered out.

The volumes in this series therefore take as their central purpose the important task of exploring the various ways—good and bad, effective and ineffective, complex and simple—that litigation in the courts has shaped the evolution of particular legal controversies for which we as a people are "on trial." And, more importantly, the volumes do all this in a manner accessible to the general reader seeking to comprehend the topic as a whole.

These twin goals—analytical and educational—shape the structure and layout of the volumes in the series. Each book consists of two parts. The first provides an explanatory essay in four chapters. Chapter One introduces the issues, controversies, events, and participants associated with the legal controversy at hand. Chapter Two explores the social, economic, political, and/or historical background to this topic. Chapter Three describes in detail the various court decisions and actions that have shaped the current status of the legal controversy under examination. In some cases this will be done through a close examination of a few representative cases; in others by a broader but less detailed narrative of the course of judicial action. Chapter Four discusses the impact of these cases on American law—their doctrinal legacy—as well as on American society—their historical, sociological, and political legacy.

Part Two, in turn, provides selective supplementary materials designed to help readers to more fully comprehend the topics covered in the chapters of Part One. First are documents aimed at helping the reader better appreciate both the issues and the process by which adjudication shaped these matters. Selected documents might include court opinions (excerpted or whole), interviews, newspaper accounts, and/or selected secondary essays. Next comes an alphabetically formatted glossary providing entries on the people, laws, and, terms, and concepts important to an understanding of the topic. A chronology next provides the reader an easily referenced listing of the major developments covered in the book, and a table of cases lists the major court decisions cited. And lastly, an annotated bibliography describes the key works in the field, directing a reader seeking a more detailed examination of the topic to the appropriate sources.

In closing, as you read the books in this series, keep in mind the purposefully controversial nature of the topics covered within. The authors in the series have not chosen easy nor agreeable topics to explore. Much of what you read may trouble you, and should. Yet it is precisely these sorts of contentious topics that need the most historical analysis and scrutiny. For it is here that we are still "on trial"—and all too often, as regards these matters, the jury is still out.

Charles L. Zelden
Ft. Lauderdale, Florida

Preface

It is my purpose in preparing this volume to provide students, through its text and documents, a sense of the historical development of the legal control of obscenity and pornography, and a sense of the complexity of the issue at various moments in the course of Anglo-American history. This work is an intellectual introduction to the problems and possibilities of public policymaking regarding pornography. Although allegedly pornographic and obscene materials have been on trial for offending sensibilities and good morals, this volume suggests that what is on trial in antipornography litigations is the level of tolerance in society at a particular time for questionable books, painting, prints, magazines, films, cable television programming, and other images. As students assess the history of antipornography litigation, they are also assessing the shifting social and cultural values of American society over time.

Few social problems in modern American society can generate the intense debate and emotions that obscenity can. On one side of the debate are those who find any hint of the risqué or indecent too much to bear. On the other side are those who want absolutely no legal restrictions placed on allegedly obscene and indecent materials. As a result, public policymakers are either accused of doing too little to halt the circulation of obscenity in the culture or of being too aggressive in restricting obscenity in the culture. As the most recent case law suggests, technology has not helped to solve this perhaps intractable problem of obscenity; instead, it has complicated matters. Suggestive images and texts have become ubiquitous in American culture, being used to sell or promote a wide variety of products and services. As a result, popular sensitivities have changed about what is appropriate and what is not. As this volume suggests, the conventions guiding what is and what is not "obscene" are more an evolving process of judicial definition and cultural reflection than a set of hard-and-fast rules. As a result, those seeking an absolute resolution of this social problem one way or the other will continue to be frustrated by the common-law, case-by-case development of obscenity jurisprudence. If the reader of this volume achieves an appreciation of that incremental process over time, then I will have succeeded.

Acknowledgments

Although I acknowledge the assistance of many in the production of this volume, I accept any errors as my own.

First, I am grateful to Alicia Merritt at ABC-CLIO for her interest in my book and in the topic generally, and for gently but firmly keeping me on task. In this and other respects, I have enjoyed good fortune that all authors should have. Second, I thank the series editor, Charles Zelden, who is both an outstanding editor and a good friend: His eagle eye, penchant for asking hard questions, and invariable patience with my occasional tardiness improved each successive draft. Another careful reader of the early drafts who steered me away from the shoals of disaster is Prof. Claudine Ferrell of Mary Washington College. Her comments, always supportive and good-humored, helped refine my writing and thinking on these issues. I thank the students in my Constitutional and Legal History classes at the University of Louisville and the law students at the Brandeis School of Law for serving as a sounding board, listening to my interpretations, and punching holes in my arguments. I thank Rita Hettinger and Lee Keeling, current staff members in the History Department at Louisville, for covering for me when I was writing this book (and letting my paperwork as department chair slide). I am grateful also to Prof. William E. Nelson and his family for welcoming me into their home in the summers and, in exchange for yard work, offering me their warmth, friendship, and cross-examination about my "real" work. I thank my sister Julie, her husband Hank Badger, and their daughter Bess, as well as my father Howard Mackey, for their great tolerance of this latest writing project and the infrequency of my visits. (Perhaps now that the book is finished, Dad and I can sneak away to scare the fish in the lower Chesapeake Bay.) My largest debt of gratitude, though, is to Kelly Kane, who two and a half years ago joined me in Louisville on a permanent basis, and in doing so improved my scholarship, my life, and me.

Thomas C. Mackey
Louisville, Kentucky

Part One

1
Introduction

Prostitution's red-light districts have faded from public consciousness as streetwalking in most cities in the United States has been brought under control and largely marginalized. Similarly, as the consumption of distilled alcohol has diminished, most have come to view alcoholism as a familiar and unexciting social problem. But a related social problem, growing out of the same social and personal forces as the others, still occasionally grips the public's attention—pornography. Pornography and obscene materials challenge Americans and their social and legal traditions in ways that the prostitution and alcohol abuse never did. Although drink and prostitution are easy to identify, pornography raises difficult questions. What is "obscene"? What is "pornography"? More important, whose standard should guide public policy about this social problem and its regulation? Compounding the difficulties inherent in defining and deciding what is and is not pornographic, attempts to control offensive published materials raise First Amendment issues about what sorts of materials are protected forms of political speech (and, therefore, not liable to be restricted, regulated, or suppressed). Identifying what may be or may not be pornographic, or even deciding who should make decisions about what is or is not pornographic, is difficult and vexing. The number of potential "correct" answers is almost as great as the vast number of those asking the questions. Ultimately, obscenity is in the eye of the beholder. The intrinsic difficulty of defining the obscene or pornographic was implicit in Associate Justice Potter Stewart's declaration in *Jacobellis v. Ohio* (378 U.S. 184 [1964]), "I know it when I see it." This famous statement nicely encapsulates the frustrations of policymakers, legislators, and judges; however, it fails to provide any guideline for the crafting of public policy controlling pornographic materials in a modern, secular, pluralist society.

Pornography is not a new social problem. Although pornography can be found in new forms and formats such as VHS tapes and DVD disks, and on a seemingly endless list of Internet sites, pornography is an age-old cultural phenomenon that has been debated and fought over throughout human history. From the ancient world to the present, what is and what is not considered "obscene" has varied according to the historical context—the values of the particular time, culture, and society. The historical context, which is embodied in the developed legal, social, moral, political, and economic values of an era, provides the template upon which public policies regarding social problems are formed. This context is especially true of policies on obscenity. For example, books banned as pornographic or obscene in one era might be hailed as great works of art in another era, or in a different culture of the same period. Historical context informs and shapes the norms of every society and every period, and only by uncovering the core values of that society and period can historians and students begin to understand policies on topics such as pornography.

Pornography as Sex, Sex as Pornography

Of course, part of the problem of dealing with pornography and obscenity is the subject they illustrate—sex. Until relatively recently in Anglo-American culture, sex and sexuality have been hidden, even forbidden, topics. Respectable persons of good character, especially women, simply did not address the issue openly or publicly. Although sex and sexuality could be and were obliquely referred to or indirectly alluded to in literature, mainstream music, and popular culture, the traditional social taboos stigmatized or forbade their direct mention or graphic depiction. Yet today sexual topics and literary descriptions of sexual encounters flourish to a degree that would have been unimaginable in the nineteenth century, as authors such as Thomas Hardy, Jane Eyre, and Charles Dickens have been replaced by authors such as Erica Jong, Jacqueline Suzanne, Arthur Miller, and the more serious but still shocking James Joyce.

During the latter half of the twentieth century, social values and sensitivities in the United States dramatically changed. Concerns about the power of government at all levels to suppress and limit creative and artistic expression developed into an ever expanding, hyperinflated rights consciousness within American society. With the rise of mass marketing, sex was increasingly exploited to sell products, and a large segment of the society gradually became numb to sexual images that would have scandalized consumers in the first half of the century. Today's commonplace images of scantily clad women in fashion and news magazines, employed to sell everything from lingerie to automobiles, would have caused a sensation and been suppressed in the nineteenth century. Furthermore, the "men's magazine" so widely available today was the underground "skin magazine" of the early twentieth century. This same phenomenon of today's norm being yesterday's suppressed issue can be seen in popular movies: Scenes that would have been banned as obscene in the 1960s have become commonplace, and innumerable X-rated videos are widely available for purchase or rent.

The mass production of cheap paperback books and magazine made obscene printed materials affordable to the average person. Although skin magazines and picture books had existed prior to the middle of the twentieth century, it was only after midcentury that a magazine like *Playboy,* featuring seminude or nude women, could be openly marketed and purchased. Although the sexual images in such magazines were more explicit than those found in advertising and the "legitimate" media, the differences were minor. Gradually, what had once seemed scandalous came to be seen as merely risqué. In the new moral and sexual world of the latter twentieth century, Hugh Hefner, the founder of *Playboy,* amassed a fortune by creating an aura of sophistication around late-night parties and scantily clad women. This business would have shocked and outraged American society ten years earlier, and it did shock and outrage a large part of society in the 1950s. Yet *Playboy* and other magazines of its ilk were not completely repressed as obscene; instead, by the end of the century an inversion of values had occurred. What had been stigmatized—not only the public flaunting of sexuality but also the consumption of alcohol, tobacco, and other taboo substances in group revelry—became socially accepted norms. This inversion of values—this collapse of the old system of values amid the emergence of a new values system—provides the cultural context for the story told here. The new values system continues to evolve as the courts struggle to craft and clarify the law on trades that profit from sex. Despite the multiplication of magazines like *Playboy,* Americans still have difficulty confronting sex and sexuality, particularly in public fora. American law and jurisprudence reflect the general unease in dealing with such issues.

Individual Rights versus Communal Responsibility

Because pornography deals with sex and sexuality, the regulation or suppression of pornography raises the issue of individual or group values and tastes, versus the responsibility, even duty, of state and federal governments to oppose vice and encourage positive social behavior. Problems arise when it becomes necessary for government and the courts to decide where to draw the line between appropriate and inappropriate images. One person might view the statue of the nude David by Michelangelo as an example of high art during the Renaissance. Another might see it as an overly graphic depiction of the nude male form that poses a moral threat to society's standards and ought not be seen, especially by children. Although some might trust in individual "common sense" and "good taste" to govern such matters, history suggests that artists and innovative thinkers throughout the ages have actively sought to shock the sensibilities of their contemporaries, and flouted social standards. More conservative social forces, in turn, often have resisted adapting their views on such matters, remained stalwart even in the face of general social and cultural change. This area of competing social values is where the dilemma for government policy arises.

In the United States, the state and federal levels of government share responsibility for promoting the common weal; but just as government authority can be wielded to promote the good society, it also can be wielded to repress social and cultural innovation. Deciding where the line ought to be drawn between the appropriate and the inappropriate has bedeviled social reformers, legislators, and judges for the past two centuries. Both the opponents and the defenders of materials deemed pornographic have turned to the law, and to legal institutions such as the courts, as the forum best suited to achieving their social goals.

The defenders of pornography turn to the First Amendment's protection of free speech and expression. Basing their arguments on the fact that many ideas initially censored by the Anglo-American tradition have come in time to be seen as fundamental to individual liberty, they contend that an individual's right to view allegedly obscene materials is constitutionally protected. Adults ought to be allowed to decide for themselves what books, articles, movies, or shows they will see, say the defenders of pornography, adopting a libertarian stance (at least on this issue). Government should have no role in deciding what they may read or view.

Opponents of pornography likewise have enlisted the law in pursuit of their goal of restricting the obscene and the profane. Anti-pornography interest groups have filed lawsuits and have lobbied for new local, state, or national statutes restricting allegedly obscene materials, thereby forcing judges, particularly those at the federal level, to decide what is obscene and pornographic and what is not.

The Effect of Rights Consciousness

Recently, the state of Utah has approached the definition of what is obscene in a new fashion. Making a definition is difficult because decisions on obscenity often encounter the charge of censorship and certainly the Anglo-American history of obscenity has seen its share of book censorship. In January 2001, Utah created and funded a new office in its state government: "obscenity and pornography complaints ombudsman." This position pays $75,000 a year. A 41-year-old lawyer, Paula J. Houston, was the first appointee to the position. As the *New York Times* reported, Utah has given her the responsibility of helping local Utah "communities determine their own standards for controlling sexually explicit materials and activities without violating the First Amendment" (*New York Times,* March 24, 2001, A8). In a state where 70 percent of the population belongs to the same religious group—the Latter-Day Saints, or Mormons—diversity is not a pressing issue. Houston is reportedly counting on her Mormon background to assist her in her new duties as Utah's "porn czar."

Establishing community standards for regulating obscenity is a good deal easier in Utah, with its relatively homogeneous population, than in the state just west of Utah: California. California is much larger and has a far more diverse economy and population. It is likely that materials that are legally available in California will be banned and suppressed in Utah. Adult-oriented businesses and even public libraries will have to abide by the letter of the laws and regulations established by Congress, the federal judiciary, and the Utah legislature and courts in order to avoid prosecution for obscenity. If events do take such a course in Utah, then other small and relatively homogeneous states may follow its example. In that case, we will see a new round of reform efforts aimed at defining obscenity as a fundamental social problem and at crafting new public policies and responses to regulate and suppress it.

Because the appointment of a "porn czar" in Utah occurred so recently, information on further developments will have to be gleaned from newspapers such as the *New York Times* and from World Wide Web sites such as cnn.com, usatoday.com, and other on-line media sources. However, in order to understand these current events, we will need to know the historical context. In that regard, there is no substitute for reading and assessing the primary sources of obscenity jurisprudence, such as the relevant state and federal statutes and judicial decisions discussed in the following chapters.

The task facing the courts—that of drawing the line between the legal and illegal, the appropriate and the obscene—has become ever more difficult over the course of the twentieth century, with the increasing breakdown of traditional morality and the increasing ethnic and cultural diversity of populations. Deciding upon and trying to enforce one set of morals in a society that is deeply divided by race, sexuality, politics, and economic status has proven enormously difficult. Cultural pluralism—although it is viewed by many in the United States as a strength—complicates, and may even completely prevent, the definition of appropriate modes of behavior and forms of self-expression. Pluralism implies toleration of a wide variety of beliefs and behaviors; but how far can toleration be pushed without negating all standards of appropriateness? Homosexuality is highly offensive to many in the United States who consider themselves Christians, especially to members of fundamentalist denominations. Asking such citizens to tolerate homosexuality is appropriate, because the United States is a secular society. But should part of the taxes paid by those Christian citizens support allegedly obscene or profane art depicting homosexual acts, via funding by the National Endowment for the Arts or the state humanities and arts councils? Americans do not live in a world of total justice; lines have to drawn and decisions made about the hard issues of obscene materials and pornography. How Americans have made those decisions, working within the Anglo-American legal tradition, is a key part of the story told in this book.

Another approach to understanding the current challenge of pornography in the United States is to take account of the legal context within which the debate over pornography and obscenity occurs. By the late twentieth century, Americans had developed a high degree of what scholars call "rights consciousness." Rights consciousness encompasses an understanding and appreciation of the fact that every public policy affects some group or groups of citizens positively and others negatively. Public policies ought then to be crafted with an eye toward achieving the desired policy goal without infringing upon or ignoring the rights of those who may be negatively affected. Growing out of the nation's spotty record of the treatment of black Americans in all aspects of life from voting rights to fair housing rights to civil rights, by the end of the twentieth century "rights" had expanded to include previously neglected groups of Americans such as the disabled, and previously undiscovered rights such as entitlement to social security. This sensitivity to individual and group rights reverberates throughout the society and legal culture. In such a rights-conscious society, wherein interest groups are always sniffing the wind for threats of censorship and other infringements on their freedom, any clear-cut definition of, say, the obscene, becomes blurred. A kind of libertarianism has become the rule in American law, in which political speech is protected by the First Amendment, and obscenity, although not protected, is assigned a loose definition that shifts with the passage of time. Therefore, persons or interest groups wishing to battle pornography bear the burden of demonstrating that the products they seek to ban are truly obscene and not legitimate books, articles, pamphlets, or art objects protected by the First Amendment. This standard is a difficult hurdle to clear.

Controversies about pornography have arisen, as legal controversies always do, on the fringes of society, and yet have strongly challenged the courts and established legal doctrines. For example, in the 1991 United States Supreme Court case *Michael Barnes v. Glen Theatre, Inc.*, 501 U.S. 560, the justices confronted the question of whether nude dancing was a form of "speech" and expression, and if so, whether it was protected by the First Amendment freedom of speech clause? Although in this case the Supreme Court decided that nude dancing was not protected speech, what is interesting is that such an argument could be made, taken seriously, and reach the highest court in the land. In previous eras in U.S. history, such behavior would have been regulated or suppressed by local authorities; but in the current rights-conscious society, suppression or regulation of behavior is not so easy. Litigants often ask legislators and judges to balance the needs of society on the one hand and the individual's or group's rights (in this example, all nude dancers and their "right" to earn a living) on the other hand. On its face, this issue may appear trivial. On closer inspection, though, larger principles are at stake, such as the protection of individual and group rights against infringement by others. The matter is further complicated by the involvement of various levels of bureaucracy and government. Such is the policymaking arena within which U.S. legislators, interest groups, and judges seek to deal with the social problem of morally offensive materials.

Pornography and obscenity are old and contentious issues in Anglo-American culture. They challenge the culture and courts to decide where to draw the line between acceptable and unacceptable materials. It is the purpose of this volume to provide a sense of the historical development of the problem of pornography and obscenity and a sense of the complexity of the issue at various points in Anglo-American history. This work is an intellectual introduction to the problems and possibilities of public policy making on pornography. Although allegedly pornographic and obscene materials often have been on trial for offending popular sensibilities and good morals, this volume suggests that what is actually on trial in anti-pornography litigations is the level of tolerance in society at the given moment in time for books, paintings, prints, magazines, films, and images that diverge from norms of taste. As readers become acquainted with the history of antipornography litigation, they also will become more aware of the shifting social and cultural values of American society over time.

The subjectivity of all concepts of "appropriateness" has long frustrated policymakers and antipornography reformers, who have been unable to come up with definitive, permanent answers to questions as fundamental as the definition of pornography, let alone what action, if any, should be taken with regard to materials found by the courts to be obscene. Should such materials be regulated, limited, or completely suppressed? How reformers and public authorities have employed the law in grappling with these questions is the subject of the following chapters.

References and Further Reading

Alexander, Donald. 1989. *The Politics of Pornography.* Chicago: University of Chicago Press.

Burnham, John C. 1993. *Bad Habits: Drinking, Smoking, Taking Drugs, Gambling, Sexual Misbehavior, and Swearing in American History.* New York: New York University Press.

Clor, Harry. 1969. *Obscenity and Public Morality.* Chicago: University of Chicago Press.

Easton, Susan M. 1994. *The Problem of Pornography: Regulation and the Right to Free Speech.* London: Routledge.

Ernst, Morris L., and Alan U. Schwartz. 1964. *Censorship: The Search for the Obscene.* New York: Macmillan.

Kobylka, Joseph F. 1991. *The Politics of Obscenity: Group Litigation in the Time of Legal Change.* Westport, CT: Greenwood Press.

Schauer, Frederick F. 1976. *The Law of Obscenity.* Washington, DC: Bureau of National Affairs.

2

Historical Background

Although much of the debate over the legal control of pornography (called "obscenity" when involved in litigation) occurred in the twentieth century, the roots of this debate lie deep in the British and American legal traditions. This chapter provides an overview of the British legal approach to controlling objectionable materials and of the subsequent evolution of legal tradition and case law in America from the colonial period to the 1930s. This chapter also introduces the important role played by privately funded antipornography interest groups and by reformers such as the U.S. Post Office's special agent Anthony Comstock in shaping the pornography debate. Their successes and failures set the stage for the burst of judicial activity on the question of obscenity in the latter half of the twentieth century, which is the core of this book.

The historical record examined here shows that local and state officials, drawing on the received traditions of British common law and motivated to action by ever growing political pressure from civic reformers, pursued a policy of suppression of pornographic materials from the eighteenth century through the 1930s. Local and state courts, in turn, buttressed this policy with judicial doctrines that sought to protect the weak from the "moral threats" posed by such offensive materials. Yet, ironically, the imprecision of these eighteenth- and nineteenth-century statutory and judicial standards led to a sweeping reassessment of the law of obscenity in the last two-thirds of the twentieth century—a reassessment whose evolving content undermined the very concept of a single standard for identifying obscenity and resulted in the current less protective and highly contested obscenity standard.

Control of Objectionable Materials
under British Common Law

In England as elsewhere in Europe, church officials traditionally policed public morality. Prior to the Protestant Reformation in the sixteenth century, the Roman Catholic Church oversaw private morals and public behavior, acting in the interest—as was then widely believed—of preserving immortal human souls jeopardized by immorality. Obscenity and pornography were sinful and immoral, and punishing sinful and immoral behavior was the responsibility of the churches. The perpetrators were expected to reform their wayward behavior under church supervision and control. Petty sinners typically confessed their infractions to the priests and were made to do penance for them. More serious offenders—heretics, adulterers, and blasphemers—were prosecuted in the church courts, which typically meted out harsher punishments.

So events stood for hundreds of years. However, spurred on by the invention of the printing press and the spread of the printed word in Europe, the Protestant Reformation soon changed the Catholic Church's central role as the locus of oversight of individual morals. Personal morality increasingly became the responsibility of local religious congregations or of the individual. Before long, the diversity of opinion within these communities undermined the universal definition of sin, upon which church supervision of morals was based. To protect the community's interest in establishing the public peace and ensuring public morality, secular authorities became more involved in defining and prosecuting moral offenses. In England, King Henry VIII initiated this shift in 1536 by establishing a state-sanctioned church independent of the Roman papacy (the Church of England, also known as the Anglican Church). Many other European nations embraced various other Protestant denominations. Of course, these changes did not occur overnight but took place gradually, over decades and centuries. From today's vantage point, governmental oversight of individual and public morals is one of the most important albeit unintended effects of the Protestant Reformation.

The transfer of moral jurisdiction from the universal church to individuals, local communities, and states was accompanied by the increasingly common assumption that government had a positive duty to guard the public's morals through its power to make and enforce the law. In practice, this duty took the form of the common law's regulation of taverns, inns, and public houses, and its suppression of disorderly houses of prostitution. (Common law in Great Britain and the United States is the body of law created by judicial decisions, which reflects and embodies the customs and traditions of the locality and the state.) The duty to oversee public morality translated into the need to control obscene books and other offensive materials held to undermine the community by their inherent threat to public morality and decency. Control of such material in England and Great Britain became the responsibility of local authorities, who prosecuted its creators under the common-law charge of "obscene libel."

Throughout the late eighteenth and the nineteenth centuries, magistrates and local justices of the peace actually concerned themselves little with policing such material, despite the flourishing trade in "underground" books, pamphlets, and woodprints across Britain. A noted diarist of seventeenth-century London, Samuel Pepys, wrote in an entry dated February 8, 1668, that he had visited his local bookseller and discovered the small book *L'Escholle des Filles*. He found it "the most bawdy, lewd book I ever saw." Concerned lest he be seen with this book, Pepys wrote, he had purchased a copy with a plain binding. He planned anyway to burn the book after reading it. In an entry made the next day, he reported that he indeed had burned the book the very same night (Latham and Matthews, eds. 1976, 21–22, 57–59).

Pepys's experience was not an isolated case. A healthy market existed in Britain and France for cheaply printed, luridly written small books and pamphlets, many of which included graphic descriptions of sexual encounters involving priests and monks. Such tales had the dual purpose of titillating readers and of undermining the popular authority of the Roman Catholic clergy. They were implicitly political in their anti-Catholicism and explicitly sexual in their content. This mixture of political and moral messages bedeviled legislators and judges who later sought to craft policies regulating such "obscene" materials.

Prior to the middle of the nineteenth century, prosecutions of obscene materials in Great Britain rested for the most part with local authorities. Direct governmental prosecution and censorship of obscene materials occurred under the common law protecting the general welfare of the realm, which was based on such principles as the presumption of innocence until guilt is proven, and the ancient right of trial by a jury of one's peers. Under common law, local justices of the peace could summarily deal with obscene materials. More serious offenses—for example, those involving assault or grand theft—were dealt with in quarter sessions in Great Britain (and local district courts in the American colonies and later states). Prosecutions on grounds of obscenity at first occurred only occasionally and generated little public concern. They also generated little consensus on the proper definition of obscene materials and whether the law had any role to play in limiting their production and dissemination. For example, an English judge in 1708 decided that a questionable book was not indictable under common law, because if an offense had occurred, it was a spiritual offense and not an offense recognized by the secular courts. Yet another English judge in 1725 decided that Richard Curl had committed the common-law crime of publishing obscenity with his pamphlet entitled *Venus in the Cloister, or the Nun in Her Smock.* Although several other similar prosecutions occurred, the issue of obscenity was almost always handled by the local courts, employing the local interpretation of the common law.

This decentralized approach to controlling obscene materials lasted in Great Britain until 1857, when Parliament enacted the Obscene Publications Act. Passed at the urging of reformers who feared that immoral literature threatened the health and morality of society, this law, also known as Lord Campbell's Act (after the member of Parliament who introduced the bill), was Parliament's first statutory effort to regulate obscene publications. Lord Campbell's proposal recognized the common-law offense of "obscene libel" and sought to bolster the restrictions against obscenity by raising the offense to the level of statutory law. Enforcement of these new antiobscenity provisions would remain at the local level, where justices of the peace and magistrates could maintain surveillance over their jurisdictions, but under the oversight of Parliament. The sponsors of this statute entitled "An act for more effectually preventing the sale of obscene books, pictures, prints, and other articles" justified its passage by stating, "It is expedient to give additional powers for the suppression of the trade in obscene books, prints, drawings, and other obscene articles" (Obscene Publications [Lord Campbell's] Act, 20 and 21 Vict., c 83 [1857]).

Given the context of mid-Victorian-era culture, which is reputed to have valued high standards of public morality, it is perhaps surprising that the Lord Chancellor of the time, Lord Campbell, believed the bill necessary. On the floor of the House of Lords, Lord Campbell defended his bill, arguing that it aimed to curb only those works "written for the single purpose of corrupting the morals of youth and of a nature calculated to shock the common feelings of decency in a well regulated mind" (146 *Hansard Parliamentary Debates,* 3rd Series, 1857, p. 327). As the details of the statute made clear, Parliament created with this act no new offense at common law but rather provided local magistrates new powers to confiscate allegedly obscene materials: If the magistrate found the confiscated materials to be obscene, then he could order the destruction of those materials. To be prosecuted under the statute, one did not have to sell dubious materials but merely to be discovered with them in one's possession, or to make them available for others to view or read. If the magistrate found the confiscated materials unobjectionable, then the materials would be returned to their owner. However, the grant to local authorities of sweeping new powers of search and seizure evoked opposition from members of the legal press.

In the parlance of the nineteenth century, Lord Campbell's bill was a police measure to better protect the health, safety, welfare, and morals of the society. Aimed at the cheap pornography in circulation, this act made such obscene materials subject to seizure and confiscation because of the moral and social threat they posed to society. As Member of Parliament John Roebuck stated the issue, Lord Campbell's bill was "an attempt to make people virtuous by Act of Parliament" (Hunter et al. 1993, 63). Passage of Lord Campbell's law was only a first step in the fight against obscene materials. Up next was the statute's interpretation by the courts. For although the statute made clear local government's powers to combat obscenity, it did little to narrow the definition of "obscene publication." That step came in the leading nineteenth-century case on obscenity, *Regina v. Benjamin Hicklin* (1868). *Hicklin* gave rise to the first in a series of judicial tests of obscenity that emerged in England and the United States during the late nineteenth and the early twentieth centuries.

The *Hicklin* Test

Arising to Great Britain's highest court (the Queen's Bench) from a prosecution under Lord Campbell's Act in 1867, *Regina v. Hicklin* involved an anti-Catholic pamphlet sold and circulated by the Protestant Electoral Union. This group sought to "protest against those teachings and practices which are un-English, immoral, and blasphemous, to maintain the Protestantism of the Bible and the liberty of England." Further, the Protestant Electoral Union supported electing as members of Parliament men who shared their anti-Catholic sentiments and who wished to "expose and defeat the deep-laid machinations of the Jesuits, and resist grants of money for Romish purposes" (*Regina v. Hicklin,* Law Reporter 3 Queen's Bench 360 [1868]). To these ends they had published a pamphlet entitled "The Confessional Unmasked," which purported to reveal the depravity of the Catholic priesthood and its abuse of the confessional. Pursuant to Lord Campbell's Act, a complaint was made to two justices of the peace, who issued a warrant for the seizure of the pamphlet. Constables then seized 252 copies, and the justices ordered them destroyed as provided for under the statute. An appeals court blocked the destruction of the pamphlets pending a decision by the Queen's Bench on whether the pamphlets were obscene under the statute.

After hearing arguments and taking briefs in the case, Chief Justice Sir Alexander James Edmund Cockburn delivered the unanimous opinion of the Queen's Bench. He began his ruling by supporting the decision of the justices of the peace to seize and condemn the pamphlet as a violation of Lord Campbell's Act. The Queen's Bench found the pamphlet obscene, and "by reason of the obscene matter in it, calculated to produce a pernicious effect in depraving and debauching the minds of the persons into whose hands it might come." Further, the court held that the argument that the pamphlet was aimed at exposing abuses in the Roman Catholic Church was not a sufficient legal justification of the pamphlet's generally obscene content. Cockburn declared inapplicable in this case the defense's suggestion (commonly encountered in obscenity cases) that occasional "immodest" or "immoral" passages might serve a legitimate purpose in otherwise respectable written materials. The pamphlet in question, he argued, could hardly be characterized in this way. Seeking to draw a clear distinction between respectable and obscene publications, the chief justice proposed the definition now known as the *Hicklin* test. In his words: "I think the test of obscenity is this: whether the tendency of the matter charged as obscenity is to deprave and corrupt those whose minds are open to such immoral influences, and into whose hands a publication of this sort might fall" (*Regina v. Hicklin*, 371).

Cockburn made clear who he thought was most at risk from obscene materials. This pamphlet, and by implication all obscene materials, "would suggest to the minds of the young of either sex, or even to persons of more advanced years, thoughts of the most impure and libidinous character" (*Regina v. Hicklin*, 371). Offensive published materials threatened children, young adults, and the morally vulnerable and impressionable of all ages; therefore, those materials constituted a punishable offense under the Obscene Publications Act of 1857. Any argument that the pamphlet revealed corruption or abuses within the Roman Catholic Church failed to change the fundamental tendency of the pamphlet, which was to present obscene material. Since such obscenity endangered the morality of the very young and of adults of tender sensibilities (i.e., women), the pamphlet was indictable and actionable under the statute. The Queen's Bench supported the findings of the justices of the peace and remanded the case to them for action (destruction of the confiscated pamphlets). With *Hicklin*, the judicial definition of obscenity as published material that has a tendency to corrupt and deprave the mind of the young and adults of tender sensibilities entered the Anglo-American legal tradition. It proved to have a long life in the law in both the United Kingdom and the United States.

Historical context is important to understanding the *Hicklin* decision. Although the concept of "obscenity" is difficult to define, the Queen's Bench had no difficulty in agreeing on a definition. This certainty was produced by the historical context. For mid-Victorian Great Britain, defining obscenity was not difficult because the judges believed that public morality was a legitimate concern of the government and that morality directly affected the health of the commonwealth. Because obscene pamphlets, words, or images could damage the character of the young and impressionable, it was proper for the law, the courts, and the state to protect such persons from obscenity. Pornography threatened the moral body politic through its immoral influences. Further, pornography presented such a threat that the state had a responsibility, even a duty, to suppress pornography and obscenity so as to ensure a moral community. Although this moral certitude of obscenity's nature and harmful effects has not endured in Anglo-American popular culture, the assumption that obscenity poses a threat to society and therefore ought to be limited if not utterly suppressed remains embedded in the legal culture.

Control of Objectionable Materials in the United States

From the Colonial Period through the Early Years of Independence

Over the course of the first 208 years of the history of British North America, from the founding of the first permanent settlement at Jamestown, Virginia, in 1607, to 1815, no government in either the colonies or the states concerned itself with the issue of obscenity. For the most part, obscenity did not draw legislative attention because families, churches, congregations, and localities oversaw and policed the moral quality of their neighborhoods and localities. Localism and a concurrent commitment to the local control of moral problems formed the historical context of early America. Nongovernmental authorities such as churches and congregations were expected to exercise moral oversight. This tradition was the case in Puritan and congregational New England as well as in the Quaker areas of Pennsylvania and New Jersey. Even in those regions where a state-established church existed, such as Virginia (where the Church of England had official status), county and local governments merely assisted churches in maintaining and guaranteeing the moral quality of their localities. Questionable published materials certainly existed in colonial and in the early national United States. No less a figure than Philadelphia printer, Enlightenment scientist, and Revolutionary Benjamin Franklin was known to have composed and privately circulated off-color and suggestive poems and stories. Yet only when such materials became widely known and available in a locality were the authorities moved to suppress their dissemination; and even then, they usually did so through social pressure rather than by formal prosecution under the law.

The first legal case that dealt with obscene materials is believed to have arisen in Philadelphia in 1815. This case gave rise to the first judicial discussion of obscenity and tested the power of the common law to suppress such materials in the United States. At its March session, the Philadelphia grand jury found that Jesse Sharpless and five of his business associates "unlawfully, wickedly, and scandalously *did exhibit, and show for money, to persons ... a certain lewd, wicked, scandalous, infamous, and obscene painting.*" This allegedly obscene painting was described as "*representing a man in an obscene, imrudent, and indecent posture with a woman.*" The grand jury indictment then described the harmful potential of this painting "to manifest corruption and subversion of youth, and other citizens of this commonwealth, to the evil example of all others in like case offending, and against the peace and dignity of the commonwealth of *Pennsylvania*" (*Commonwealth v. Jesse Sharpless,* 2 Serg. and R [Pa.] [1815] 91, 92).

At trial, Sharpless lost. He appealed to the Pennsylvania Supreme Court, arguing that the indictment against him did not specify an indictable act under common law nor did it allege that the offense occurred in a public place. In addition, he argued that the picture was exhibited in a private house. Noting the past difficulties encountered by the British legal establishment in deciding which cases should be handled by the secular courts and which by the ecclesiastical courts, Chief Justice William Tilghman declared that in the United States, without a legal history of church courts, moral offenses were the responsibility of secular courts. And because "there is no act punishing the offence charged against the defendants ... the case must be decided upon the principles of the common law." Tilghman then restated the common-law rule, finding that "actions of *public indecency* were always indictable, as tending to corrupt the public morals." Public exposure was indictable even during what Tilghman described as the "profligate reign of Charles II," the allegedly hedonistic era in British history that followed the post–civil war restoration of the monarchy. Tilghman asserted that "courts are guardians of the public morals, and therefore have jurisdiction in such cases" as public exposure and the publication of indecent books. Therefore, an action would be indictable as damaging of the public morals even if it were not committed in public, because it was the "*nature of the offense*" that ran afoul of the common law: the threat to the public morals (*Commonwealth v. Sharpless,* 102).

In the case at hand, Tilghman held that "a picture tends to excite lust as strongly as writing; and the *shewing* of a picture, is as much a *publication,* as the *selling* of a book." That Sharpless had displayed the work in a private house made no difference: "The law is not to be evaded by an artifice of that kind," the judge warned. If showing the picture in a private room did make a difference, then individuals could be taken one by one into a private room, "there inflaming their passions by the exhibition of lascivious pictures." Tilghman continued: "In the eyes of the law, this would be a *publication,* and a most pernicious one." He then dismissed Sharpless's argument that the indictment did not adequately describe the picture: "Must the indictment describe minutely, the attitude and posture of the figures? I am for paying some respect to the chastity of our records" (*Commonwealth v. Sharpless,* 103). In the end, Sharpless's appeal failed, and the Pennsylvania Supreme Court upheld his conviction.

In effect, all Chief Justice Tilghman did in *Commonwealth v. Sharpless* was restate the common-law rule that courts could and should take notice of offenses to the public morals. Offensive pictures or behavior threatened to corrupt the youth and "other citizens of the commonwealth." Under common law, even those exhibiting obscene materials in a private dwelling could be prosecuted in order to prevent such corruption. This decision nicely encapsulates the early American approach to the control of obscenity: Let the localities and the local courts employing the common law control any threats to morals in their neighborhoods.

And so matters remained for the next six years. Despite the lack of uniform enforcement standards for obscenity, books as well as pictures often ran afoul of local courts and prosecutors. In 1821, Massachusetts prosecuted Peter Holmes for debauching and corrupting the public morals and threatening youth by publishing and delivering to three persons the notorious book about prostitution, John Cleland's eighteenth-century *Memoirs of a Woman of Pleasure.* In this case, the state claimed that the book threatened society by creating "in their minds inordinate and lustful desires" and "manifest corruption and subversion of the youth and other good citizens of said commonwealth . . . in contempt of law." As described by the court reporter, this book was "lewd, wicked, and obscene that the same would be offensive to the Court here, and improper to be placed upon the record" (*Commonwealth v. Peter Holmes,* 17 Mass. 336 [1821]).

Holmes challenged and appealed his conviction to the Massachusetts Supreme Court, attacking the validity of the indictment against him on the grounds that the Massachusetts Court of Common Pleas lacked jurisdiction to try such offenses against the public morals. Chief Justice Isaac Parker found Holmes's appeal without merit. He traced the institutional history of the Court of Common Pleas back to the earliest colonial courts, the British common-law courts, which routinely dealt with local misdemeanors such as moral offenses. Justice Parker argued that after the Revolution and the adoption of the common law by the new state courts, lower local courts continued to have jurisdiction over offenses such as publishing and distributing obscene libel. Therefore, this local court held the proper jurisdiction, and it certainly had the power and duty to protect the community from moral threats posed by obscene publications. Chief Justice Parker upheld the validity of the indictment against Holmes, and thereby Holmes's conviction, for publishing and distributing an obscene book.

Holmes's case demonstrated and reinforced the common-law tradition of local control over such moral issues, finding that the district courts possessed sufficient power to deal with misdemeanors. Although the general quality of early-nineteenth-century indictments would not pass judicial scrutiny today, within the context of their time they reflected the legal value of local control of local moral problems and the expectation that district courts could best police local morality. However, as the nation grew and developed and a mass culture and society gradually emerged, the task of controlling obscene material became more difficult and more complex. And as the nature of the problem changed, new solutions had to be devised.

Nonjudicial Responses in the Mid- to Late-Nineteenth Century

Between the *Holmes* decision and the adoption of the *Hicklin* test in 1879, a number of other restrictions on obscene material and pornography emerged. A few states, such as Connecticut in 1834 and Massachusetts in 1835, passed statutes outlawing "indecent" literature. Congress first became involved when it passed the Customs Act of 1842, prohibiting the importation of "all indecent and obscene prints, paintings, lithographs, engravings, and transparencies" (Ernst and Schwartz 1964, 19–20). Interestingly, this federal statute prohibited pictures and prints but did not extend to allegedly obscene books and pamphlets. In 1865, Congress shifted its focus from prohibiting the importation of obscene pictorial materials to prohibiting the interstate commerce of such materials through the U.S. mail. However, this statute lacked enforcement power, and prosecution could occur only after the obscene materials had actually traveled through the mails. In 1873, a newly formed interest group, the Committee (later, Society) for the Suppression of Vice, together with the Young Men's Christian Association (YMCA), lobbied Congress to close the loopholes in the 1865 statute. Their efforts resulted in further restrictions on the use of the mails to distribute a wide variety of objectionable materials. As described in the 1873 revised statute, "Every obscene, lewd, lascivious, or filthy book, pamphlet, picture, paper, letter writing, print, or other publication of an indecent character . . . is declared to be nonmailable matter and shall not be conveyed in the mails or delivered from any post office or by any letter carrier" (Ernst and Schwartz 1964, 32–33).

In addition to such obscene materials, this federal statute also prohibited using the mails to send any information on abortion or drugs or devices that produced an abortion, or drugs or medicines claiming to prevent contraception; and/or advertisements for drugs or devices that produced or claimed to produce an abortion. First-time offenders of this federal statute faced a fine of as much as $5,000 and could be jailed for up to five years. Repeat offenders were fined up to $10,000 and could be jailed for as many as ten years. This statute, however, was not generally enforced until one of the leaders of the antiobscenity lobby, Anthony Comstock, an ex–grocery clerk from the state of New York, volunteered for appointment as a "special agent" of the Postal Service. Nothing would be the same thereafter. Comstock aggressively pursued obscene materials. His Society for the Suppression of Vice received part of the fines collected by the federal government in its successful prosecution of obscene materials, and Comstock and his antipornography interest group flourished until his death in 1915, and beyond.

Essentially, Comstock became the nation's moral overseer, policing and searching the mails for obscenity, and prosecuting those using who polluted the mails with prohibited items. On January 1, 1874, he reported that in less than a year he had seized and destroyed 194,000 obscene pictures and photographs, 134,000 pounds of books, 14,200 stereo plates, 60,300 "rubber items" (probably condoms), 5,500 stacks of cards, and 31,150 boxes of substances claimed to be aphrodisiacs (Ernst and Schwartz 1964, 34).

As these figures suggest, the federal "Comstock Law" was no paper tiger. Anyone using the mails to distribute obscenity or information on

abortion ran the risks of confiscation, a heavy fine, and/or imprisonment. Nor was the New York Society for the Suppression of Vice the
only reform group pushing for governmental suppression of obscene
materials. By the dawn of the twentieth century, numerous antivice
societies were operating in the growing urban centers of the northern
and western United States. Moral reformers identified a wide range of
social threats needing attention by privately funded, nongovernmental
interest groups. Such groups expected that the laws of the states and
the federal government would assist them in their moral reform
efforts, and they often lobbied the state legislatures and Congress for
more effective laws attacking vice in American cities. The most important of these so-called vice societies formed in the major cities of the
northeastern United States in the 1870s and spread from there across
the country. In 1873 (the same year in which the New York Society for
the Suppression of Vice formed), for example, the New England Society for the Suppression of Vice was established. This group is perhaps
better remembered by the name it adopted a few years later, the New
England Watch and Ward Society. In general, these societies sought to
oversee public morals by waging a campaign against obscene books,
pamphlets, prints, and paintings. They filed lawsuits and actively lobbied public officials to join their campaign against harmful books and
other obscene materials. These societies believed that the moral quality
of the city and the public was so important that it justified the censorship of morally offensive books, pictures, and objects.

Concurrently with these efforts, other antivice groups also
attacked other social problems that they saw as related to obscenity.
For example, antipoverty reformers grappled with the problem of the
poor. Such reformers debated about the moral character of the poor
and the poor's ability to reform themselves. Urban masses provided
plenty of fodder for social and moral reformers—from overcrowd-
ing, to alcohol and tobacco use, to prostitution and bawdy houses.
Numerous organizations sprang up in reaction to these social problems, including the YMCA, the Women's Christian Temperance
Union (WCTU), the Anti-Saloon League, and the Salvation Army, as
well as lesser-known groups such as New York City's Committee of
Fifteen (1900–1901), which was formed to investigate fake hotels
catering to prostitution. Also important among these groups was the
long-lived successor to the Committee of Fifteen, the Committee of
Fourteen (1905–1932), which waged many campaigns against prostitution during its existence.

What united all of these diverse anti-vice societies—not to mention government officials—was their firm belief that only through repression of moral threats such as pornography and prostitution could the moral character of society and of individuals be protected and preserved. Only within a morally pure environment could the poor improve themselves and their families. Moral threats formed such an insidious problem that the only public policy that they could envision was suppression of the moral threats through law. And this is where the Comstock Law and other legislative reactions to pornography entered the picture. For with the passage of the Comstock Law and other anti-obscenity acts, the federal policy toward obscenity became one of suppression. This policy remained in place until well into the twentieth century. But although the case law and legal doctrines that are examined and analyzed in this book are important, one must keep in mind that the larger cultural and historical context supported and encouraged these developments.

Antipornography in the Federal Courts Prior to 1940

While Comstock pursued obscene materials under the new federal statute, localities and states still occasionally initiated the prosecution of purveyors of pornography; but the most important case law of the late nineteenth century arose within the federal court system. In the habeas corpus case *Ex parte Jackson* (1877), a unanimous U.S. Supreme Court upheld Congress's plenary power to establish regulations for the U.S. Postal Service. Although this case dealt with the interstate mailing of lottery tickets contrary to federal statute, it established the rule that Congress could exclude morally objectionable materials such as lottery tickets—and by implication, obscene materials—from the mail.

Of equal significance was the case prompted on November 12, 1878, when a man by the last name of Bennett deposited into the mails two copies of a book entitled *Cupid's Yokes, or The Binding Forces of Conjugal Life,* described in the indictment as "so lewd, obscene, and lascivious that the same would be offensive to the court" (*United States v. Bennett,* 24 F.Cas. 1093 [1879]). Anthony Comstock uncovered this abuse of the mails, and the federal prosecutor in the eastern district of New York State prosecuted Bennett under the Comstock Law. At trial, the jury found Bennett guilty. He then appealed.

Bennett's appeal, *United States v. Bennett,* reached only the federal circuit court level; but the circuit court's opinion was significant because the decision in this case adopted the *Hicklin* test for obscenity and incorporated it into U.S. judicial doctrine. Bennett argued that the indictment against him was flawed because the material in question was a pamphlet and not a book as specified in the statute. Associate Supreme Court Justice Samuel Blatchford, presiding judge in the circuit court, dismissed this contention as lacking substance. After reviewing the relevant British and American precedents (such as *Holmes* and *Sharpless*), he reviewed the trial judge's lengthy charge to the jury, in which the judge spoke approvingly of Comstock's actions. In his charge, the trial judge had dismissed Bennett's argument about freedom of the press, saying, "Freedom of the press does not include freedom to use the mails for the purpose of distributing obscene literature, and no right or privilege of the press is infringed by the exclusion of obscene literature from the mails." This analysis accurately reflected the state of the law on expression in the late 1800s, the justice ruled.

Blatchford then took up Bennett's argument that "obscene" was not adequately defined in the indictment. At this point, Blatchford took the precedent-setting step of incorporating England's *Hicklin* test into American law. After reviewing Chief Justice Cockburn's decision in *Hicklin,* Blatchford remarked that Cockburn's decision "seems to us very sound" (*United States v. Bennett,* 1104). Blatchford then ruled that *Cupid's Yoke* met the *Hicklin* test of having a tendency to deprave and corrupt susceptible persons. Based on their finding that all of Bennett's allegations of problems with his indictment and of errors at trial lacked substance, Blatchford and the rest of the circuit court denied his request for a new trial and upheld his conviction. More importantly, England's *Hicklin* test had been incorporated into American law as the legal rule in obscenity cases.

This acceptance of the British obscenity rule into American law was consolidated in the 1896 Supreme Court case of *Rosen v. United States.* Lew Rosen published a small paper entitled *Broadway.* When he placed the April 15, 1893, issue in the mails for distribution to subscribers, he ran afoul of the Comstock Law because the newspaper contained revealing pictures of women. As described in the decision, these pictures were "partially covered with lampblack that could be easily erased with a piece of bread. The object of sending them out in that condition was, of course, to excite a curiosity to know what was thus concealed." (The hypothetical "piece of bread" was particularly significant, because it was an object that any young child, seated at a table on which the newspaper might be left lying, would have readily at hand.) At trial, the jury found Rosen guilty of using the mails to post "an obscene, lewd, or lascivious book, pamphlet, picture, paper, writing, print, or other publication of an indecent character" as established by the Comstock Law. Rosen's lawyer objected to the charge and indictment against his client, but the trial judge overruled these objections and sentenced Rosen to prison at hard labor for thirteen months. He also required Rosen to pay a fine of one dollar (*Rosen v. United States,* 161 U.S. 29 [1896], 31).

Rosen quickly appealed his conviction, and the case came before the U.S. Supreme Court on October 29, 1895. On January 27, 1896, in a 7–2 decision, Associate Justice John Marshall Harlan delivered the majority opinion for the Court. Reviewing the facts of the case, the trial record, and the precedents dealing with obscenity such as *Sharpless, Holmes,* and *Bennett,* Harlan found no error in the indictment against Rosen and no constitutional problem with the Comstock Law. Harlan then reviewed the trial judge's charge to the jury, which quoted *Hicklin,* saying, "The test of obscenity is whether the tendency of the matter is to deprave and corrupt the morals of those whose minds are open to such influence and into whose hands a publication of this sort may fall." This test of obscenity, the justice ruled, was entirely appropriate. Finding no error in the indictment, the trial record, the judge's charge to the jury, or the federal statute, the Supreme Court upheld Rosen's conviction (*Rosen v. United States,* 43).

This conclusion was acceptable in general to the whole Court, even the dissenting justices. Tellingly, although Associate Justices Edward D. White and George Shiras dissented from the Court's decision, they did not object to the use of the *Hicklin* test. Instead, they dissented on the grounds that the indictment against Rosen was not as clear and specific as it ought to have been and therefore Rosen had been denied his Fifth Amendment right to a proper indictment. Thus, the Supreme Court's confirmation of the lower court's decision in *Rosen* established the rule that it was illegal to mail any material that a jury might find provocative to a child.

Six weeks later, on March 9, 1896, the Supreme Court handed down a decision in *Swearingen v. United States* that overturned a conviction under the Comstock Act. In the process, the Court clarified the law's definition of obscenity and limited its application to sexual matters. On September 21, 1894, Dan K. Swearingen had published and mailed a newspaper in Burlington, Kansas. In it was an editorial that the federal prosecutor charged was of an "obscene, lewd, and lascivious character" and therefore nonmailable under the Comstock Act. This offensive article, in current parlance "an op-ed" piece, slandered the character and reputation of Kansas politicians. Swearingen objected to the indictment brought against him and pleaded not guilty. At trial, the jury found him guilty of violating the Comstock Act. Swearingen then asked for a new trial. The trial judge overruled his objections, denied his request for a new trial, and sentenced Swearingen to serve one year in prison, to pay the costs of his prosecution, and to pay a $50 fine. Swearingen appealed his conviction through the federal system, submitting a request for a writ of error to the U.S. Supreme Court on October 12, 1895.

In a 5–4 decision, Associate Justice Shiras wrote for the majority of the Court in overturning Swearingen's conviction. (Four justices—John Marshall Harlan, Horace Gray, Henry Billings Brown, and Edward D. White—disagreed, but did so without a written dissent.) Shiras declared unfounded the charge that Swearingen's editorial was obscene. He interpreted the phrase in the Comstock Act— "obscene, lewd, or lascivious"—"as describing one and the same offense." In other words, these words should be read together as describing one type of offensive materials. Continuing his analysis, Shiras held that these three words "signify that form of immorality which has relation to sexual impurity, and have the same meaning as is given them at common law in prosecutions for obscene libel." The editorial attacking anti-Populist politicians in Kansas did not fulfill this definition of "obscene, lewd, and lascivious." Although the language of the editorial was "exceeding coarse and vulgar," the Court's majority did not "perceive in it anything of a lewd, lascivious and obscene tendency, calculated to corrupt and debauch the mind and morals of those into whose hands it might fall" (*Swearingen v. United States,* 161 U.S. 446 [1896], 451). Therefore, the Supreme Court reversed Swearingen's conviction and ordered that he be granted a new trial.

The law on freedom of speech and press had hardly been developed in 1896. Had *Swearingen* been heard in a later decade, it would have been dealt with as a routine case of protected political speech. But in 1896, the case set a precedent, giving rise to a new rule:

"Obscenity" did not extend to language that was merely "coarse and vulgar." *Bennett, Jackson, Rosen,* and *Swearingen* were relatively minor cases; but the legal rules established in them, such as the use of the *Hicklin* test, proved important in the future of anti-obscenity prosecutions.

Questions and Concerns: Antipornography Challenged by the Courts

Despite the strength of the antivice societies and their success in enlisting the legal and political establishments to suppress "obscene" materials, in the early twentieth century at least one federal judge questioned the appropriateness of the *Hicklin* test. In *United States v. Kennerley* (1913), noted federal district Judge Learned Hand first spoke of the problems inherent in the *Hicklin* obscenity test when he produced a written opinion overruling Kennerley's request to throw out the indictment against him. Hand took notice of the *Hicklin* standard for defining obscenity and stated that he could not simply disregard it. However, he said, "the rule laid down, however consonant it may be with mid-Victorian morals, does not seem to me to answer to the understanding and morality of the present time." As he explained in a now famous passage:

> I question whether in the end men will regard that as obscene which is honestly relevant to the adequate expression of innocent ideas, and whether they will not believe that truth and beauty are too precious to society at large to be mutilated in the interests of those most likely to pervert them to base uses.

He continued:

> Indeed, it seems hardly likely that we are even to-day so lukewarm in our interest in letters and serious discussion as to be content to reduce our treatment of sex to the standard of a child's library in the supposed interest of a salacious few, or that shame will for long prevent us from adequate portrayal of some of the most serious and beautiful sides of life.

Reducing the test group for obscenity to the youngest and most sensitive members of the society, Hand concluded, limited full, frank, and honest discussion of some of the most important aspects of life. *Hicklin* had a chilling effect, to use lawyers' language, on writings and publications, because under the *Hicklin* test one could never know what writings or images might be offensive and might open one up to prosecution for obscenity. As Judge Hand succinctly stated, "To put thought in leash to the average conscience of the time is perhaps tolerable, but to fetter it by the necessities of the lowest and least capable seems a fatal policy" (*United States v. Kennerley,* 209 F. 119 [1913], 121). Judge Hand did not overrule the *Hicklin* test, but he did question its relevance in the twentieth century; and in so ruling, he established the basis on which later judges would critique and undermine the test.

Judge Hand's concerns and his skepticism about the utility of the *Hicklin* test confronted the courts repeatedly as twentieth-century authors addressed previously taboo or private matters in an increasingly provocative manner. Serious and important literature tended more and more frequently to challenge the limits of the acceptable. But few publishing events in the twentieth century generated as much controversy as the publication of James Joyce's 1924 masterpiece *Ulysses.* Originally published overseas, it was banned in 1933 from importation into the United States on the grounds that it contained offensive language, including passages that were graphically sexual. Joyce had indeed employed language usually heard only on the roughest streets in the toughest neighborhoods; but he had done so in order authentically to convey the inner life and struggles of his characters. On this basis, the publisher decided to challenge the ban in federal court.

Federal district Judge John M. Woolsey's opinion on the banning of *Ulysses* in *United States v. One Book Called "Ulysses"* (1933) suggested a new standard for judging whether or not a literary work was obscene. After reading the entire book through once, and then rereading the passages of the book that the federal government most objected to, Woolsey found that viewed as a whole, *Ulysses* was not obscene: "Reading 'Ulysses' in its entirety, as a book must be read on such a test as this, did not tend to excite sexual impulses or lustful thoughts" (*United States v. One Book Called "Ulysses,"* 5 F.Supp. 182 [1933], 185). He conceded that parts of the book "seem to me to be disgusting," but, he continued, "I have not found anything that I consider to be dirt for dirt's sake." Woolsey found that Joyce had not written with "pornographic intent." If the book were evaluated in its entirety by a "reasonable man," then it could not be found obscene but instead must be declared "a sincere and serious attempt to devise a new literary method for the observation and description of mankind." Woolsey acknowledged that the language and imagery in the book made it "a rather strong draught to ask some sensitive, though normal, persons to take"; but he did not believe that this could or should be taken to mean that the work was pornographic or obscene. In other words, the *Hicklin* test was an inadequate standard for a finding of obscenity. Woolsey reversed the lower court's decision banning the importation of the book into the United States.

The legal challenge to *Ulysses* was not immediately laid to rest: The federal government appealed Woolsey's decision to the Second Circuit Court of Appeals, on whose bench sat Judges Augustus Hand (Learned Hand's cousin), Learned Hand, and Martin T. Manton. But on August 7, 1934, this federal circuit court handed down a 2–1 decision (in *United States v. One Book Entitled* Ulysses *by James Joyce*) supporting Woolsey's decision and adopting his "work as a whole" doctrine in obscenity cases. Writing for the majority, Augustus Hand followed the same general line of reasoning Woolsey had, and reached the same conclusions. Hand wrote: "That numerous long passages in *Ulysses* contain matter that is obscene under any fair definition of the word cannot be gainsaid; yet they are relevant to the purpose of depicting the thoughts of characters and are introduced to give meaning to the whole, rather than to portray filth for its own sake. . . . The book as a whole is not pornographic, and, while in not a few spots it is coarse, blasphemous, and obscene, it does not, in our opinion tend to promote lust." Therefore, it was the opinion of the court's majority that "*Ulysses* is a book of originality and sincerity of treatment and that it has not the effect of promoting lust. Accordingly it does not fall within the statute, even though it justly may offend many" (*United States v. One Book Entitled* Ulysses *by James Joyce*, 72 F.2d 705 [1934], 708–709). *Ulysses* thereupon entered the United States and became a classic in "stream-of-consciousness" literature of the twentieth century.

The circuit court's ruling in *Ulysses* was a landmark decision in the realm of free speech, and it strongly influenced the ongoing debate over the proper definition of "obscene" materials. Yet the rethinking of obscenity was not unanimous, even in the circuit court. Judge Manton dissented from the "work as a whole" doctrine, and he would have confirmed the decision banning *Ulysses*. Manton found it easy to label the work obscene; the book's "characterization as obscene should be quite unanimous by all who read it," he wrote. Manton reviewed and approved of the *Hicklin* test for obscenity, adopting the position that literature and fiction should uplift and inspire readers, and not lower them to the lowest and basest common denominator. As Manton understood the relationship between author and reader: "Literature exists for the sake of the people, to refresh the weary, to console the sad, to hearten the dull and downcast, to increase man's interest in the world, his joy of living, and his sympathy in all sorts and conditions of men. Art for art's sake is heartless and soon grows artless; art for the public market is not art at all, but commerce; art for the people is a noble, vital, and permanent element of human life" (*United States v. One Book Entitled* Ulysses *by James Joyce,* 711). *Ulysses* failed to inspire Judge Manton; and its occasional coarseness and strong sexual imagery crossed the line into obscenity. For these reasons he believed that it ought to be banned and suppressed. What the Judges Hand found to be high art and literature, Judge Manton found to be low trash and obscenity. This split exactly reflects the ongoing difference of opinion regarding "obscenity."

Two years later, the Second Circuit Court of Appeals delivered the last word on the *Hicklin* test. At issue in the 1936 case of *United States v. Levine* was the use of the mails to distribute five allegedly obscene books. Levine appealed his conviction, arguing that the *Hicklin* standard was no longer good law in the United States. The Second Circuit agreed. Judge Learned Hand disposed of the *Hicklin* test, saying, "This earlier doctrine necessarily presupposes that the evil against which the statute is directed so much outweighs all interests of art, letters, or science, that they must yield to the mere possibility that some prurient person may get a sensual gratification from reading or seeing what to most people is innocent and may be delightful or enlightening." Hand continued, "No civilized community not fanatically puritanical would tolerate such an imposition, and we do not believe that the courts that have declared it, would ever have applied it consistently." In other words, the *Hicklin* test was too narrow. It denied legitimate materials to reasonable people, and no court or judge could be expected to support and perpetuate such a narrow and confining legal doctrine. "[A] work must be taken as a whole, its merits weighed against its defects," argued Judge Hand, confirming the new standard for determining obscenity. More has to be assessed in obscenity cases than just the possible effects of some material on the most sensitive and youngest members of the community: "If it is old, its accepted place in the arts must be regarded; if new, the opinions of competent critics in published reviews or the like may be considered; what counts is its effect, not upon any particular class, but upon all those whom it is likely to reach" (*United States v. Levine*, 83 F.2d 156, 157 [1936]). Obscenity, then, entailed more than alleged effects on the weak-minded or the hypersensitive. The work as a whole, and any reviews of that work, should be considered when struggling with the difficult question of obscenity. Because the trial judge employed the *Hicklin* test and because he erred in his charge to the jury, the Second Circuit reversed Levine's conviction and ordered a new trial based on this new legal rule of obscenity.

Conclusion

This review of the early history of the law of obscenity reveals a picture of evolving legal rules and approaches to combat the problem of pornography. From the origins of obscenity as the common-law crime of "obscene libel," prosecuted by local officials, to the emergence of the *Hicklin* doctrine in Great Britain in 1868, the control of obscenity fell to local authorities to discover and prosecute. American colonial and early national developments mirrored those in Britain with regard to local prosecution under common law. But as the United States became more cosmopolitan, as the anonymous cities and the market for pornography grew, as publishing became cheaper and easier, and as antivice interest groups formed to combat the social problem of pornography, Congress became involved. By denying the importation of allegedly obscene materials and declaring obscene materials "nonmailable," Congress crafted obscenity policy and pursued the suppression of obscenity. Nevertheless, over time, the *Hicklin* test proved less useful than nineteenth-century judges had considered it. New cases arose, and new judges began to question the assumptions contained in *Hicklin*. In the 1930s, American appellate judges discarded the *Hicklin* test and established in its place the "work as a whole" test. This test too was discarded later in the twentieth century, as the U.S. federal courts (especially the Supreme Court) struggled to craft an obscenity rule flexible enough to allow the publication and dissemination of legitimate literary and scientific materials but stringent enough to stigmatize and limit the circulation of pornographic materials. The attempt to strike a balance between openness and restrictiveness in the legal rules of obscenity is the topic of the next chapter.

References and Further Reading

Bates, Anna Louise. 1995. *Weeder in the Garden of the Lord: Anthony Comstock's Life and Career.* Lanham, MD: University Press of America.

Beisel, Nicola Kay. 1997. *Imperiled Innocents: Anthony Comstock and Family Reproduction in Victorian America.* Princeton: Princeton University Press.

Boyer, Paul S. 1968. *Purity in Print: The Vice-Society Movement and Book Censorship in America.* New York: Charles Scribner's Sons.

———. 1978. *Urban Masses and Moral Order in America, 1820–1920.* Cambridge, MA: Harvard University Press.

Broun, Heywood. 1927. *Anthony Comstock: Roundsman of the Lord.* New York: Literary Guild of America.

The Committee of Fifteen. 1979 [1901]. *The Social Evil, with Special Reference to Conditions Existing in the City of New York.* New York: G. P. Putnam's Sons; reprint New York: Garland.

Ernst, Morris L., and Alan U. Schwartz. 1964. *Censorship: The Search for the Obscene.* New York: Macmillan.

Griffith, Kathryn. 1973. *Judge Learned Hand and the Role of the Judiciary.* Norman: University of Oklahoma Press.

Gunther, Gerald. 1994. *Learned Hand: The Man and the Judge.* New York: Knopf.

Hixson, Richard F. 1996. *Pornography and the Justices: The Supreme Court and the Intractable Obscenity Problem.* Carbondale: Southern Illinois University Press.

Horowitz, Helen Lefkowitz. 2000. "Victoria Woodhull, Anthony Comstock, and Conflict over Sex in the United States in the 1870s." *Journal of American History* 87 (September): 403–434.

Hunt, Lynn, ed. 1993. *The Invention of Pornography: Obscenity and the Origins of Modernity, 1500–1800.* New York: Zone Books.

Hunter, Ian, David Sauders, and Dugald Williamson. 1993. *On Pornography: Literature, Sexuality, and Obscenity Law.* New York: St. Martin's Press.

Latham, Robert, and William Matthews, eds. 1976. *The Diary of Samuel Pepys, IX, 1668–1669.* Berkeley: University of California Press.

Nelson, Marcia. 1983. *The Remarkable Hands: An Affectionate Portrait.* New York: Foundation of the Federal Bar Council.

Schwartz, Joel. 2000. *Fighting Poverty with Virtue: Moral Reform and America's Urban Poor, 1825–2000.* Bloomington: Indiana University Press.

Tine, Andrea. 2000. "Black Market Birth Control: Contraception Entrepreneurship and Criminality in the Gilded Age." *Journal of American History* 87 (September): 435–459.

3
Cases

From their common-law origins to the early twentieth century, obscenity and pornography existed as a social problem for the courts and legal authorities to regulate and suppress. The law was a reflection of the larger culture: Because the Anglo-American culture of the nineteenth century believed that society ought to use the power of government to keep immoral materials from undermining the character of children and sensitive adults, policymakers pursued the suppression of such materials. The *Hicklin* doctrine, created by a judicial decision in the English courts (and adopted soon after by U.S. courts), established the authority of the legislature to act against allegedly immoral materials; yet it also established the precedent of judicial oversight of those legislative initiatives. In time, judges in the United States (e.g., Learned and Augustus Hand) began to raise questions about the *Hicklin* doctrine—in particular, its overt policy of suppression. This chapter surveys and analyzes the leading issues and case law on obscenity from 1957 to the present. Within that time frame, the changing social context in the United States provided the U.S. Supreme Court an opportunity to craft new judicial doctrines to control obscene materials. As tolerance of obscenity gradually increased in the culture, the legal restrictions on pornography became less severe; and as an increasingly rights-conscious judiciary questioned the limits, manners, and wisdom of suppressing pornography through law, the questions soon led to answers. Federal judges such as U.S. Supreme

Court Associate Justice William J. Brennan took the lead in allowing the pornography genie out of the bottle.

Just as the twentieth century brought enormous technological changes, moving from the age of steam power to the age of nuclear power, it also brought enormous legal, social, and cultural changes. In 1900, few Americans would have questioned the power, authority, and duty of the state and federal governments to root out and suppress pornographic materials. Yet, by 2000, an inversion of values had occurred, and materials that people in 1900 would have considered highly obscene—for example, pictures of nude women—were sold freely across the counter at most convenience stores throughout the nation. This inversion of values, and the varied public policies that accompanied it, did not occur in a vacuum. Among the causes behind these moral shifts can be counted the relocation of the bulk of the population from rural areas to urban and suburban areas; the growing affluence of the population with disposable income; the emergence of the United States as one of two superpowers in the world (and after 1990, the primary superpower); the emergence of race- and gender-based interest groups pressing for "rights" against the majority population; and the communications revolution fostered by radio, television, and the Internet, which connected far-flung locales and facilitated the rapid dissemination of ideas, fashions, and values. To an unprecedented degree, the media had become the primary transmitter of social and moral values to the population. Although the traditional transmitters of values (family and religion) did not disappear, their sway and influence ebbed before the flash and excitement generated by the new technologies. Radio, television, and cinematic representations of "art" challenged older notions of appropriate and inappropriate behavior as the social barriers fell; what had been shocking became commonplace, and the lines between appropriate and inappropriate behavior blurred. This fluid, relativist cultural dynamic, in turn, called into question the boundaries and definitions of what was and what was not "obscene."

Ultimately, legislatures and courts responded in kind. They questioned older legal doctrines and brought forth new legal rules, doctrines, and guidelines that reflected the new social values and new levels of materials accepted or tolerated in the culture. Yet even before this shift occurred, other areas of law important to the judicial reevaluation of obscenity underwent important changes—changes upon which federal judges would build the new judicial doctrines on obscenity.

One such area was the law of speech and press. Some knowledge of First Amendment history is necessary in order to understand the legal context in which legislators, judges, and justices tackled questions of obscenity in the middle to late twentieth century. This chapter starts, then, with a short review of the major changes and doctrines of speech and press issues that set the stage for the key changes in the case law on obscenity. Then, to provide a sense of the sheer magnitude of social and legal change, a brief review of the changing nature of personal rights in the United States follows. Mirroring the rise of liberalism in the country, new judicial doctrines emerged to reflect societal values. The federal courts began to develop national standards for the treatment of citizens by governmental authorities in their localities, not only in regards to free speech and press but also regarding issues of criminal rights and personal morality. Because the social problem of pornography touched on all these modern American values, this part of the story starts with them.

Speech, Press, and the Incorporation Doctrine: A Review

It is not well known that before the twentieth century, in most circumstances, the *federal* Bill of Rights limited only the actions of the *federal* government and not the behavior of state and local governments in the United States. Nor did it limit the private actions of individuals. As interpreted by the courts of the day, only state constitutions and state bills of rights protected people from abuses of state power and regulated relationships between individuals. The federal Bill of Rights was for federal misconduct alone. This concept, known as federalism (the division of duties and responsibilities between different levels of government), strictly defined and limited the claims an individual could make upon the national government for protection. It was not the national government's job to police civil liberties. However, with the success of the Union in the Civil War and the subsequent passage of the Civil War amendments to the U.S. Constitution (especially the Fourteenth Amendment, which established the primacy of national citizenship and due process and equal protection of the law), the entire concept of federalism changed. In the process, a new constitution emerged—one that could be interpreted as promising the active defense of individual rights by the federal government. Still, for most of the late nineteenth and early twentieth centuries, the idea of a consolidated government centered in Washington, D.C., remained more promise than reality; the older tradition of allowing states to oversee the nature and quality of rights of persons within their borders would continue well into the twentieth century. In fact, it would take a "great war" to alter this situation, shifting the balance of power toward the federal government and prompting the federal courts to assume a greater role in the oversight of the rights of individual citizens within states. This "great war" was World War I.

When the United States entered World War I in April 1917, the administration of President Woodrow Wilson was concerned about potential disloyalty among the large immigrant populations of German, Austrian, and Hungarian Americans. The question of internal security became pressing. In response, Congress passed two pieces of legislation: the Espionage Act of 1917 and the Sedition Act of 1918. The Sedition Act was aimed at limiting speech that might hinder or harm the nation's war efforts. By the terms of the Act, it was a felony to "disrupt or discourage recruiting or enlistment service, or utter, print, or publish disloyal, profane, scurrilous, or abusive language about the form of government, the Constitution, soldiers and sailors, flag, or uniform of the armed forces, or by word or act support or favor the cause of the German Empire or its allies in the present war, or by word or act oppose the cause of the United States" (Murphy 1979, 83). Federal district attorneys used this clause to close German-language and pacifist newspapers and to prosecute those who opposed America's participation in the Great War. These federal prosecutions led to convictions under the Sedition Act; those convicted appealed, arguing that the Sedition Act violated the free speech and press rights guaranteed in the First Amendment. And so the issue came before the Supreme Court.

One such case, *Schenck v. United States,* was decided in the spring of 1919. Charles Schenck, who had printed and circulated leaflets opposing the war and had been arrested, tried, and convicted under the Sedition Act, had appealed his conviction to the U.S. Supreme Court. In a unanimous opinion Associate Justice Oliver Wendell Holmes, Jr., upheld the Sedition Act as constitutional. Holmes explained that free speech was not an absolute right at all times, and that especially in times of war, limitations on speech might be appropriate. In explaining when limitations on speech would be appropriate, Holmes crafted the famous "clear and present danger" doctrine:

"The question in each case," he held, "is whether the words are used in such circumstances and are of such a nature as to create a clear and present danger that they will bring about the substantive evils that Congress has a right to prevent. It is a question of proximity and degree" (249 U.S. 47, 52). This was the first significant case in which the Supreme Court had interpreted the free speech clause of the First Amendment to mean that some restrictions on speech were constitutional. On this basis the Court later upheld other convictions under the Sedition Act.

But by the fall of 1919, Holmes had changed his mind about the clear and present danger doctrine. In the case *Abrams v. United States* (1919), Associate Justice John H. Clarke and six other members of the Court upheld the Sedition Act on the grounds that Jacob Abrams's pamphlet constituted a clear and present danger to national security. Justice Holmes and Associate Justice Louis D. Brandeis dissented. Over the summer, Holmes had become concerned that federal prosecutors, guided by the standard of clear and present danger, would act too aggressively in censoring political speech. As a result, he argued that this standard should be replaced by an even more restrictive one: "imminent danger." Although Holmes failed to carry the rest of the Court with him in moving to a new standard for curtailing political speech, his passionate defense of speech liberties would resonate during the rest of the century and influence later constitutional developments.

Meanwhile, although the Court's decisions in *Schenck* and *Abrams* clearly upheld federal governmental limits on some types of *political* speech in wartime, they had left unclarified the First Amendment's bearing on peacetime, nonpolitical speech (such as pornography). A major breakthrough in defining the First Amendment's peacetime coverage occurred in 1925, in *Gitlow v. New York*. In 1917, Benjamin Gitlow had been convicted, under New York's Criminal Anarchy Law of 1902, for publishing an editorial in a socialist newspaper, allegedly advocating the violent overthrow of the government. Gitlow appealed his conviction to the U.S. Supreme Court, arguing that the First Amendment of the Bill of Rights provided *federal* protection to freedom of the press against prosecution by the states. As he had in *Abrams,* Justice Holmes, with the concurrence of Justice Brandeis, penned a passionate defense of civil liberties; but the majority of the Court upheld both Gitlow's conviction and New York's Criminal Anarchy Law.

Yet from this case emerged a significant advance in First Amendment doctrine—surprising, given that the majority had followed the line of reasoning in *Schenk*. Associate Justice Edward T. Sanford announced this breakthrough in the Court's thinking when he wrote: "For the present purposes, we may and do assume that freedom of speech and of the press—which are protected by the First Amendment from abridgement by Congress—are among the fundamental personal rights and 'liberties' protected by the due process clause of the Fourteenth Amendment from impairment by the states" (268 U.S. 652, 666). With *Gitlow*, the Supreme Court had incorporated the speech and press clause of the First Amendment against the states through the due process clause of the Fourteenth Amendment. (That is to say, the Supreme Court held that the Fourteenth Amendment's limitations on *state* governmental action mirrored the limits imposed on the *federal* government by the First Amendment.) Henceforth, the idea that the Fourteenth Amendment protected First Amendment rights of free speech and press from state interference would be known as the "*Gitlow* assumption." Although the Court found no violation of the right to free speech either in the state statute or in Gitlow's conviction under that statute, it clearly signaled that such a violation might exist in other cases.

In 1931, in *Yetta Stromberg v. California*, the Supreme Court found just such an occurrence, and for the first time it struck down a *state* law as a violation of the First Amendment guarantee of free speech. That same year, state restrictions on freedom of the press came under Supreme Court scrutiny in *Near v. Minnesota* (1931). Jay Near published a scandal sheet that revealed corruption in public office and maligned the character of public officials. In response, local authorities employed a Minnesota statute that allowed the state to suppress malicious, scandalous, or defamatory newspapers. Near appealed, and Chief Justice Charles Evans Hughes held that Minnesota's statute violated the First Amendment right to freedom of the press as applied to the states in *Gitlow:* the states could not exercise prior restraint against publications.

In sum, in the thirty years following *Gitlow*, the Supreme Court established a new era in constitutional law by selectively applying parts of the federal Bill of Rights against the states, in defense of the liberties of individuals. Through incorporation, the Court changed American law and constitutionalism and encouraged a rights-conscious culture. This rights-consciousness is the context within which the most serious challenges to governmental restrictions on obscenity have arisen.

Cultural and Legal Liberalism

During the tenure of Chief Justice Earl Warren (1953–1969), the U.S. Supreme Court employed the incorporation doctrine to expand the rights of individuals and interest groups. This trend reflected the growing rights-conscious political atmosphere of the middle to late twentieth century. In order to understand the changes in obscenity law in the United States in the post–World War II era, it is necessary to understand the legal doctrine of incorporation and the Court's willingness to provide strict scrutiny of invasions of speech and press rights. It is also necessary to appreciate other legal and constitutional events and developments—ones related to a wide range of individual and group rights—in order to understand the Court's response to pornography during this period. With the New Deal, the balance of political power began to shift from individual citizens and from the states toward the federal government in Washington, D.C. The trend accelerated during World War II, due to the need for centralized governmental power to fight and win that war as well as the subsequent Cold War against communism. Issues that previously had been state concerns or even private personal concerns became the business of the U.S. Congress and ultimately resulted in federal legislation. Traditionally local issues, such as school integration or segregation, apportionment of the state legislature, state criminal procedures, and personal choices in birth control and abortion, came under the control of federal law and generated new federal legal doctrine. A review of a few key cases provides the legal and constitutional context necessary to understand how changes in obscenity law mirrored the changing cultural and legal environment underlying late-twentieth-century liberalism.

As World War II came to a close, revelations of two major sets of events shocked many Americans: the Holocaust in Europe, and the federally sanctioned internment of Japanese Americans in the United States. These events suggested that if governments gained too much power, they would increasingly ignore individual liberties—especially those of minority populations. Events in Europe made clear the dangers inherent in the concentration of too much power in government hands; and events in the United States showed that what had happened in Europe could also happen in America—even if only in an attenuated form. These events caused American lawyers and judges to reconsider the treatment of minorities.

Even before the war, black Americans, led by the Legal Defense Fund (LDF) of the National Association for the Advancement of Colored People (NAACP), had started a judicial campaign seeking rulings that made clear the unconstitutionality of racial segregation and race-based discrimination. Their efforts in the courts came to a head in 1954, with the most important Supreme Court decision of the twentieth century, *Linda Brown v. Board of Education of Topeka.* In this case the Supreme Court unanimously ruled that segregated public schools were unconstitutional. The Court followed up this decision the next year, in *Linda Brown v. Board of Education of Topeka II,* by declaring that segregation in schools had to end "with all deliberate speed," and delegating to federal district court judges the task of overseeing the desegregation of the public schools (349 U.S. 294). Resistance to *Brown* emerged throughout the South and in the border states. It erupted into overt confrontation in Little Rock, Arkansas, in 1957–1958, over the desegregation of the Central High School. Litigation over Arkansas' opposition reached the Supreme Court in 1958, with *Cooper v. Aaron.* In this case the court unanimously upheld the power of the federal government to order the desegregation of schools and to defend the Fourteenth Amendment's promise of equal protection for all citizens under the law.

Ten years later, in *Green v. County School Board of New Kent County* (1968), the Supreme Court held that the mere destruction of segregation was not enough; active desegregation and integration of segregated schools were required. That decision, in turn, led to judicial sanctioning of forced busing of schoolchildren to achieve racial integration in the public schools, as directed in *Swann v. Charlotte-Mecklenberg County Board of Education* (1970). Four years later, in the case of *Milliken v. Bradley,* the Supreme Court limited the reach of the federal courts in traditionally local issues such as school policy. The Court rejected a comprehensive plan for metropolitan schools of the Detroit area as too far-reaching. Nonetheless, by 1974 a great deal of power to control public and private behavior within the states had been transferred to the federal courts. Federal courts could go to great lengths to guarantee citizens equality of access to public schools; however, with the *Bradley* ruling, the Court also made clear the limits on this federal judicial power.

A similar progression of ideas attended debate over the thorny question of political representation. Beginning in 1962, the Supreme Court limited the states' ability to draw their own legislative district lines for state and federal voting districts—first, in the case of *Baker v. Carr,* and then in *Gray v. Sanders* (1963) and *Reynolds v. Sims* (1964). In *Baker,* Justice Brennan held for the six-justice majority that states that did not reapportion their district lines with some regard for population equality between rural and urban districts violated the equal protection clause of the Fourteenth Amendment. In *Gray,* Associate Justice William O. Douglas held that the district lines and the primary voting system used in Georgia failed to provide equal protection to all voters and thus violated the ideal of "one person, one vote" (372 U.S. 368, 381). This developing line of judicial thinking reached its apex the next year in *Reynolds v. Sims* (1964). In an 8–1 decision written by Chief Justice Warren, the Court held that representation in state legislatures must be based substantially on population only; states could not craft any other system of apportionment (for example, the federal model whereby membership in one house is based on geography) without violating the equal protection clause. In all of these cases, Associate Justice John M. Harlan dissented, arguing that apportionment was a political question, that the federal courts lacked jurisdiction in such matters, and that the Court improperly limited the traditional powers of the states to control their own political affairs. *Baker, Gray,* and *Reynolds* have become accepted parts of constitutional law; but at the time, as Harlan's dissents indicate, they evidenced a new and controversial level of federal oversight over state behavior.

The same was true of the Court's oversight of the rights of those accused of crimes. State criminal law procedures came under Supreme Court scrutiny in many cases, the two most famous being *Escobedo v. Illinois* (1964) and *Miranda v. Arizona* (1966). In *Escobedo,* by a vote of 5–4, the Court ruled that a police procedure denying the accused access to a lawyer was unconstitutional. Associate Justice Arthur J. Goldberg, who wrote the majority opinion, left open the question of when during the arrest, interrogation, and charging process those accused were to be apprised of their rights. As a result, the Court later agreed to hear another case dealing with the rights of the accused, a case whose name became inextricably linked with those rights: *Miranda.* Again by a 5–4 vote, the Court reached a decision that clarified and expanded upon *Escobedo.* Chief Justice Warren held that once suspects were in "custodial interrogation," they had the right to be informed that anything they said could be used against them in a court of law; that they could choose to remain silent; that they could talk with a lawyer before answering any questions from the police, and have a lawyer present during police questioning; and that a lawyer would be provided by the government if they could not afford one (384 U.S. 436). The majority opinion in this case laid down the procedure followed by policeman across the country when making an arrest.

Highly controversial then and since, the Court's decision in *Miranda* can be read in at least two ways: as a requirement that the rights of the accused be respected no matter what their social status or how heinous the crimes they are believed to have committed; or as yet another intrusion by the federal courts into local and state traditions, aiding criminals and handicapping the police in their battle against crime. Either way, the ruling increased the already extensive role of the federal courts in defining and shaping private actions and state government policies.

This period of judicial activism on behalf of liberal causes, federal power, and individual and group rights continued and expanded into many issues affecting daily life. Judicial liberalism perhaps reached its zenith with a 1965 decision *(Griswold v. Connecticut)* in which the Supreme Court announced that it had just discovered a right to privacy in the Bill of Rights, and with the even more controversial decision in *Roe v. Wade* (1973), wherein the Court asserted that a woman's right to an abortion was a constitutionally protected matter of privacy.

Justice Douglas wrote the majority opinion in the 7–2 decision in *Griswold v. Connecticut.* In 1879, Connecticut had passed a law prohibiting the use of any sort of contraception, even by married couples. When the statute had been challenged in the past, the Supreme Court had declined to consider the issue, and had disposed of all such cases on procedural or technical grounds. But in 1965, the Warren Court accepted a challenge to the statute. Although the word *privacy* appears nowhere in the U.S. Constitution, a majority of the justices struck down the statute on the grounds that it violated the constitutionally protected "right to privacy" of married persons. Following a loose interpretation of the Constitution, Justice Douglas distinguished an aura of rights that existed around and was associated with specific guarantees in the Bill of Rights. As he put it, "Specific guarantees . . . have penumbras, formed by emanations from those guarantees that help give them life and substance." Douglas listed the First, Third, Fourth, Fifth, and Ninth Amendments as the location of "zones of privacy" that the states may not intrude upon (381 U.S. 479, 484). Other members of the majority concurred and wrote that some rights were fundamental, that they existed within the Constitution and Bill of Rights and emanated from the vague Ninth Amendment. But regardless of the exact location of these "zones of privacy," the Court declared, the Connecticut statute limiting married people's access to contraception had trespassed on them.

Next up was *Roe v Wade.* In this case, in a decision as difficult as *Griswold* and expanding on *Griswold*'s assumptions of "zones of privacy" in which the states and the federal government could not intrude, the Supreme Court tackled the divisive issue of abortion rights. Few decisions reflect the changing social and cultural world of the United States more vividly than *Roe.* Some states in the 1970s retained severe, nineteenth-century restrictions on abortion, whereas others had revised their statutes to allow abortions in specific situations. In *Roe,* the Court examined a restrictive Texas statute and a more permissive Georgia statute. In a 7–2 decision, the Court held that the states did have an interest in restricting abortions; however, the states could not completely outlaw abortions, because of the private nature of pregnancy and a woman's right to control her own body. According to Associate Justice Harry Blackmun, who wrote for the majority, only in the last three months of pregnancy could the states prohibit abortions. In the second trimester, the state and the individual shared an interest in the outcome of pregnancy, and the state could provide some guidelines that might slightly limit a woman's right to abort. However, in the first trimester, the state possessed no authority to restrict abortions. Although Chief Justice Warren Burger claimed in his concurring opinion that the Court's decision should not be interpreted as supporting abortion-on-demand, many did interpret the decision in that way. Once granted, a woman's right to privacy applied to the states through the due process clause of the Fourteenth Amendment; thus, the Court's decision effectively limited how the states could regulate this issue.

The decision generated immediate controversy and has since been under unceasing popular, scholarly, and legal attack. Although the

Court in subsequent cases clarified and limited the breadth of its opinion in *Roe,* the fundamental issue—a woman's right to an abortion—is still the focus of political and legal wrangling. The *Roe* decision shows how pliable the law can be in the hands of the Supreme Court justices. It also suggests how much more tolerant American culture and society have become of previously stigmatized behaviors.

In sum, judicial liberalism reflected the social, moral, and cultural changes that swept across the United States in the 1950s, 1960s, and 1970s. Complementing the rise of judicial liberalism was a drift toward restricting the actions of the states and expanding the power of the federal government and the federal judiciary. It was within this legal and social culture that the next wave of case law questioning obscenity restrictions and the toleration of pornography occurred.

Litigating Obscenity from 1942 to 1974

In the common-law tradition of case-by-case, incremental development and decisionmaking, the richest area of obscenity jurisprudence evolved from a First Amendment speech litigation case that held significant ramifications for obscenity and pornography. *Chaplinsky v. New Hampshire* was one of two cases heard by the U.S. Supreme Court in the early 1940s that involved Jehovah's Witnesses. The Court in this case upheld Walter Chaplinsky's conviction by the state for using "offensive words" while promoting his religious beliefs. During the late 1930s, Chaplinsky allegedly had called hecklers on the street "God damn fascists"; referred to the Rochester city government as "Fascists or Fascist agents"; and described organized religion as a "racket" (315 U.S. 568). Arrested and tried under a New Hampshire statute regulating public speech, Chaplinsky was convicted by the jury. He appealed through the state court system and later to the U.S. Supreme Court. However, Associate Justice Frank Murphy, writing for a unanimous court, upheld Chaplinsky's conviction in 1942.

Murphy agreed with Chaplinsky that the First Amendment had been incorporated against the states through the due process clause of the Fourteenth Amendment, but reminded him that "the right to free speech is not absolute at all times and under all circumstances." Political speech was protected; but "there are certain well-defined and narrowly limited classes of speech, the prevention and punishment of which have never been thought to raise any Constitutional problem." Murphy then listed speech that was not protected by the First Amendment as including "the lewd and obscene, the profane, the libelous, and the insulting or 'fighting' words—those which by their very utterance inflict injury or tend to incite an immediate breach of the peace." For the first time, the Supreme Court explicitly stated in *Chaplinsky v. New Hampshire* that obscenity was not protected speech; such speech could be punished, limited, and regulated by state statute. Obscene words are "no essential part of any exposition of ideas, and are of such slight social value as a step to truth that any benefit that may be derived from them is clearly outweighed by the social interest in order and morality" (315 U.S. 568, 572). In *Chaplinsky,* the Supreme Court clarified the line between protected and unprotected expression in the realm of obscenity and profanity. This division would assist future judges in assessing the relative levels of constitutional protection afforded various obscene and pornographic materials.

In 1957, the Supreme Court handed down its decision in *Butler v. Michigan*—what media historian Richard F. Nixon called "the last nail in the *Hicklin* coffin" (352 U.S. 380). Michigan had a statute making it a crime to sell a book that contained "immoral, lewd, or lascivious language, prints, figures, or descriptions" that tended to "the corruption of the morals of youth," or to provide "to the general public a book the trial judge finds to have a potentially deleterious influence on youth." Writing for the majority of eight justices, with Associate Justice Hugo Black concurring, Associate Justice Felix Frankfurter found that the legislation was "not reasonably restricted to the evil with which it is said to deal. The incident of this enactment is to reduce the adult population of Michigan to reading only what is fit for children." To prevent adults from seeing such materials because they *might* corrupt youth was to go too far. In Frankfurter's words, "Surely, this is to burn down the house to roast the pig" (352 U.S. 380, 383). Frankfurter thereby put an end to the use of the *Hicklin* doctrine in U.S. constitutional law. What would replace the *Hicklin* doctrine in obscenity cases was not yet known, but it soon became clear.

Modern judicial discussion of the problem of obscenity and pornography began on June 24, 1957, when the Supreme Court handed down two cases: *Kingsley Books, Inc., et al. v. Brown, Corporation Counsel* and *Samuel Roth v. United States.* These cases— one dealing with a state statute that allowed cities to seize and destroy "obscene" materials and the other with a federal statute barring obscene materials from the mail—opened a new line of argument and case law on the issue of obscenity. In *Kingsley,* a New York statute authorized municipalities to enjoin "the sale or distribution of obscene written and printed matter." If the local judge in this civil administrative procedure (not criminal procedure) thereafter found the material to be obscene, the material had to be destroyed. Kingsley Books violated the statute, was enjoined, and appealed the injunction on First Amendment grounds. Justice Frankfurter wrote for the majority, upholding the regulation as a valid exercise of the state's police power. For the majority, the issue was one of methods of suppressing obscene materials. If New York chose to allow injunctions as well as criminal prosecutions against those who sold and distributed obscene material, then New York could do so; it was, Frankfurter wrote, "a matter within the legislature's range of choice."

In dissent, Chief Justice Warren argued that this case was not about "criminal obscenity" but rather about banning some books by court order. In Warren's opinion, *Kingsley* placed the content of the book on trial, and no judicial standard existed for judging the quality or offensiveness of the book. "It is the conduct of the individual that should be judged," Warren argued, "not the quality of art or literature." He argued that in the absence of a judicial determination of what was and was not illegal or objectionable, the books in question should not be destroyed. "It savors too much of book burning," he wrote (354 U.S. 436, 446). This concern arose again in later case law.

Also dissenting, Associate Justice Brennan argued that the lack of a jury trial was a fatal error in New York's procedure. Only through a jury trial could allegedly obscene material be judged; and the standard for judging, Brennan proposed, was "whether to the average person, applying the contemporary community standards, the dominant theme of the material taken as a whole appeals to prurient interests." Brennan considered the jury a particularly appropriate means for judging obscenity, because his judge-made standard "call[ed] for an appraisal of material according to the average person's application of contemporary community standards." Brennan conceded, "Reasonable men may differ whether the material is obscene" (354 U.S. 436, 448); but this fact made the jury's input all the more important.

Kingsley signaled that the Supreme Court was heading toward a major change in obscenity law. That change became clear in the other obscenity case decided that day, *Roth v. United States.* Justice Brennan's opinion in *Roth* created a new judicial standard for defining obscenity and thus opened a new chapter in obscenity jurisprudence. His decision also reflected the changing social and cultural sentiments of the post–World War II United States, as well as a faith that federal power could solve most social problems. Brennan's goal was to establish a single, national judicial standard for determining what constituted obscenity; in the long run, this goal proved elusive and perhaps naïve.

Roth v. United States dealt with an 1876 federal law known as the Comstock Act, which made obscene, lewd, lascivious, filthy, or indecent material nonmailable and which imposed punishment on anyone who attempted to use the mails to distribute such material. (*Roth*'s companion case, *Alberts v. California,* dealt with a California statute that made it illegal to sell or advertise obscene or indecent material.) Defendants in both cases had lost at the trial level and pushed their appeals through the state and federal courts to the U.S. Supreme Court. In both cases the facts confronted the justices with the question of what was or was not obscene, and also whether the state and federal statutes were valid regulations. In a 5–4 decision, the majority upheld both statutes as constitutional. Justice Brennan wrote for the majority, addressing the concern that regulation of obscenity might infringe upon or limit legitimate First Amendment rights, and trying to put that concern to rest. He argued that "all ideas having the slightest redeeming social importance—unorthodox ideas, controversial ideas, even ideas hateful to the prevailing climate of opinion—have the full protection of the guarantees" of the First Amendment. Nevertheless, the First Amendment was not unlimited. He continued, "Implicit in the history of the First Amendment is the rejection of obscenity as utterly without redeeming social importance." As evidence that obscenity (in his famous words) was "utterly without redeeming social value," Brennan cited colonial statutes and *Chaplinsky v. New Hampshire* (1942). In interesting *dicta* (language not necessary for the disposition of the case but included as explanation or justification), Brennan drew a distinction between the sexual and the obscene, noting that the two were not synonymous:

> Obscene material is material that deals with sex in a manner appealing to prurient interest. The mere portrayal of sex in works of art, literature, or science is no reason to deny such works the constitutional protection of freedom of speech and press. Sex, a great and mysterious

motive force in human life, has indisputably been a subject of absorbing interest to mankind through the ages; it is one of the vital problems of human interest and public concern.

Moving on, Brennan then explained that social benefits of freedom of speech and press "have contributed greatly to the development and well-being of our free society and are indispensable to its continued growth." It was the responsibility of the U.S. Supreme Court to safeguard those freedoms from erosion by Congress and the states. To do so, the Court needed "standards for judging obscenity [that] safeguard the protection of speech and press for material which does not treat sex in a manner appealing to prurient interest" (354 U.S. 476, 488).

Brennan concluded by taking judicial notice of the old *Hicklin* test and holding that it had been rejected and replaced by a new judicial standard, an update of Judge John M. Woolsey's ruling in *Ulysses* in 1933: *"whether to the average person, applying contemporary community standards, the dominant theme of the material taken as a whole appeals to prurient interest"* (354 U.S. 476, 489; emphasis added). Whereas the *Hicklin* test considered the effects upon susceptible persons of isolated passages in written or published materials, Brennan's new *Roth* test avoided that narrowness and was therefore considered constitutionally sound. With this new test, the Court upheld Roth's conviction, the federal statute granting the Post Office the power to bar from the mails obscene materials, and California's statute. This new standard became the new baseline for judicial decisionmaking on what was and what was not "obscene" and "utterly without redeeming social importance." Trial judges and juries could administer this new standard in their deliberations.

Chief Justice Warren concurred in the result in *Roth* but expressed concern about the potential breadth of Brennan's new obscenity standard. Justice John Marshall Harlan II agreed with the Court's majority in *Alberts*, continuing his tradition of allowing the states to control issues such as obscenity; but he dissented in *Roth*, believing that the regulation of obscenity was not a federal issue. Given the vast diversity of opinion in the United States, Harlan did not believe that a single, national standard defining obscenity—a standard that could only be judicially determined and federally imposed—was appropriate. As Harlan argued, "The dangers of federal censorship in this field are far greater than anything the States may do." If one state banned a book and a neighboring state did not, Harlan argued, some citizens could still read the banned book, and the great experiment of American federalism could still proceed unhindered in the forty-eight "social laboratories" that were the individual states (354 U.S. 476, 505).

Justices Douglas and Black dissented from the majority opinion, arguing that all federal and state statutes against obscenity violated the First Amendment guarantee of free speech and press, which prohibited any regulation of message content. They pointed out that Brennan's language was vague, and they questioned the meaning of phrases such as "contemporary community standards" and "appealing to prurient interests." Douglas worried that "the test that suppresses a cheap tract today can suppress a literary gem tomorrow. All it need do is to incite a lascivious thought or arouse a lustful desire." To Douglas's mind, "the list of books that judges or juries can place in that category is endless." Douglas, joined by Black, concluded that they would give the First Amendment a broader interpretation: "I have the same confidence in the ability of our people to reject noxious literature as I have in their capacity to sort out the true from the false in theology, economics, politics, or any other field" (354 U.S. 476, 514).

Roth is a landmark case not only because the Court upheld the federal and state statutes in question but also because a new judicial standard was established defining obscenity. The new, five-part "test" stated that a determination of obscenity (1) relied on the viewpoint of the average reasonable person, (2) depended on community standards of acceptability, (3) could be made only for those works that had questionable material as their predominant theme, (4) must be based on the entirety of the particular work, and (5) must excite individuals' prurient interests. Brennan's phrase "utterly without redeeming social importance" became as important to a finding of obscenity as was this new, five-part test, since many of the new pulp magazines (including *Playboy*) could argue that they contained *some* socially redeeming material and therefore could not be banned from the mails or prosecuted by the states. Thus, instead of reinforcing restrictions on obscenity and the mailing of allegedly obscene materials, *Roth v. United States* became the reason such materials could be sent through the mail without interference. Unintentionally, *Roth* led to a liberalization of restrictions on pornography and the greater circulation and availability of obscene materials. Only so-called hard-core pornography was unprotected by the Constitution and failed to pass Brennan's *Roth* standard. Restrictions on obscenity, since *Roth,* cannot be tightened.

With this liberalization of the rules of pornography, people and entities that had been prosecuted earlier under state or federal statutes appealed their convictions, on the grounds that under the new judge-made rules of obscenity, they had committed no violation. In *Kingsley International Pictures Corp. v. Regents of the University of New York* (1959) the justices decided that a film could not be banned from a college campus because its content included a depiction of adultery. In that same year, *Smith v. California* "added more variables," in the words of obscenity scholar Hixson, to the *Roth* standard (Hixson 1996, 28). In *Smith,* a divided Supreme Court decided that a Los Angeles ordinance that made a bookseller criminally liable if he or she had an "obscene" book in the store was unconstitutionally broad and vague. This ordinance would make the bookseller a self-censor and inhibit the circulation of ideas, the justices ruled. However, little consensus existed among the justices on the appropriate definition of obscenity: five different concurring opinions and dissents were filed. Although a majority agreed that the ordinance went too far, the grounds for such a finding were not at all clear.

Community standards, prevailing literary standards, questions of search-and-seizure, exceptions for films, and judicial concerns about local and state censorship all emerged as separate threads in the Supreme Court's decisions after *Roth*. In 1961, the Supreme Court called into question whether motion pictures could be censored at all, even as its 5–4 decision in *Times Film Corp. v. Chicago* upheld Chicago's policy of requiring films shown in the city to be submitted to a local board of censors. At issue in the case was not obscenity directly but whether decisions about morality were, in fact, appropriately handled by administrative boards. Dissenters argued that the freedom of speech prohibited all such oversight by localities because the censor would do more damage than the films being shown. As Chief Justice Warren argued in the dissent, "The censor's sword pierces deeply into the heart of free expression" (365 U.S. 43, 75). Four years later, the Court limited *Times Film Corp.* when it found that a Maryland regulation on film submission violated the First Amendment. In 1968, the Supreme Court essentially reversed the position it had defended in *Times Film Corp.* when it found in *Teitel*

Film Corp. v. Cusack that Chicago's film censorship program violated the First and Fourteenth Amendments.

The Court also heard a number of other cases, involving media other than film, in which the process by which police seized allegedly obscene materials was in question. A 1961 Missouri procedure that allowed for the sweeping seizure of allegedly obscene books and magazines, based on the flimsiest knowledge of the contents of those books and magazines, by a judge who had not even examined them, went too far and threatened freedom of expression, in the justices' view. States could seize materials under the *Roth* standard, the justices held, but the court or the police had to have prior evidence that the materials were pornographic as defined in *Roth*. Absent such support, seizure was improper.

This confusing picture needed further clarification, which the Court sought to provide in another major case in 1962, only five years after *Roth*. Unfortunately, its effort was only marginally successful. In June 1962, the Supreme Court handed down a decision in *Manual Enterprises, Inc., et al. v. Day, Postmaster General* in which the justices questioned the reach of the Comstock Law and the meaning of the *Roth* definition of obscenity. Herman L. Womack published a series of magazines that featured photos of nude and seminude men and that provided the names of the men pictured and the names and addresses of the photographers. These magazines also carried advertisements of independent photographers who had similar images for sale. Womack mailed these magazines to Chicago addresses. As required by federal law, the postmaster in Alexandria, Virginia, intercepted the magazines and determined that their content made the magazines "nonmailable" under the Comstock Act: that is, they were obscene and provided information for procuring obscene materials. Womack appealed.

No single opinion appeared in *Manual* (although the Court's division was 8–1), but Justice Harlan, joined by Associate Justice Potter Stewart, provided the fullest analysis. Harlan added a new dimension to the *Roth* standard: Before it could be declared obscene, material must not only be found to appeal to "prurient interest" but also to be "patently offensive." As Harlan explained, "These magazines cannot be deemed so offensive on their face as to affront current community standards of decency—a quality that we shall hereafter refer to as 'patent offensiveness' or 'indecency.'" And if these magazines were not obscene, then they did not violate the Comstock Act. Harlan next addressed the issue of which "community" was the relevant one for deciding "community standards." Supporting national community standards for judging obscenity, he argued, "We think the proper test under this federal statute, reaching as it does to all parts of the United States whose population reflects many different ethnic and cultural backgrounds, is a national standard of decency." Localism no longer mattered, and even state standards no longer held sway with the Supreme Court; one moral size fit all Americans. Harlan left open the question of whether Congress could make exceptions, saying only that the federal courts "need not decide whether Congress could constitutionally prescribe a lesser geographical framework for judging this issue [of community standards] which would not have the intolerable consequence of denying some sections of the country access to material, there deemed acceptable, which in others might be considered offensive to prevailing community standards of decency"(370 U.S. 478, 488).

On the question of providing information to others on where to procure obscene material, the justices decided that the government had not demonstrated that the publisher knew that the advertisements were offering obscene materials for sale; therefore, the prosecution of Manual Enterprises failed on this count as well. Justice Brennan, joined by Chief Justice Warren and Justice Douglas, concurred but asserted that the Comstock Act did not authorize the postmaster to make a determination of obscenity; rather, that determination had to be made by a jury. Associate Justice Tom Clark dissented, arguing that the federal statute was clear, that the materials were obscene and therefore nonmailable under the statute. These widely divergent concurring and dissenting opinions revealed the Court's ongoing confusion regarding the laws governing obscenity. *Manual Enterprises* both clarified and expanded *Roth* (materials had to appeal to prurient interest and be patently offensive), but it also confused *Roth* by suggesting that only a national standard of obscenity was constitutionally permissible. Later case law further expanded and elaborated on these interpretive problems.

In the years after the *Roth* decision in 1957, the justices and their court came under a great deal of scrutiny and criticism not only for their activism in the areas of criminal procedure and apportionment but also for their decisions loosening the rules of obscenity and allowing greater circulation of pornography. This criticism came from both the popular press and the legal profession. As a result, the

Supreme Court ventured yet again into the tangle of obscenity in 1964, in the case of *Jacobellis v. Ohio*. Nico Jacobellis managed a movie theatre in Cleveland Heights, Ohio, that showed a French film entitled *Les Amants* (The Lovers), which contained questionable material toward its end. Ohio prosecuted Jacobellis for possessing and exhibiting an obscene film, and the jury found him guilty. After appealing his conviction through the Ohio courts (all of which upheld his conviction and the state statute under which he was convicted), Jacobellis appealed to the Supreme Court. His attorneys argued that the film was not obscene under the *Roth* standard and that the Ohio statute unconstitutionally violated the freedom-of-expression guarantees of the First and Fourteenth Amendments.

In a 6–3 decision, with five of the justices registering separate opinions (as was becoming the norm in obscenity cases), Justice Brennan, joined by Associate Justice Goldberg, delivered the most important Court opinion in this case (although none of the divergent opinions technically can be called the opinion of the Court). Since he had penned the earlier *Roth* decision, it is not surprising that Brennan upheld the *Roth* test of obscenity. In addition, he defined what constituted "the community"; held that the Supreme Court possessed a constitutional duty to decide obscenity cases; and decided that the film in this case was not obscene. Brennan then responded to criticism that the justices ought not be involved in defining and determining what was "obscene," leaving such matters instead to juries. Brennan admitted that the argument for the Court's avoiding such cases was "appealing, since it would lift from our shoulders a difficult, recurring, and unpleasant task." "But," he continued, "we cannot accept [the argument]. Such an abnegation of judicial supervision in this field would be inconsistent with our duty to uphold the constitutional guarantees." Because obscenity was excluded from constitutional protection, "the question whether a particular work is obscene necessarily implicates an issue of constitutional law." Wherever "rights" were at issue, the Supreme Court had a constitutional duty to fulfill. Brennan denied that the Court's majority was acting as censor in crafting judicial guidelines for determining what was "obscene." (In his dissent, Chief Justice Warren had made this claim against the majority's decision.) Instead, Brennan argued, the Court was acting to defend the freedom of expression. Brennan reaffirmed "the principle that, in 'obscenity' cases as in all others involving rights derived from the First Amendment guarantees of free expression, this Court cannot avoid making an independent constitutional judgment on the facts of the case as to whether the material involved is constitutionally protected." In shorthand: The Supreme Court had a responsibility, even a duty, to define and defend "rights"; it had no choice but to confront the issue of obscenity.

Next Justice Brennan defended his *Roth* standard. After restating the standard—whether to the average person, applying contemporary community standards, the dominant theme of the material taken as a whole appeals to prurient interest—Brennan conceded that the definition was "not perfect." On the other hand, he also believed that "any substitute would raise equally difficult problems," and for that reason the Court reaffirmed the *Roth* standard as the rule for the Court. He also reaffirmed that obscenity was excluded from constitutional protection because it was "utterly without redeeming social importance," and confirmed that the portrayal of sex in written materials and films was not necessarily obscene. Brennan stuck by his *Roth* standard.

He then launched into a discussion of which "community" ought to be the standard for judging "community standards," immediately disposing of the argument that the local community whence the case arose mattered most. Where the case began did not matter, in Brennan's view. He interpreted language used by federal district Judge Learned Hand in the 1913 *Kennerley* decision to mean that the "community" implied not the locality or even the state where the case originated but "society at large; . . . the public, or people in general." The definition of obscenity should not vary from place to place, county to county, or state to state, but rather should apply to the entire United States. In connection with this line of thought, Brennan referred to Justice Harlan's statement in *Manual Enterprises* that without a national standard some sections of the country would have access to materials that other sections would lack. What was needed and what Brennan announced in *Jacobellis* was a national standard of obscenity. "An allegedly obscene work," he stressed, "must be determined on the basis of a national standard" (378 U.S. 184, 195). Alluding to one of the great constitutional cases from the early nineteenth century, *McCulloch v. Maryland* (1819)—in which Chief Justice John Marshall reminded the country, "It is a Constitution we are expounding" (17 U.S. 316, 407)—and in an attempt to lend his decision greater weight, Justice Brennan added, "It is, after all, a national Constitution we are expounding" (378 U.S. 184, 195).

Brennan then described the film at issue, noted that reviewers had favorably reviewed it, and commented that it had been shown widely across the country. He then held that the last scene of the film was not obscene under his *Roth* standard, and he reversed Jacobellis's conviction.

Justice Potter Stewart wrote a separate, concurring opinion in *Jacobellis* that has since been much quoted. He conceded that *Roth* could be read "in a variety of ways" and that the Supreme Court was "trying to define what may be indefinable." Arguing that under *Roth* criminal prosecution of obscenity was limited to "hard-core pornography," he explained: "I shall not today attempt further to define the kinds of material I understand to be embraced within that shorthand description; and perhaps I could never succeed in intelligently doing so. But I know it when I see it, and the motion picture involved in this case is not that" (378 U.S. 184, 197). "I know it when I see it" captures the frustration experienced by the justices in attempting to define the obscene in terms that were appropriately narrow and yet applicable nationwide.

In dissent, Chief Justice Warren, joined by Justice Clark, agreed that Brennan's *Roth* standard was an appropriate guide for judges and courts, but did not agree that this meant a national standard was needed. "Community standards" in *Roth* meant the local community, "not a national standard." Warren argued convincingly that "there is no provable 'national standard,' and perhaps there should be none." Further, Warren opposed the casting of the U.S. Supreme Court in the role of moral censor for the nation. Once a trial court had determined some material to be "obscene," Warren would not then have an appellate court—especially not the Supreme Court—reviewing materials and making a judgment on whether they were obscene or not. He opposed the Supreme Court's becoming "the Super Censor of all of the obscenity purveyed throughout the Nation" (378 U.S. 184, 203). Also dissenting, Justice Harlan argued that the states, not the federal government, ought to make the decision about what was or was not obscene. He would uphold the Ohio obscenity statute.

Jacobellis restated the *Roth* rule, expanded the community that would judge a work, and revealed the deep divisions among the justices on the difficulties of defining a general standard of obscenity. The lack of consensus on the Court, in turn, reflected the absence of a social consensus on the appropriate limits of censorship and the nature of obscenity. Justice Stewart might have known it when he saw it; but did anyone else agree that what he saw was obscene?

The split in the Supreme Court continued in the next major decision on obscenity, reached two years later, in *A Book Named "John Cleland's Memoirs of a Woman of Pleasure" et al. v. Attorney General of Massachusetts* (1966). As they had in *Jacobellis*, the justices in *Memoirs of a Woman of Pleasure* delivered several opinions, none of which can rightly be called the opinion of the Court. Of the nine justices, seven of them wrote separate opinions in *Memoirs*. The case arose in Massachusetts, where a state statute allowed the state attorney general to bring a civil equity suit to have a book declared "obscene." At issue was a new edition of *Memoirs of a Woman of Pleasure*, better known as *Fanny Hill*—a story about a prostitute, originally published about 1750. At trial, the judge ruled that the book was obscene. The Massachusetts Supreme Judicial Court agreed, finding that *Fanny Hill* met the requirements set forth by the *Roth* test. The book's publisher, G. P. Putnam's Sons, then appealed to the United States Supreme Court.

Perhaps influenced by the written and oral arguments of the publisher's counsel Charles Rembar, Brennan in writing his opinion (in which he was joined by Chief Justice Warren and Associate Justice Abe Fortas) changed key words in the *Roth* test. In *Memoirs*, Brennan restated the test as follows: "(a) the dominant theme of the material taken as a whole appeals to a prurient interest in sex; (b) the material is patently offensive because it affronts contemporary community standards relating to the description or representation of sexual matters; and (c) the material is utterly without redeeming social *value*" (383 U.S. 413, 418).

In *Roth* the language had read, "utterly without redeeming social *importance*." Supposedly a book could have "value" without being "important"—and that was exactly the error made by the Massachusetts court when it held that the book had little social value as literature and historical artifact. According to Brennan's new version of the *Roth* test, even a little social value was enough to prevent the book's suppression as an obscene work. As a result, the finding in Massachusetts that *Memoirs* was obscene had to be reversed (383 U.S. 413, 421).

Yet a consensus on obscenity continued to elude the justices. In dissent, Justice Clark spoke of how troubled he was by obscenity cases as well as by the material involved in them. "I have 'stomached' past cases," he lamented, "for almost 10 years without much outcry. Though I am not known to be a purist—or a shrinking violet—this book is too much even for me" (383 U.S. 413, 441). He went on to describe the book in some detail, in order to demonstrate that it possessed no conceivable social importance and ought to have been suppressed. Justices Harlan and White would have deferred to the state of Massachusetts to decide whether the work was obscene; and since the Supreme Judicial Court had determined that it was, they would have supported the lower court's finding. Whether to continue along the path of crafting a national obscenity standard or to defer to state policies was one of the central dilemmas facing the Supreme Court justices in the 1960s.

Two years after the decision in *Memoirs,* in April 1968, the justices deferred to and upheld a state's restriction on access of allegedly obscene materials to minors. This decision, handed down in *Ginsberg v. New York,* evoked sharply dissenting views among the justices—once again demonstrating the growing stresses and strains on the Court over the issue of obscenity. In October 1965, a 16-year-old boy had bought two "girlie" magazines at Sam's Stationery and Luncheonette, run by Sam Ginsberg in Bellmore, Long Island, New York. According to the facts presented in the dissenting opinion, the boy's mother told him to buy the magazines so that Ginsberg's store could be prosecuted. After he bought the magazines, she complained to authorities, and New York prosecuted Ginsberg under a state statute making it a crime to sell obscene materials to minors. At trial without a jury, the judge found the sale to the 16-year-old violated the statute, which forbade the knowing sale to a minor under 17 years of age of "'(a) any picture ... [which] depicts nudity ... and which is harmful to minors,' and '(b) any ... magazine which contains ... [such pictures] ... and which, taken as a whole is harmful to minors.'" Ginsberg turned to the appellate court in New York, which affirmed his conviction; a subsequent appeal to the state supreme court, the New York Court of Appeals, was denied. At that point, Ginsberg appealed to the U.S. Supreme Court, challenging the constitutionality of the state's statute.

Justice Brennan wrote the majority opinion in *Ginsberg,* upholding both the conviction and the statute. In doing so, he restated the *Roth* rule that obscenity did not lie within the area of protected speech or press upheld by the First Amendment freedom of expression clauses. Ginsberg's lawyers had argued for "the broad proposition that the scope of the constitutional freedom of expression secured to a citizen to read or see material concerned with sex cannot be made to depend upon whether the citizen is an adult or a minor." But the Court's majority rejected this argument. Insuring the "well-being" of children constituted a legitimate reason for the state statute, because the exposure of minors to such materials might harm them, the justices ruled. Of course, parents possessed the primary responsibility for raising their children; yet parents could expect the law to assist them in that task by prohibiting the sale of such materials to children under 17 years old. Should there be any parents who did not welcome such assistance from the state, as Brennan pointed out, "the prohibition against sales to minors does not bar parents who so desire from purchasing the magazines for their children"(390 U.S. 629, 639). Therefore, New York had a rational basis for the statute: the safeguarding of minors from harm. Brennan found that the state statute was sufficiently narrow, and he upheld the constitutionality of the statute even though it created one standard of obscenity for children and another for adults.

Justice Stewart concurred with the majority's decision, adding, "A child—like someone in a captive audience—is not possessed of that full capacity for individual choice which is the presupposition for First Amendment guarantees." On the basis of this presupposition, he explained, the state denied other rights to children, such as marriage and voting—restrictions that would be "intolerable for adults" (390 U.S. 629, 650). Should not the same standard apply to obscene materials? Justices Douglas and Black dissented from the decision. Douglas argued, "Big Brother can no more say what a person shall listen to or read than he can say what shall be published." He claimed to find materials like those involved in the Ginsberg case "exceedingly dull and boring," but said he could understand how some people might become concerned about such materials. Even so, he feared the involvement of any level of government in censoring people's reading or viewing materials. In Douglas's view, the First Amendment "was designed to keep the state and the hands of state officials off the printing presses of America and off the distribution of all printed literature." Only a constitutional amendment, he believed, could authorize the federal government or the states to censor even immoral reading materials. And governmental censorship would necessarily depend on the "neurosis of the censor," leading to arbitrariness—the unequal application of the law. The desire to avoid such pitfalls led Douglas to his absolutist position on the freedom-of-expression clauses: no regulation or suppression was acceptable. "Today," he wrote, "this Court sits as the Nation's board of censors." And, he continued, "I do not know of any group in the country less qualified, first, to know what obscenity is when they see it, and second, to have any considered judgment as to what the deleterious or beneficial impact of a particular publication may be on minds of either young or old" (390 U.S. 629, 656).

In a controversial dissent, Justice Abe Fortas also diverged from the majority's decision in *Ginsberg.* He believed that the majority was wrong in finding no need to scrutinize the state's determination of obscenity in conjunction with the age of the consumer to whom the allegedly obscene materials were distributed: "The Court avoids facing the problem whether the magazines in the present case are 'obscene' when viewed by a 16-year-old boy, although not 'obscene' when viewed by someone 17 years of age or older." He accepted the general concept of variable obscenity—"what is not obscene for an adult may be obscene for a child"—but believed that the difference between the two categories had yet to be adequately described and defined by law. Although the states had the power to differentiate between adults and children, they could not do so on "an arbitrary, free-wheeling basis." Nor could the sellers of printed matter be expected to distinguish on sight between 16- and 17-year-olds, at the risk of lawsuit and the loss of their livelihood and freedom: "Bookselling should not be a hazardous profession." Furthermore, although the marketing of obscene materials to children was inappropriate, Fortas found equally inadmissible the "undefined and unlimited approval of state censorship in this area [that] denies to children free access to books and works of art to which many parents may wish their children to have uninhibited access." To avoid these difficulties, Fortas proposed a new rule for the prosecution of obscenity cases like *Ginsberg:* that a seller of allegedly obscene materials must be proven to have sold those materials *with full knowledge and forethought* to children. If such intent on the part of the seller could not be proven (as it could not in *Ginsberg*), then the prosecution must fail (390 U.S. 629, 674). Fortas's opinion failed to persuade the Court and left the general public with the impression that he was "soft" on pornography. This dissent later would come back to haunt him.

Memoirs and *Ginsberg* demonstrated to the legal profession and to the country just how badly divided the Supreme Court was on the issue of obscenity and how the justices of the Supreme Court adjusted their rules to fit the evolving legal and social context. Public opinion was equally divided. By the middle to late 1960s, the tensions in the country over the Vietnam War, student activism, the civil rights movement, and the judicial activism of the Supreme Court had polarized much of the country. Obscenity continued to be featured in the headlines.

In 1968, in Hollywood, California, in response to pressure from concerned parents and politicians, the Motion Picture Association adopted a self-imposed rating system for judging the content of movies: the current system of G, PG, R, and X for hard-core pornography (PG-13 was added later). This development occurred as mainstream American cinema became more and more explicit in the treatment and depiction of sex. Also stirring up discussion was the opinion of Justice Fortas in *Ginsberg*. Fortas was intensely scrutinized by the media and federal politicians, who believed him tolerant of pornography. The criticism was unfounded, but it damaged his reputation: In 1968, when President Lyndon B. Johnson nominated Fortas to succeed Earl Warren as chief justice of the Supreme Court, the nomination was defeated in the Senate, in large measure due to the perception that he was "soft" on obscenity.

The next major decision by the Supreme Court on obscenity, in *Stanley v. Georgia* (1969), was unusual in that it was unanimous. The Court used the occasion to enunciate a new rule in United States law: that private possession of pornography was not a crime. Georgia police had obtained a warrant to search Robert Stanley's home for evidence of bookmaking. In the course of their search, officers found three reels of eight-millimeter film in a desk drawer. They viewed the reels, using a projector and screen found in Stanley's living room, and concluded that the films were obscene. Georgia then charged Stanley with possession of obscene materials. He was tried before a jury and convicted. He appealed the conviction, claiming that the state statute making it illegal to possess such materials violated the First and Fourteenth Amendments to the federal Constitution. Associate Justice Thurgood Marshall, supported by six other members of the Court, upheld Stanley's argument and declared the Georgia statute unconstitutional. Because *Roth* did not apply to the issue confronted in this case, which was the mere possession of obscenity, Marshall referred to the 1965 "right-to-privacy" case of *Griswold v. Connecticut,* saying that that decision established the rule that "the Constitution protects the right to receive information and ideas." Such a right, claimed the Court's majority, was "fundamental to our free society" and "free, except in very limited circumstances, from unwanted governmental intrusions into one's privacy." Georgia claimed that the presence of "obscene" materials justified the state's intrusion into Stanley's home, but the Court found this argument "insufficient." As Marshall stated the issue:

> Whatever may be the justifications for other statutes regulating obscenity, we do not think they reach into the privacy of one's home. If the First Amendment means anything, it means that a State has no business telling a man, sitting alone in his own home, what books he may read or what films he may watch. Our whole constitutional heritage rebels at the thought of giving government the power to control men's minds.

To Georgia's argument that it wished to limit exposure to obscenity because such exposure might lead to "deviant sexual behavior or crimes of sexual violence," Marshall was dismissive; no evidence existed establishing a link between obscenity and deviant antisocial behavior. Georgia could "no more prohibit mere possession of obscene matter on the ground that it may lead to antisocial conduct than it may prohibit possession of chemistry books on the ground that they may lead to the manufacture of homemade spirits." Anticipating criticism of this decision—with critics arguing that *Stanley* would prohibit the states from applying any regulations on obscenity—Marshall pointed out, "The States retain broad power to regulate obscenity; that power simply does not extend to mere possession by the individual in the privacy of his own home."

Justices Stewart, Brennan, and White concurred with the result reached by their brethren; yet they would have reversed Stanley's conviction on other, procedural grounds. They would have reversed because the police searching his house were not authorized by their search warrant to search for obscenity; rather, the warrant authorized them to search only for bookmaking paraphernalia. Under the 1961 landmark case of *Mapp v. Ohio,* which extended the exclusionary rule in police searches against the states through the Fourteenth Amendment, the viewing and the seizure of the films by police were illegal. The Supreme Court overturned Stanley's conviction, declared Georgia's statute prohibiting the possession of obscene materials unconstitutional, and extended the right to privacy to cover the possession of pornographic materials.

After the ruling in *Stanley,* many feared that obscenity would be marching into every home. Many Americans' fears about the further liberalization of the law on pornography appeared to be coming true when in September 1970 the President's Commission on Obscenity and Pornography, established by Congress in 1967 and appointed by President Johnson in 1968, issued its *Report* to President Richard M. Nixon. The *Report* recommended that adults be given greater access to materials previously defined as obscene, because no evidence existed linking access to obscenity with delinquent or criminal behavior among adults. Following the lead of the Supreme Court, the *Report* urged the repeal of state laws prohibiting adult access to obscenity and recommended that all levels of government not interfere with the rights of adults "to read, obtain, or view explicit sexual material" (Hixson, 1996). Given how divisive the issue was at the time, it is unsurprising that the *Report* received mixed reviews and soon became a historical relic of 1960s liberalism.

As a legal and social issue, obscenity would not go away. Two years later the Supreme Court again sought to clarify the law on obscenity and its own prior obscenity standards. On May 3, 1971, the Court handed down two decisions in this area: *United States v. Reidel* and *United States v. Thirty-Seven Photographs.* Both cases arose because of the Court's *Stanley* ruling that mere private possession of obscenity could not be made a crime. That ruling raised the question of why, if possession of pornography was not a crime, its distribution through the mails or importation into the country from overseas was still a criminal offense? In *Reidel,* in a 7–2 decision, with Justice White writing for the majority, the Court held that Congress possessed the power to regulate the distribution of obscenity through the mails even to individuals who stated that they were adults over 21. *Stanley*'s constitutional right to possess obscene materials in the privacy of one's home did not, by extension, denote a First Amendment right to sell and deliver such material. One might own such materials, but Congress could regulate or ban the use of the mails to distribute such materials. Signaling that the Court was growing weary of the obscenity issue, Justice White noted that obscenity prosecutions and decisions had become so complicated and costly that "basic reassessment is not only wise but essential," and that such reassessment had to come from the legislative branch of government, not the courts. If reassessment were necessary, he argued, then the task "lies with those who pass, repeal, and amend statutes and ordinances" (402 U.S. 351, 357). In other words, he hoped that the legislative branch might provide the Court a path out of the obscenity thicket.

Not only could Congress prohibit the use of the mails to deliver pornography, but as announced in a 6–3 decision in *Thirty-Seven Photographs,* Congress could prevent the importation of obscenity into the country even for private use. In a fractured opinion that also dealt with a procedural question involved with the prosecution, six justices agreed that their *Stanley* opinion did not interfere with Congress's power to regulate or prohibit obscene materials from entering the country as part of the stream of commerce. Justice Stewart concurred in the result of this decision but wondered if it was the proper case for deciding whether the federal government could seize such materials at the border when the materials were intended for a private use as opposed to commercial distribution.

What *Reidel* and *Thirty-Seven Photographs* demonstrated was that the Supreme Court was tired of dealing with the issue of obscenity and all of the varied questions that arose in connection with it. Their actions and decisions had established the Court as the national censor, but their rulings had established a contradictory rule. Persons might legally possess pornography, but the distribution of obscenity could still be regulated. In other words, one could possess obscene materials, if one could somehow obtain them.

With time and retirements—of Warren in 1969 and Fortas in 1970—the Court's activist, social-liberal stance on the obscenity issue began to fade, and its role as censor fell into decline. Two linked Court decisions announced on June 21, 1973, signaled a reaction against and step away from the *Roth/Jacobellis/Memoirs* rules. Chief Justice Burger wrote the majority opinions in both *Miller v. California* and *Paris Adult Theatre I et al. v. Slaton, District Attorney, et al.,* and these cases should be read together; the justices themselves referred to their opinions in each case in tandem.

Miller changed both the nature of the arguments about obscenity and the judicial standards for judging it. This case began when Marvin Miller sent a mass, unsolicited mailing to a variety of people in California, informing them of the availability of "adult material" with titles such as "Man-Women" and "An Illustrated History of Pornography." This adult material consisted of brochures with "pictures and drawings very explicitly depicting men and women in groups of two or more engaging in a variety of sexual activities." A manager of a restaurant in Newport Beach, California, and his mother had received these brochures, opened them, and complained to the police about their contents. California prosecuted Miller for violating a state statute that made it illegal to knowingly distribute obscene material. At trial, the judge followed the guidelines previously laid down by the Supreme Court: that "(a) the dominant theme of the material taken as a whole appealed to a prurient interest in sex, (b) the material was patently offensive because it affronted contemporary standards . . . and (c) the material was utterly without redeeming social value"(413 U.S. 15). Ignoring *Roth,* the judge instructed the jury to apply the contemporary community standards of the *state* in determining whether the materials were obscene. After deliberation, the jury found Miller guilty of knowingly distributing obscene materials. Miller appealed. California's appellate court affirmed his conviction, and he then appealed to the U.S. Supreme Court, arguing that the trial judge had misapplied the Supreme Court's earlier guidelines, and asserting a First Amendment right to expression.

In a 5–4 decision, Chief Justice Burger with the support of Justices White, Blackmun, Powell, and Rehnquist reworked the obscenity test into five new or modified requirements, vacated Miller's conviction, and remanded the case to the trial judge for retrial using the new standards of obscenity just handed down by the Court. First, the Court reaffirmed that obscenity was not protected speech and press under the First Amendment. Second, the Court held that the standards for the states to follow in determining what was or was not obscene and subject to regulation were "(a) whether the average person, applying contemporary community standards, would find that the work, taken as a whole, appealed to the prurient interest, (b) whether the work depicted or described, in a patently offensive way, sexual conduct specifically defined by the applicable state law . . . and (c) whether the work, taken as a whole, lacked serious literary, artistic, political, or scientific value." This last point was something new in obscenity jurisprudence, a major change in the obscenity test pattern. Third in the Court's five new obscenity standards points was the removal of the requirement that the states had to demonstrate that the material was "utterly without redeeming social value." Fourth, the majority held that state regulation of obscenity "must define the sexual conduct as to which depiction or description was proscribed, providing fair notice as to what public and commercial activities would bring prosecution." In other words, regulations by the states must be as specific as possible and provide due notice to the public and commercial interests as to what was and was not allowed. Lastly, the Court ruled that the phrase "contemporary community standards" *did not* mean national standards but rather the community standards of the locality (413 U.S. 15).

Seeking to end the Court's role as national censor, *Miller* dropped the *Memoirs* standard of "utterly without redeeming social value" and reaffirmed the harder standard temporarily abandoned by the Warren Court that the First Amendment did not protect obscenity. Further, the Court's majority argued, it was not the Court's role to propose what regulatory schemes the states might adopt. Nevertheless, Burger provided "a few plain examples of what a state statute could define for regulation under part 2(b) of the standard announced in this opinion: (a) Patently offensive representations or descriptions of ultimate sexual acts, normal and perverted, actual or simulated; (b) Patently offensive representations or descriptions of masturbation, excretory functions, and lewd exhibition of the genitals."

Although knowing that any lines drawn would be controversial and disputed, the Court's goal was to better draw the lines between acceptable and unacceptable materials: "At a minimum prurient, patently offensive depiction or description of sexual conduct must have serious literary, artistic, political, or scientific value to merit First Amendment protection." Graphic depictions of human anatomy in medical books were an example of materials that the First Amendment would protect; X-rated materials were not. And who would make such sensitive determinations? This majority held that "we must continue to rely on the jury system, accompanied by the safeguards that judges, rules of evidence, presumption of innocence, and other protective features provide, as we do with rape, murder, and a host of other offenses against society and its individual members." Burger believed that these new standards would affect and limit only hard-core pornography as defined by the states, and that the states had to provide fair notice to the dealer of such materials and to his public that such materials might bring prosecution (413 U.S. 15, 27).

In explaining his opinion, Chief Justice Burger further noted that not since the 1957 *Roth* case had a majority of the Court "agreed on concrete guidelines to isolate 'hard core' pornography from expression protected by the First Amendment." Case law and Justice Brennan's liberalization of obscenity had brought only confusion to the state and federal courts and placed a strain on those courts to deal with the issue of obscenity. This new standard, the Court's majority understood, "may not be an easy road, free from difficulty. But no amount of 'fatigue' should lead us to adopt a convenient 'institutional' rationale—an absolutist, 'anything goes' view of the First Amendment—because it will lighten our burdens" (413 U.S. 15, 29). In other words, the Court's role was to tackle the controversial and hard cases such as were presented in obscenity trials, and the Court could not shirk that responsibility—especially since the Court had involved itself in the first place with *Roth*.

On the perennial question of whether there should be a single, national standard of obscenity answering to the national Constitution, Burger held that "fundamental First Amendment limitations on the powers of the States do not vary from community to community, but this does not mean that there are, or should or can be, fixed, uniform national standards of precisely what appeals to the 'prurient interest' or is 'patently offensive.'. . . These are essentially questions of fact," the majority in *Miller* held, "and our Nation is simply too big and too diverse for this Court to reasonably expect that such standards could be articulated for all 50 States in a single formulation." America's unique diversity prevented the establishment of a centrally defined set of community standard. As Burger wrote: "To require a State to structure obscenity proceedings around evidence of a national 'community standard' would be an exercise in futility. It is neither realistic nor constitutionally sound to read the First Amendment as requiring that the people of Maine or Mississippi to accept public depictions of conduct found tolerable in Las Vegas or New York City." Juries should determine obscenity based on local and state community standards, not some mythical national standard (413 U.S. 15, 32).

Justice Brennan criticized the Court's majority in *Miller* for inaugurating a new wave of repression by means of its decision; the Court's majority found such charges to be nonsense. To the majority, "to equate the free and robust exchange of ideas and political debate with commercial exploitation of obscene material demeans the grand conception of the First Amendment and its high purposes in the historic struggle for freedom." Furthermore, in the majority view

There is no evidence, empirical or historical, that the stern 19th century censorship of public distribution and display of material relating to sex . . . in any way limited or affected expression of serious literary, artistic, political, or scientific ideas. On the contrary, it is beyond question that the era following Thomas Jefferson to Theodore Roosevelt was an "extraordinary vigorous period" not just in economics and politics, but in *belles lettres* and in "the outlying fields of social and political philosophies." We do not see the harsh hand of censorship of ideas—good or bad, sound or unsound—and "repression" of political liberty lurking in every regulation of commercial exploitation of human interest in sex.

Times change, and the justices in the majority understood that. "One can concede that the 'sexual revolution' of recent years may have had useful byproducts in striking layers of prudery from a subject long irrationally kept from needed ventilation," Burger wrote. "But it does not follow that no regulation of patently offensive 'hard core' materials is needed or permissible; civilized people do not allow unregulated access to heroin because it is a derivative of medicinal morphine." The Court's majority thus vacated Miller's conviction and remanded the case for retrial under these new standards (413 U.S. 15, 36).

Four justices dissented in *Miller*, fearing government-sponsored repression. Justice Douglas argued that the First Amendment made no exceptions for obscenity and did not permit the government to ban materials that *some* persons found offensive. In this respect he maintained his earlier, absolutist position. Further, he argued that before any obscenity regulations could be adopted, a constitutional amendment, not a judicial decision, was necessary. Lastly, he argued that criminal prosecution of obscenity should have to wait until all civil prosecutions were completed, so that defendants would know that their conduct was criminal. Douglas acknowledged, "The Court has worked hard to define obscenity and concededly has failed." He continued, "Obscenity—which even we cannot define with precision—is a hodge-podge." Yet, "to send men to jail for violating standards they cannot understand, construe, and apply is a monstrous thing to do in a Nation dedicated to fair trials and due process" (413 U.S. 15, 44). In the end, Douglas figuratively threw his hands in the air and conceded that perhaps it was beyond the ability of the justices to establish and administer obscenity standards, in which case only the people, acting through the clumsy procedure of constitutional amendment, could do so.

Justice Brennan, joined by Justices Stewart and Marshall, also dissented in *Miller*. However, he deferred the bulk and substance of his dissent to *Miller*'s companion case, *Paris Adult Theatre I*. Handed down the same day as *Miller*, the opinion of the majority of the Court in *Paris Adult Theatre I v. Slaton* applied the new *Miller* standard to Georgia litigation. This case presented new twists and turns in its fact structure that, in turn, affected the Court's decision. In December 1970, local prosecutors in Fulton County, Georgia, had filed civil suit alleging that the Paris Adult Theatre I was exhibiting obscene films in violation of Georgia law. At trial, the defendants produced the films in question, as well as photographs of the outside of the theater. These photographs showed a sign on the building, declaring that it showed "Atlanta's Finest Mature Feature Films"; on the door was posted a second sign, saying: "Adult Theatre—You must be 21 and able to prove it. If viewing the nude body offends you, Please Do Not Enter." At trial, the judge viewed the films, took testimony from officers who paid a fee to view the films, and decided that although the films were obscene under Georgia law, "the display of these films in a commercial theatre, when surrounded by requisite notice to the public of their nature and by reasonable protection against the exposure of these films to minors, is constitutionally permissible" (413 U.S. 49, 53). Georgia appealed the trial judge's decision (a procedure allowed under Georgia procedural guidelines), and the Georgia Supreme Court unanimously reversed the trial judge. Georgia's Supreme Court held that the films were obscene and therefore were not protected by the First Amendment. According to the Georgia Supreme Court, the 1969 *Stanley v. Georgia* decision of the U.S. Supreme Court did not apply to this case, because these materials were being offered to the public instead of being viewed by the individual in the privacy of the home. "The films in this case," the state high court declared, "leave little to the imagination" and should have been enjoined (413 U.S. 49, 53). Paris Adult Theatre appealed this decision to the U.S. Supreme Court.

Chief Justice Warren Burger delivered the deciding opinion in the case. The Court again was split, 5–4. Applying the *Miller* standards for judging obscenity, Chief Justice Burger elaborated and clarified issues raised by the case, vacated the decision against the theater, and sent the case back for retrial employing the new *Miller* standards.

Early in his opinion, Burger castigated the trial judge's action: "We categorically disapprove the theory that obscene, pornographic films acquire constitutional immunity from state regulation simply because they are exhibited for consenting adults," he wrote. The Georgia Supreme Court had been correct in rejecting this argument. He restated the general rule that "the States have a long-recognized legitimate interest in regulating the use of obscene material in local commerce and in all places of local accommodation, as long as these regulations do not run afoul of specific constitutional prohibitions." States held this power in order to protect minors and mere passersby from such offending materials and signs. Nor was this power unique to obscenity. Burger examined a series of other areas, such as regulations of unscrupulous business affairs, federal securities law, and anti–forced prostitution laws, where the state could legislate to protect innocent persons from injury and the states did not have to demonstrate conclusive proof between the action and the alleged injury. He concluded:

> The sum of experience, including that of the past two decades, affords an ample basis for legislatures to conclude that a sensitive, key relationship of human existence, central to family life, community welfare, and the development of human personality, can be debased and distorted by crass commercial exploitation of sex. Nothing in the Constitution prohibits a State from reaching such a conclusion and acting on it legislatively simply because there is no conclusive evidence or empirical data. (413 U.S. 49, 63)

Having dispatched the argument that states had to show a link between obscenity and antisocial behavior, he moved on to the defense's argument that states and the Supreme Court ought to adopt a hands-off, laissez-faire attitude toward obscenity. This argument, too, Burger found unacceptable. States could adopt laws and regulations of human behavior to protect the public health and public places. In fact, confirmed Burger, the states could indeed adopt a hands-off policy in matters of obscenity, "but nothing in the Constitution *compels* the States to do so with regard to matters falling within state jurisdiction" (413 U.S. 49, 64). If the states decided that they preferred a public policy of regulating obscenity with reasonable regulations within constitutional boundaries, they were permitted to pursue such a policy.

Burger then took up the defense's argument that the state law making it a crime to view obscene films in a theater violated the right to privacy. Commercial ventures such as movie theaters had consistently been held to be public places, and their use therefore could be regulated by the state. As Burger put the issue, "Conduct or depictions of conduct that the state police power can prohibit on a public street do not become automatically protected by the Constitution merely because the conduct is moved to a bar or a 'live' theater stage, any more than a 'live' performance of a man and woman locked in a sexual embrace at high noon in Times Square is protected by the Constitution because they simultaneously engage in a valid political dialogue."

Lastly, the Court took up the argument that Georgia's statute and the Court's rules for judging obscenity sought to control the thoughts of persons. Again, the Court dismissed this argument. Burger pointed out that under the *Miller* rules, "preventing unlimited display or distribution of obscene material, which by definition lacks any serious literary, artistic, political, or scientific value as communication . . . is distinct from control of reason and the intellect" (413 U.S. 49, 67). Obscenity jurisprudence limited obviously obscene materials such as hard-core pornography, not genuine and socially significant exchanges of ideas. Further, the fact that the materials were shown only to adults made no difference, because the state always has the power to protect the community from materials whose presence injures the community as a whole, endangers public safety, or endangers public decency.

Summing up, Burger held that obscenity and commerce in obscene materials were not protected by the First Amendment. States possessed the power to regulate the "depiction and description of specifically defined sexual conduct." The Court held that "the States have a legitimate interest in regulating commerce in obscene materials and in regulating exhibition of obscene material in places of public accommodation, including so-called 'adult' theatres from which minors are excluded" (413 U.S. 49, 69). Therefore, Georgia could establish regulations controlling places such as the Paris Adult Theatre, as long as those regulations conformed to the guidelines established in the Supreme Court's decision in *Miller*.

As in *Miller*, Justice Douglas dissented in a rambling statement that repeated his previous absolutist position that the First Amendment protected obscenity from all governmental regulations because the solution for obscenity (government oversight and regulation) raised the spectre of government censorship of ideas. "Art and literature reflect tastes," Douglas wrote, "and tastes, like musical appreciation, are hardly reducible to precise definitions. That is one reason I have always felt that 'obscenity' was not an exception to the First Amendment." He further argued (incorrectly) that obscenity was not a crime prior to the adoption of the federal Constitution, and that before the federal government could allow the states and localities to limit expression, the people would have to propose and ratify a constitutional amendment providing for such action. In modern life, Douglas stated, people encounter a wide variety of behaviors that cause offense, such as some "political pronouncements, sociological themes, and . . . stories of official misconduct." As he explained, "One of the most offensive experiences of my life was a visit to a nation where bookstalls were filled only with books on mathematics and books on religion." True, he personally would guide his children or wards away from such theaters; but he feared that government oversight of moral threats to the community constituted a greater threat than did smut and pornography. Douglas conceded that when people formed communities, more social controls became necessary. But, he continued, "Our society—unlike most in the world—presupposes that freedom and liberty are in a frame of reference that makes the individual, not government, the keeper of his tastes, beliefs, and ideas. That is the philosophy of the First Amendment; and it is the article of faith that sets us apart from most nations of the world" (413 U.S. 49, 73).

Justice Brennan's dissent in *Paris Adult Theatre I,* in which he was joined by Justices Stewart and Marshall, was aimed both at this case and at the new *Miller v. California* standard. Chief Justice Burger's majority decision and rule in *Miller* brought an end to Brennan's activism in the area of obscenity, and Brennan knew that he had lost. But in his dissent, he again analyzed the issue of obscenity and defended his liberal approach. The task was not easy. "This case," he stated, "requires the Court to confront once again the vexing problem of reconciling state efforts to suppress sexually oriented expression with the protections of the First Amendment . . . . No other aspect of the First Amendment has, in recent years, demanded so substantial a commitment of our time, generated such disharmony of views, and remained so resistant to the formulation of stable and manageable standards." This "vexing problem" required the Supreme

Court to struggle with the tensions between the values of free expression and the equally valued desired to regulate the distribution and access to obscenity.

After reviewing the facts and the history of the case, Brennan acknowledged that the "existence of something called 'obscenity' is still a long and painful step from agreement on a workable definition of the term." After sketching the judicial history of obscenity from the 1957 decision in *Roth* through the new guidelines proposed by the *Miller* majority, he agreed that the Supreme Court had failed to adequately establish clear standards for lower federal courts and the states to follow. What resulted was "hopeless confusion." He wrote:

> After 16 years of experimentation and debate I am reluctantly forced to the conclusion that none of the available formulas, including the one announced today, can reduce the vagueness to a tolerable level while at the same time striking an acceptable balance between the protections of the First and Fourteenth Amendments, on the one hand, and on the other the asserted state interest in regulating the dissemination of certain sexually oriented materials. Any effort to draw a constitutionally acceptable boundary on state power must resort to such indefinite concepts as "prurient interest," "patently offensive," "serious literary value," and the like. The meaning of these concepts necessarily varies with the experience, outlook, and even idiosyncrasies of the person defining them. Although we assume that obscenity does exist and we "know it when [we] see it," . . . we are manifestly unable to describe it in advance except by reference to concepts so elusive that they fail to distinguish clearly between protected and unprotected speech.

With this statement, Justice Brennan admitted defeat, but at the same time he vowed to continue the battle to define obscenity. He feared that any language adopted by the Supreme Court would be vague, open to interpretation by lawyers, judges, and justices, and thus might lead to the repression of materials that did not deal with sexual matters. It would fail to provide due notice to people engaged in the commerce of such materials that their actions might bring criminal prosecutions. The justices had sought to craft a narrow definition of obscenity so as not to interfere with legitimate forms of expression. Yet the vague language that resulted from their fear of limiting speech and press rights had created uncertainty in the state and lower federal courts about what the standards of obscenity were and how those standards ought to be applied. Hence, new, clearer standards were needed.

Brennan reviewed the new standards announced in *Miller;* he believed that to a high degree they paralleled his own standards in *Memoirs.* To his way of thinking, the key difference came in the third component of the *Memoirs* test, which held that materials had to be "utterly without redeeming social value." In *Miller,* that component was recast as lacking "serious literary, artistic, political, or scientific value." Justice Brennan believed that the new language would lead to repression, that it would permit "far more sweeping suppression of sexually oriented expression, including expression that would surely be held protected under our current formulation." For under this new *Miller* formulation, Brennan continued, the same problems remained; they were merely restyled. Who would decide, and on what grounds, what had "serious literary, artistic, political, or scientific value"?

Further, claimed Brennan, the *Miller* standard left the ultimate determination of obscenity in the hands of the U.S. Supreme Court, because every prosecution for obscenity raised the First Amendment issue of the possible repression of legitimate expression. He considered the option of leaving obscenity determinations to the people sitting in the jury box in the appropriate locality, but he found that option unsatisfactory as well—firstly, because appeals would still arise from such jury decisions, and "the approach would expose much protected, sexually oriented expression to the vagaries of jury determinations." More importantly, any gain made by lifting the burden of such cases off the state and federal courts, he felt, would not be sufficient to "offset . . . the unprecedented infringement of First Amendment rights." The same could be said of Douglas's First Amendment absolutism, which prohibited the suppression of allegedly obscene materials. Such absolutism eliminated the states from obscenity regulation, but not the federal government and the federal courts; the latter would still have to make a case-by-case determination of obscenity, judged against the First Amendment. The Supreme Court could not simply abandon its oversight of the states' and the federal government's regulations of obscenity, Brennan argued; therefore, Douglas's approach could not be adopted (413 U.S. 49, 102).

Having reviewed obscenity's history from its common-law origins through the *Hicklin* test and on to *Roth* and *Memoirs,* Brennan took up the premise enunciated by the lower court in *Paris Adult Theatre I:* that the state had a legitimate interest and duty to shield children and unconsenting adults from such displays of obscenity. Brennan found this basis for upholding the statute unpersuasive, given the threat the statute represented to First Amendment freedoms. As he described the problem: "Even a legitimate, sharply focused state concern for the morality of the community cannot . . . justify an assault on the protections of the First Amendment. . . . Where the state interest in regulation of morality is vague and ill defined, interference with guarantees of the First Amendment is even more difficult to justify."

Brennan still believed that the cure was worse than the illness—that government regulation of expression posed a greater danger to the states and the culture than did the presence of obscenity. "While I cannot say that interests of the State—apart from the question of juveniles and unconsenting adults—are trivial or nonexistent, I am compelled to conclude that these interests cannot justify the substantial damage to constitutional rights and to this Nation's judicial machinery that inevitably results from state efforts to bar distribution even of unprotected material to consenting adults," noted Brennan. All levels of government were powerless to protect the community from obscenity, in his view—unless the purveyors of the obscene materials specifically targeted, or made no effort to avoid exposing, children and nonconsenting adults. "I would hold, therefore, that at least in the absence of distribution to juveniles or obtrusive exposure to unconsenting adults, the First and Fourteenth Amendments prohibit the State and Federal Governments from attempting wholly to suppress sexually oriented materials on the basis of allegedly 'obscene' contents." Suppression of pornography and obscenity as a public policy failed to pass constitutional scrutiny, although under certain circumstances government could justifiably take action to regulate "the manner of distribution of sexually oriented materials." On this basis, Brennan would have reversed the Georgia Supreme Court decision, maintained his own *Roth/Memoirs* standards, and returned the case to trial court for rehearing.

A masterful example of Brennan's constitutional philosophy—what stood out in Brennan's *Paris* dissent—was his concession that his own tinkering with obscenity definitions had created bottlenecks and problems for the state and federal courts (not to mention local prosecutors), and his insistence that the suppression of obscenity threatened fundamental First Amendment rights. Although the majority in *Miller* allowed local and state regulation of obscenity in line with local community standards, Brennan feared arbitrary prosecutions from locality to locality and state to state. He continued to believe that he, and he alone, could craft a national judicial rule to be applied uniformly throughout the country and that the threat to the freedom of expression came from the localities and the states, not from judicially imposed standards. He failed to appreciate how one national standard, created and enforced by the unelected and unaccountable federal judiciary, created no less a threat to the freedom of expression as it overrode local preferences and wishes. If political democracy really means that the people in a community decide for themselves the important questions of their era, then Brennan's schemes damaged the American tradition of localism, federalism, and the First Amendment while associating freedom of expression with the tawdry business of obscenity. In his sincere effort to do social good, Justice Brennan's judicial activism had confused the issue and tainted the reputation of his Court.

It would be only one year before *Miller*'s obscenity test reached the Supreme Court for interpretation. This time, both sides in the obscenity debate would be able to claim victory in the outcome of the litigation, especially Brennan. In *Jenkins v. Georgia*, a 5–4 decision was handed down on June 24, 1974. Justice William Rehnquist wrote the majority opinion, joined by Justices Burger, White, Blackmun, and Powell. Justice Douglas again wrote a dissent, as did Justice Brennan, who was joined by Justice Marshall. At issue in this first major test of the Court's 1973 *Miller* rule was the film *Carnal Knowledge*. Although the film was suggestive and did contain brief nudity, it certainly did not fall into the category of "hard-core" pornography. At issue was the reach of the *Miller* test and whether it would have the effect of suppressing suggestive but not overtly graphic films.

In 1971, in Dougherty County, Georgia, a jury convicted a theater manager, Billy Jenkins, of showing an obscene movie, *Carnal Knowledge,* in violation of the Georgia obscenity statute. This conviction occurred *before* the U.S. Supreme Court had handed down its *Miller* opinion in 1971. On appeal, the Georgia Supreme Court upheld Jenkins's conviction, noting that it had taken place under the older, *Memoirs* standards, which were more restrictive than the *Miller* standard. Jenkins then appealed to the U.S. Supreme Court, challenging his conviction under the older obscenity rules and arguing that the film was not obscene and that therefore his conviction should be overturned.

Justice Rehnquist quickly cut to the heart of the matter, holding that "defendants convicted prior to the announcement of our *Miller* decisions but whose convictions were on direct appeal at that time should receive any benefit available to them." For the majority, he found *Carnal Knowledge* not to be obscene under the *Miller* test; therefore, the First and Fourteenth Amendments required that Jenkins's conviction be overturned. Of greater importance in this case, however, was the question of whether the Constitution required juries to be instructed to apply "a hypothetical statewide community." Here Rehnquist held that the *Miller* decision approved the use of such a community standard but did not mandate it. In fact, Rehnquist approved of the trial judge's instructions to the jury to "apply 'community' standards without specifying what 'community.'" He continued, "*Miller* held it was constitutionally permissible to permit jurors to rely on the understanding of the community from which they came as to contemporary community standards, and the States have considerable latitude in framing statutes under this element of the *Miller* decision" (418 U.S. 153, 157). Under *Miller*, the justices therefore concluded, states should be granted leeway in crafting obscenity standards to fit their own individualized needs, social values, and legal traditions.

Rehnquist discussed *Miller* in light of the facts of *Jenkins*. Questions of what was "patently offensive" and what appealed to "prurient interest" were indeed issues of fact for juries to decide by the standards of their locality. But that power to decide obscenity was not unrestrained; juries did not possess "unbridled discretion" in determining obscenity. In *Miller*, the Court had suggested examples of what a state might define as obscene, although its list of examples was not exhaustive. That list "was certainly intended to fix substantive constitutional limitations, deriving from the First Amendment, on the type of material subject to such a determination." And even if a jury had been properly charged and had unanimously agreed upon a verdict, the verdict "would be wholly at odds with this aspect of *Miller* to uphold an obscenity conviction based upon a defendant's depiction of a woman with a bare midriff" (418 U.S. 153, 161). More than that would be needed in order to deem an image obscene.

Rehnquist mentioned that the members of the Supreme Court had viewed the movie and had seen nothing in it that violated the *Miller* standards; it was "simply not the 'public portrayal of hard core sexual conduct for its own sake, and for the ensuing commercial gain' which we said was punishable in *Miller*"(418 U.S. 153, 161). Having applied the *Miller* standard to this prosecution and to this film and having found both that the standard was reasonable and the film was not obscene, the majority of the Court reversed Jenkins's conviction. *Miller* had passed its first constitutional challenge: The Court's majority had found it practical and useful in providing the states and local juries guidance for making a determination of obscenity.

Concurring, Justice Douglas referred back to his dissent in *Paris Adult Theatre I* and once again restated his belief that the First Amendment banned any state or federal restrictions on obscenity. Also concurring, Justice Brennan pointed out that at least some of the predictions in his dissent in *Paris Adult Theatre I* had come to fruition in *Jenkins*—five members of the United States Supreme Court ultimately had made the decision of what was and what was not obscene—and as he almost gleefully pointed out, "The Court's new formulation does not extricate us from the mire of case-by-case determinations of obscenity." Not only did the Court still have to look at whether the material was "patently offensive," but it also had to consider whether "the work, taken as a whole, [lacked] serious literary, artistic, political, or scientific value," as laid down in *Miller*. To do so, the justices actually would have to view the work. As Brennan pointed out in *Paris Adult Theatre I*, no one would know what was obscene "until at least five members of this Court, applying inevitably obscure standards, have pronounced it so"(418 U.S. 153, 164).

To Brennan's eyes, the *Miller* majority had sought to remove the justices from making the determination of obscenity, yet ironically, the majority opinion in *Miller* ensured that the justices would remain central in the controversy. Brennan closed by saying that he believed that the First and Fourteenth Amendments prohibited the suppression of materials on the grounds of their allegedly obscene contents but did not prohibit attempts to prevent the distribution of such materials to children and unconsenting adults. Not surprisingly, although he dissented from the majority decision in *Jenkins*, he concurred with the result: the reversal of Jenkins's conviction.

And so events stood as the new and enormous outburst of judicial decisionmaking on the issue of obscenity during the sixteen-year period between *Roth* in 1957 and *Miller* in 1973 (or, a bit more accurately, the seventeen-year period from *Roth* to *Jenkins* in 1974) came to an end. This pattern of liberalization and centralization of decisionmaking, followed by a reaction and an effort to return decisionmaking to the states and localities, mirrored the rise and fall of the turbulent era of the 1960s, when cultural liberalism held sway in the United States. Led by Justice William Brennan, in a bold and unsuccessful display of judicial hubris, the Court cast aside all vestiges of older traditions regarding the control and regulation of obscenity, such as the tradition of localism and deference to the states in the prosecution and definition of obscenity. The Court had hoped to modernize obscenity jurisprudence; but instead, judicial liberalism in obscenity managed only to further muddy the waters and entangle the Court in endless questions and problems of definition. As political power and economic decisions became more and more centralized in the federal government, the justices of the Supreme Court sought to update and dust off what appeared to be a "backward" area of the law. Their liberalization of the law of obscenity paralleled the loosening and changing of the nation's moral codes and attitudes, a process both participated in by the Supreme Court and advanced by the Court's decisions. Not until the political landscape changed in the early 1970s was this liberalization checked. But the obscenity genie was out of the bottle, and once released, it would not be put back. By the 1970s, Americans were witnessing more frequent and more explicit sexual imagery on television, in cinema, in popular music, and in the printed word than ever before. What might have been shocking in the late 1950s was becoming commonplace by the 1970s, although many Americans objected to this trend. And at the center of the controversy stood the justices of the U.S. Supreme Court and their varied attempts to deal with the problem of obscenity in a free society. At the end of this dramatic period of smoke and fire about obscenity, in 1964, Justice Potter Stewart penned what has proved the most honest of statements about obscenity: "But I know it when I see it."

Although Chief Justice Burger's *Miller* standard signaled yet another change in obscenity policy and a reformulation of obscenity, the issue did not end in 1973 or with *Jenkins* in 1974. New technologies emerged, such as pay-per-view cable television and the Internet, and new questions arose that challenged the states, the state courts, and the Supreme Court obscenity rules. As a result, the states and the Supreme Court have continued to revisit the issue of obscenity. A whole new age of pornography was dawning, and soon everybody was going to "see it" and "know it."

Litigating Obscenity from 1974 to the Present

From 1974 to the present, obscenity and pornography have persisted in American culture and have continued to present thorny problems to courts and judges. More and more legislators and judges have approached obscenity as a First Amendment freedom-of-expression issue rather than a moral issue to be resolved by society. As a result, the limits of obscene speech have become a hotly contested area in First Amendment law.

Underlying this doctrinal shift has been a massive growth in the availability of pornography. During this period, electronic technology altered the delivery of obscene materials. People began to employ commonplace modes of communication such as the telephone and cable television to deliver messages and programming such as phone sex and pornographic films. Other businesses flourished as well, such as the so-called "adult clubs" that offered all-nude dancing. These activities have been defended as forms of expression deserving of First Amendment protection. The presence of pornography on the Internet led the U.S. Congress to pass the Telecommunications Act of 1996, which includes the better-known Communications Decency Act of 1996.

Modern technology complicates obscenity jurisprudence. The range and graphic capability of new media expand the scope of the problem almost infinitely. Because each new medium raises different issues, the Supreme Court has been forced to continue its tradition of case-by-case decisionmaking on obscenity. Although a number of general judicial doctrines have been devised to test whether a particular regulation of obscenity is valid, no single, overarching rule or consensus has emerged. As a result, obscenity regulation continues to challenge localities, states, and the federal judiciary to define and redefine the obscene and the most appropriate measures for dealing with it.

The renewed judicial focus on the dilemmas of obscenity regulation began in a gray area of the law of obscenity: broadcasting. The law on broadcasting is a large and complex subject. In 1978, the U.S. Supreme Court decided *Federal Communications Commission v. Pacifica Foundation,* in which it began to draw a line between appropriate and inappropriate speech on the airwaves. (Since that time, the broadcast media and the culture have blurred this line; but it is important to know where the discussion of obscenity on the airwaves began.) Because the airwaves are public property and because broadcasts cross state borders, Congress and its creation, the Federal Communications Commission (FCC), have established a series of laws and regulations governing the use of the airwaves. Chapter 18 of the United States Code, § 1464 (1976 ed.), prohibited the use of "any obscene, indecent, or profane language by means of radio communications." On Tuesday, October 30, 1973, about 2 P.M., a radio station owned by the Pacifica Foundation broadcast a twelve-minute monologue by comedian George Carlin on the topic "filthy words." As Carlin explained to his audience, these were "the words you couldn't say on the public, ah, airwaves, um, the ones you definitely wouldn't say, ever" (438 U.S. 726, 729). After a brief prologue, Carlin proceeded with his routine, which was liberally laced with repeated expletives. Carlin originally had presented this monologue before an appreciative California audience, and the performance had been recorded for later broadcast. But some in his radio audience were less receptive.

A father driving in his car with his young son accidentally tuned in to the broadcast, and later complained to the FCC. Pacifica responded to the complaint by explaining that the sketch was part of a longer program examining society's attitudes toward language. Furthermore, it had been preceded by a warning to listeners that the sketch contained "sensitive language which might be regarded as offensive to some." The company had received no other complaints about the program or the Carlin monologue. On February 21, 1975, the FCC granted the complaint and threatened Pacifica with administrative sanctions—specifically, a review of the station's license to broadcast. The FCC also stated that it was undertaking a thorough review of its regulation of the airwaves, given the growing number of complaints it was receiving about indecent speech. After a review of the Carlin monologue, the Commission concluded that it contained "certain words [that] depicted sexual and excretory activities in a patently offensive manner," which were broadcast "at a time when children were undoubtedly in the audience (i.e., in the early afternoon)" and which were used repetitively. Thus, the FCC concluded,

"We therefore hold that the language as broadcast was indecent and prohibited by 18 U.S.C. § 1464." In response to further questions about this administrative ruling, the FCC explained that it "never intended to place an absolute prohibition on the broadcast of this type of language, but rather sought to channel it to times of day when children most likely would not be exposed to it."

Pacifica appealed the FCC's rulings to the Court of Appeals for the District of Columbia Circuit, in which a three-judge panel reversed the opinion of the FCC despite disagreement among the judges. Because of that disagreement on Circuit, the Supreme Court agreed to hear and decide the case. Associate Justice John Paul Stevens wrote the opinion of the Court, but the justices split a number of ways, agreeing in part and disagreeing in part. Additionally, Justices William Brennan, Thurgood Marshall, and Byron R. White dissented from the Court's opinion.

After reviewing the history of the case, Justice Stevens narrowed the issues before the Court to whether judicial review reached further than the FCC's determination of indecency; whether the FCC's order violated the anticensorship guidelines of §326; whether the broadcast was indecent within §1464; and whether the FCC's order violated the free speech clauses of the First Amendment. Justice Stevens reviewed the history of §326 and found that it prohibited the FCC from censoring broadcasts in advance of their distribution via the airwaves. But, he continued, this restriction "has never been construed to deny the Commission the power to review the content of completed broadcasts in the performance of its regulatory duties." Therefore, §326 did not limit the Commission's authority "to impose sanctions on licensees who engage in obscene, indecent, or profane broadcasting." The Court found that the Commission had acted properly.

On the question of §1464—whether the afternoon broadcast of the "Filthy Words" monologue was indecent within the meaning of the statute—Stevens pointed out that Pacifica did not challenge the FCC's finding that the afternoon broadcast of the piece was "patently offensive." Pacifica did challenge the finding that the broadcast was indecent, because of the "absence of prurient appeal." But after reviewing Pacifica's argument, construction of the statute, and relevant precedent, Justice Stevens found the argument without substance, because prurient appeal was not an essential component of indecent language. The FCC found that Pacifica had broadcast indecent language, and this conclusion was correct.

Justice Stevens then took up the constitutional arguments. Pacifica had argued: "The Commission's construction of the statutory language broadly encompasses so much constitutionally protected speech that reversal is required even if Pacifica's broadcast of the 'Filthy Words' monologue is not itself protected by the First Amendment. Second, Pacifica argues that inasmuch as the recording is not obscene, the Constitution forbids any abridgement of the right to broadcast it on the radio." Justice Stevens dismissed the first argument, noting that the FCC's decision was appropriately narrow, being limited to the specific factual context. After all, he stated, "indecency is largely a function of context—it cannot be adequately judged in the abstract." So Pacifica's first argument failed because the speech used in the monologue, in the context, was indecent. Pacifica broadcast the speech at an inappropriate time, and the FCC acted correctly in finding the speech indecent and fining Pacifica accordingly. Pacifica's second argument also failed, because the First Amendment does not protect all speech, only political speech. A broadcast that contains "patently offensive words dealing with sex and excretion may be regulated because of its content." If the FCC had found Carlin's speech offensive because of its political content, then Pacifica might have had a stronger argument. But the FCC found the "Filthy Words" monologue indecent because of the obscene character of the words. In some other context, he argued, even these words might be protected speech; but they were not such, in the context of this case. Justice Stevens then took notice of the unique and powerful role the broadcast media play in modern American life, and of the pervasiveness of their messages. The warning before the broadcast, that it contained words that some might find offensive, was insufficient because people could tune in at any point during the broadcast and might miss the warning. Changing the tuner after hearing the offensive words would not remedy the damage already done to the listener. The broadcaster therefore could be held liable for the indecent broadcast. As Justice Stevens noted, "Broadcasting is uniquely accessible to children, even those too young to read." Children who cannot read enlarge their vocabulary by repeating the language they hear. Broadcasts like Carlin's monologue threatened the children in the audience, and thus "amply justify special treatment of indecent broadcasting."

Lest anyone misunderstand the decision of the Court or think that the ruling was too broad, Justice Stevens concluded with a statement emphasizing the narrowness of the decision. This case did not involve a "two-way radio conversion between a cab driver and a dispatcher, or a telecast of an Elizabethan comedy." An "occasional expletive" in those contexts would not be sufficient to bring sanctions to a broadcast. A "host of variables" is required before sanctions would be appropriate. One of the most important variables, whether the speech occurs in a radio or television broadcast or in a closed-circuit system, is the time of day. Stevens then approvingly quoted Associate Justice George Sutherland's statement in a nuisance case, that a "nuisance may be merely a right thing in the wrong place—like a pig in the parlor instead of the barnyard." He continued: "We simply hold that when the Commission finds that a pig has entered the parlor, the exercise of its regulatory power does not depend on proof that the pig is obscene." Therefore, the Supreme Court upheld the FCC's actions and overturned the Court of Appeals decision. Carlin's monologue was indecent.

Concurring in part and dissenting in part, Associate Justice Lewis Powell was joined in part by Associate Justice Harry A. Blackmun. Justice Powell supported the decision as it pertained to the power of the media to reach into the home and affect children. He found Pacifica's argument that ruling against them would reduce adults "to hearing only what is fit for children" significant, and asserted that that argument ought to be considered. But he also found their argument insufficient "to leave the Commission powerless to act in circumstances such as those in this case." As he pointed out, even if the broadcast were barred, adults could still purchase the album, attend Carlin's performance, or read a transcript of his monologue. He also noted that neither the Court's decision nor the Commission's decision prohibited Pacifica from broadcasting the performance at night or broadcasting a discussion of contemporary language. He dissented from the part of Justice Stevens's decision that privileged language protected by the First Amendment—"political" speech—over language that was less valuable and was not protected by the First Amendment (obscenity). He believed that this determination depended so heavily on context, that such a typology was inappropriate. He said he doubted this decision would prevent anyone wishing to hear or receive Carlin's monologue from doing so and "making for himself a value judgment as to the merit of the message and words."

In dissent, Associate Justice Brennan, joined by Justice Marshall, could hardly control his disgust with the Court's majority decision:

"I find," he wrote, "the Court's misapplication of fundamental First Amendment principles so patent, and its attempt to impose its notions of propriety on the whole of the American people so misguided, that I am unable to remain silent." As reviewed in the previous section, this statement is highly ironic, because Justice Brennan spilled a great deal of ink in the 1950s and 1960s, attempting to impose his notions of propriety on U.S. law and on the American people. Unfortunately for Brennan, the tide had changed and left him in dissent. He opposed the "time, place, and manner" restrictions on obscene speech that the FCC enforced in this case. Furthermore, he believed that the two reasons the Court cited for supporting the FCC's sanctions—the pervasive nature of the media, and the effects of indecent language on children—did not justify the intrusions into free speech rights. Instead of viewing the FCC's decision as a reasonable restriction of obscene speech on the radio, Justice Brennan believed that "the censor is all too discernable here."

Regarding the issue of protecting children, Justice Brennan realized that many parents would "find understandable as well as commendable the Court's sympathy with the FCC's desire to prevent offensive broadcasts from reaching the ears of unsupervised children." In doing so, however, those parents and the Court were supporting censorship of the airwaves, with which Brennan could not agree. Further, he argued, "Some parents may actually find Mr. Carlin's unabashed attitude toward the seven 'dirty words' healthy, and deem it desirable to expose their children to the manner in which Mr. Carlin defuses the taboo surrounding the words." He conceded that the number of such dubious parents may constitute "a minority of the American public," but their small numbers did not alter his point that those parents had the right to raise their children as they saw fit, had not "the Court's regrettable decision" prevented them from doing so.

Justice Brennan discerned only disaster in the Court's upholding of the Commission's penalties against Pacifica; the ruling would cast a chilling effect upon other kinds of speech. Henceforth, he conjectured, any four-letter word might be purged from the radio waves by the regulatory authorities, who might go so far as to ban "a myriad of literary works, novels, poems, and plays by the likes of Shakespeare, Joyce, Hemingway, Ben Jonson, Henry Fielding, Robert Burns, and Chaucer." Warming to his own rhetoric, Brennan claimed that this decision could lead to the banning of broadcasts of the Nixon tapes and even of parts of the Bible. Instead of allowing a government agency to decide what is and what is not offensive, Brennan would have denied the federal government and its agencies *any* power to police the airwaves. Instead, he preferred to leave such decisions "in a public free to choose those communications worthy of its attention from a marketplace unsullied by the censor's hand."

Brennan concluded by severely criticizing his fellow justices for their decision. "I find equally disturbing," he wrote, "a depressing inability to appreciate that in our land of cultural pluralism, there are many who think, act, and talk differently from the Members of this Court, and who do not share their fragile sensibilities." Only "acute ethnocentric myopia" could account for a decision that approves censorship because of the words contained in the communication. This decision, he alleged in Marxist-like language, was nothing more than "another of the dominant culture's inevitable efforts to force those groups who do not share its mores to conform to its way of thinking, acting, and speaking." Brennan closed with an allusion to Pacifica's explanation that Carlin was satirizing as "harmless and essentially silly our attitudes towards those words." He said Carlin and Pacifica might well find the Court decision silly, and he hoped the Court's decision would prove harmless (438 U.S. 726, 777).

Time has demonstrated that Justice Brennan's fears were unfounded. Since *Federal Communications Commission v. Pacifica Foundation,* no massive wave of federal censorship has occurred; in fact, in retrospect and given the crudities regularly heard on the radio and television in the early twenty-first century, Brennan appears more and more to be a man of little faith. *Pacifica* did not open a Pandora's box of censorship.

Although government censorship has not materialized, another impulse toward censorship has surfaced, motivated by the melding of late-twentieth-century rights consciousness with a militant feminist antipornography agenda. This impulse, predictably, brought the issue of pornography back into the courtroom. In the early 1980s, two of the most extreme and noted leaders of the feminist movement, Professor Catharine MacKinnon (then of the University of Minnesota Law School) and Andrea Dworkin, drafted a proposed municipal ordinance that defined pornography as a violation of the civil rights of women. In December 1983, they presented their proposal to the Minneapolis City Council for discussion. They also took their idea to Indianapolis, Indiana, where it had a public hearing in

April 1984, and to Los Angeles, California, where the proposal received a public hearing in April 1985. Minneapolis (in 1983) and Indianapolis (in 1984) both passed a version of this ordinance, defining pornography as a civil rights violation. Because these ordinances affected a form of speech, their fates rested with the courts; and Indianapolis's ordinance became a test case for use of a civil rights argument to limit and prohibit pornography. Although the test case failed judicial scrutiny, the arguments for and against such ordinances, and the judicial reasoning overturning the ordinances, demonstrate the limits of tolerable speech and obscenity within the culture and the dilemma of pornography on trial.

Indianapolis's ordinance took the form of an amendment to the "Human Relations; Equal Opportunity" section of the municipal code. In the sections on "Findings," the amended revised code read:

(2) Pornography is a discriminatory practice based on sex which denies women equal opportunities in society. Pornography is central in creating and maintaining sex as a basis for discrimination. Pornography is a systematic practice of exploitation and subordination based on sex which differentially harms women. The bigotry and contempt it promotes, with the acts of aggression it fosters, harm women's opportunities for equality in rights in employment, education, access to and use of public accommodations, and acquisition of real property; promote rape, battery, child abuse, kidnapping, and prostitution and inhibit just enforcement of laws against such acts; and contribute significantly to restricting women in particular from full exercise of citizenship and participation in public life, including in neighborhoods.

The ordinance continued that its purpose was "to prevent and prohibit all discriminatory practices of sexual subordination or inequality through pornography." In detailed language, the Indianapolis ordinance defined and outlawed "trafficking in pornography," "coercion into pornographic performance," "forcing pornography on a person," and "assault or physical attack due to pornography." Defenses against such charges were also specified. This ordinance then entered the thorny area of defining pornography. "Pornography shall mean," the ordinance specified, "the graphic sexually explicit subordination of women, whether in pictures or in words" and then presented a series of situations that fit that description, such as when "women are presented as sexual objects who enjoy pain or humiliation" (MacKinnon and Dworkin 1997, 444).

With this ordinance, feminist groups wished to test the limits of civil rights; in other words, did women in the United States have a civil right to live in a society where no pornography existed and where local governments possessed the power to suppress and eliminate all depictions of women that might be "pornographic" in the name of guaranteeing social equality for women? However deliberately crafted, the Indianapolis ordinance and its close cousin in Minneapolis potentially constituted a form of censorship. So the question became whether such restrictions on speech and press would stand if challenged in the courts.

And challenged they were. On May Day, May 1, 1984, the Indianapolis City Council passed its ordinance, and Mayor William Hudnut signed it into law. But before it could take effect, a coalition of groups filed suit in federal district court to stop its implementation, claiming that it violated the First Amendment clauses guaranteeing free speech and press. At trial, Judge Sarah E. Baker agreed with the plaintiffs that the Indianapolis ordinance regulated speech instead of the conduct involved in producing pornography. Speech could be regulated *only* if Indianapolis proved a compelling interest in reducing sex discrimination by this ordinance; but the city had failed to do so. In addition, Judge Baker held that the ordinance was vague, overly broad, and established a prior restraint of speech; in sum, the ordinance was unconstitutional. Indianapolis decided to defend its antipornography ordinance, and appealed the district judge's decision to the Seventh Circuit Court of Appeals, which would give the ordinance its most thorough judicial analysis.

After hearing arguments on June 14, 1985, the federal appellate judges handed down their opinion in *American Booksellers Association, Inc., et al. v. William H. Hudnut, III* on August 27, 1985. In a unanimous opinion, the federal appeals court upheld the district court's finding that the Indianapolis ordinance was too broad and violated the First Amendment. Judge Frank H. Easterbrook, who wrote the opinion for the court, started by pointing out that Indianapolis's definition of "pornography" differed from "obscenity" as defined by the Supreme Court in the 1973 case of *Miller v. California.* In that case, to be found obscene a publication had to be "taken as a whole, appeal to prurient interest, must contain patently offensive depictions or descriptions of specified sexual conduct and on the whole have no serious literary, artistic, political, or scientific value." In contrast, the Indianapolis ordinance defined pornography as "the graphic sexually explicit subordination of women, whether in pictures or words" (771 F.2d 323, 324). Indianapolis's ordinance had not referred to the obscenity standards set forth in *Miller*. The defenders of the ordinance claimed that that omission was a strength rather than a weakness. "Pornography influences attitudes, and the statute is a way to alter the socialization of men and women rather than to vindicate community standards of offensiveness." In reply, Easterbrook noted that various feminist groups offered "friends of the court" briefs, some supporting and others attacking the ordinance. He was unclear how printed works that depicted women as "submissive objects for conquest and domination" in literary works as diverse as James Joyce's *Ulysses* and Homer's *Iliad* would fare under the ordinance; but he dismissed the need to balance the arguments for and against the ordinance, its methods, or its goals. Instead, the Seventh Court of Appeals found that "the ordinance discriminates on the ground of the content of the speech." As Easterbrook stated the issue:

> Speech treating women in an approved way—in sexual encounters "premised on equality"—is lawful no matter how sexually explicit. Speech treating women in the disapproved way—as subversive in matters sexual or as enjoying humiliation—is unlawful no matter how significant the literary, artistic, or political qualities of the work taken as a whole. The state may not ordain preferred viewpoints in this way. The Constitution forbids the state to declare one perspective right and silence opponents.

Shifting his focus, Easterbrook next reviewed some of the legal history of free speech in the United States. "If there is any fixed star in our constitutional constellation," he wrote, quoting the Supreme Court in the 1943 flag salute case of *West Virginia State Board of Education v. Barnette,* "it is that no official, high or petty, can prescribe what shall be orthodox in politics, nationalism, religion, or other matters of opinion or force citizens to confess by word or act their faith therein." He cited the Nazi regime of Germany as a repressive government that suppressed its own citizens, and he cited the discrimination promulgated by the Ku Klux Klan in the United

States as another example of groups limiting speech liberties. Yet, Easterbrook pointed out, because of the First Amendment such groups within the United States could put forward their ideas without interference from local, state, or federal government. In the United States, although such beliefs might be offensive and gross, political speech was nevertheless protected from unreasonable government regulation. Indianapolis's pornography ordinance forbade speech that "subordinates" women "no matter how great the literary or political value of the work taken as a whole," whereas speech that portrayed women in positions of equality, "no matter how graphic the sexual content," was lawful. Easterbrook could not agree: "This is thought control. It establishes an 'approved' view of women, of how they may react to sexual encounters, or how the sexes may relate to each other." This type of "thought control" by government was outside of the American tradition and violated the First Amendment (771 F.2d 323, 328).

Still, Easterbrook did not dismiss the ordinance's premises out of hand. Indianapolis claimed that the ordinance was valid because pornography affected thoughts. As Easterbrook paraphrased the argument: "Men who see women depicted as subordinate are more likely to treat them so. Pornography is an aspect of dominance . . . . In this view pornography is not an idea; pornography is the injury." To the feminists backing the ordinance, the alleged injury justified the prohibition; but to the Seventh Circuit Court of Appeals, this understanding of pornography only underlined the importance and power of pornography as speech. And the appropriate solution in dealing with speech disliked by one or another interest group was not government censorship of that speech, as provided in this ordinance, but rather freer speech, which could bring about social change. If pornography was powerful speech, so too was speech that tackled the multidimensional questions surrounding speech and pornography; and that sort of discussion was the appropriate avenue to follow in dealing with pornography in society. What Easterbrook could not tolerate was an answer that "leaves the government in control of all of the institutions of culture, the great censor and director of which thoughts are good for us" (771 F.2d 323, 330). What the culture needed was a healthy and robust popular dialogue about what was appropriate and what was not. Only a strong commitment to the value of freedom of speech would guarantee that people and interest groups could challenge the dominant traditions of the culture.

Easterbrook concluded that the definition of pornography in the Indianapolis ordinance was unconstitutional and that no amount of tinkering with the language could save the ordinance. It was too broad and too vague, as the district court had found. Other aspects of the ordinance might be salvageable; but any changes would have to be made with an eye toward bringing the ordinance into compliance with the First Amendment and the Supreme Court's guidelines for defining obscenity. Not surprisingly, Indianapolis appealed this federal circuit court decision, but the U.S. Supreme Court summarily affirmed the Easterbrook decision. With the summary judgment by the Supreme Court, the litigation against the Indianapolis ordinance ended. To date, Indianapolis has not tried to amend its ordinance; nor have other, similar ordinances been either enforced or challenged. The social and legal values attached to maintaining speech and press liberties overrode the attempt to enforce the feminist viewpoint of obscenity's social effects.

Instead of trying to curb pornography by attacking it as a violation of civil rights, many cities and towns in the United States have instead sought to deal with the presence of pornography through the city's power over land use via zoning laws. But in a rights-conscious society even zoning raises the issue of whether the zoning regulations affecting "adult businesses" are truly aimed at regulating how persons use their private real property or are actually a form of speech censorship.

In 1976, the U.S. Supreme Court took up this issue in *Young, Mayor of Detroit, et al. v. American Mini Theatres, Inc., et al.* Detroit's ordinance prohibited the location of an adult theater within 1,000 feet of specified regulated areas such as churches and schools or 500 feet of a residential zone. The city's goal was to prevent such businesses from congregating in one area of the city. Ruling for a plurality of the Court, Justice John Paul Stevens accepted this logic, holding that such restrictions did not constitute a violation of the First or the Fourteenth Amendments; rather, he saw them as merely routine and valid land use regulations tailored appropriately to meet the stated need of the city.

So events would stand until *City of Renton et al. v. Playtime Theatres, Inc., et al.*—a case similar to *Young*—reached the Supreme Court in 1986. In this case, the city of Renton, Washington, passed an ordinance that prohibited adult theaters from locating within 1,000 feet of any residential zone, single- or multiple-family dwelling, church, park, or school. Playtime Theatres challenged the ordinance, arguing that this restriction violated the speech and press clauses of the First Amendment. Unlike Detroit, which sought to disperse adult theaters from one area of the city, Renton sought to congregate such businesses within a specific area of the municipal boundary in order to protect other parts of the city. At trial, the district judge found for the City of Renton, and Playtime Theatres appealed to the Ninth Circuit Court of Appeals. This court reversed the district judge and held that the zoning ordinance "constituted a restriction of speech" and that "the city had failed to make a sufficient showing of a substantial government interest in support of the ordinance" (475 U.S. 41). Renton then appealed to the U.S. Supreme Court, which heard arguments in this case on November 12, 1985, and handed down its decision on February 25, 1986.

In a 7–2 decision, the Supreme Court reversed the Ninth Circuit Court of Appeals and upheld Renton's ordinance. Relying on the 1976 *Young* decision, Justice Rehnquist wrote in the opinion of the Court that because the Renton ordinance, like Detroit's, did not totally ban such businesses but merely established zoning guidelines where such places *could* exist, the zoning regulation formed an appropriate "time, place, and manner" regulation. Normally, Rehnquist wrote, restrictions of speech are presumptively held to be violations of the First Amendment; but "content-neutral" restrictions, such as regulations affecting time, place, and manner, can be acceptable if they serve a "substantial governmental interest" and do not "unreasonably limit alternative avenues of communications." Renton's ordinance was not aimed at limiting the content of the films—that would violate the First Amendment—but rather aimed to control "the *secondary effects* of such theaters on the surrounding community." Secondary effects of such places included loitering, petty crime, minor assaults, and other unsavory, negative urban conditions the ordinance sought to prevent. As the chief justice viewed the situation, this zoning ordinance was not aimed at limiting or suppressing pornography as a form of speech but rather at preventing crime and maintaining property values within the city. As a result, "the Renton ordinance is completely consistent with our definition of 'content-neutral' speech regulations" (475 U.S. 41, 48).

Having decided that the Renton ordinance was "content-neutral," Rehnquist then asked whether the ordinance was designed to serve a "substantial governmental interest and allowed for reasonable alternative avenues of communication." In other words, did the ordinance achieve its goals while allowing for other possible avenues of speech? To the question of whether Renton's decision to congregate adult businesses in one location was a substantial governmental interest, Rehnquist answered that it was. As he wrote, "Cities may regulate adult theaters by dispersing them, as in Detroit, or by effectively concentrating them, as in Renton." And were reasonable alternative avenues of communication available to the businesses? Here the majority again supported the federal district judge's finding that at least 520 acres of the city were open to these businesses. And although some of that land already had buildings on it, Rehnquist held that the theaters would have to operate in the real estate market, vying with other businesses for choice locations. As a result, a reasonable alternative avenue of communication did exist for these businesses. Overall, then, "the Renton ordinance represented a valid governmental response to the 'admittedly serious problems' created by adult theaters." The Supreme Court reversed the Ninth Circuit decision and upheld Renton's districting ordinance (475 U.S. 41, 54).

Justices William Brennan and Thurgood Marshall dissented from the majority opinion in *Renton*, arguing that the ordinance was not "content-neutral," and that even if it had been, the city had failed to demonstrate a substantial governmental interest fulfilled by the ordinance. Nor did the city provide adequate alternative avenues of communication. "Renton's zoning ordinance selectively imposes limitations on the location of a movie theater based exclusively on the content of the films shown there," Brennan stated. In his tradition of defending the First Amendment against any and all restrictions, Brennan opposed Renton's ordinance and the majority's decision to uphold the ordinance. Because this ordinance affected only adult theaters, he and the other dissenters claimed the ordinance had the effect of limiting the *content* of films shown at such places. Therefore, the restriction on adult theaters violated such businesses' First Amendment rights and ought to be struck down. Unpersuaded by the city's contention that its goal was not to restrict speech but rather to control crime and social problems, Brennan declared, "The ordinance is patently unconstitutional."

Even assuming for the sake of argument that the ordinance was a valid time, place, and manner regulation, it would still fail, according to Brennan, because nothing in the record demonstrated that the ordinance advanced a substantial government interest. Merely voicing a concern for maintaining the quality of urban life was an insufficient demonstration; Renton had provided no evidence that this ordinance did, in fact, help maintain the quality of urban life. Neither did the dissenters believe that Renton had provided sufficient alternative avenues of communication for these adult businesses. Insufficient land and property existed to support these businesses, they found, and these businesses did not operate "on equal footing with other prospective purchasers and lessees"; therefore, the ordinance must fail on these grounds as well (475 U.S. 41, 65). As a result, Justices Brennan and Marshall would have upheld the Ninth Circuit Court of Appeals decision and overturned the Renton, Washington, ordinance.

The issue of pornography and obscenity next arose before the Supreme Court three years later, propelled by advancing technology and the law's response to problems created by this advance, as it had been in *Federal Communications Commission v. Pacifica* (1978). On June 23, 1989, the Supreme Court handed down a 6–3 decision in *Sable Communications of California v. Federal Communications Commission,* informally known as the "dial-a-porn" case. This case, which technically revolved around the legal regulation of "indecent" and "obscene" speech, became a vehicle for the Court's further exploration of the nexus of technology, obscenity, and law.

The case originated in 1988, when Congress amended Section 223(b) of the Communications Act of 1937, also known as 47 United States Code §223(b), and imposed a ban on all indecent and obscene interstate telephone conversations that had a commercial basis. Since 1983, Sable Communications of California had been "offering sexually oriented prerecorded telephone messages (popularly known as 'dial-a-porn') through the Pacific Bell network." When Congress amended the Communications Act of 1937, Sable sued to stop the enforcement of the revisions, describing them as a "blanket prohibition on indecent as well as obscene interstate commercial telephone messages" (492 U.S. 115, 118). At the district court level, the judge denied Sable's request to overturn the obscenity amendments of the Communications Act but granted Sable's request to strike down the indecent speech provisions of §223(b) because they were overly broad and violated speech liberties protected by the First Amendment. Sable appealed to the Ninth Circuit, and through an administrative process, with the consent of the FCC, then brought the case directly to the U.S. Supreme Court, which heard arguments on April 19, 1989.

Justice Byron White wrote the opinion for the majority. He reviewed FCC regulations on telephone communications as well as earlier congressional amendments to the 1934 Communications Act that were aimed at regulating the use of telephone technology to deliver obscene materials for commercial purposes. Various methods previously had been proposed for regulating dial-a-porn, such as limiting the time of day when such services could be accessed (known as time channeling), or requiring payment by credit card (screening) before messages could be transmitted. Access codes or user identification codes as well as message scrambling (requiring that the consumer have a descrambler) had also been tried by the industry and encouraged by the Federal Communications Commission. These gatekeeping methods balanced the need to allow consenting adults access to messages (i.e., to avoid violating the First Amendment rights of patrons and producers) against the need to screen out minors, but they were not foolproof. In April 1988, responding to fears that minors might still gain access to dial-a-porn in spite of the technical obstacles, Congress passed a complete ban on all dial-a-porn communications for commercial purposes. Sable Communications of California then challenged this total prohibition.

Justice White had no difficulty upholding the federal government's restriction against obscene communications, because legal precedent had established that the First Amendment does not protect obscene materials or speech. He cited *Paris Adult Theatre I v. Slaton* (1973) for support. Further, the majority denied that §223(b) had established a national community standard and thereby had violated the Court's *Miller v. California* (1973) standard. Instead, they found that Congress had acted well within its power to prohibit the circulation of obscene materials. It was Sable's responsibility to tailor its messages to meet the community standards requirement of the Court's *Miller* rule.

However, the majority could not support the total ban on "indecent," as opposed to "obscene," commercial speech. As White stated the issue: "The District Court concluded that while the Government has a legitimate interest in protecting children from exposure to indecent dial-a-porn messages, §223(b) was not sufficiently narrowly drawn to serve that purpose and thus violated the First Amendment. We agree." He continued, "Sexual expression which is indecent but not obscene is protected by the First Amendment." He pointed out that the commercial exchange of such messages among adults is not a criminal offense (492 U.S. 115, 126). In this case, the revised statute was too broadly drawn, as a result of which adults were denied access to merely indecent prerecorded messages. Quoting Justice Felix Frankfurter in *Butler v. Michigan*, White said, "Surely this is to burn down the house to roast the pig" (352 U.S. 380).

Yet another legal precedent undermined the federal government's defense of the 1988 revisions to the 1934 Communications Act: *Federal Communications Commission v. Pacifica* (1978). Pacifica did not "involve a total ban on broadcasting indecent material"; rather, it sought only to channel such broadcasts to times of the day when minors would be least likely to encounter such language on the public airwaves (438 U.S. 726). As White further explained, "Placing a telephone call is not the same as turning on a radio and being taken by surprise by an indecent message" (492 U.S. 115, 128). Thus, the federal government's claim that *Pacifica* supported the total ban on dial-a-porn failed to convince a majority of the justices.

Supporters of the total ban on dial-a-porn services argued that it was the only reasonable method available to the federal government to prevent minors from gaining access, and that the federal courts ought to defer to the decisions of the elected and accountable branches of government in such matters. To this the majority responded, "We find the argument quite unpersuasive." White pointed out that the FCC and the Court of Appeals in earlier cases had found the various methods of gatekeeping satisfactory; they served the government's compelling interest in protecting children. No evidence existed that new rules were needed to shield youngsters from messages to which they should not have access. And, as for deferring to congressional decisions, White reminded the parties that it was the Supreme Court's task "to decide whether Congress has violated the Constitution." This task was especially true in matters involving the First Amendment. As a result, "because the statute's denial of adult access to telephone messages which are indecent but not obscene far exceeds that which is necessary to limit the access of minors to such messages, we hold that the ban does not survive constitutional scrutiny" (492 U.S. 115, 131). Therefore, the Supreme Court upheld the district court's decision to strike down the part of §223(b) dealing with indecent speech while upholding the section of that revised statute dealing with obscene speech. Congress could legislate the commercial use of the interstate telephone lines; but in doing so, it could not violate speech liberties protected by the First Amendment.

Justices Brennan, Marshall, and Stevens dissented from the majority's decision and instead made a case for the threat of federal government censorship implicit in §223(b). Brennan in particular supported the majority's decision to strike down the part of §223(b) dealing with only "indecent" speech, but he dissented from the majority's decision to let stand the restrictions on "obscene" speech. He wrote, "I have long been convinced that the exaction of criminal penalties for the distribution of obscene materials to consenting adults is constitutionally intolerable." He feared that the federal government, in its attempt to limit obscene materials to minors, would in fact censor materials that adults might want to view. Brennan and the dissenters found that the total ban on indecent and obscene telephone messages for commercial purposes was too "heavy-handed" in regard to indecent speech, but the same could be said of obscene speech as well. They would reverse the district court's findings "because this criminal statute curtails freedom of speech far more radically than the Government interest in preventing harm to minors could possibly license" (492 U.S. 115, 135). As a result, §223(b) of the 1934 Communications Act ought to be declared unconstitutional, a violation of the speech liberties of the First Amendment.

Although Brennan and the other dissenters worried about the power of government to restrict commercial speech such as dial-a-porn services to adults, the majority sought to craft a balance between limiting such services to minors and allowing adults access. It proved a difficult balance for the justices.

The issues did not get any easier with the passage of time and continual innovations in technology. Cable television created yet another complex set of problems with regard to obscenity for the justices to sort through. At issue in *Denver Area Educational Telecommunications Consortium, Inc., et al. v. Federal Communications Commission* (1996) were sections of the Cable Television Consumer Protection and Competition Act (CTCPCA) of 1992. Once again, technology complicated obscenity jurisprudence. By the 1980s, cable television had been available on a limited basis in a number of places for a long time. In the 1990s, however, because of advances in cable technology (cable television has the advantage over broadcast television in that it can carry literally hundreds of television broadcasts into a home or an office) and greater consumer demand, cable television had become widespread. Many new cable networks emerged to fill the demand, some of which carried "adult" content. In order to protect children from televised pornography, in 1992 Congress passed the CTCPCA. Like other forms of speech, these government regulations of cable television broadcasts came under First Amendment attack for limiting what adults could view, and when.

Three sections of the CTCPCA constituted the heart of this litigation. First, §10(a) of the Act "*permitted* a cable system operator to prohibit broadcasting . . . of programming that the operator reasonably believed to describe or depict sexual or excretory activities or organs in a patently offensive manner." Section 10(b) "*required* cable systems operators which decided to permit such 'patently offensive' programming to (a) segregate such programming on a single channel, and (b) block that channel from viewer access in advance and in writing." Lastly, §10(c) "permitted a cable system operator to *prohibit* the broadcasting of such programming on public access channels," public access channels being those channels "set aside for public, educational, or governmental purposes" (518 U.S. 727). After the Federal Communications Commission established guidelines for implementing these sections of the 1992 Cable Act, public access programmers and viewers of such programs brought suit in the U.S. Court of Appeals for the District of Columbia, seeking judicial review of the reasonableness and constitutionality of the regulations. At first, a panel of the appeals court found that these sections of the Act violated the First Amendment; but when the Court of Appeals heard the case *en banc,* the court found the statute and the regulations consistent with the First Amendment. Because of this split in the decisions of the appeals court, the U.S. Supreme Court agreed to hear the case on February 21, 1996.

When the Supreme Court handed down its decision on June 28, 1996, opinion was fragmented. Justice Steven Breyer wrote the judgment of the Court, but five other justices also wrote lengthy separate opinions. Seven members of the Supreme Court agreed that §10(a) was consistent with the First Amendment's free speech guarantees and was valid; six justices agreed that §10(b) violated the First Amendment's free speech guarantees; and five justices agreed that §10(c) also violated the First Amendment. As these voting patterns suggest, the splits among the justices make it difficult to describe the rationale of the Court's decision. Nevertheless, Justice Breyer's opinion provided some idea of the Supreme Court's understanding of the issues involved in the broadcast of obscenity via cable television.

Telecommunications regulations are highly complex and must balance a wide variety of social, cultural, and economic interests. Because of this complexity, the justices sought to craft as narrow a decision as possible. Breyer and six others decided that §10(a) was consistent with the First Amendment. Breyer wrote that the need to protect children from exposure "to patently offensive sex-related material" constituted a sufficiently significant justification for the statute. Next, because the statute was permissive, it provided "congressional permission for cable operators to regulate programming that, but for an Act of Congress, would have had no path of access to cable channels free of an operator's control." By this Act, cable operators could choose which channels to carry on their systems; without the Act, they might be forced to carry any channel, regardless of local needs and circumstances. Thus this permissive language allowed flexibility to the statute and cable operators, and was valid. Next Breyer relied on *FCC v. Pacifica* (1978) for guidance. He pointed out that in *Pacifica* the Supreme Court upheld a definition of "indecent" materials inclusive of "language that describes in terms patently offensive as measured by contemporary community standards for the broadcast medium, sexual or excretory activities and organs, at times of day when there is a reasonable risk that children may be in the audience." After review, the justice upheld this language as constitutional because "broadcasting is uniquely accessible to children," and children were likely to be listening to an afternoon radio broadcast. Children had similar easy access to cable television, and stations might confront children with inappropriate material with little or no prior warning. In fact, Breyer pointed out, cable viewers were more likely "to sample more channels before settling on a program," because of the range of stations available on cable, making them "more susceptible to random exposure to unwanted materials." Limiting that potential for exposure justified this section of the statute.

Breyer further argued that the permissive nature of the statute "means that it likely restricts speech less than, not more than, the ban at issue in *Pacifica.*" This flexibility allowed cable operators "not to ban broadcasts, but, say, to rearrange broadcast times to better fit the desires of adult audiences while lessening the risks to children." He continued, "In all of these respects, the permissive nature of the approach taken by Congress renders this measure appropriate as a means of achieving the underlying purpose of protecting children." More succinctly, Breyer wrote, "The existence of this complex balance of interests persuades us that the permissive nature of the provision, coupled with its viewpoint-neutral application, is a constitutionally permissible way to protect children from the type of sexual material that concerned Congress, while accommodating . . . the First Amendment interests served by the access requirements" (518 U.S. 727, 747).

As a result, the Supreme Court upheld §10(a) of the 1992 Act as constitutional. Sections 10(b) and 10(c), however, did not pass constitutional examination. Section 10(b) provided for the "segregate and block" requirements of the Act, and the Court found that this section had "obvious restrictive effects" on viewers and operators. This regulation meant that viewers "cannot decide to watch a single program without considerable advance planning." Viewers and programmer could not select programs "day by day (or through 'surfing,' minute by minute)." Further, the "written notice" provisions of the regulation would tend to deter viewers, for fear that their names would be placed on lists of subscribers; and cable operators who wished to operate strictly at night might be banned altogether. "We do not agree," wrote Breyer, "that the 'segregate and block' requirements properly accommodate the speech restrictions they impose and the legitimate objective they seek to attain." Lastly, this section of the 1992 Act was not narrowly or reasonably tailored to meet the legitimate objective of protecting children, so it failed on those grounds as well. In other words, section 10(b) might have been well meant, but it was extreme and "overly restrictive" and therefore violated the First Amendment (518 U.S. 727, 760).

A majority of the Court found that §10(c) also violated the First Amendment by permitting cable operators to prohibit indecent programming on public access channels—as opposed to the leased channels in §10(a)—because it could not be demonstrated that such a prohibition protected children. As Breyer and four of his brethren explained, "We conclude that the Government cannot sustain its burden of showing that §10(c) is necessary to protect children or that it is appropriately tailored to secure that end" (518 U.S. 727, 766). Therefore, this third provision of the Cable Television Consumer Protection and Competition Act of 1992 was unconstitutional.

Having stated that §10(a) could still stand and be enforced even though enforcement of sections 10(b) and 10(c) would have to end, Breyer and the majority reversed the Court of Appeals decision on §10(b) and (c) and upheld the Court of Appeals on §10(a). Cable operators could choose to prohibit indecent programming over leased channels, but not public access channels, to serve the social goal of protecting children from obscenity. Justices Stevens, Souter, O'Connor, Kennedy, and Thomas all wrote separate opinions. Each of them concurred in part or dissented in part with Breyer's opinion, and each did so on slightly different grounds. Nevertheless, Breyer's opinion set forth the Court's judgment on what cable television operators could and could not carry on their systems, and thereby established the current legal guidelines for cable operators.

Technology challenged the Supreme Court yet again in the 1997 decision of *Janet Reno, Attorney General of the United States, et al. v. American Civil Liberties Union et al.* This time the technology used to deliver obscenity to customers was not the television or the radio but personal computers and the Internet. During the early to middle 1990s, purchases of personal computers multiplied in the United States. By 1997, the Court estimated, 40 million people were using the Internet, and that figure was expected to rise to 200 million by 1999. More and more American families owned personal computers, and children were learning not only to use computers but also to program them. Some colleges and universities even required students to own a personal computer. Linking all of these computers together was the Internet.

As this discussion clearly shows, every medium of human communication has been used to display, print, or show pornographic, obscene, or indecent images and/or ideas; the Internet proved no different. As described in the case notes in *Reno,* the Internet is "an international network of interconnected computers that enables millions of people to communicate with one another in 'cyberspace' and to access vast amounts of information from around the world"; further, the Internet was "a unique and wholly new medium of worldwide human communication" (521 U.S. 844, 850). Some of that information might be obscene; that dilemma, in turn, has led to the problem of how to prevent children from accessing obscene or pornographic images on a World Wide Web site. Congress responded to this social concern by passing the Telecommunications Act of 1996, Title V of which was known as the Communications Decency Act (CDA) of 1996. The CDA was immediately challenged in court.

Defenders of the Internet and of free speech had particular concerns with sections 223(a) and 223(d) of the CDA. Section 223(a) made it a federal crime to knowingly transmit by personal computer "'obscene or indecent' communications to any recipient under 18 years of age"; and §223(d) made it a federal crime to send to anyone under 18 years of age "communications that, in context, depict or describe, in terms 'patently offensive' as measured by contemporary community standards, sexual or excretory activities or organs." This statute established the maximum penalty for violating these sections as two years in prison. Given the complicated and technical nature of computer communications, the statute spelled out possible defenses against charges contained in 223(a) and 223(d). Affirmative defenses would be available to those who took "good faith, reasonable, effective, and appropriate actions to restrict access to minors to the prohibited communications" or to restrict access to minors by, for example, requiring proof of age "such as a verified credit card or an adult identification number or code" (521 U.S. 844).

On February 8, 1996, just after President William J. Clinton signed the bill into law, the American Civil Liberties Union and other plaintiffs filed two suits to stop the implementation of Title V, alleging that §223(a) and §223(d) unconstitutionally violated the First Amendment free speech rights of Americans. A three-judge federal district court in the Eastern District of Pennsylvania agreed to consider these two challenges jointly. After hearing the arguments, they issued a unanimous opinion that those sections of the CDA infringed upon the First Amendment and were therefore unconstitutional. Pursuant to the provisions in the CDA, a direct appeal was taken to the U.S. Supreme Court, which heard arguments on March 19, 1997.

On June 26, 1997, Justice Stevens handed down the opinion of the Court's seven-member majority, striking down key sections of the CDA; Justices O'Connor and Rehnquist dissented in part and concurred in part. Stevens began by tracing the history of the Internet, and explaining how it worked. He described the World Wide Web, Web browsers, E-mail, list-serves, and chat rooms, and alluded to the wide range of information available on-line through the Web. Quoting from the district court opinion, he described the nature of the "sexually explicit material" available on the Web as "extend[ing] from the modestly titillating to the hardest core." He noted that most sexually explicit Web sites contain a warning about their content. Stevens then reviewed the methods of age verification available to site operators and pointed out the weaknesses of such systems. He wrote, again quoting from the lower court's finding of facts, "Even if credit card verification or adult password verification were implemented, the Government presented no testimony as to how such systems could ensure that the user of the password or credit card is in fact over 18" (521 U.S. 844, 857).

Stevens then reviewed the legislative and judicial history of *Reno v. ACLU* and called the Telecommunications Act of 1996 "an unusually important legislative enactment." He took judicial notice of the fact that Title V—the Communications Decency Act—contained provisions that Congress added after regular debate on the bill had closed. Senators added both §223(a) and §223(d) from the Senate floor, during debates. By taking judicial notice of these additions, Stevens suggested that these amendments were already questionable in their motivation, and he left no doubt that the justices viewed the disputed sections of the CDA as overly broad and unconstitutional.

Justice Stevens examined the argument by the federal government favoring the CDA and reviewed each of the major decisions it relied on to support the constitutionality of the CDA: *Ginsberg v. New York* (1968), *FCC v. Pacifica Foundation* (1978), and *Renton v. Playtime Theatres, Inc.* (1986). In each of these earlier cases, Stevens demonstrated that the alleged precedent did not fit the facts of the case at hand (to use a legal term, he "distinguished" the precedent from the case at hand). More troubling for Stevens and the majority was the vagueness of sections 223(a) and 223(d). Since the statute failed to define terms such as "indecent," the justices worried that topics such as "birth control practices, homosexuality, the First Amendment issues raised by the Appendix to our *Pacifica* opinion, or the consequences of prison rape would not violate the CDA." These questions suggested to Stevens that Congress had not tailored the disputed sections sufficiently to the goal of protecting minors from immoral materials on the Internet. These concerns led the majority to state bluntly, "The CDA is a content-based regulation of speech." The government's claim that the statute met the Supreme Court's *Miller v. California* (1973) guidelines did not convince. Although *Miller* sought to craft rules for judging when materials were or were not obscene and indecent, the CDA sought to censor speech and therefore bore a burden that went beyond mere definition. As Stevens stated, "The CDA lacks the precision that the First Amendment requires when a statute regulates the content of speech" (521 U.S. 844, 874).

Concerning age verification, Stevens supported the district court's finding that security systems based on credit card numbers and passwords were inadequate to prevent children from accessing obscenity on the Web. In addition, he pointed out that such measures would also "inevitably curtail a significant amount of adult communication on the Internet." In Stevens's view, this overbreadth of the statute was a fatal flaw. He supported the district court's finding that "the CDA places an unacceptably heavy burden on protected speech" and that the proposed defenses of the statute did not measure up. In *Sable Communications of California, Inc. v. FCC* (1989), Stevens had argued, "We remarked that the speech restrictions at issue there amounted to 'burning down the house to roast the pig.' The CDA, casting a far darker shadow over free speech, threatens to torch a large segment of the Internet community." And that the Supreme Court could not allow.

Finally, to the government's last argument—that because obscene material was driving people away from using the Internet, the CDA was a valid regulation to ensure the wholesome quality and the viability of the medium—was dismissed by the majority as "singularly unpersuasive." Stevens wrote: "We presume that governmental regulation of speech is more likely to interfere with the free exchange of ideas than to encourage it. The interest in encouraging freedom of expression in a democratic society outweighs any theoretical but unproven benefit of censorship" (521 U.S. 844, 885). Not surprisingly, the Supreme Court affirmed the district court's decision declaring sections 223(a) and 223(d) of the Communications Decency Act of 1996 unconstitutional.

Justice O'Connor, joined by Justice Rehnquist, dissented in part, arguing that these sections formed a type of "zoning restriction," establishing an adults-only area on the Internet. These sections might be valid. Her reading of the statute led her to question the statute insofar as it affected the First Amendment rights of adults, not in that it protected children. The statute's "'indecency transmission' and 'specific persons' provisions prohibit[ing] the use of indecent speech in communications between an adult and one or more minors can and should be sustained," O'Connor argued (521 U.S. 844, 896). Nevertheless, the majority of the Court disagreed with this analysis, and no further litigation along these lines has yet come forward.

Television and obscenity again came before the Supreme Court just after the turn of the twenty-first century. In May 2000, the Supreme Court handed down another decision dealing with the Telecommunications Act (TCA) of 1996 and furthering its ongoing discussion and analysis of technology, obscenity, and the limits of the First Amendment. Section 505 of the TCA was at issue in *United States et al. v. Playboy Entertainment Group, Inc.* This section sought to remedy a problem with cable television signals, a problem known as "signal bleed." Although cable operators employ special scrambling technology to ensure that only paying customers receive their programming, this technology is not perfect. Some of the audio and/or visual portions of the scrambled program can occasionally still be seen and heard. Signal bleed was a problem primarily with channels dedicated to sexually oriented programming, because the signal bleed could be seen and heard by children and nonconsenting adults. Section 505 required cable operators to follow one of two options to combat signal bleed: (1) fully scramble or otherwise block those channels, or (2) "time channel" such programming to hours when children would be less likely to be watching. In order to comply with §505, most cable operators had chosen to time channel such programming, which meant that during two-thirds of the day no viewer could receive adult programming.

Playboy Entertainment Group, Inc., brought suit in the Federal District Court of Delaware, challenging the constitutionality of §505. Playboy Entertainment Group, Inc., owned, produced, and transmitted programming such as Playboy Television, AdulTVision, Adam & Eve, and Spice, and the 505 restrictions deprived them of their First Amendment rights while limiting their income. At first a three-judge panel denied Playboy's request for a preliminary injunction, and the U.S. Supreme Court upheld that denial. After a full trial of the issues, however, the district court held that §505 was a content-based restriction on speech and concluded that although §505 addressed a compelling governmental interest, a less restrictive method of regulation existed that would be more in line with the First Amendment. That less restrictive method was §504 of the Telecommunications Act of 1996, which required cable operators to block unwanted channels at the request of individual households. The district court found §505 unconstitutional, and instead it imposed the requirement that cable operators provide adequate notice of §504 to cable subscribers.

The federal government appealed this decision to the U.S. Supreme Court, which heard arguments on November 30, 1999. On May 22, 2000, the Supreme Court handed down its 5–4 decision. Justice Kennedy wrote the majority opinion and Justices Stevens, Souter, Thomas, and Ginsburg joined him. In a long and rambling opinion, the majority upheld and elaborated upon the district court's findings. Kennedy began with a review of the signal bleed problem and other technological issues involved in cable television. Although digital television offered a remedy for signal bleed, that technology was not widely available. Having established the problems and reviewed the findings of the district court, Kennedy elaborated on some of the Court's understandings. First, he emphasized, "We shall assume that many adults themselves would find the material highly offensive" and that when such material enters homes where it might be seen or heard by children, both reasons constituted sufficient reason to regulate "sexually explicit adult programming or other programming that is indecent." Second, all the parties as well as all the judges and justices agreed, "Playboy's programming has First Amendment protection." Adults could view Playboy's programming, the government could not prevent children from seeing or hearing such programming if they had their parents' consent, and Playboy had a right to transmit such programming. Its programming might be indecent, but it was not obscene; therefore, the First Amendment protected Playboy from unreasonable governmental regulations.

Next, Kennedy pointed out that the speech in question was "defined by its content" and that the statute sought to restrict that speech because of its content. Therefore, the statute was a content-based restriction on speech and would have to undergo strict scrutiny by the justices. Not only was §505 a content-based restriction, but the statute singled out specific programmers for restrictions—those "primarily dedicated to sexually oriented programming." In fact, and in a bit of an unusual move, Kennedy noted that California Senator Diane Feinstein of California referred to Playboy by name as just the sort of programmer the legislators sought to curb. Justice Kennedy added, "Laws designed or intended to suppress or restrict the expression of specific speakers contradict basic First Amendment principles."

Examining the statute and its effects more closely, the majority recognized that time channeling had become the only reasonable manner for cable operators to comply with §505. Yet, that regulation silenced protected speech for two-thirds of the day, regardless of whether children or nonconsenting adults were in the household. This chilling effect to speech made the majority uncomfortable. As they wrote, "To prohibit this much speech is a significant restriction of communication between speakers and willing adult listeners, communication which enjoys First Amendment protection." Although this regulation did not ban the speech outright, it clearly placed an undue burden on that speech. For all these reasons, Kennedy and the majority determined that §505 was a content-based speech restriction. In order to be a valid regulation of content-based speech, the regulation had to be "narrowly tailored to promote a compelling Government interest." The majority found that this requirement was not met.

Kennedy continued: "Our precedents teach three principles. Where the designed benefit of a content-based speech restriction is to shield the sensitivities of listeners, the general rule is that the right of expression prevails, even when no less restrictive alternative exists." For this reason, the justices had to strictly scrutinize the statute. After reviewing possible precedents, such as *Denver Area Educational Telecommunications Consortium, Inc., v. FCC* (1996), *Sable Communication of California, Inc. v. FCC* (1989), and *FCC v. Pacifica Foundation* (1978), the Court noted a key difference between cable systems and other media: "Cable systems have the capacity to block unwanted channels on a household-by-household basis." Called "target blocking," this form of regulation "enables the Government to support parental authority without affecting the First Amendment interests of speakers and willing listeners." Target blocking was a "less restrictive" option than banning obscene or offensive speech on cable, and if target blocking was feasible, then the federal government could not ban such programming and speech. Was target blocking feasible? During the time frame when §505 was in litigation, a survey of cable operators showed that fewer than 0.5 percent of cable subscribers requested target blocking. As a result, when target blocking was the sole regulation, the Court found, "the public greeted it with a collective yawn." This survey suggested either that not many Americans were concerned with the speech that entered their households via the television cable systems, or they did not know about or understand target blocking.

Justice Kennedy then proceeded *in dicta* to deliver a short lecture in answer to critics of the Supreme Court who claimed that the justices were too "soft" on pornography. He pointed out that in speech cases the normal assumption by the Court—that laws passed by the Congress were constitutional—was, in fact, reversed. In speech cases, the government bore the burden of demonstrating the constitutionality of its laws. In a political democracy, speech is so important that reversing the burden of proof is necessary. Through speech "we bring . . . beliefs to bear on Government and on society"; and citizens are "entitled to seek out or reject certain ideas or influences without Government interference or control." Anticipating another wave of public criticism, Kennedy provided an extraordinary defense of the Supreme Court's obscenity jurisprudence.

> When students first encounter American free speech jurisprudence, they might think it is influenced by the philosophy that one idea is as good as any other, and that in art and literature objective standards of style, taste, decorum, beauty, and esthetics are deemed by the Constitution to be inappropriate, indeed unattainable. Quite the opposite is true. The Constitution no more enforces a relativistic philosophy or moral nihilism than it does any other point of view. The Constitution exists precisely so that opinions and judgments, including esthetic and moral judgments about art and literature, can be formed, tested, and expressed. What the Constitution says is that these judgments are for the individual to make, not for the government to decree, even with the mandate or approval of a majority. Technology expands the capacity to choose; and we deny the productive potential of this revolution if we assume the government is best positioned to make these choices for us.

This remarkable statement was an obvious effort to defend the Court from the accusation that it was largely responsible for the moral decay of the country since the 1960s. Not so, claimed Kennedy. The Court sought only to provide an open forum for the discussion of thoughts and ideas (no matter how offensive or obscene), necessary for the optimal functioning of the democratic political system. What the population did with that forum would determine the outcome. As a result, he continued, "It is rare that a regulation restricting speech because of its content will ever be permissible." Thus, the burden fell on the federal government to demonstrate why §505's content-based speech restriction should be upheld (120 S.Ct. 1878, 1889).

Justice Kennedy provided the fullest defense of the Supreme Court's obscenity jurisprudence to date. When he shifted back to the case at hand, he took up the district court's exploration for the lack of individual blocking requests. Three possible explanations existed:

first, "individual blocking might not be an effective alternative, due to technological or other limitations"; second, "although an adequate advertised blocking provision might have been effective, §504 as written did not require sufficient notice to make it so"; and third, the actual signal bleed problem might be of far less concern than the government had supposed. At the district level, the court found the first and last possibilities were "equally consistent" with the record; in other words, individual household block might not be effective due to technological limitations, and the problem of signal bleed might not have been as great as first thought. On the second issue, notification of individual household blocking, the district court held that the record was "not clear" as to whether §504 had been given a "fighting chance." "The case, then," according to the majority, "was at best a draw." They added, "Unless the District Court's findings are clearly erroneous, the tie goes to free expression."

Reviewing the district court's decision, the Court found only the thinnest of evidence that signal bleed was a social problem of the first order. Nor did Court find the federal government's arguments that §504's individual household blocking requirement would be as restrictive as §505. Instead, the Court majority supported the district court's findings that household blocking had not been sufficiently advertised or implemented. A "publicized §504, which has the real possibility of promoting more open disclosure and the choice of an effective blocking system, would provide parents the information needed to engage in active supervision," the Court found.

Keeping children away from obscene images and programming might be a compelling governmental interest, but was §505 an appropriate remedy? The federal district court, supported by the Supreme Court, decided it was not. A less restrictive method of preventing minors access to adult programs existed—individual household blocking, as provided for in §504—and that method was the most appropriate for dealing with this social problem. Kennedy reminded the Court and his legal audience that even if the speech at issue was not all that important, the Supreme Court still could not permit it to receive less protection than other kinds of speech. He continued: "The history of the law of free expression is one of vindication in cases involving speech that many citizens may find shabby, offensive, or even ugly. If television broadcasts can expose children to the real risk of harmful exposure to indecent materials, even in their own home and without parental consent, there is a problem that the Government can address. It must do so, however, in a way consistent with First Amendment principles. Here the Government has not met the burden the First Amendment imposes" (120 S.Ct. 1878, 1893). Thus, the district court's findings stood, §505 was declared unconstitutional, and the less restrictive method of individual household block in §504 was approved and upheld as the appropriate remedy.

Four justices dissented from the majority opinion, raising important questions. Justice Scalia, joined by Justices Rehnquist and O'Connor, agreed with the other dissenters that §505 was supported by a compelling state interest and was narrowly tailored to meet that legitimate end; but he believed that this section could be upheld on even simpler grounds: that it "regulates the business of obscenity." Scalia pointed out that the Supreme Court had restricted "commercial entities" that engaged in "the sordid business of pandering," and referred to the 1968 case of *Ginsberg v. United States.* The sale of obscene or even merely indecent materials such as Playboy's constituted an activity undeserving of any First Amendment review or protection. Section 505 was not overly broad, because it was limited to programming that "describes or depicts sexual or excretory activities or organs in a *patently offensive manner* as measured by contemporary community standards [for cable television]" and applied only to those channels that are *"primarily dedicated* to sexually oriented programming" (emphasis added by Scalia)—to businesses such as Playboy Entertainment Group, Inc., which produced and transmitted "Playboy Television," "virtually 100 percent sexually explicit adult programming." Scalia quoted from some of Playboy's own advertising, which encouraged viewers to "enjoy the sexiest, hottest adult movies in the privacy of your own home." The following text appeared in promotional material for one particular movie: "Little miss country girls are aching for a quick roll in the hay! Watch southern hospitality pull out all the stops as the ravin' nymphos tear down the barn and light up the big country sky." These juvenile rants amused Scalia, but he correctly pointed out that no matter how juvenile they might be, it was certainly "marketing sex," and Congress could highly regulate, even block, businesses that trafficked in sex. Scalia understood that "contemporary American society has chosen to permit such commercial exploitation." However, that was a cultural and a social choice, not a choice mandated by the Constitution. In Scalia's view, given that the federal government could block such transmissions constitutionally, time channeling formed a perfectly valid approach to dealing with obscenity on cable television (120 S.Ct. 1878, 1897).

Justice Breyer separately dissented from the majority view, arguing that §505 formed a valid and narrowly tailored remedy for the problem of obscenity on cable TV. He argued that the rules guiding the Supreme Court in deciding such cases were not at issue; all the justices agreed on the rules to be applied. But Breyer disagreed that §505 went too far in restricting speech liberties. This statute, he argued, "places a *burden* on adult channel speech by requiring the relevant cable operator either to use better scrambling technology, or, if that technology is too expensive, to broadcast only between 10 P.M. and 6 A.M." This flexibility, combined with the fact that the statute affected only those businesses that broadcast "virtually 100 percent sexually explicit material," meant that §505 was appropriately tailored to meet the compelling need as formulated by Congress.

Breyer further disagreed with the district court's finding, supported by the majority of the Supreme Court, that the federal government had not proved the seriousness of the problem. He estimated that as many as "29 million children are potentially exposed to audio and video bleed from adult programming." To Breyer, this figure suggested the need for §505 and its restrictions. He and the other dissenters all disagreed with the majority finding that the federal government had failed to demonstrate the absence of a "less restrictive alternative." The dissenters held that §504 presented as many problems as §505 without providing the benefits of §505, which limited "adult cable channels to children whose parents may be unaware of what they are watching, whose parents cannot easily supervise television viewing habits, whose parents do not know of their §504 'opt-out' rights, or whose parents are simply unavailable at critical times. In this respect, §505 serves the same interests as laws that deny children access to adult cabarets or X-rated movies." "This legislative objective is perfectly legitimate," Breyer emphasized.

Breyer and the other dissenters feared that the district court's and the majority's decision would manage to harm children while seeking to protect adult First Amendment liberties. "To rely primarily upon law that bans speech for adults is to overlook the special need to protect children," the dissenters alleged. Although Congress had taken seriously its role of "maintaining adult access to sexually explicit channels," the Supreme Court had undone that work. "By finding 'adequate alternatives' where there are none," Breyer argued, "the Court reduces Congress' protective power to the vanishing point. That is not what the First Amendment demands" (120 S.Ct. 1878, 1904).

In his dissent, Breyer provided a child-protective analysis of §505 and found that section an appropriate response and remedy to the social problem of obscenity and indecency on cable television and the access of children to those channels. Whereas the Court's majority balanced adult access to adult programming on cable television against children's access to obscenity and found §505 too restrictive and §504 less restrictive and therefore appropriate, the minority in *United States v. Playboy* found the restrictions imposed by §505 appropriate, constitutional, and valid. Time will tell whether their concerns were well founded.

Conclusion

The most recent obscenity decisions and legal rules suggest that the challenge of obscenity and pornography is still very much alive in American society and culture. Americans have not yet reached a consensus on the best policy to pursue regarding obscenity. It is not surprising, then, that the federal courts continue to disagree on this issue. Technological developments and innovations such as the telephone, cable television, and the Internet have provided new methods of delivering offensive material to many Americans in their cars and in their homes. Congress has responded to the social problem of obscenity through a number of important statutes; and in response, the U.S. Supreme Court has continued its case-by-case arbitration between the defenders of regulation and the advocates of First Amendment freedoms. It is not easy to balance the many technological, legal, cultural, and societal issues involved in obscenity litigation, and federal legislators and judges struggle mightily to accomplish that task. The results so far have not been to everyone's liking, nor are they likely to be in the future.

References and Further Reading

The general outlines of the incorporation of the Bill of Rights and the rise of a rights-conscious society in the twentieth-century United States can be traced in the standard textbooks in the field, such as Alfred H. Kelly et al., *The American Constitution: Its Origins and Development,* 7th ed. (New York: W. W. Norton, 1991); and Melvin I. Urofsky and Paul Finkelman, *A March of Liberty: A Constitutional History of the United States,* 2nd ed. (New York: Oxford University Press, 2002). The best work on World War I and freedom of speech and press is Paul L. Murphy, *World War I and the Origin of Civil Liberties in the United States* (New York: W. W. Norton, 1979). For a solid interpretation of a leading case of that era, see Richard Polenberg, *Fighting Faiths: The Abrams Case, the Supreme Court, and Free Speech* (New York: Penguin, 1987).

The Warren Court, its decisions, and the 1960s were and remain controversial. As a result, a large literature exists on Warren and his Court. Good introductions to the subject include Alan J. Matusow, *The Unraveling of America* (New York: Harper & Row, 1984); William E. Leuchtenburg, *A Troubled Feast: American Society since 1945* (Boston: Little, Brown, 1979); Lucas A. Powe, Jr., *The Warren Court and American Politics* (Cambridge, MA: Belknap Press, 2000); Bernard Schwartz, ed., *The Warren Court: A Retrospective* (New York: Oxford University Press, 1993); G. Edward White, *Earl Warren: A Public Life* (New York: Oxford University Press, 1982); and Ed Cray, *Chief Justice: A Biography of Earl Warren* (New York: Simon & Schuster, 1997).

On the Supreme Court under Chief Justice Warren Burger, see Charles M. Lamb and Stephen H. Halpern, eds., *The Burger Court: Political and Judicial Profiles* (Champaign: University of Illinois Press, 1991); Melvin I. Urofsky, *The Continuity of Change: The Supreme Court and Individual Liberties, 1953–1986* (Belmont, CA: Wadsworth, 1991); Bernard Schwartz, *The Ascent of Pragmatism: The Burger Court in Action* (Reading, MA: Addison-Wesley, 1990). The feminist critique of obscenity law and pornography can be found in Catharine A. MacKinnon and Andrea Dworkin, eds., *In Harm's Way: The Pornography Civil Rights Hearings* (Cambridge, MA: Harvard University Press, 1997).

Perhaps the best book currently available on obscenity is Richard F. Hixson, *Pornography and the Justices: The Supreme Court and the Intractable Obscenity Problem* (Carbondale: Southern Illinois University Press, 1996). Civil liberties lawyer Charles Rembar participated in some of these key cases and later published an interesting book explaining his position on obscenity, *The End of Obscenity: The Trials of Lady Chatterly, Tropic of Cancer, and Fanny Hill* (New York: Random House, 1968). Other useful works are Harry Clor, *Obscenity and Public Morality* (Chicago: University of Chicago Press, 1969); Ian Hunter, David Sauders, and Dugald Williamson, *On Pornography: Literature, Sexuality and Obscenity Law* (New York: St. Martin's Press, 1993).

For the most recent case law and reactions to those decisions, see the *New York Times.* If prudently used, some Web sites also can be useful. Of course, the best source for the current rules on obscenity are the case records published in the *United States Reports.*

4

Impact and Legacy

In *Butler v. Michigan* (1957), U.S. Supreme Court Justice Felix Frankfurter wrote the decision striking down a Michigan statute that made it illegal to "sell ... distribute or offer for sale, any book or magazine ... containing obscene, immoral, lewd or lascivious language ... manifestly tending to the corruption of the morals of youth." Michigan defended the statute by claiming that it was promoting the general welfare by "quarantining the general reading public against books not too rugged for grown men and women in order to shield juvenile innocence." Frankfurter disagreed. "Surely, this is to burn the house to roast the pig," he complained. Since its 1957 decisions in *Butler* and *Samuel Roth v. United States,* the U.S. Supreme Court has sought to refine the judicial rules for dealing with the difficult and emotionally charged issues of obscenity and pornography without burning down the First Amendment house.

Numerous challenges have arisen to the doctrines and rules developed by the Supreme Court—from new state statutes and municipal ordinances to new technologies such as cable television and the Internet. Few social behaviors, it would seem, are as adaptable to changing social situations and electronic and print technologies as pornography. As the social problem of obscenity and pornography mutates in response to new social and legal pressures, the new mutations create new challenges for state and federal legislators as well as state and federal judges and justices. By the early twenty-first century, the justices of the Supreme Court understood pornography as an issue of speech and press liberties, a part of First Amendment jurisprudence. Preferring to leave the moral issues surrounding pornography to political majorities in the states and Congress or to individuals to decide according to their own religious and personal values, the justices seek to maintain elbow room in the culture for "adult material" while protecting children and the liberties of expression. Their decisions have never pleased everyone; but the Supreme Court justices have navigated the dangerous shallows of obscenity without losing their way and without losing their institutional legitimacy as final arbiter of this difficult issue.

One recent and important interpreter of the law of obscenity, Richard F. Hixson, asserted, "In the end, the mood of the Court at any given time, influenced by public opinion and precedent will determine the degree to which pornography will be tolerated legally." He urged the justices of the Supreme Court "to give less time to defining obscenity . . . and even less time limiting speech protection on the basis of possible effects." Because pornography is difficult and perhaps even impossible to define, it is better to deal with obscenity as a speech issue than as a social harm issue, Hixson argued—particularly because social harm is equally difficult to define and measure. Following the lead of Justice William J. Brennan, Hixson believes that "obscenity is an issue for the individual, not the collective"; therefore, government's role is merely to protect minors and nonconsenting adults from unwanted exposure to it (Hixson 1996, 232).

Yet this nearly libertarian approach—government ought to have no role, or at most a highly limited role, in dealing with obscenity—abandons one of the key duties and expectations of establishing and forming government: the maintenance and oversight of a civil community. Is there no public interest in the control of pornography? Hixson's and Justice Brennan's hands-off position at first blush might appear a viable option; but on closer examination, that illusion fades. To acknowledge that government needs to safeguard children and nonconsenting adults from obscenity ironically harkens back to the first judicial standard that guided English judges and policymakers dealing with pornography: Chief Judge Alexander James Edmund Cockburn's 1868 *Hicklin* rule, that obscenity consists of materials that have a tendency to deprave and corrupt susceptible persons. Responsible and prudent scholars, lawyers, and policymakers have agreed and continue to agree that children ought to be screened from obscenity and that adults who eschew such materials ought to be able to rely on their local, county, state, or federal government to dramatically limit or suppress such materials. Therein lies the continuing dilemma: the protection of the young and nonconsenting, which mandates governmental oversight and control of obscenity, versus the potential fear that such oversight and control might damage the speech rights of publishers, distributors, and consumers of such materials. It is clear that the public does have an interest in the production, distribution, and circulation of allegedly obscene materials, and equally clear that courts and legislators ought to be involved in these difficult issues. *Laissez-faire* is not an option in public policy and jurisprudence on obscenity.

As the previous chapters have demonstrated, the question of which community standards should be followed—local or national—has been central to obscenity jurisprudence. According to the common law, which continued to be applied well into the nineteenth century in Great Britain and the United States, local governments bore the responsibility for dealing with local obscenity, pornography, and other dangers to public morality (such as those presented by taverns, gambling halls, and bawdy houses). That tradition gradually was altered as the states passed statutes restricting obscenity; but the prosecution of pornography still lay in the offended community's hands. The burden of responsibility began to shift with the 1964 case *Nico Jacobellis v. Ohio,* in which Justice Brennan held that national standards regarding obscenity were needed and that the federal judiciary ought to define and establish those standards. Because the country had become a nation and because every citizen in every state across the nation deserved the same treatment and protections under the law, obscenity standards also had to be national in scope, argued Brennan. This position was a dramatic departure from the traditional doctrine allowing localities to decide for themselves what was and was not obscene and what to prosecute or not to prosecute. Although this decision was controversial at the time, a majority of justices in the 1960s supported the idea of a national standard. But in 1973, in *Miller v. California,* after the addition of a new chief justice and a shift in public opinion toward tighter restrictions on obscenity, Brennan lost his majority support, and the Court established the current doctrine of "community standards." This doctrine is essentially a return to the rule of localities. Yet the U.S. Supreme Court justices continue to be called on to resolve disputes resulting from efforts by local government to control obscenity, and in doing so, they must strike a delicate balance: on the one hand, they must uphold the First Amendment right of freedom of expression, and on the other hand, they must respect the community desire to limit or suppress obscenity and pornography. Thus, *Miller* did not end legal controversies over obscenity; it merely reestablished the importance of the local community in setting and enforcing the rules on obscenity.

In more recent obscenity jurisprudence, nothing has challenged and frustrated state and federal legislators and state and federal judges more than the application of modern technology to the distribution of pornography. Not only have old technologies been put to new uses (as has the telephone, by the "dial-a-porn" businesses); new technologies have emerged, such as cable television and the Internet, and with them, new opportunities for the production and distribution of obscene materials. Just as every available communications medium in the past was used to deliver obscene messages and images—newspapers, books, magazines, broadsides, pamphlets, and film, to name but a few—so too the most recent forms of communication technology also lend themselves to that use. As a result, litigation on obscenity is again proliferating, and new legal challenges constantly rise to the Supreme Court. From the justices' decisions, based on adaptations of older obscenity rules to the new uses of technology, arise new legal doctrines and rules reflecting the current social norms. In this case-by-case, cumulative development of legal precedent, we can see the common law at work. The old axiom that law follows social and technological changes is clearly demonstrated in the area of obscenity jurisprudence.

Obscenity and its associated issues and problems continue to encourage experimentation by the states. The best example of state experimentation with pornography control occurred in Utah. In 2000, Utah established and funded a new state office, Obscenity and Pornography Complaints Ombudsman, to advise local governments on rules and guidelines for obscenity law, to suggest approaches and possible local ordinances for dealing with obscenity, and if necessary, to prosecute obscenity and pornography in the state. In Utah, given that two-thirds of the population are Mormons who follow the strict behavioral code of the Church of Jesus Christ of Latter-Day Saints (which forbids the use of alcohol, tobacco, and caffeine, as well as sexual relations outside of marriage), it is not surprising that such a state office would be established and funded at $150,000 per year for the director and one assistant.

Appointed to this post was Paula Houston, a 41-year-old single woman. A Mormon Church member with a law degree from Brigham Young University, Houston had fifteen years of experience as a state prosecutor in Salt Lake City. As a prosecutor, Houston successfully had tried cases against allegedly obscene material and its distribution in Utah. Most of the complaints she has fielded since occupying the office of ombudsman have not dealt with magazines such as *Playboy* or *Penthouse* or even with hard-core pornography; instead, they have been aimed at risqué advertising in women's magazines such as *Cosmopolitan*. Outrage often has been triggered by publicly displayed images of scantily clad high-fashion models, such as that in a Victoria's Secret ad at a local mall, featuring "a nude woman covering her breasts with her hands." A petition with 1,000 signatures was sent to Houston's office, protesting the appearance of that particular image in such a public place. Meanwhile, newspaper and Internet sites reported that Houston was at work on a moral nuisance law that "would allow property to be confiscated from businesses such as brothels or pornographic video stores" (October 15, 2001, "Porn Czar fields 1,500 complaints," http://www.usatoday.com).

U.S. Attorney General John Ashcroft, the various state attorneys general, and civil liberties groups such as the American Civil Liberties Union are closely monitoring this Utah experiment for successes, failures, and abuses. However, whatever the experiment's eventual results, it seems doubtful that they will be replicable in many other states, given that most states lack a sufficiently broad popular consensus on the definition of prosecutable obscenity. Nevertheless, the developments in Utah are interesting in that they may signal a trend of increasing public pressure on state policymakers to control obscenity.

Two cases that the Supreme Court recently agreed to hear may be especially significant in this regard. In May 2001, the Cable News Network reported that the Supreme Court had accepted the case of *John Ashcroft v. American Civil Liberties Union*, which revolves around efforts to limit children's access to on-line pornography. At issue is a section of the 1998 Child Online Protection Act that makes it a crime "to knowingly place objectionable material where a child could find it on the World Wide Web." The ACLU challenged the statute on the grounds that it violates the freedom-of-expression guarantees of the First Amendment ("Supreme Court to consider online porn," *www.cnn.com,* cited May 21, 2001).

In an even more complex and murky case, the Supreme Court heard arguments on October 30, 2001, in *John Ashcroft, Attorney General et al. v. The Free Speech Coalition et al.,* on whether Congress could regulate computer-simulated images of child pornography. In 1996, Congress passed the Child Pornography Prevention Act (CPPA), a section of which outlawed any visual depiction that "appears to be" children in sexually explicit situations, or that is advertised so that it "conveys the impression" that someone under 18 is involved (18 U.S.C. § 2251). In other words, can fake, computer-generated images of children involved in explicit sexual behavior be banned? On April 16, 2002, in a 6–3 decision, the Supreme Court upheld the Ninth Federal Circuit Court of Appeals finding that this section of the CPPA was unconstitutional (122 S.Ct. 1389). For the majority, Justice Anthony Kennedy wrote that the ban on virtual child pornography was overbroad "since it proscribed speech that was neither child pornography nor obscene and thus abridged the freedom to engage in a substantial amount of lawful speech." Kennedy noted that "the visual depiction of teenage sexual activity was a common theme in acclaimed artistic works and a fact of modern society" and this section of this statute "prohibited speech which recorded no crime and created no victims." Further, the majority held that the federal government could not ban protected virtual child pornography as a means to enforce the government's proper ban on actual child pornography. Justice Sandra Day O'Connor, joined by Chief Justice Rehnquist and Justice Scalia, dissented arguing that because "the computer-generated images are virtually indistinguishable from real children" then such images ought to be banned. They believed that virtual child pornography should be suppressed and would have upheld this section of the CPPA. These cases provide continuing evidence of the increasing complexity of the obscenity and pornography issues confronting the judicial system and United States culture.

Conclusion

Regardless of the future twists and turns in obscenity litigation and jurisprudence, legislators, interest groups, judges, and justices will have to craft their responses to conform to their own time and culture. Toleration or repression of obscenity in the United States has been and continues to be tied to the values of the larger culture. Today's routine images seen in television commercials, heard on the radio, or viewed on the Internet would have shocked the majority of Americans fifty years ago. In time, even the current, comparatively permissive attitudes may begin to seem quaint, squeamish, and repressed. But by that time, the rules and guidelines for the production, distribution, delivery, and possession of allegedly obscene materials will have shifted to meet the needs of that era. Litigation aimed at drawing and redrawing the line between appropriate and inappropriate materials can be interpreted as the effort of the legal culture to adjust to the social values of the moment. Changing social and moral values continually set new standards for obscenity and pornography in the United States. In the process, neither First Amendment freedoms nor restrictions on obscenity ever fully triumph; instead, a new equilibrium is established for a time between the two opposing forces.

Part Two

Documents

Commonwealth v. Sharpless (1815)

Before U.S. appellate courts adopted the Hicklin *test, localities prosecuted obscene publications through traditional common-law actions. When defense attorneys raised questions about whether British common law had been adopted into the new American states during or after the Revolution, state judges consistently held that the common law was in force in their states. As a result, prosecutions for selling or displaying obscenity did occur, and prosecutors employed the common-law standards and rules to achieve convictions. In this case, Jesse Sharpless had displayed an allegedly obscene painting to the public and was prosecuted under the common law for the display. He appealed on a variety of grounds reviewed by the Court.*

CHIEF JUSTICE TILGHMAN delivered the opinion of the Court.

This is an indictment against *Jesse Sharpless* and others, for exhibiting an indecent picture to divers persons for money. The defendant consented, that a verdict should go against them, and afterwards moved in arrest of judgment for several reasons:

1: "That the matter laid in the indictment is not an indictable offense." It was denied, in the first place, that even a *public* exhibition of an indecent picture was indictable; but supposing it to be so, it was insisted, that this indictment contained no charge of a *public* exhibition. In *England,* there are some acts of immorality, such as adultery, of which the ecclesiastical courts have taken cognizance from very ancient times, and in such cases, although they tended to the corruption of the public morals, the temporal courts have not assumed juris-

diction. This occasioned some uncertainty in the law; some difficulty
in discriminating between the offenses punishable in the temporal and
ecclesiastical courts. Although there was not ground for this distinction in a country like ours, where there was no ecclesiastical jurisdiction, yet the common law principle was suppose to be in force, and to
get rid of it, punishments were inflicted by acts of assembly. There is
no act punishing the offense charged against the defendants, and therefore the case must be decided upon the principles of the common law.
That actions of *public indecency,* were always indictable, as tending to
corrupt the public morals, I can have no doubt; because even in the
profligate reign of *Charles* II. Sir *Charles Sedley* was punished by
imprisonment and a heavy fine, for standing naked in a balcony, in a
public part of the city of *London*. It is true, that, besides his shameful
exhibition, it is mentioned in some of the reports of that case, that he
threw down bottles, containing offensive liquor, among the people;
but we have the highest authority for saying, that the most criminal
part of his conduct, and that which principally drew upon him the
vengeance of the law, was the *expose of his person* . . . . Neither is there
any doubt, that the publication of *an indecent book* is indictable.
[Tilghman then reviewed the pertinent British common law.] Now to
apply these principles to the present case. The defendants are charged
with *exhibiting and shewing to sundry persons, for money, a lewd,
scandalous, and obscene painting.* A picture tends to incite lust as
strongly as a writing; and the *shewing* of a picture, is as much a *publication,* as the *selling* of a book. *Curl* was convicted of selling a book. It
is true, the indictment charged the act to have been in a *public shop,*
but that can make no difference. The mischief was no greater than if he
had taken the purchaser into a *private room,* and sold him the book
there. The law is not to be evaded by an artifice of that kind. If the privacy of the room was a protection, all the youth of the city might be
corrupted by taking them one by one into a chamber, and there
inflaming their passions by the exhibition of lascivious pictures. In the
eyes of the law, this would be a *publication,* and a most pernicious one.
Then, although it is not said in the indictment, in express terms, that
the defendants published the painting, yet the averment is substantially the same, that is to say, that they exhibited it to sundry persons
for money; for that in law is a *publication.*

2. The second reason in arrest of judgment is, that the picture is not
sufficiently described in the indictment. It is described as *a lewd and
obscene painting, representing a man in an obscene, imprudent, and*

indecent posture with a woman. We do not know, that the picture had any name, and therefore it might be impossible to designate it by name. What then is expected? Must the indictment describe minutely, the attitude and posture of the figures? I am for paying some respect to the chastity of our records. These are circumstances which may be well omitted. Whether the picture was really indecent, the jury must judge from the *evidence,* or if necessary from *inspection.* The witnesses could identify it. I am of opinion that the description is sufficient.

3. The third and last reason is, that the indictment does not lay the defendants' *house* to be a *nuisance,* nor the act of the defendants to be the *common nuisance* of all the citizens, &c. The answer is plain. It is not an indictment for a *nuisance,* but for an action of evil example, tending to the corruption of the youth, and other citizens of the commonwealth, and against the peace, &c. In describing the offense of this kind, the technical word *nuisance* would have been improper. My opinion is, that the indictment is good, and therefore the judgment should not be arrested.

Commonwealth v. Holmes (1821)

Jurisdictional questions continued to bedevil judges and state courts confronting appeals from obscenity convictions. When the states formed during the Revolution, did the new state courts inherit the common-law jurisdictions possessed by the colonial courts and British courts? This question arose as a challenge to Peter Holmes's conviction for publishing John Cleland's infamous book Memoirs of a Woman of Pleasure. *At trial, Holmes was convicted of publishing obscenity. He appealed this conviction to the Supreme Court of Massachusetts.*

CHIEF JUSTICE PARKER delivered the opinion of the Court.

The second and fifth counts in this indictment are certainly good; for it can never be required that an obscene book and picture should be displayed upon the records of the Court; which must be done if the description in these counts is insufficient. This would be to require that the public itself should give permanency and notoriety to indecency, in order to punish it. These counts being good, it is unnecessary to give an opinion upon the others; since, if there be good and bad counts in the same indictment, a general verdict of guilty returned, the verdict must be applied to the good ones.

The only objection which has seemed to require much consideration, is that which is founded upon a supposed want of jurisdiction of this offense in the Court of Common Pleas, at which court the indictment was found. A short history of our judicial tribunals will show clearly that this objection must also fail.

It is conceded that, by the statute of 1803, c. 155, the courts of common pleas, in whatever shapes they have existed since the passage of that act, have enjoyed all the criminal jurisdiction before lawfully exercised by the Court of General Sessions of the Peace. The inquiry then is, what jurisdiction this last-mentioned court had in criminal matters, before the statute was enacted.

The jurisdiction of the Court of Sessions, under the present constitution, was established by the statute of 1782, c. 14. By this statute, the justices of that court "are empowered to hear and determine all matters relative to the conservation of the peace, and the punishment of such offenses as are cognizable by them at common-law, or by the acts and laws of the legislature; and to give judgment, order, or sentence thereon, as the law directs, and to award execution accordingly."

The existing power of this Court, whether at the common law or by legislative act, before the adoption of the constitution, must be sought for, in order to ascertain its present jurisdiction.

By the common law, the Court of Sessions of the Peace in *England* had jurisdiction of all misdemeanors, and indeed of all felonies, the punishment of which was not capital. This Court, however, could not try any offense newly created by statute, unless jurisdiction was expressly given to it. The offense of libel is an offense at common law, of which the Court of Sessions originally has jurisdiction, without doubt.

But we are rather to look at the common law of our own country, which at the time of the adoption of the constitution, may as well have existed in the form of statutes and ordinances of the colonial and provincial legislatures, as in any other way. By the provisional act of 11 Will. III. c. 1, a court of general sessions of the peace was constituted within each county, who were "empowered to hear and determine all matters relating to the conservation of the peace, and punishment of offenders, and whatsoever is by them cognizable according to law; and to give judgment and ward execution therein." Even this early provision rests upon some preexisting power, resulting from the common law of antecedent legislative acts. By the third section of this act, a provision is made for the summoning of jurors to attend this

Court. An earlier provincial act provides for the attendance upon said Court of a grand inquest, whose duty it is made to inquire and duly present the breach of all such good and wholesome laws, as are or shall be established within the province, and all such misdemeanors as are proper to their inquiry and the jurisdiction of the Court.

One step further back brings us to colonial judicial establishments, in which will be found the principles and fundamental qualities of the several judicial tribunals since created. As all legislative, so all judicial power seems to have been exercised by the whole body of the people, for a year or two after the arrival of the first colonists. When a representative legislature succeeded to this simple democracy, it exercised judicial power, both criminal and civil. But in the year 1639 this crude system was superseded by the Court of Assistants, to which was given jurisdiction by appeal in civil actions, and original in all criminal suits which extended to life, member, or banishment. And at the same time county courts were established, with jurisdiction civil and criminal, not extending to life, member, or banishment; which was reversed to the Court of Assistants.

This county court was the parent of the courts of common pleas, and of the general sessions of the peace; enjoying the powers of both, as now exercised. And its criminal jurisdiction was analogous to that practically exercised by the Court of Quarter Sessions in *England;* to which the colonial legislatures undoubtedly had reference, in determining its jurisdiction. In the year 1699, the provincial legislature divided the criminal and civil jurisdiction between the Court of Common Pleas and the Court of Sessions; both of which were at that time established by law, and have continued ever since, with various modifications, until the whole criminal jurisdiction of the Court of Sessions was, in 1804, transferred to the Court of Common Pleas. Thus the county court was abolished.

It then appears, by tracing back our judicial history, that the Court of Common Pleas has criminal jurisdiction, in every thing which does not relate to life, member, or banishment; except such crimes as have been since constituted by law, or the punishment of which, by statute, is to be administered by the Supreme Judicial Court. And this is the case with respect to all punishments by hard labor; and in many instances, where fine and imprisonment are the punishment jurisdiction is given only to the court last mentioned.

The offense, of which the defendant stands convicted, is a misdemeanor, the punishment of which does not extend to life, member, or banishment; nor is the offense created by statute; so that it is clearly cognizable by the Court of Common Pleas, as organized when the indictment was presented.

Regina v. Hicklin (1868)

Obscenity jurisprudence can be said to have started with Chief Justice Cockburn's 1868 decision in Regina v. Hicklin. *According to common law, publishing an allegedly obscene book or print was indictable as a breach of the common peace or as an obscene libel. But prosecutions of obscene materials occurred only occasionally and were almost always handled at the most local level.*

Yet an increase in allegedly immoral published materials circulating in Victorian England led to a call in 1857 for a parliamentary statute to curb such immoral materials. Reformers argued that obscenity threatened the moral health and character of the individuals exposed to such texts and images. In turn, those immoral individuals lowered and threatened the overall moral character of English culture. Parliament responded and passed the Obscene Publications Act, better known as Lord Campbell's Act (20 & 21 Vict. c. 83). Prosecutions commenced under this statute, and in 1868 the judges of the Queen's Bench, the highest judicial tribunal in Great Britain, had their first chance to interpret and define "obscenity." Hicklin had been convicted of selling an anti-Catholic pamphlet that was alleged to be obscene. The Recorder reversed the decision of the Magistrates, and Hicklin appealed to the Queen's Bench.

The RT. HONORABLE CHIEF JUSTICE COCKBURN delivered the opinion of the Court.

We have considered this matter, and we are of opinion that the judgment of the learned recorder must be reversed, and the decision of the magistrates affirmed. This was a proceeding under 20 & 21 Vict. C. 83, s. 1 where by it is provided that, in respect to obscene books, &c, kept to be sold or distributed, magistrates may order the seizure and condemnation of such works, in case they are of the opinion that the publication of them would have been the subject-matter of an indictment at law, and that such a prosecution ought to have been instituted. Now, it is found here as a fact that the work which is the subject-matter of the present proceeding was, to a considerable extent, an

obscene publication, and, by reason of the obscene matter in it, calculated to produce a pernicious effect in depraving and debauching the
minds of the persons into whose hands it might come. The magistrates
must have been of the opinion that the work was a fit and proper subject for indictment. We must take the latter finding of the magistrates
to have been adopted by the learned recorder when he reversed their
decision, because it is not upon that ground that he reversed it; he
leaves that ground untouched, but he reversed the magistrates' decision upon the ground that, although this work was an obscene publication, and although its tendency upon the public mind was that suggested upon the part of the information, yet that immediate intention
of the appellant was not so to affect the public mind, but to expose the
practices and errors of the confessional system in the Roman Catholic
Church. Now, we must take it, upon the finding of the recorder, that
such was the motive of the appellant in distributing this publication;
that his intention was honestly and a bona fide to expose the errors
and practices of the Roman Catholic Church in the matter of confession; and upon that ground of motive the recorder thought an indictment could not have been sustained, inasmuch as to the maintenance
of the indictment it would have been necessary that the intention
should be alleged and proved, namely, that of corrupting the public
mind by the obscene matter in question. In that respect I differ from
the recorder. I think that if there be an infraction of the law the intention to break the law must be inferred, and the criminal character of
the publication is not affected or qualified by there being some ulterior object in view (which is the immediate and primary object of the
parties) of a different and of an honest character. It is quite clear that
the publishing of an obscene book is an offense against the law of the
land. It is perfectly true, as has been pointed out by Mr. Kydd [plain-
tiff's attorney], that there are a great many publications of high repute
in the literary productions of this country the tendency of which is
immodest, and, if you please, immoral, and possibly there might have
been subject-matter for indictment in many of the works which have
been referred to. But it is not to be said, because there are in many
standard and established works objectionable passages, that therefore
the law is not as alleged on the part of the prosecution, namely, that
obscene works are the subject-matter of indictment; and I think the
test of obscenity is this, whether the tendency of the matter charged as
obscenity is to deprave and corrupt those whose minds are open to
such immoral influences, and into whose hands a publication of this

sort may fall. Now, with regard to this work, it is quite certain that it would suggest to the minds of the young of either sex, or even to persons of more advanced years, thoughts of a most impure and libidinous character. The very reason why this work is put forward to expose the practices of the Roman Catholic confessional is the tendency of questions, involving practices and propensities of a certain description, to do mischief to the minds of those to whom such questions are addressed, by suggesting thoughts and desires which otherwise would not have occurred to their minds . . . . But, then, it is said for the appellant, "Yes, but his purpose was not to deprave the public mind; his purpose was to expose the errors of the Roman Catholic religion especially in the matter of the confessional." Be it so. The question then presents itself in this simple form: May you commit an offense against the law in order that thereby you may effect some ulterior object which you have in view, which may be an honest and even a laudable one? My answer is, emphatically, no. The law says, you shall not publish an obscene work. An obscene work is here published, and a work of obscenity which is so clear and decided, that it is impossible to suppose that the man who published it must not have known and seen that the effect upon the minds of many of those into whose hands it would come would be of a mischievous and demoralizing character . . . . It seems to me that the effect of this work is mischievous and against the law, and is not to be justified because the immediate object of the publication is not to deprave the public mind, but, it may be, to destroy and extirpate Roman Catholicism. I think the old sound and honest maxim, that you shall not do evil that good may come, is applicable in law as well as in morals; and here we have a certain and positive evil produced for the purpose of effecting an uncertain, remote, and very doubtful good . . . . I am of opinion, as the learned recorder has found, that this is an obscene publication. I hold that, where a man publishes a work manifestly obscene, he must be taken to have had the intention which is implied from that act; and that, as soon as you have an illegal act thus established, . . . it does not lie in the mouth of the man who does it to say "Well, I was breaking the law, but I was breaking it for some wholesome and salutary purpose." The law does not allow that; you must abide by the law, and if you would accomplish your object, you must do it in a legal manner, or let it alone; you must not do it in a manner which illegal. I think, therefore, that the recorder's judgment must be reversed, and the order must stand.

Ex Parte Jackson (1877)

In the 1870s, interest groups such as the Society for the Suppression of Vice, and the Young Men's Christian Association, lobbied Congress for legislation to stop the use of the U.S. mails to disseminate allegedly obscene materials. These materials included immoral books and prints but also birth control information and devices such as condoms. Spearheaded by Anthony Comstock (and popularly known as the "Comstock Law"), this legislation required postmasters to remove such materials from the mail. Repeat offenders under this act could be fined up to $10,000, be sentenced to ten years in jail, or both. Comstock became a "special agent" of the Post Office and spent a good deal of his life pursuing pornographers and people who distributed birth control information and aids. In this case, which was heard by the U.S. Supreme Court, Jackson challenged Congress's ability to establish rules and regulations for the operation of the Postal Service.

MR. JUSTICE FIELD delivered the opinion of the Court.

The power vested in Congress 'to establish post-offices and post-roads' has been practically construed, since the foundation of the government, to authorize not merely the designation of the routes over which the mail shall be carried, and the offices where letters and other documents shall be received to be distributed or forwarded, but the carriage of the mail, and all measures necessary to secure its safe and speedy transit, and the prompt delivery of its contents. The validity of legislation prescribing what should be carried, and its weight and form, and the charges to which it should be subjected, has never been questioned. What should be mailable has varied at different times, changing with the facility of transportation over the post-roads. At one time, only letters, newspapers, magazines, pamphlets, and other printed matter, not exceeding eight ounces in weight, were carried; afterwards books were added to the list; and now small packages of merchandise, not exceeding a prescribed weight, as well as books and printed matter of all kinds, are transported in the mail. The power possessed by Congress embraces the regulation of the entire postal system of the country. The right to designate what shall be carried necessarily involves the right to determine what shall be excluded. The difficulty attending the subject arises, not from the want of power in Congress to prescribe regulations as to what shall constitute mail matter, but from the necessity of enforcing them consistently with rights reserved to the people, of far greater importance than the transportation of the mail. In their enforcement a distinction is to be made between different kinds of mail matter—between what is intended to be kept free from inspection, such as letters, and sealed packages subject to letter postage; and what is open to inspection, such as newspapers, magazines, pamphlet, and other printed matter, purposely left in a condition to be examined. Letters and sealed packages of this kind in the mail are as fully guarded from examination and inspection, except as to their outward form and weight, as if they were retained by the parties forwarding them in their own domiciles. The constitutional guaranty of the right of the people to be secure in their papers against unreasonable searches and seizures extends to their papers, thus closed against inspection, wherever they may be. Whilst in the mail, they can only be opened and examined under like warrant, issued upon similar oath or affirmation, particularly describing the thing to be seized, as is required when papers are subjected to search in one's own household. No law of Congress can place in the hands of officials connected with the postal service any authority to invade the secrecy of letters and such sealed packages in the mail; and all regulations adopted as to mail matter of this kind must be in subordination to the great principle embodied in the fourth amendment of the Constitution.

Nor can any regulations be enforced against the transportation of printed matter in the mail, which is open to examination, so as to interfere in any manner with the freedom of the press. Liberty of circulating is as essential to that freedom as liberty of publishing; indeed, without the circulation, the publication would be of little value. If, therefore, printed matter be excluded from the mails, its transportation in any other way cannot be forbidden by Congress.

[Field then reviewed at length the 1830s controversy denying the mails to abolitionists as they sought to spread their anti-slavery message.] . . . In excluding various articles from the mail, the object of Congress has not been to interfere with the freedom of the press, or with any other rights of the people; but to refuse its facilities for the distribution of matter deemed injurious to the public morals. Thus, by the act of March 3, 1873, Congress declared 'that no obscene, lewd, or lascivious book, pamphlet, picture, paper, print, or other publication of an indecent character, or any article or thing designed or intended for the prevention of conception or procuring of abortion, nor any article or thing intended or adapted for any indecent or immoral use or nature, nor any written or printed card, circular,

book, pamphlet, advertisement, or notice of any kind, giving information, directly or indirectly, where, or how, or of whom, or by what
means, either of the things before mentioned may be obtained or
made, nor any letter upon the envelope of which, or postal-card upon
which indecent or scurrilous epithets may be written or printed, shall
be carried in the mail; and any person who shall knowingly deposit,
or cause to be deposited, for mailing or delivery, any of the hereinbefore mentioned articles or things, . . . shall be deemed guilty of a misdemeanor, and, on conviction thereof, shall, for every offence, be
fined not less than $100, nor more than $5,000, or imprisonment at
hard labor not less than one year nor more than ten years, or both, in
the discretion of the judge.'

All that Congress meant by this act was that the mail should not be
used to transport such corrupting publications and articles, and that
any one who attempted to use it for that purpose should be punished.
The same inhibition has been extended to circulars concerning lotteries—institutions which are supposed to have a demoralizing influence
upon the people. There is no question before us as to the evidence
upon which the conviction of the petitioner was had; nor does it
appear whether the envelope in which the prohibited circular was
deposited in the mail was sealed or left open for examination. The only
question for our determination relates to the constitutionality of the
act; and of that we have no doubt.

As there is an exemplified copy of the record of the petitioner's
indictment and conviction accompanying the petition, the merits of
his case have been considered at his request upon this application; and,
as we are of opinion that his imprisonment is legal, no object would be
subserved by issuing the writs; they are therefore

Denied.

United States v. Bennett (1879)

Chief Justice Cockburn's rule in Hicklin *did not stay in Great Britain.
It was not uncommon for courts in the United States to pay attention
to legal developments in English courts, and a new judicial doctrine
such as the* Hicklin *rule was no secret. When the opportunity arose,
judges in the United States adopted the* Hicklin *standard and applied
it in their jurisdictions. Over time, the* Hicklin *rule became the standard in the United States as well as in Great Britain.*

*In this case, Bennett had tried to mail two copies of an allegedly
obscene book. Anthony Comstock discovered the mailing, and the
prosecutor in the eastern district of New York prosecuted Bennett for
using the mails to distribute an obscene publication. After conviction,
Bennett appealed. The U.S. Circuit Court of Appeals upheld his conviction.*

MR. JUSTICE BLATCHFORD delivered the opinion of the Court.

The indictment against the defendant contains two Counts. The
first count avers, that the defendant, "on the twelfth day of November,
in the year of our Lord one thousand eight hundred and seventy-eight,
at the Southern district of New York, and within the jurisdiction of
this court, did unlawfully and knowingly deposit, and cause to be
deposited, in the mail of the United States, then and there, for mailing
and delivery, a certain obscene, lewd and lascivious book, called
'Cupid's Yokes, or The Binding Forces of Conjugal Life,' which said
book is so lewd, obscene and lascivious, that the same would be offensive to the court here, and improper to be placed upon the records
thereof; Wherefore, the jurors aforesaid do not set forth the same in
this indictment; which said book was then and there enclosed in a
paper wrapper, which said wrapper was then and there addressed and
directed as follows: G. Brackett, Box 202, Granville, N.Y." The second
count avers, that the defendant, "on the twelfth day of November, in
the year of our Lord one thousand eight hundred and seventy-eight, at
the Southern district of New York, and within the jurisdiction of this
court, unlawfully and knowingly did deposit, and cause to be
deposited, in the mail of the United States, then and there, for mailing
and delivery, a certain publication of an indecent character, called
'Cupid's Yokes, or The Binding Forces of Conjugal Life,' which said
publication is so indecent that the same would be offensive to the
court here, and improper to be placed on the records thereof; wherefore, the jurors aforesaid do not set forth the same in this indictment;
which said publication was then and there enclosed in a wrapper,
which said wrapper was then and there addressed and directed as follows, to wit: G. Brackett, Box 202, Granville, N.Y." The defendant
was tried at one of the exclusively criminal terms of this court, held
under the provisions of sections 613 and 658 of the Revised Statutes,
by the district judge for the Eastern district of New York. The jury
rendered a verdict of guilty, and the defendant has moved for a new
trial, on a case and exceptions, and also to set aside the verdict, and for

an arrest of judgment upon the same, the motion being made at an exclusively criminal term, held under the same sections, by the circuit judge for the Second judicial circuit, and the district judges for the Southern and Eastern districts of New York.

The statute under which this indictment proceeds is section 3893 of the Revised Statutes, as amended by section 1 of the act of July 12, 1876 (19 Stat. 90) [the revised Comstock Act]. It provides as follows: "Every obscene, lewd or lascivious book, pamphlet, picture, paper, writing, print, or other publication of an indecent character, are hereby declared to be non-mailable matter, and shall not be conveyed in the mails, nor delivered from any post office, nor by any letter carrier, and any person who shall knowingly deposit, or cause to be deposited, for mailing or delivery, anything declared by this section to be non-mailable matter shall be deemed guilty of a misdemeanor, and shall, for each and every offence, be fined not less than one hundred dollars nor more than five thousand dollars, or imprisoned at hard labor not less than one year nor more than ten years, or both, at the discretion of the court." The question of the constitutionality of this statute, so far as the offences charged in this indictment are concerned, seems to us to have been definitely settled by the decision of the Supreme Court in *Ex parte Jackson*. That decision related to a statute excluding from the mail letters and circulars concerning lotteries, but the views of the court apply fully to the present case.

[Discusses relevant case law] . . . In *Com. v. Holmes,* the indictment was for an offence at common law—publishing an obscene print, in a book, and also for publishing such book. The second count did not set forth the book or any part of it, but alleged that it was so obscene that it would be offensive to the court and improper to be placed on the records thereof, and that, therefore, the jurors did not set it forth in the indictment. The fifth count described the print. The defendant, after conviction, moved in arrest of judgment, because, in certain counts, no part of the book was set forth, and because, in certain other counts, the print was not so particularly described as it ought to have been, so that the jury might judge whether the same was obscene. The court said: "The second and fifth counts in this indictment are certainly good for it can never be required that an obscene book and picture should be displayed upon the records of the court, which must be done if the description in these counts is insufficient. This would be to require that the public itself should give permanency and notoriety to indecency, in order to punish it."

. . .In *Com. v. Sharpless,* the indictment charged that the defendant "did exhibit and show for money to persons, to the inquest aforesaid unknown, a certain lewd, wicked, scandalous, infamous, and obscene painting, representing a man in an obscene, impudent and indecent posture with a woman." After a verdict against the defendant, a motion in arrest of judgment was made, on the ground that the picture was not sufficiently described in the indictment. On this point, Tilghman, C.J., says: "We do not know that the picture had any name, and, therefore, it might be impossible to designate it by name. What, then, is expected? Must the indictment describe minutely the attitude and posture of the figures? I am for paying some respect to the chastity of our records. These are circumstances which may be well omitted. Whether the picture was really indecent the jury might judge from the evidence, or, if necessary, from inspection. The witnesses could identify it. I am of opinion that the description is sufficient." The motion in arrest was overruled.

. . .We are unable to recognize the force of the suggestion, that the defendant, in the case of an indictment for depositing an obscene book in the mail, is entitled to take the opinion of the court by demurrer, as to whether the matter alleged to be obscene is obscene. The suggestion referred to has never been regarded, in the American cases, as of sufficient weight to lead to a following of the present English rule. The true view, we think, is, that if, in a case like the present one, any question can be raised to the court, it can only be the question whether, on the matter alleged to be obscene, a verdict that it is obscene would be set aside as clearly against evidence and reason. This question can be fully raised before the trial, by a motion to be made on the indictment and a bill of particulars. Under all other circumstances, it is for the jury to say whether the matter is obscene or not.

. . .The [trial] court charged the jury as follows: "The statute under which the defendant is indicted provides, that 'every obscene, lewd, or lascivious book or pamphlet, picture, paper, writing, print, or other publication of an indecent character' is non-mailable matter, and shall not be conveyed in the mails, nor delivered from any post office, nor by any letter-carrier; and that any person who shall knowingly deposit, or cause to be deposited, for mailing or delivery, anything so declared to be non-mailable matter, shall be guilty of an offence, and liable to the punishment stated. The object of this statute was to prevent the employment of the mails of the United States for the purpose of disseminating obscene literature. The necessity of such a statute is obvious to any person who has paid attention to the facts. If you think what the United States mails are, how they are protected by the law, where they go, the secrecy attending their operations, you will at once see, that, for the distribution of matter of any kind upon paper, there is no other engine of equal power. It is the machine best adapted to the dissemination of obscene literature, because of the fact that it reaches every person, and letters delivered by the mail can be received in secret by the person to whom they are addressed, whether in their own or in fictitious names. For this reason the mails have been used, and the extent to which they have been used for that purpose is appalling to one acquainted with the facts. These facts have been made known to the Congress of the United States, the government of the United States alone being charged with the carrying of the mails, and it being competent for the Congress of the United States to say what shall be and what shall not be carried in the mails, whereupon Congress declared that obscene matter should not be so carried. Nobody can question the justice, the wisdom, the necessity of such a statute. This statute does not undertake to regulate the publication of matter. Matter of any kind may be published, and not violate this law. It does not undertake to regulate the dissemination of obscene matter. Such matter may be sent by express, without violating any law of the United States. But what the United States government says is, that the mails of the United States shall not be devoted to this purpose. It is a law to protect the community against the abuse of that powerful engine, the United States mail. The constitutionality of the law is not a question here. The statute is the law of the land, and it is to be enforced by the courts, to be obeyed by the citizens. Under this statute, this defendant is charged with having deposited in the mail an obscene book or publication. . . . This is not a question of religion, nor a question of the freedom of the press. There is no such question involved in this prosecution. This defendant may entertain peculiar views on the subject of religion; he may be an infidel; he may have peculiar and improper notions on the marriage relation; he may be a freethinker; he may be whatever he pleases; that should have no effect upon your deliberations. Whatever may be his beliefs or opinions, he is entitled here to a verdict at your hands, impartially, upon the simple fact involved in this case, and upon no other fact. . . . You are not, therefore, called upon by your verdict to express your opinion in regard to any doctrines alluded to in this publication. All men in this country, so far as this statute is concerned, have a right to their opinions. They may publish them; this man may entertain the opinions expressed in this book, or he may not. Freelovers and freethinkers have a right to their views, and they may express them, and they may publish them; but they cannot publish them in connection with obscene matter, and then send that matter through the mails. If, in the discussion of any doctrine, any man uses obscene matter, he cannot send it through the mails of the United States, without violating the law. Of course, freedom of the press, which, I think, was alluded to, has nothing to do with this case. Freedom of the press does not include freedom to use the mails for the purpose of distributing obscene literature, and no right or privilege of the press is infringed by the exclusion of obscene literature from the mails. . . .The only question, therefore, which you are called upon to decide, is, whether or not the book is obscene, lewd or lascivious, or of an indecent character. . . . You see, then, that all you are called upon to determine in this case is, whether the marked passages in this book are obscene, lewd or of an indecent character. Now, I give you the test by which you are to determine the question. It is a test which has been often applied, and has passed the examination of many courts, and I repeat it here, as the test to be used by you. . . . This is the test of obscenity, within the meaning of the statute: It is, whether the tendency of the matter is to deprave and corrupt the morals of those whose minds are open to such influences, and into whose hands a publication of this sort may fall. If you believe such to be the tendency of the matter in these marked passages, you must find the book obscene. If you find that such is not the tendency of the matter in these marked passages, you must find the book not obscene, and acquit the prisoner. . . . Now, gentlemen, I have given you the test; it is not a question whether it would corrupt the morals, tend to deprave your minds or the minds of every person; it is a question whether it tends to deprave the minds of those open to such influences and into whose hands a publication of this character might come. It is within the law if it would suggest impure and libidinous thoughts in the young and the inexperienced. There has been some comment on the fact, that, in many libraries you may find books which contain more objectionable matter, it is said, than this book contains. It may be so; it is not material here. When such books are brought before you, you will be able to determine whether it is lawful to mail them or not. . . . The question is, the tendency of this book. If you find that the tendency of the passages marked in this book is to deprave and corrupt the morals of those whose minds are open to such influences, and into whose hands a publication of this sort may fall, it is your duty to convict the defendant, notwithstanding the fact that there may be many worse books in every library of this city . . . ."

It is contended, that the court erred in what it said to the jury as to the test of obscenity within the meaning of the statute; that it substituted the stated test for the words of the statute; that the stated test was, as a definition, erroneous, and was not a definition of obscenity; that it was a definition of an effect and not of the word "obscenity"; that, because an essay tends to deprave and corrupt the morals of society, it does not follow that it is obscene; that, while all obscenity tends to immorality, all immorality is not obscenity; and that essays on the drama, gluttony, inebriety, gaming, cock fighting, horse racing, polygamy, divorce or blasphemy, advocating or palliating any of them might tend "to deprave and corrupt the morals of those whose minds are open to such influences and into whose hands a publication of this sort may fall," but they would not necessarily be obscene.

In saying that the "test of obscenity, within the meaning of the statute," is, as to "whether the tendency of the matter is to deprave and corrupt the morals of those whose minds are open to such influences, and into whose hands a publication of this sort may fall," the court substantially said, that the matter must be regarded as obscene, if it would have a tendency to suggest impure and libidinous thoughts in the minds of those open to the influence of such thoughts, and thus deprave and corrupt their morals, if they should read such matter. It was not an erroneous statement of the test of obscenity, nor did the court give an erroneous definition of obscenity, or a definition different from that of the first request to charge. It gave a definition substantially agreeing with that of such request.

In *Reg. v. Hicklin,* the question arose as to what was an " obscene" book, within a statute authorizing the destruction of obscene books. The book in question was, to a considerable extent, an obscene publication, and, by reason of the obscene matter in it, was calculated to produce a pernicious effect, in depraving and debauching the minds of the persons into whose hands it might come. It was contended, however, that, although such was the tendency of the book upon the public mind, yet, as the immediate intention of the person selling it was not so to affect the public mind, but to expose certain alleged practices and errors of a religious system, the book was not obscene. . . . In the present case, the remarks made by the court, in its charge, as to the test of obscenity, were made in reference to suggestions like those made in the *Hicklin* case. It was contended, that the motive and object of the book were material. On this question the court said: "The question is, whether this man mailed an obscene book; not why he mailed it. His motive may have been ever so pure; if the book he mailed was obscene, he is guilty. You see, then, that all you are called upon to determine in this case is, whether the marked passages in this book are obscene, lewd, or of an indecent character. Now, I give you the test by which you are to determine this question. It is a test which has been often applied, has passed the examination of many courts, and I repeat it here, as the test to be used by you. You will apply this test to these marked passages, and, if, judged by this test, you find any of them to be obscene or of an indecent character, it will be your duty to find the prisoner guilty. If you do not find them, judged by this test, to be obscene or of an indecent character, it will be your duty to acquit him. This is the test of obscenity, within the meaning of the statute: It is whether, &c." The test there stated is substantially the same as that stated by Cockburn, C.J. . . .

After a careful consideration of all the points presented, we are unanimously of opinion, that the motion for a new trial, and to set aside the verdict, and for an arrest of judgment upon the same, must be denied.

Rosen v. United States (1896)

Although the Hicklin *doctrine had entered U.S. law in* United States v. Bennett *in 1879, the U.S. Supreme Court had not dealt directly with the issue. In this case, the Court examined both the Comstock Law and the* Hicklin *doctrine and decided that both the statute and the judge-made rule were constitutional. In this 7–2 decision, the Court took formal notice of the* Hicklin *doctrine, and thereby made it the law of the land.*

This case involved the sending of an allegedly immoral newspaper through the mails. Lew Rosen published a newspaper that included immoral pictures obscured by a coating of lampblack. This covering could easily be removed. He was prosecuted for sending an obscene newspaper through the mails and was convicted. Rosen appealed, and the case eventually was heard by the U.S. Supreme Court.

MR. JUSTICE HARLAN delivered the opinion of the Court.

The plaintiff in error was indicted under section 3893 of the Revised Statutes, providing that 'every obscene, lewd, or lascivious book, pamphlet, picture, paper, writing, print, or other publication of an indecent character, . . . and every article or thing intended or adapted for any indecent or immoral use, and every written or printed card, circular, book, pamphlet, advertisement, or notice of any kind giving information, directly or indirectly, where or how, or of whom, or by what means, any of the hereinbefore mentioned matters, articles, or things may be obtained or made, . . . are hereby declared to be non-mailable matter, and shall not be conveyed in the mails, nor delivered from any post office nor by any letter carrier; and any person who shall knowingly deposit, or cause to be deposited, for mailing or delivery, anything declared by this section to be non-mailable matter, and any person who shall knowingly take the same, or cause the same to be taken, from the mails, for the purpose of circulating, or disposing of, or of aiding in the circulation or disposition of the same, shall be deemed guilty of a misdemeanor, and shall for each and every offense be fined not less than one hundred dollars nor more than five thousand dollars, or imprisoned at hard labor not less than one year nor more than ten years, or both, at the discretion of the court. . . .'

The defendant pleaded not guilty, and the trial was entered upon without objection in any form to the indictment as not sufficiently informing the defendant of the nature of the charge against him.

A verdict of guilty having been returned, the accused moved for a new trial, upon the ground, among others, that the indictment was fatally defective in matters of substance. That motion was denied.

The defendant thereupon moved in arrest of judgment, upon the ground that the indictment did not charge that he knew at the time what were the contents of the paper deposited in the mail, and alleged to be lewd, obscene, and lascivious. This motion was also denied, and the accused was sentenced to imprisonment at hard labor during a period of 13 months, and to pay a fine of one dollar.

The paper 'Broadway,' referred to in the indictment, was produced in evidence, first, by the United States, and afterwards by the accused. The copy read in evidence by the government was the one which, it was admitted at the trial, the defendant had caused to be deposited in the mail. The pictures of females appearing in that copy were, by direction of the defendant, partially covered with lampblack, that could be easily erased with a piece of bread. The object of sending them out in that condition was, of course, to excite a curiosity to know what was thus concealed. The accused read in evidence a copy that he characterized as a 'clean' one, and in which the pictures of females, in different attitudes of indecency, were not obscured by lampblack.

[The Court then reviewed Rosen's indictment.] We are of opinion that the indictment sufficiently informed the accused of the nature and cause of the accusation against him, and that there was no legal ground for an arrest of the judgment.

At the trial below, the defendant, by his counsel, asked the court to instruct the jury that he should be acquitted if they entertained a reasonable doubt whether he knew that the paper or publication referred to in the indictment was obscene. This request was refused, and an exception was taken to the ruling of the court.

. . . It is also assigned for error that the court left it to the jury to say whether the paper in question was obscene, when it was for the court, as a matter of law, to determine that question. If the court had instructed the jury as matter of law that the paper described in the indictment was obscene, lewd, and lascivious, no error would have been committed; for the paper itself was in evidence, it was of the class excluded from the mails, and there was no dispute as to its contents. It has long been the settled doctrine of this court that the evidence before the jury, if clear and uncontradicted upon any issue made by the parties, presented a question of law in respect of which the court could, without usurping the functions of the jury, instruct them as to the principles applicable to the case made by such evidence. Even if we should hold that the court ought to have instructed the jury, as matter of law, that the paper was, within the meaning of the statute, obscene, lewd, and lascivious, it would not follow that the judgment should, for that reason, be reversed, because it is clear that no injury came to the defendant by submitting the question of the character of the paper to the jury. But it is proper to add that it was competent for the court below, in its discretion, and even if it had been inclined to regard the paper as obscene, lewd, and lascivious, to submit to the jury the general question of the nature of the paper, accompanied by instructions indicating the principles or rules by which they should be guided in determining what was an obscene, lewd, or lascivious paper within the contemplation of the statute under which the indictment was framed. That was what the court did when it charged the jury that 'the test of obscenity is whether the tendency of the matter is to deprave and corrupt the morals of those whose minds are open to such influence, and into whose hands a publication of this sort may fall.' 'Would it,' the court said, 'suggest or convey lewd thoughts and lascivious thoughts to the young and inexperienced?' In view of the character of the paper, as an inspection of it will instantly disclose, the test prescribed for the jury was quite as liberal as the defendant had any right to demand.

. . . We find no error of law in the record, and the judgment is affirmed.

Swearingen v. United States (1896)

The Hicklin *rule did not reach so far as to prohibit merely offensive language. Where to draw the line of what was and what was not "obscene" started to become clear with the decision in* Swearingen. *In this case, Dan K. Swearingen had published a newspaper and sent copies of it through the mails to subscribers. The newspaper contained an article castigating local politicians for corruptness and generally criticizing the character and reputation of several powerful politicians. He was charged with violating the Comstock Act by sending the offensive article through the mails, and at trial he was convicted. He then appealed to the U.S. Supreme Court.*

MR. JUSTICE SHIRAS delivered the opinion of the Court.

The record discloses that the defendant was, in the month of September, 1894, the editor and publisher of a newspaper called 'The Burlington Courier,' and was indicted for having mailed several copies of the paper, containing the article set forth in the previous statement, addressed to different persons.

The bill of exceptions shows that, at the trial, the government offered the article in question in evidence, and that the defendant objected, for the reasons that no public offense was stated in the indictment, that there was a misjoinder of offenses, and that the words of said newspaper article did not constitute unmailable matter. These objections were overruled, and an exception was allowed. The article was then read to the jury, and evidence was offered and received tending to show that on September 21, 1894, copies of the newspaper containing the said article were mailed by employees of the defendant, addressed severally to Riggs, Cowgill, and Lane, who were regular subscribers to the paper, and whose names were on the mail list. . . . The defendant offered no evidence, and the court charged the jury that the newspaper article in evidence, which the defendant admitted he published, was obscene and unmailable matter, and that the only thing for the jury to pass upon was whether the evidence satisfied them, beyond a reasonable doubt, that the defendant deposited, or caused to be deposited, in the post office at Burlington, Kan., newspapers containing said article. To the rulings of the court overruling the motions, and to the charge, exceptions were taken and allowed.

As we think that the court erred in charging the jury that the newspaper article in question was obscene and unmailable matter, it will not be necessary for us to consider the merits of those assignments which allege error in the admission of evidence.

This prosecution was brought under section 3893 of the Revised Statutes, which declares that 'every obscene, lewd or lascivious book, pamphlet, picture, paper, writing, or other publication of an indecent character . . . are hereby declared to be non-mailable matter, and shall not be conveyed in the mails, nor delivered from any post office, nor by any letter carrier; and any person who shall knowingly deposit or cause to be deposited, for mailing or delivery, anything declared by this section to be non-mailable matter, and any person who shall knowingly take the same or cause the same to be taken from the mails for the purpose of circulating or disposing of or aiding in the circulation or disposition of the same, shall be deemed guilty of a misdemeanor, and shall, for each and every offense, be fined not less than one hundred dollars nor more than five thousand dollars, or be imprisoned at hard labor not less than one year nor more than ten years, or both, at the discretion of the court.' The indictment contained three counts, in each of which the offense charged was the mailing of a copy of a newspaper containing the article described in the previous statement, and which was alleged to be 'an obscene, lewd, and lascivious article.'

As already stated, the court charged the jury that the newspaper article was obscene and unmailable matter, and that the only question for the jury to pass upon was whether the defendant deposited the same in the post office at Burlington, Kan.

The language of the statute is that 'every obscene, lewd or lascivious book or paper' is unmailable, from which it might be inferred that each of those epithets pointed out a distinct offense. But the indictment alleges that the newspaper article in question was obscene, lewd, and lascivious. If each adjective in the statute described a distinct offense, then these counts would be bad for duplicity, and the defendant's motion in arrest of judgment for that reason ought to have been sustained. We, however, prefer to regard the words 'obscene, lewd or lascivious,' used in the statute, as describing one and the same offense. That was evidently the view of the pleader and of the court below, and we think this is an admissible construction.

. . . Assuming that it was within the province of the judge to determine whether the publication in question was obscene, lewd, and lascivious, within the meaning of the statute, we do not agree with the court below in thinking that the language and tenor of this newspaper article brought it within such meaning. The offense aimed at, in that portion of the statute we are now considering, was the use of the mails to circulate or deliver matter to corrupt the morals of the people. The words 'obscene,' 'lewd,' and 'lascivious,' as used in the statute, signify that form of immorality which has relation to sexual impurity, and have the same meaning as is given them at common law in prosecutions for obscene libel. As the statute is highly penal, it should not be held to embrace language unless it is fairly within its letter and spirit.

Referring to this newspaper article, as found in the record, it is undeniable that its language is exceedingly coarse and vulgar, and, as applied to an individual person, plainly libelous; but we cannot perceive in it anything of a lewd, lascivious, and obscene tendency, calculated to corrupt and debauch the minds and morals of those into whose hands it might fall.

The judgment of the court below is reversed, and the cause remanded, with instructions to set aside the verdict and award a new trial.

United States v. Kennerley (1913)

In spite of broad acceptance of Hicklin, *not everyone agreed that its rules were the best or the wisest. By the early twentieth century, sensibilities had changed and* Hicklin's *standards started to appear too restrictive.*

Noted federal district Judge Learned Hand took advantage of the opportunity afforded him by the case of United States v. Kennerley *to discuss the problems with the* Hicklin *test.*

DISTRICT JUDGE HAND delivered the opinion of the Court.

It seems to have been thought in *U.S. v. Bennett,* that in an indictment of this sort the question whether the case must go to the jury could be raised in advance of the trial by inspection of the book, after it had been made a part of the record, by bill of particulars. However, in *Dunlop v. U.S.,* the Supreme Court said that the book does not ever become a part of the record, and that therefore, "if the indictment be not demurrable upon its face, it would not become so by the addition of a bill of particulars." The same rule is laid down in *U.S. v. Clarke.* It is a little questionable in my mind whether Mr. Boyle's consent that the book should be considered as a part of the indictment really effects any more than if it had been produced by bill of particulars. However, as the result from any point of view is the same, I have considered the case as though the book had been set out in extenso.

Whatever be the rule in England, in this country the jury must determine under instructions whether the book is obscene. The court's only power is to decide whether the book is so clearly innocent that the jury should not pass upon it at all. The same question arises as would arise upon motion to direct a verdict at the close of the case. *Swearingen v. U.S.,* did not decide that the court is finally to interpret the words, but that matter was left open, because the instructions in any case misinterpreted the statute. The question here is, therefore, whether the jury might find the book obscene under proper instructions. Lord Cockburn laid down a test in *Reg. v. Hicklin,* in these words: "Whether the tendency of the matter charged as obscenity is to deprave and corrupt those whose minds are open to such immoral influences and into whose hands a publication of this sort may fall."

That test has been accepted by the lower federal courts until it would be no longer proper for me to disregard it. Under this rule, such parts of this book as pages 169 and 170 might be found obscene, because they certainly might tend to corrupt the morals of those into whose hands it might come and whose minds were open to such immoral influences. Indeed, it would be just those who would be most likely to concern themselves with those parts alone, forgetting their setting and their relevancy to the book as a whole.

While, therefore, the demurrer must be overruled, I hope it is not improper for me to say that the rule as laid down, however consonant it may be with mid-Victorian morals, does not seem to me to answer to the understanding and morality of the present time, as conveyed by the words, "obscene, lewd, or lascivious." I question whether in the end men will regard that as obscene which is honestly relevant to the adequate expression of innocent ideas, and whether they will not believe that truth and beauty are too precious to society at large to be mutilated in the interests of those most likely to pervert them to base uses. Indeed, it seems hardly likely that we are even to-day so luke-warm in our interest in letters or serious discussion as to be content to reduce our treatment of sex to the standard of a child's library in the supposed interest of a salacious few, or that shame will for long prevent us from adequate portrayal of some of the most serious and beautiful sides of human nature. That such latitude gives opportunity for its abuse is true enough; there will be, as there are, plenty who will misuse the privilege as a cover for lewdness and a stalking horse from which to strike at purity, but that is true to-day and only involves us in the same question of fact which we hope that we have the power to answer.

Yet, if the time is not yet when men think innocent all that which is honestly germane to a pure subject, however little it may mince its words, still I scarcely think that they would forbid all which might corrupt the most corruptible, or that society is prepared to accept for its own limitations those which may perhaps be necessary to the weakest of its members. If there be no abstract definition, such as I have suggested, should not the word "obscene" be allowed to indicate the present critical point in the compromise between candor and shame at which the community may have arrived here and now? If letters must, like other kinds of conduct, be subject to the social sense of what is right, it would seem that a jury should in each case establish the standard much as they do in cases of negligence. To put thought in leash to the average conscience of the time is perhaps tolerable, but to fetter it by the necessities of the lowest and least capable seems a fatal policy.

Nor is it an objection, I think, that such an interpretation gives to the words of the statute a varying meaning from time to time. Such words as these do not embalm the precise morals of an age or place; while they presuppose that some things will always be shocking to the public taste, the vague subject-matter is left to the gradual development of general notions about what is decent. A jury is especially the organ with which to feel the content comprised within such words at any given time, but to do so they must be free to follow the colloquial connotations which they have drawn up instinctively from life and common speech.

Demurrer overruled.

United States v. One Book Called "Ulysses" (1933)

Today considered a masterpiece of stream-of-consciousness literature, James Joyce's novel Ulysses *was initially banned from importation into the United States due to the rough language the author had used in certain passages of the book.*

Building on Judge Learned Hand's opinion in Kennerley, *Judge John M. Woolsey of the U.S. District Court for the Southern District of New York examined the* Hicklin *standard and found it wanting. His precedent-setting decision established a new, narrower standard for determining obscenity.*

DISTRICT JUDGE WOOLSEY delivered the opinion of the Court.

The motion for a decree dismissing the libel herein is granted, and, consequently, of course, the government's motion for a decree of forfeiture and destruction is denied.

Accordingly a decree dismissing the libel without costs may be entered herein.

I have read "Ulysses" once in its entirety and I have read those passages of which the government particularly complains several times. In fact, for many weeks, my spare time has been devoted to the consideration of the decision which my duty would require me to make in this matter.

"Ulysses" is not an easy book to read or to understand. But there has been much written about it, and in order properly to approach the consideration of it, it is advisable to read a number of other books which have now become its satellites. The study of "Ulysses" is, therefore, a heavy task.

The reputation of "Ulysses" in the literary world, however, warranted my taking such time as was necessary to enable me to satisfy myself as to the intent with which the book was written, for, of course, in any case where a book is claimed to be obscene it must first be determined, whether the intent with which it was written was what is called, according to the usual phrase, pornographic, that is, written for the purpose of exploiting obscenity.

If the conclusion is that the book is pornographic, that is the end of the inquiry and forfeiture must follow.

But in "Ulysses," in spite of its unusual frankness, I do not detect anywhere the leer of the sensualist. I hold, therefore, that it is not pornographic.

In writing "Ulysses," Joyce sought to make a serious experiment in a new, if not wholly novel, literary genre. He takes persons of the lower middle class living in Dublin in 1904 and seeks, not only to describe what they did on a certain day early in June of that year as they went about the city bent on their usual occupations, but also to tell what many of them thought about the while.

Joyce has attempted—it seems to me, with astonishing success—to show how the screen of consciousness with its ever-shifting kaleidoscopic impressions carries, as it were on a plastic palimpsest, not only what is in the focus of each man's observation of the actual things about him, but also in a penumbral zone residua of past impressions, some recent and some drawn up by association from the domain of the subconscious. He shows how each of these impressions affects the life and behavior of the character which he is describing . . . .

The words which are criticized as dirty are old Saxon words known to almost all men and, I venture, to many women, and are such words as would be naturally and habitually used, I believe, by the types of folk whose life, physical and mental, Joyce is seeking to describe. In respect of the recurrent emergence of the theme of sex in the minds of his characters, it must always be remembered that his locale was Celtic and his season spring.

Whether or not one enjoys such a technique as Joyce uses is a matter of taste on which disagreement or argument is futile, but to subject that technique to the standards of some other technique seems to me to be little short of absurd.

Accordingly, I hold that "Ulysses" is a sincere and honest book, and I think that the criticisms of it are entirely disposed of by its rationale.

Furthermore, "Ulysses" is an amazing tour de force when one considers the success which has been in the main achieved with such a difficult objective as Joyce set for himself. As I have stated, "Ulysses" is not an easy book to read. It is brilliant and dull, intelligible and obscure, by turns. In many places it seems to me to be disgusting, but although it contains, as I have mentioned above, many words usually considered dirty, I have not found anything that I consider to be dirt for dirt's sake. Each word of the book contributes like a bit of mosaic to the detail of the picture which Joyce is seeking to construct for his readers.

If one does not wish to associate with such folk as Joyce describes, that is one's own choice. In order to avoid indirect contact with them one may not wish to read "Ulysses"; that is quite understandable. But when such a great artist in words, as Joyce undoubtedly is, seeks to draw a true picture of the lower middle class in a European city, ought it to be impossible for the American public legally to see that picture?

To answer this question it is not sufficient merely to find, as I have found above, that Joyce did not write "Ulysses" with what is commonly called pornographic intent. I must endeavor to apply a more objective standard to his book in order to determine its effect in the result, irrespective of the intent with which it was written.

The statute under which the libel is filed only denounces, in so far as we are here concerned, the importation into the United States from any foreign country of "any obscene book." It does not marshal against books the spectrum of condemnatory adjectives found, commonly, in laws dealing with matters of this kind. I am, therefore, only required to determine whether "Ulysses" is obscene within the legal definition of that word.

The meaning of the word "obscene" as legally defined by the courts is: Tending to stir the sex impulses or to lead to sexually impure and lustful thoughts.

Whether a particular book would tend to excite such impulses and thoughts must be tested by the court's opinion as to its effect on a person with average sex instincts—what the French would call *l'homme moyen sensuel*—who plays, in this branch of legal inquiry, the same role of hypothetical reagent as does the "reasonable man" in the law of torts and "the man learned in the art" on questions of invention in patent law. . . .

After I had made my decision in regard to the aspect of "Ulysses," now under consideration, I checked my impressions with two friends of mine who in my opinion answered to the above-stated requirement for my reagent.

These literary assessors—as I might properly describe them—were called on separately, and neither knew that I was consulting the other. They are men whose opinion on literature and on life I value most highly. They had both read "Ulysses," and, of course, were wholly unconnected with this cause.

Without letting either of my assessors know what my decision was, I gave to each of them the legal definition of *obscene* and asked each whether in his opinion "Ulysses" was obscene within that definition.

I was interested to find that they both agreed with my opinion: That reading "Ulysses" in its entirety, as a book must be read on such a test as this, did not tend to excite sexual impulses or lustful thoughts, but that its net effect on them was only that of a somewhat tragic and very powerful commentary on the inner lives of men and women.

It is only with the normal person that the law is concerned. Such a test as I have described, therefore, is the only proper test of obscenity in the case of a book like "Ulysses" which is a sincere and serious attempt to devise a new literary method for the observation and description of mankind.

I am quite aware that owing to some of its scenes "Ulysses" is a rather strong draught to ask some sensitive, though normal, persons to take. But my considered opinion, after long reflection, is that, whilst in many places the effect of "Ulysses" on the reader undoubtedly is somewhat emetic, nowhere does it tend to be an aphrodisiac.

"Ulysses" may, therefore, be admitted into the United States.

United States v. One Book Entitled Ulysses by James Joyce (1934)

Dissatisfied with Judge Woolsey's district court decision, the federal government appealed his decision to the Second Circuit Court of Appeals. The three-judge circuit court was composed of Augustus Hand, Learned Hand, and Martin T. Manton. Augustus Hand wrote the opinion in this case, which upheld Woolsey's and further undercut the Hicklin *rule. Augustus Hand's "work as a whole" standard provided an alternative to the limiting* Hicklin *rule, although Judge Manton's dissent took the opposite position that James Joyce's* Ulysses *was unworthy of special treatment or the undermining of the* Hicklin *rule.*

CIRCUIT JUDGE HAND delivered the opinion of the Court.

This appeal raises sharply the question of the proper interpretation of section 305 (a) of the Tariff Act of 1930. That section provides that "all persons are prohibited from importing into the United States from any foreign country any obscene book, pamphlet, paper, writing, advertisement, circular, print, picture, drawing, or other representation, figure, or image on or of paper or other material," and directs that, upon the appearance of any such book or matter at any customs office, the collector shall seize it and inform the district attorney, who shall institute proceedings for forfeiture. In accordance with the statute, the collector seized *Ulysses,* a book written by James Joyce, and the United States filed a libel for forfeiture. The claimant, Random House, Inc., the publisher of the American edition, intervened in the cause and filed its answer denying that the book was obscene and was subject to confiscation and praying that it be admitted into the United States. The case came on for trial before Woolsey, J., who found that the book, taken as a whole, "did not tend to excite sexual impulses or lustful thoughts but that its net effect was only that of a somewhat tragic and very powerful commentary on the inner lives of men and women." He accordingly granted a decree adjudging that the book was "not of the character the entry of which is prohibited under the provision of section 305 of the Tariff Act of 1930" and dismissing the libel, from which this appeal has been taken.

James Joyce, the author of *Ulysses,* may be regarded as a pioneer among those writers who have adopted the "stream of consciousness" method of presenting fiction, which has attracted considerable attention in academic and literary circles. In this field *Ulysses* is rated as a book of considerable power by persons whose opinions are entitled to weight. Indeed it has become a sort of contemporary classic, dealing with a new subject-matter. It attempts to depict the thoughts and lay bare the souls of a number of people, some of them intellectuals and some social outcasts and nothing more, with a literalism that leaves nothing unsaid. Certain of its passages are of beauty and undoubted distinction, while others are of a vulgarity that is extreme and the book as a whole has a realism characteristic of the present age. It is supposed to portray the thoughts of the principal characters during a period of about eighteen hours.

We may discount the laudation of *Ulysses* by some of its admirers and reject the view that it will permanently stand among the great works of literature, but it is fair to say that it is a sincere portrayal with skillful artistry of the "streams of consciousness" of its characters. Though the depiction happily is not of the "stream of consciousness" of all men and perhaps of only those of a morbid type, it seems to be sincere, truthful, relevant to the subject, and executed with real art. Joyce, in the words of *Paradise Lost,* has dealt with "things unattempted yet in prose or rime"—with things that very likely might better have remained "unattempted"—but his book shows originality and is a work of symmetry and excellent craftsmanship of a sort. The question before us is whether such a book of artistic merit and scientific insight should be regarded as "obscene" within section 305 (a) of the Tariff Act.

That numerous long passages in *Ulysses* contain matter that is obscene under any fair definition of the word cannot be gainsaid; yet they are relevant to the purpose of depicting the thoughts of the characters and are introduced to give meaning to the whole, rather than to promote lust or portray filth for its own sake. The net effect even of portions most open to attack, such as the closing monologue of the wife of Leopold Bloom, is pitiful and tragic, rather than lustful. The book depicts the souls of men and women that are by turns bewildered and keenly apprehensive, sordid and aspiring, ugly and beautiful, hateful and loving. In the end one feels, more than anything else, pity and sorrow for the confusion, misery, and degradation of humanity. Page after page of the book is, or seems to be, incomprehensible. But many passages show the trained hand of an artist, who can at one moment adapt to perfection the style of an ancient chronicler, and at another become a veritable personification of Thomas Carlyle. In numerous places there are found originality, beauty, and distinction. The book as a whole is not pornographic, and, while in not a few spots it is coarse, blasphemous, and obscene, it does not, in our opinion, tend to promote lust. The erotic passages are submerged in the book as a whole and have little resultant effect. If these are to make the book subject to confiscation, by the same test *Venus and Adonis, Hamlet, Romeo and Juliet,* and the story told in the Eighth Book of the *Odyssey* by the bard Demodocus of how Ares and Aphrodite were entrapped in a net spread by the outraged Hephaestus amid the laughter of the immortal gods, as well as many other classics, would have to be suppressed. Indeed, it may be questioned whether the obscene passages in *Romeo and Juliet* were as necessary to the development of the play as those in the monologue of Mrs. Bloom are to the depiction of the latter's tortured soul.

It is unnecessary to add illustrations to show that, in the administration of statutes aimed at the suppression of immoral books, standard works of literature have not been barred merely because they contained some obscene passages, and that confiscation for such a reason would destroy much that is precious in order to benefit a few.

It is settled, at least so far as this court is concerned, that works of physiology, medicine, science, and sex instruction are not within the statute, though to some extent and among some persons they may tend to promote lustful thoughts. We think the same immunity should apply to literature as to science, where the presentation, when viewed objectively, is sincere, and the erotic matter is not introduced to promote lust and does not furnish the dominant note of the publication. The question in each case is whether a publication taken as a whole has a libidinous effect. The book before us has such portentous length, is written with such evident truthfulness in its depiction of certain types of humanity, and is so little erotic in its result, that it does not fall within the forbidden class.

. . . But it is argued that *United States v. Bennett* stands in the way of what has been said, and it certainly does. There a court held that the offending paragraphs in a book could be taken from their context and the book judged by them alone, and that the test of obscenity was whether the tendency of these passages in themselves was "to deprave the minds of those open to such influences and into whose hands a publication of this character might come." The opinion was founded upon a dictum of Cockburn, C.J., in *Regina v. Hicklin,* where half of a book written to attack alleged practices of the confession was obscene and contained "a great deal which there cannot be any necessity for in any legitimate argument on the confessional." . . . The rigorous doctrines laid down in that case are inconsistent with our own decision and, in our opinion, do not represent the law. They would exclude much of the great works of literature and involve an impracticability that cannot be imputed to Congress and would in the case of many books containing obscene passages inevitably require the court that uttered them to restrict their applicability.

It is true that the motive of an author to promote good morals is not the test of whether a book is obscene, and it may also be true that the applicability of the statute does not depend on the persons to whom a publication is likely to be distributed. The importation of obscene books is prohibited generally, and no provision is made permitting such importation because of the character of those to whom they are sold. While any construction of the statute that will fit all cases is difficult, we believe that the proper test of whether a given book is obscene is its dominant effect. In applying this test, relevancy of the objectionable parts to the theme, the established reputation of the work in the estimation of approved critics, if the book is modern, and the verdict of the past, if it is ancient, are persuasive pieces of evidence; for works of art are not likely to sustain a high position with no better warrant for their existence than their obscene content.

It may be that *Ulysses* will not last as a substantial contribution to literature, and it is certainly easy to believe that, in spite of the opinion of Joyce's laudators, the immortals will still reign, but the same thing may be said of current works of art and music and of many other serious efforts of the mind. Art certainly cannot advance under compulsion to traditional forms, and nothing in such a field is more stifling to progress than limitation of the right to experiment with a new technique. . . . We think that *Ulysses* is a book of originality and sincerity of treatment and that it has not the effect of promoting lust. Accordingly it does not fall within the statute, even though it justly may offend many.

Decree affirmed.

DISSENT: MANTON, Circuit Judge.

I dissent. This libel, filed against the book *Ulysses* prays for a decree of forfeiture, and it is based upon the claim that the book's entry into the United States is prohibited by section 305 (a) of the Tariff Act of 1930. On motion of appellee, the court below entered an order dismissing the libel, and the collector of customs was ordered to release the book. The motion was considered on the pleadings and a stipulation entered into by the parties.

The sole question presented is whether or not the book is obscene within section 305 (a). . . .

Who can doubt the obscenity of this book after a reading of the pages referred to, which are too indecent to add as a footnote to this opinion? Its characterization as obscene should be quite unanimous by all who read it.

In the year 1868 in *Regina v. Hicklin*, Cockburn C.J., stated that "the test of obscenity is this, whether the tendency of the matter charged as obscenity is to deprave and corrupt those whose minds are open to such immoral influences, and into whose hands a publication of this sort may fall."

In 1879, in *United States v. Bennett*, Judge Blatchford, later a justice of the Supreme Court, approved the rule of the Hicklin Case and held a charge to a jury proper which embodied the test of that case. The Bennett Case clearly holds the test of obscenity, within the meaning of the statute, is "whether the tendency of the matter is to deprave and corrupt the morals of those whose minds are open to such influences, and into whose hands a publication of this sort may fall." The court held that the object of the use of the obscene words was not a subject for consideration.

Judge Blatchford's decision met with approval in *Rosen v. United States*. The court had under consideration an indictment charging the accused with depositing obscene literature in the mails. There instructions to the jury requested that conviction could not be had although the defendant may have had knowledge or notice of the contents of the letter "unless he knew or believed that such paper could be properly or justly characterized as obscene, lewd, and lascivious." The court said the statute was not to be so interpreted. . . .

Thus the court sustained a charge having a test as to whether or no the publications depraved the morals of the ordinary reader or tended to lower the standards of civilization. The tendency of the matter to deprave and corrupt the morals of those whose minds are open to such influence and into whose hands the publication of this sort may fall, has become the test thoroughly entrenched in the federal courts. . . .

Ulysses is a work of fiction. It may not be compared with books involving medical subjects or description of certain physical or biological facts. It is written for alleged amusement of the reader only. The characters described in the thoughts of the author may in some instances be true, but, be it truthful or otherwise, a book that is obscene is not rendered less so by the statement of truthful fact. . . . The gist of the holding is that a book is not to be declared obscene if it is "an accurate exposition of the relevant facts of the sex side of life in decent language and in manifestly serious and disinterested spirit." A work of obvious benefit to the community was never intended to be within the purview of the statute. No matter what may be said on the side of letters, the effect on the community can and must be the sole determining factor. . . .

Congress passed this statute against obscenity for the protection of the great mass of our people; the unusual literator can, or thinks he can, protect himself. The people do not exist for the sake of literature, to give the author fame, the publisher wealth, and the book a market. On the contrary, literature exists for the sake of the people, to refresh the weary, to console the sad, to hearten the dull and downcast, to increase man's interest in the world, his joy of living, and his sympathy in all sorts and conditions of men. Art for art's sake is heartless and soon grows artless; art for the public market is not art at all, but commerce; art for the people's service is a noble, vital, and permanent element of human life.

The public is content with the standard of salability; the prigs with the standard of preciosity. The people need and deserve a moral standard; it should be a point of honor with men of letters to maintain it. Masterpieces have never been produced by men given to obscenity or lustful thoughts—men who have no Master. Reverence for good work is the foundation of literary character. A refusal to imitate obscenity or to load a book with it is an author's professional chastity.

Good work in literature has its permanent mark; it is like all good work, noble and lasting. It requires a human aim—to cheer, console, purify, or ennoble the life of people. Without this aim, literature has never sent an arrow close to the mark. It is by good work only that men of letters can justify their right to a place in the world.

Under the authoritative decisions and considering the substance involved in this appeal, it is my opinion that the decree should be reversed.

United States v. Levine (1936)

Hicklin *had been dealt heavy blows, yet it still existed as a possible standard for judging obscenity. In this case, Judge Learned Hand delivered almost the last word on the* Hicklin *rule. Not only had judicial opinion turned against it, but the culture had shifted as well. Contrasting with mid-nineteenth-century culture, a greater toleration for what had previously been considered "obscene" had emerged by the 1930s. As a result,* Hicklin *was teetering on the brink of extinction. In this case, Levine had been convicted of sending five allegedly obscene books through the mails and had appealed to the Second Circuit Court of Appeals.*

CIRCUIT JUDGE HAND delivered the opinion of the Court.

The defendant was indicted in one count for posting an obscene circular, and in eight subsequent counts for posting obscene circulars advertising obscene books. The jury brought in a verdict of guilty only on the eighth count and the others were dismissed; the circular laid in that count was alleged to have advertised five books, of which only three are before us; they are entitled, "Secret Museum of Anthropology," "Crossways of Sex" and "Black Lust." The first is a reproduction of a collection of photographs, for the most part of nude female savages of different parts of the world; the legitimacy of its pretensions as serious anthropology is, to say the most, extremely tenuous, and, while in the hands of adults it could not be considered obscene, it might be undesirable in those of children or youths. The second book professes to be a scientific treatise on sexual pathology; again its good-faith is more than questionable; for example, the author, a supposititious scientist, remains anonymous. It could have no value to psychiatrists or others genuinely interested in the subject, and in the hands of children it might be injurious. The third is a work of fiction of considerable merit, but patently erotic, describing the adventures of an English girl captured by the Dervishes at the fall of Khartoum and kept in a harem until the Battle of Omdurman, when she is killed. It purports to be a study in sadism and masochism, and would rouse libidinous feelings in almost any reader. . . .

The defendant took a number of exceptions during the trial with most of which we need not concern ourselves, because they will not reappear upon the next trial, which must be had because we cannot accept the charge. The judge first said that the statute was directed against stimulating sensuality, and that this was not to be measured by its effect, either upon "the highly educated" or upon the "highly prudish," but "on the usual, average human mind." This was well enough, so far as it went, but later he in substance took it back. There was a class, he said, "found in every community, the young and immature, the ignorant and those who are sensually inclined"; the statute was meant to protect these and the jury should regard the effect of the books on their minds, rather than on those of "people of a high order of intelligence and those who have reached mature years." If the books contained a "single passage" such as would "excite lustful or sensual desires" in the minds of those "into whose hands they might come," the statute condemned them. This the defendant challenged and the judge said he would modify it, but he did not; the attempted modification was in substance a repetition of what he had said before. The standard so put before the jury was indeed within the doctrine laid down in *Regina v. Hicklin* and *United States v. Bennett,* though the Supreme Court has never approved it. *Rosen v. U.S.* has at times been supposed to do so, and the charge then before the court did indeed follow *Regina v. Hicklin,* so that the accused might have raised the point now at bar. But he did not; his only complaint, which the court overruled, was that the judge should not have left it to the jury at all to say whether the publication was obscene, but should have decided the question himself. It is true that *United States v. Bennett,* has been followed but without considering the point specifically, merely repeating the phrase that the decisive question was the effect upon any persons into whose hands the book might fall. At times even in these decisions, there were intimations that the standard might depend upon those to whom the publication was addressed. . . .

This earlier doctrine necessarily presupposed that the evil against which the statute is directed so much outweighs all interests of art, letters or science, that they must yield to the mere possibility that some prurient person may get a sensual gratification from reading or seeing what to most people is innocent and may be delightful or enlightening. No civilized community not fanatically puritanical would tolerate such an imposition, and we do not believe that the courts that have declared it, would ever have applied it consistently. As so often happens, the problem is to find a passable compromise between opposing interests, whose relative importance, like that of all social or personal values, is incommensurable. We impose such a duty upon a jury because the standard they fix is likely to be an acceptable mesne, and because in such matters a mesne most nearly satisfies the moral demands of the community. There can never be constitutive principles for such judgments, or indeed more than cautions to avoid the personal aberrations of the jurors. We mentioned some of these in *United States v. One Book Entitled "Ulysses,"* the work must be taken as a whole, its merits weighed against its defects; if it is old, its accepted place in the arts must be regarded; if new, the opinions of competent critics in published reviews or the like may be considered; what counts is its effect, not upon any particular class, but upon all those whom it is likely to reach. Thus "obscenity" is a function of many variables, and the verdict of the jury is not the conclusion of a syllogism of which they are to find only the minor premiss, but really a small bit of legislation ad hoc, like the standard of care.

The case was not tried on this theory; on the contrary the judge supposed that a book or picture was obscene or innocent by an absolute standard independent of its readers; moreover he thought that a single passage might condemn it, regardless of its merits as a whole. He was in error as to both points, and the only question is whether the mistakes were serious enough to upset the conviction.... But even when the crime consists of a single sale, and so may be judged by possible injury to the buyer, the book must be taken as a whole. In this case the jury may find "Crossways of Sex" and "Black Lust" obscene when sent to any reader; "Secret Museum of Anthropology" can be so regarded only if sent to youths. The standard must be the likelihood that the work will so much arouse the salacity of the reader to whom it is sent as to outweigh any literary, scientific or other merits it may have in that reader's hands; of this the jury is the arbiter....

Judgment reversed; new trial ordered.

Butler v. Michigan (1957)

Although the Hicklin *rule had lost much of its relevance, judicial rules die hard, and* Hicklin *was no exception. But as American culture shifted toward greater toleration for risqué materials and topics and as new litigation reached the U.S. Supreme Court, the justices had the opportunity to finally slay* Hicklin.

At issue in this case was a state statute that encapsulated the Hicklin *rule. The justices had to decide whether the statute was a valid regulation of obscenity. Justice Frankfurter, writing for the Court, said the statute went too far, burning down the house in order to roast the pig.*

MR. JUSTICE FRANKFURTER delivered the opinion of the Court.

This appeal from a judgment of conviction entered by the Recorder's Court of the City of Detroit, Michigan challenges the constitutionality of the following provision, 343, of the Michigan Penal Code:

"Any person who shall import, print, publish, sell, possess with the intent to sell, design, prepare, loan, give away, distribute or offer for sale, any book, magazine, newspaper, writing, pamphlet, ballad, printed paper, print, picture, drawing, photograph, publication or other thing, including any recordings, containing obscene, immoral, lewd or lascivious language, or obscene, immoral, lewd or lascivious prints, pictures, figures or descriptions, tending to incite minors to violent or depraved or immoral acts, manifestly tending to the corruption of the morals of youth, or shall introduce into any family, school or place of education or shall buy, procure, receive or have in his possession, any such book, pamphlet, magazine, newspaper, writing, ballad, printed paper, print, picture, drawing, photograph, publication or other thing, either for the purpose of sale, exhibition, loan or circulation, or with intent to introduce the same into any family, school or place of education, shall be guilty of a misdemeanor."

Appellant was charged with its violation for selling to a police officer what the trial judge characterized as "a book containing obscene, immoral, lewd, lascivious language, or descriptions, tending to incite minors to violent or depraved or immoral acts, manifestly tending to the corruption of the morals of youth." Appellant moved to dismiss the proceeding on the claim that application of 343 unduly restricted freedom of speech as protected by the Due Process Clause of the Fourteenth

Amendment in that the statute (1) prohibited distribution of a book to the general public on the basis of the undesirable influence it may have upon youth; (2) damned a book and proscribed its sale merely because of some isolated passages that appeared objectionable when divorced from the book as a whole; and (3) failed to provide a sufficiently definite standard of guilt. After hearing the evidence, the trial judge denied the motion, and, in an oral opinion, held that "the defendant is guilty because he sold a book in the City of Detroit containing this language [the passages deemed offensive], and also because the Court feels that even viewing the book as a whole, it [the objectionable language] was not necessary to the proper development of the theme of the book nor of the conflict expressed therein." Appellant was fined $100.

Pressing his federal claims, appellant applied for leave to appeal to the Supreme Court of Michigan. Although the State consented to the granting of the application "because the issues involved in this case are of great public interest, and because it appears that further clarification of the language of . . . [the statute] is necessary," leave to appeal was denied. In view of this denial, the appeal is here from the Recorder's Court of Detroit. We noted probable jurisdiction.

Appellant's argument here took a wide sweep. We need not follow him. Thus, it is unnecessary to dissect the remarks of the trial judge in order to determine whether he construed 343 to ban the distribution of books merely because certain of their passages, when viewed in isolation, were deemed objectionable. Likewise, we are free to put aside the claim that the Michigan law falls within the doctrine whereby a New York obscenity statute was found invalid in *Winters v. New York*.

It is clear on the record that appellant was convicted because Michigan, by 343, made it an offense for him to make available for the general reading public (and he in fact sold to a police officer) a book that the trial judge found to have a potentially deleterious influence upon youth. The State insists that, by thus quarantining the general reading public against books not too rugged for grown men and women in order to shield juvenile innocence, it is exercising its power to promote the general welfare. Surely, this is to burn the house to roast the pig. Indeed, the Solicitor General of Michigan has, with characteristic candor, advised the Court that Michigan has a statute specifically designed to protect its children against obscene matter "tending to the corruption of the morals of youth." But the appellant was not convicted for violating this statute.

We have before us legislation not reasonably restricted to the evil with which it is said to deal. The incidence of this enactment is to reduce the adult population of Michigan to reading only what is fit for children. It thereby arbitrarily curtails one of those liberties of the individual, now enshrined in the Due Process Clause of the Fourteenth Amendment, that history has attested as the indispensable conditions for the maintenance and progress of a free society. We are constrained to reverse this conviction.

Reversed.

Kingsley Books v. Brown (1957)

Modern obscenity jurisprudence starts with Kingsley Books *and the subsequent case,* Roth v. United States. *The modern legal debate on the definition of obscenity is grounded in these two cases. In* Kingsley Books, *a New York State statute allowed localities to enjoin the sale and distribution of obscene materials by administrative procedure. If a judge found the materials to be obscene, then those materials had to be destroyed. The validity of this procedure was at issue. Justice Frankfurter, writing for the U.S. Supreme Court, voiced concern that it could appear to be a form of judicial book-burning and -banning— a concern raised among the justices also by subsequent cases.*

MR. JUSTICE FRANKFURTER delivered the opinion of the Court.

This is a proceeding under 22-a of the New York Code of Criminal Procedure, as amended in 1954. This section supplements the existing conventional criminal provision dealing with pornography by authorizing the chief executive, or legal officer, of a municipality to invoke a "limited injunctive remedy," under closely defined procedural safeguards, against the sale and distribution of written and printed matter found after due trial to be obscene, and to obtain an order for the seizure, in default of surrender, of the condemned publications.

A complaint dated September 10, 1954, charged appellants with displaying for sale paper-covered obscene booklets, fourteen of which were annexed, under the general title of "Nights of Horror." The complaint prayed that appellants be enjoined from further distribution of the booklets, that they be required to surrender to the sheriff for destruction all copies in their possession, and, upon failure to do so, that the sheriff be commanded to seize and destroy those copies. The same day the appellants were ordered to show cause within four days why they should not be enjoined from distributing the booklets. Appellants consented to the granting of an injunction and did not bring the matter to issue promptly, as was their right under subdivision 2 of the challenged section, which provides that the persons sought to be enjoined "shall be entitled to a trial of the issues within one day after joinder of issue and a decision shall be rendered by the court within two days of the conclusion of the trial." After the case came to trial, the judge, sitting in equity, found that the booklets annexed to the complaint and introduced in evidence were clearly obscene—were "dirt for dirt's sake"; he enjoined their further distribution and ordered their destruction. He refused to enjoin "the sale and distribution of later issues" on the ground that "to rule against a volume not offered in evidence would . . . impose an unreasonable prior restraint upon freedom of the press."

Not challenging the construction of the statute or the finding of obscenity, appellants took a direct appeal to the New York Court of Appeals, a proceeding in which the constitutionality of the statute was the sole question open to them. That court found no constitutional infirmity: three judges supported the unanimous conclusion by detailed discussion, the other three deemed a brief disposition justified by "ample authority." A claim under the Due Process Clause of the Fourteenth Amendment made throughout the state litigation brought the case here on appeal.

Neither in the New York Court of Appeals, nor here, did appellants assail the legislation insofar as it outlaws obscenity. The claim they make lies within a very narrow compass. Their attack is upon the power of New York to employ the remedial scheme of 22-a. Authorization of an injunction, as part of this scheme, during the period within which the issue of obscenity must be promptly tried and adjudicated in an adversary proceeding for which "[a]dequate notice, judicial hearing, [and] fair determination" are assured is a safeguard against frustration of the public interest in effectuating judicial condemnation of obscene matter. It is a brake on the temptation to exploit a filthy business offered by the limited hazards of piecemeal prosecutions, sale by sale, of a publication already condemned as obscene. New York enacted this procedure on the basis of study by a joint legislative committee. Resort to this injunctive remedy, it is claimed, is beyond the constitutional power of New York in that it amounts to a prior censorship of literary product and as such is violative of that "freedom of thought, and speech" which has been "withdrawn by the Fourteenth Amendment from encroachment by the states."

In an unbroken series of cases extending over a long stretch of this Court's history, it has been accepted as a postulate that "the primary requirements of decency may be enforced against obscene publications." And so our starting point is that New York can constitutionally convict appellants of keeping for sale the booklets incontestably found to be obscene. The immediate problem then is whether New York can adopt as an auxiliary means of dealing with such obscene merchandising the procedure of 22-a.

We need not linger over the suggestion that something can be drawn out of the Due Process Clause of the Fourteenth Amendment that restricts New York to the criminal process in seeking to protect its people against the dissemination of pornography. It is not for this Court thus to limit the State in resorting to various weapons in the armory of the law. Whether proscribed conduct is to be visited by a criminal prosecution or by an injunction or by some or all of these remedies in combination, is a matter within the legislature's range of choice. If New York chooses to subject persons who disseminate obscene "literature" to criminal prosecution and also to deal with such books as deodands [items forfeited to the state] of old, or both, with due regard, of course, to appropriate opportunities for the trial of the underlying issue, it is not for us to gainsay its selection of remedies. . . .

Nor are the consequences of a judicial condemnation for obscenity under 22-a more restrictive of freedom of expression than the result of conviction for a misdemeanor. . . .

The judgment is Affirmed.

MR. CHIEF JUSTICE WARREN, dissenting.

This is not a criminal obscenity case. Nor is it a case ordering the destruction of materials disseminated by a person who has been convicted of an offense for doing so, as would be authorized under provisions in the laws of New York and other States. It is a case wherein the New York police, under a different state statute, located books which, in their opinion, were unfit for public use because of obscenity and then obtained a court order for their condemnation and destruction.

The majority opinion sanctions this proceeding. I would not. Unlike the criminal cases decided today, this New York law places the book on trial. There is totally lacking any standard in the statute for judging the book in context. The personal element basic to the criminal laws is entirely absent. In my judgment, the same object may have wholly different impact depending upon the setting in which it is placed. Under this statute, the setting is irrelevant.

It is the manner of use that should determine obscenity. It is the conduct of the individual that should be judged, not the quality of art or literature. To do otherwise is to impose a prior restraint and hence to violate the Constitution. Certainly in the absence of a prior judicial determination of illegal use, books, pictures and other objects of expression should not be destroyed. It savors too much of book burning.

I would reverse.

MR. JUSTICE BRENNAN, dissenting.

I believe the absence in this New York obscenity statute of a right to jury trial is a fatal defect. Provision for jury trials in equity causes is made by 430 of the New York Civil Practice Act, but only for discretionary jury trials, and advisory verdicts, to be followed or rejected by the trial judge as he deems fit and proper.

In *Alberts v. California* and *Roth v. United States,* the Court held to be constitutional the following standard for judging obscenity— whether to the average person, applying contemporary community standards, the dominant theme of the material taken as a whole appeals to prurient interest. The statutes there involved allowed a jury trial of right, and we did not reach the question whether the safeguards necessary for securing the freedoms of speech and press for material not obscene included a jury determination of obscenity.

The jury represents a cross-section of the community and has a special aptitude for reflecting the view of the average person. Jury trial of obscenity therefore provides a peculiarly competent application of the standard for judging obscenity which, by its definition, calls for an appraisal of material according to the average person's application of contemporary community standards. A statute which does not afford the defendant, of right, a jury determination of obscenity falls short, in my view, of giving proper effect to the standard fashioned as the necessary safeguard demanded by the freedoms of speech and press for material which is not obscene. Of course, as with jury questions generally, the trial judge must initially determine that there is a jury question; i.e., that reasonable men may differ whether the material is obscene.

I would reverse the judgment and direct the restraining order to be dissolved.

Roth v. United States and *Alberts v. California* (1957)

In this case, Associate Justice William J. Brennan, Jr., grappled for the first time with the issue of obscenity and its definition. His decision must be read as part of a larger doctrinal trend toward judicial liberalism encouraged by the Warren Court. Under Chief Justice Earl Warren (1954–1969), the U.S. Supreme Court pursued an activist jurisprudence that increased the presence of the federal government in the lives of citizens. From Brown v. Board of Education *(1954), which dealt with the issue of racial segregation, to the emotional busing cases, to political reapportionment, criminal law reform, and the discovery of a right to privacy, the Warren Court sought a new direction and relevance for the Supreme Court. Another aspect of the law that the Warren Court sought to rework was the law of obscenity.*

Brennan's decision marked a new era in the Supreme Court's history—an era marked by the assumption that the federal government could solve difficult social problems and reflecting the shifting cultural sensibilities of the 1950s. Roth *and its companion case* Alberts v. California *dealt with a prosecution under the Comstock Act of 1873, as amended in 1876, and with a similar California statute. Although a majority of the Court upheld both statutes,* Roth *is important because of the new obscenity doctrine proposed by Brennan, which signaled a new direction in obscenity jurisprudence.*

MR. JUSTICE BRENNAN delivered the opinion of the Court.

The constitutionality of a criminal obscenity statute is the question in each of these cases. In *Roth*, the primary constitutional question is whether the federal obscenity statute violates the provision of the First Amendment that "Congress shall make no law . . . abridging the freedom of speech, or of the press. . . ." In *Alberts*, the primary constitutional question is whether the obscenity provisions of the California Penal Code invade the freedoms of speech and press as they may be incorporated in the liberty protected from state action by the Due Process Clause of the Fourteenth Amendment. . . .

Roth conducted a business in New York in the publication and sale of books, photographs and magazines. He used circulars and advertising matter to solicit sales. He was convicted by a jury in the District Court for the Southern District of New York upon 4 counts of a 26-count indictment charging him with mailing obscene circulars and advertising, and an obscene book, in violation of the federal obscenity statute. His conviction was affirmed by the Court of Appeals for the Second Circuit. We granted certiorari.

Alberts conducted a mail-order business from Los Angeles. He was convicted by the Judge of the Municipal Court of the Beverly Hills Judicial District (having waived a jury trial) under a misdemeanor complaint which charged him with lewdly keeping for sale obscene and indecent books, and with writing, composing and publishing an obscene advertisement of them, in violation of the California Penal Code. The conviction was affirmed by the Appellate Department of the Superior Court of the State of California in and for the County of Los Angeles. We noted probable jurisdiction.

The dispositive question is whether obscenity is utterance within the area of protected speech and press. Although this is the first time the question has been squarely presented to this Court, either under the First Amendment or under the Fourteenth Amendment, expressions found in numerous opinions indicate that this Court has always assumed that obscenity is not protected by the freedoms of speech and press.

The guaranties of freedom of expression in effect in 10 of the 14 States which by 1792 had ratified the Constitution, gave no absolute protection for every utterance. Thirteen of the 14 States provided for the prosecution of libel, and all of those States made either blasphemy or profanity, or both, statutory crimes. As early as 1712, Massachusetts made it criminal to publish "any filthy, obscene, or profane song, pamphlet, libel or mock sermon" in imitation or mimicking of religious services. Thus, profanity and obscenity were related offenses.

In light of this history, it is apparent that the unconditional phrasing of the First Amendment was not intended to protect every utterance. This phrasing did not prevent this Court from concluding that libelous utterances are not within the area of constitutionally protected speech. At the time of the adoption of the First Amendment, obscenity law was not as fully developed as libel law, but there is sufficiently contemporaneous evidence to show that obscenity, too, was outside the protection intended for speech and press.

All ideas having even the slightest redeeming social importance—unorthodox ideas, controversial ideas, even ideas hateful to the prevailing climate of opinion—have the full protection of the guaranties, unless excludable because they encroach upon the limited area of more important interests. But implicit in the history of the First Amendment is the rejection of obscenity as utterly without redeeming social importance. This rejection for that reason is mirrored in the universal judgment that obscenity should be restrained, reflected in the international agreement of over 50 nations, in the obscenity laws of all of the 48 States, and in the 20 obscenity laws enacted by the Congress from 1842 to 1956. . . .

We hold that obscenity is not within the area of constitutionally protected speech or press.

. . . However, sex and obscenity are not synonymous. Obscene material is material which deals with sex in a manner appealing to prurient interest. The portrayal of sex, e.g., in art, literature and scientific works, is not itself sufficient reason to deny material the constitutional protection of freedom of speech and press. Sex, a great and mysterious motive force in human life, has indisputably been a subject of absorbing interest to mankind through the ages; it is one of the vital problems of human interest and public concern. . . .

The fundamental freedoms of speech and press have contributed greatly to the development and well-being of our free society and are indispensable to its continued growth. Ceaseless vigilance is the watchword to prevent their erosion by Congress or by the States. The door barring federal and state intrusion into this area cannot be left ajar; it must be kept tightly closed and opened only the slightest crack necessary to prevent encroachment upon more important interests. It is therefore vital that the standards for judging obscenity safeguard the protection of freedom of speech and press for material which does not treat sex in a manner appealing to prurient interest.

The early leading standard of obscenity allowed material to be judged merely by the effect of an isolated excerpt upon particularly susceptible persons. Some American courts adopted this standard but later decisions have rejected it and substituted this test: whether to the average person, applying contemporary community standards, the dominant theme of the material taken as a whole appeals to prurient interest. The *Hicklin* test, judging obscenity by the effect of isolated passages upon the most susceptible persons, might well encompass material legitimately treating with sex, and so it must be rejected as unconstitutionally restrictive of the freedoms of speech and press. On the other hand, the substituted standard provides safeguards adequate to withstand the charge of constitutional infirmity. . . .

In summary, then, we hold that these statutes, applied according to the proper standard for judging obscenity, do not offend constitutional safeguards against convictions based upon protected material, or fail to give men in acting adequate notice of what is prohibited. . . .

The judgments are Affirmed.

MR. CHIEF JUSTICE WARREN, concurring in the result.

I agree with the result reached by the Court in these cases, but, because we are operating in a field of expression and because broad language used here may eventually be applied to the arts and sciences and freedom of communication generally, I would limit our decision to the facts before us and to the validity of the statutes in question as applied. . . .

That there is a social problem presented by obscenity is attested by the expression of the legislatures of the forty-eight States as well as the Congress. To recognize the existence of a problem, however, does not require that we sustain any and all measures adopted to meet that problem. The history of the application of laws designed to suppress the obscene demonstrates convincingly that the power of government can be invoked under them against great art or literature, scientific treatises, or works exciting social controversy. Mistakes of the past prove that there is a strong countervailing interest to be considered in the freedoms guaranteed by the First and Fourteenth Amendments.

The line dividing the salacious or pornographic from literature or science is not straight and unwavering. Present laws depend largely upon the effect that the materials may have upon those who receive them. It is manifest that the same object may have a different impact, varying according to the part of the community it reached. But there is more to these cases. It is not the book that is on trial; it is a person. The conduct of the defendant is the central issue, not the obscenity of a book or picture. The nature of the materials is, of course, relevant as an attribute of the defendant's conduct, but the materials are thus placed in context from which they draw color and character. A wholly different result might be reached in a different setting.

. . . The defendants in both these cases were engaged in the business of purveying textual matter openly advertised to appeal to the erotic interest of their customers. They were plainly engaged in the commercial exploitation of the morbid and shameful craving for materials with prurient effect. I believe that the State and Federal Governments can constitutionally punish such conduct. That is all that these cases present to us, and that is all we need to decide.

I agree with the Court's decision in its rejection of the other contentions raised by these defendants.

MR. JUSTICE HARLAN, concurring.

I regret not to be able to join the Court's opinion [in *Roth*]. I cannot do so because I find lurking beneath its disarming generalizations a number of problems which not only leave me with serious misgivings as to the future effect of today's decisions, but which also, in my view, call for different results in these two cases.

In final analysis, the problem presented by these cases is how far, and on what terms, the state and federal governments have power to punish individuals for disseminating books considered to be undesirable because of their nature or supposed deleterious effect upon human conduct. Proceeding from the premise that "no issue is presented in either case, concerning the obscenity of the material involved," the Court finds the "dispositive question" to be "whether obscenity is utterance within the area of protected speech and press," and then holds that "obscenity" is not so protected because it is "utterly without redeeming social importance." This sweeping formula appears to me to beg the very question before us. The Court seems to assume that "obscenity" is a peculiar genus of "speech and press," which is as distinct, recognizable, and classifiable as poison ivy is among other plants. On this basis the constitutional question before us simply becomes, as the Court says, whether "obscenity," as an abstraction, is protected by the First and Fourteenth Amendments, and the question whether a particular book may be suppressed becomes a mere matter of classification, of "fact," to be entrusted to a fact-finder and insulated from independent constitutional judgment. But surely the problem cannot be solved in such a generalized fashion. Every communication has an individuality and "value" of its own. The suppression of a particular writing or other tangible form of expression is, therefore, an individual matter, and in the nature of things every such suppression raises an individual constitutional problem, in which a reviewing court must determine for itself whether the attacked expression is suppressable within constitutional standards. Since those standards do not readily lend themselves to generalized definitions, the constitutional problem in the last analysis becomes one of particularized judgments which appellate courts must make for themselves.

I do not think that reviewing courts can escape this responsibility by saying that the trier of the facts, be it a jury or a judge, has labeled the questioned matter as "obscene," for, if "obscenity" is to be suppressed, the question whether a particular work is of that character involves not really an issue of fact but a question of constitutional judgment of the most sensitive and delicate kind. Many juries might find that Joyce's "Ulysses" or Boccaccio's "Decameron" was obscene, and yet the conviction of a defendant for selling either book would raise, for me, the gravest constitutional problems, for no such verdict could convince me, without more, that these books are "utterly without redeeming social importance." In short, I do not understand how the Court can resolve the constitutional problems now before it without making its own independent judgment upon the character of the material upon which these convictions were based. I am very much afraid that the broad manner in which the Court has decided these cases will tend to obscure the peculiar responsibilities resting on state and federal courts in this field and encourage them to rely on easy labeling and jury verdicts as a substitute for facing up to the tough individual problems of constitutional judgment involved in every obscenity case.

[Analyzes the *Alberts* case.] . . . I dissent in No. 582, *Roth v. United States*.

We are faced here with the question whether the federal obscenity statute, as construed and applied in this case, violates the First Amendment to the Constitution. To me, this question is of quite a different order than one where we are dealing with state legislation under the Fourteenth Amendment. . . .

The Constitution differentiates between those areas of human conduct subject to the regulation of the States and those subject to the powers of the Federal Government. The substantive powers of the two governments, in many instances, are distinct. And in every case where we are called upon to balance the interest in free expression against other interests, it seems to me important that we should keep in the forefront the question of whether those other interests are state or federal. Since under our constitutional scheme the two are not necessarily equivalent, the balancing process must needs often produce different results. Whether a particular limitation on speech or press is to be upheld because it subserves a paramount governmental interest must, to a large extent, I think, depend on whether that government has, under the Constitution, a direct substantive interest, that is, the power to act, in the particular area involved. . . .

Not only is the federal interest in protecting the Nation against pornography attenuated, but the dangers of federal censorship in this field are far greater than anything the States may do. It has often been said that one of the great strengths of our federal system is that we have, in the forty-eight States, forty-eight experimental social laboratories. . . . Different States will have different attitudes toward the same work of literature. The same book which is freely read in one State might be classed as obscene in another. And it seems to me that no overwhelming danger to our freedom to experiment and to gratify our tastes in literature is likely to result from the suppression of a borderline book in one of the States, so long as there is no uniform nation-wide suppression of the book, and so long as other States are free to experiment with the same or bolder books.

Quite a different situation is presented, however, where the Federal Government imposes the ban. The danger is perhaps not great if the people of one State, through their legislature, decide that "Lady Chatterley's Lover" goes so far beyond the acceptable standards of candor that it will be deemed offensive and non-sellable, for the State next door is still free to make its own choice. At least we do not have one uniform standard. But the dangers to free thought and expression are truly great if the Federal Government imposes a blanket ban over the Nation on such a book. The prerogative of the States to differ on their ideas of morality will be destroyed, the ability of States to experiment will be stunted. The fact that the people of one State cannot read some of the works of D. H. Lawrence seems to me, if not wise or desirable, at least acceptable. But that no person in the United States should be allowed to do so seems to me to be intolerable, and violative of both the letter and spirit of the First Amendment.

I judge this case, then, in view of what I think is the attenuated federal interest in this field, in view of the very real danger of a deadening uniformity which can result from nation-wide federal censorship, and in view of the fact that the constitutionality of this conviction must be weighed against the First and not the Fourteenth Amendment. So viewed, I do not think that this conviction can be upheld. The petitioner was convicted under a statute which, under the judge's charge, makes it criminal to sell books which "tend to stir sexual impulses and lead to sexually impure thoughts." I cannot agree that any book which tends to stir sexual impulses and lead to sexually impure thoughts necessarily is "utterly without redeeming social importance." Not only did this charge fail to measure up to the standards which I understand the Court to approve, but as far as I can see, much of the great literature of the world could lead to conviction under such a view of the statute. Moreover, in no event do I think that the limited federal interest in this area can extend to mere "thoughts." The Federal Government has no business, whether under the postal or commerce power, to bar the sale of books because they might lead to any kind of "thoughts."

It is no answer to say, as the Court does, that obscenity is not protected speech. The point is that this statute, as here construed, defines obscenity so widely that it encompasses matters which might very well be protected speech. I do not think that the federal statute can be constitutionally construed to reach other than what the Government has termed as "hard-core" pornography. Nor do I think the statute can fairly be read as directed only at persons who are engaged in the business of catering to the prurient minded, even though their wares fall short of hard-core pornography. Such a statute would raise constitutional questions of a different order. That being so, and since in my opinion the material here involved cannot be said to be hard-core pornography, I would reverse this case with instructions to dismiss the indictment.

MR. JUSTICE DOUGLAS, with whom MR. JUSTICE BLACK concurs, dissenting.

When we sustain these convictions, we make the legality of a publication turn on the purity of thought which a book or tract instills in the mind of the reader. I do not think we can approve that standard and be faithful to the command of the First Amendment, which by its terms is a restraint on Congress and which by the Fourteenth is a restraint on the States.

In the *Roth* case the trial judge charged the jury that the statutory words "obscene, lewd and lascivious" describe "that form of immorality which has relation to sexual impurity and has a tendency to excite lustful thoughts." He stated that the term "filthy" in the statute pertains "to that sort of treatment of sexual matters in such a vulgar and indecent way, so that it tends to arouse a feeling of disgust and revulsion." He went on to say that the material "must be calculated to corrupt and debauch the minds and morals" of "the average person in the community," not those of any particular class. "You judge the circulars, pictures and publications which have been put in evidence by present-day standards of the community. You may ask yourselves does it offend the common conscience of the community by present-day standards."

The trial judge who, sitting without a jury, heard the *Alberts* case and the appellate court that sustained the judgment of conviction, took California's definition of "obscenity." That case held that a book is obscene "if it has a substantial tendency to deprave or corrupt its readers by inciting lascivious thoughts or arousing lustful desire."

By these standards punishment is inflicted for thoughts provoked, not for overt acts nor antisocial conduct. . . . The question remains, what is the constitutional test of obscenity?

. . . The test of obscenity the Court endorses today gives the censor free range over a vast domain. To allow the State to step in and punish mere speech or publication that the judge or the jury thinks has an undesirable impact on thoughts but that is not shown to be a part of unlawful action is drastically to curtail the First Amendment.

. . . If we were certain that impurity of sexual thoughts impelled to action, we would be on less dangerous ground in punishing the distributors of this sex literature. But it is by no means clear that obscene literature, as so defined, is a significant factor in influencing substantial deviations from the community standards. . . .

The standard of what offends "the common conscience of the community" conflicts, in my judgment, with the command of the First Amendment that "Congress shall make no law . . . abridging the freedom of speech, or of the press." Certainly that standard would not be an acceptable one if religion, economics, politics or philosophy were involved. How does it become a constitutional standard when literature treating with sex is concerned?

Any test that turns on what is offensive to the community's standards is too loose, too capricious, too destructive of freedom of expression to be squared with the First Amendment. Under that test, juries can censor, suppress, and punish what they don't like, provided the matter relates to "sexual impurity" or has a tendency "to excite lustful thoughts." This is community censorship in one of its worst forms. It creates a regime where in the battle between the literati and the Philistines, the Philistines are certain to win. If experience in this field teaches anything, it is that "censorship of obscenity has almost always been both irrational and indiscriminate." The test adopted here accentuates that trend.

I assume there is nothing in the Constitution which forbids Congress from using its power over the mails to proscribe conduct on the grounds of good morals. No one would suggest that the First Amendment permits nudity in public places, adultery, and other phases of sexual misconduct.

I can understand (and at times even sympathize with) programs of civic groups and church groups to protect and defend the existing moral standards of the community. I can understand the motives of the Anthony Comstocks who would impose Victorian standards on the community. When speech alone is involved, I do not think that government, consistently with the First Amendment, can become the sponsor of any of these movements. I do not think that government, consistently with the First Amendment, can throw its weight behind one school or another. Government should be concerned with antisocial conduct, not with utterances. Thus, if the First Amendment guarantee of freedom of speech and press is to mean anything in this field, it must allow protests even against the moral code that the standard of the day sets for the community. In other words, literature should not be suppressed merely because it offends the moral code of the censor.

The legality of a publication in this country should never be allowed to turn either on the purity of thought which it instills in the mind of the reader or on the degree to which it offends the community conscience. By either test the role of the censor is exalted, and society's values in literary freedom are sacrificed. . . .

Freedom of expression can be suppressed if, and to the extent that, it is so closely brigaded with illegal action as to be an inseparable part of it. As a people, we cannot afford to relax that standard. For the test that suppresses a cheap tract today can suppress a literary gem tomorrow. All it need do is to incite a lascivious thought or arouse a lustful desire. The list of books that judges or juries can place in that category is endless.

I would give the broad sweep of the First Amendment full support. I have the same confidence in the ability of our people to reject noxious literature as I have in their capacity to sort out the true from the false in theology, economics, politics, or any other field.

Manual Enterprises v. Day (1962)

While attempting to clarify the standards of the new obscenity doctrine set out by Justice Brennan in Roth, *Justice Harlan in this case unintentionally muddied them. The U.S. Supreme Court questioned just how far the Comstock Law could reach, and tried to craft a more precise definition of obscenity. In a fractured decision (there was no commonality of opinion, although the vote was 8–1), Justice Harlan added a new component to the* Roth *obscenity standard, hoping to sharpen it; yet his language produced even greater confusion.*

MR. JUSTICE HARLAN announced the judgment of the Court.

This case draws into question a ruling of the Post Office Department, sustained both by the District Court and the Court of Appeals barring from the mails a shipment of petitioners' magazines. That ruling was based on alternative determinations that the magazines (1) were themselves "obscene," and (2) gave information as to where obscene matter could be obtained, thus rendering them nonmailable under two separate provisions of 18 U.S.C. 1461, known as the Comstock Act. . . .

Petitioners are three corporations respectively engaged in publishing magazines titled MANual, Trim, and Grecian Guild Pictorial. They have offices at the same address in Washington, D.C., and a common president, one Herman L. Womack. The magazines consist largely of photographs of nude, or near-nude, male models and give the names of each model and the photographer together with the address of the latter. They also contain a number of advertisements by independent photographers offering nudist photographs for sale.

On March 25, 1960, six parcels containing an aggregate of 405 copies of the three magazines, destined from Alexandria, Virginia, to Chicago, Illinois, were detained by the Alexandria postmaster, pending a ruling by his superiors at Washington as to whether the magazines were "non-mailable." After an evidentiary hearing before the Judicial Officer of the Post Office Department there ensued the administrative and court decisions now under review.

On the issue of obscenity, as distinguished from unlawful advertising, the case comes to us with the following administrative findings, which are supported by substantial evidence and which we, and indeed the parties, for the most part, themselves, accept: (1) the magazines are not, as asserted by petitioners, physical culture or "body-building" publications, but are composed primarily, if not exclusively, for homosexuals, and have no literary, scientific or other merit; (2)

they would appeal to the "prurient interest" of such sexual deviates, but would not have any interest for sexually normal individuals; and (3) the magazines are read almost entirely by homosexuals, and possibly a few adolescent males; the ordinary male adult would not normally buy them.

On these premises, the question whether these magazines are "obscene," was thought to depend solely on a determination as to the relevant "audience" in terms of which their "prurient interest" appeal should be judged. This view of the obscenity issue evidently stemmed from the belief that in *Roth v. United States* this Court established the following single test for determining whether challenged material is obscene: "whether to the average person, applying contemporary community standards, the dominant theme of the material taken as a whole appeals to prurient interest." On this basis the Court of Appeals, rejecting the petitioners' contention that the "prurient interest" appeal of the magazines should be judged in terms of their likely impact on the "average person," even though not a likely recipient of the magazines, held that the administrative finding respecting their impact on the "average homosexual" sufficed to establish the Government's case as to their obscenity.

We do not reach the question thus thought below to be dispositive on this aspect of the case. For we find lacking in these magazines an element which, no less than "prurient interest," is essential to a valid determination of obscenity under 1461, and to which neither the Post Office Department nor the Court of Appeals addressed itself at all: These magazines cannot be deemed so offensive on their face as to affront current community standards of decency—a quality that we shall hereafter refer to as "patent offensiveness" or "indecency." Lacking that quality, the magazines cannot be deemed legally "obscene," and we need not consider the question of the proper "audience" by which their "prurient interest" appeal should be judged. . . .

Obscenity under the federal statute . . . requires proof of two distinct elements: (1) patent offensiveness; and (2) "prurient interest" appeal. Both must conjoin before challenged material can be found "obscene" under 1461. In most obscenity cases, to be sure, the two elements tend to coalesce, for that which is patently offensive will also usually carry the requisite "prurient interest" appeal. It is only in the unusual instance where, as here, the "prurient interest" appeal of the material is found limited to a particular class of persons that occasion arises for a truly independent inquiry into the question whether or not the material is patently offensive.

The Court of Appeals was mistaken in considering that *Roth* made "prurient interest" appeal the sole test of obscenity. Reading that case as dispensing with the requisite of patently offensive portrayal would be not only inconsistent with 1461 and its common-law background, but out of keeping with *Roth*'s evident purpose to tighten obscenity standards. The Court there both rejected the "isolated excerpt" and "particularly susceptible persons" tests of the *Hicklin* case, and was at pains to point out that not all portrayals of sex could be reached by obscenity laws but only those treating that subject "in a manner appealing to prurient interest." That, of course, was but a compendious way of embracing in the obscenity standard both the concept of patent offensiveness, manifested by the terms of 1461 itself, and the element of the likely corruptive effect of the challenged material, brought into federal law via *Regina v. Hicklin.*

To consider that the "obscenity" exception in "the area of constitutionally protected speech or press," does not require any determination as to the patent offensiveness of the material itself might well put the American public in jeopardy of being denied access to many worthwhile works in literature, science, or art. For one would not have to travel far even among the acknowledged masterpieces in any of these fields to find works whose "dominant theme" might, not beyond reason, be claimed to appeal to the "prurient interest" of the reader or observer. We decline to attribute to Congress any such quixotic and deadening purpose as would bar from the mails all material, not patently offensive, which stimulates impure desires relating to sex. . . . It is only material whose indecency is self-demonstrating and which, from the standpoint of its effect, may be said predominantly to appeal to the prurient interest that Congress has chosen to bar from the mails by the force of 1461.

We come then to what we consider the dispositive question on this phase of the case. Are these magazines offensive on their face?

There must first be decided the relevant "community" in terms of whose standards of decency the issue must be judged. We think that the proper test under this federal statute, reaching as it does to all parts of the United States whose population reflects many different ethnic and cultural backgrounds, is a national standard of decency. We need not decide whether Congress could constitutionally prescribe a lesser geographical framework for judging this issue which would not have the intolerable consequence of denying some sections of the country access to material, there deemed acceptable, which in others might be considered offensive to prevailing community standards of decency.

As regards the standard for judging the element of "indecency," the *Roth* case gives little guidance beyond indicating that the standard is a constitutional one which as with "prurient interest," requires taking the challenged material "as a whole." Being ultimately concerned only with the question whether the First and Fourteenth Amendments protect material that is admittedly obscene, the Court there had no occasion to explore the application of a particular obscenity standard. At least one important state court and some authoritative commentators have considered *Roth* and subsequent cases to indicate that only "hard-core" pornography can constitutionally be reached under this or similar state obscenity statutes. Whether "hard-core" pornography, or something less, be the proper test, we need go no further in the present case than to hold that the magazines in question, taken as a whole, cannot, under any permissible constitutional standard, be deemed to be beyond the pale of contemporary notions of rudimentary decency.

We cannot accept in full the Government's description of these magazines which, contrary to *Roth* tends to emphasize and in some respects overdraw certain features in several of the photographs, at the expense of what the magazines fairly taken as a whole depict. Our own independent examination of the magazines leads us to conclude that the most that can be said of them is that they are dismally unpleasant, uncouth, and tawdry. But this is not enough to make them "obscene."

. . . We conclude that the administrative ruling respecting nonmailability is improvident insofar as it depends on a determination that these magazines are obscene. . . .

In conclusion, nothing in this opinion of course remotely implies approval of the type of magazines published by these petitioners, still less of the sordid motives which prompted their publication. All we decide is that on this record these particular magazines are not subject to repression under 1461.

Reversed.

MR. JUSTICE BRENNAN, with whom THE CHIEF JUSTICE and MR. JUSTICE DOUGLAS join, concurring in the reversal.

[Reviews the facts of the cases.] We risk erosion of First Amendment liberties unless we train our vigilance upon the methods whereby obscenity is condemned no less than upon the standards whereby it is judged. Questions of procedural safeguards loom large in the wake of an order such as the one before us. Among them are: (a) whether Congress can close the mails to obscenity by any means other than prosecution of its sender; (b) whether Congress, if it can authorize exclusion of mail, can provide that obscenity be determined in the first instance in any forum except a court; and (c) whether, even if Congress could so authorize administrative censorship, it has in fact conferred upon postal authorities any power to exclude matter from the mails upon their determination of its obscene character. . . .

Whether Congress has authorized the Postmaster General to censor obscenity, is our precise question. The Government relies upon no other provision to support the constitutionally questionable power of administrative censorship of this material. That power is inferred from the declaration that every item proscribed in 1461 is "nonmailable matter and shall not be conveyed in the mails or delivered from any post office or by any letter carrier." Even granting that these words on their face permit a construction allowing the Post Office the power it asserts, their use in a criminal statute, their legislative history, and the contrast with the words and history of other provisions dealing with similar problems, raise the most serious doubt that so important and sensitive a power was granted by so perfunctory a provision. The area of obscenity is honeycombed with hazards for First Amendment guaranties, and the grave constitutional questions which would be raised by the grant of such a power should not be decided when the relevant materials are so ambiguous as to whether any such grant exists. . . . [Brennan then undertook a long review of the history of the relevant federal statutes.]

It is clear that the Post Office has long practiced administrative censorship of allegedly obscene mailings generally. . . .

We have sustained the criminal sanctions of 1461 against a challenge of unconstitutionality under the First Amendment. We have emphasized, however, that the necessity for safeguarding First Amendment protections for nonobscene materials means that Government "is not free to adopt whatever procedures it pleases for dealing with obscenity . . . without regard to the possible consequences for constitutionally protected speech." I imply no doubt that Congress could constitutionally authorize a noncriminal process in the nature of a judicial proceeding under closely defined procedural safeguards. But the suggestion that Congress may constitutionally authorize any process other than a fully judicial one immediately raises the gravest doubts. . . . I, therefore, concur in the judgment of reversal.

MR. JUSTICE CLARK, dissenting.

While those in the majority like ancient Gaul are split into three parts, the ultimate holding of the Court today, despite the clear congressional mandate found in 1461, requires the United States Post Office to be the world's largest disseminator of smut and Grand Informer of the names and places where obscene material may be obtained. The Judicial Officer of the Post Office Department, the District Court, and the Court of Appeals have all found the magazines in issue to be nonmailable on the alternative grounds that they are obscene and that they contain information on where obscene material may be obtained. The Court, however, says that these magazines must go through the mails. . . . Since in my view the Postmaster General is required by 1461 to reject nonmailable matter, I would affirm the judgment on the sole ground that the magazines contain information as to where obscene material can be obtained and thus are nonmailable. I, therefore, do not consider the question of whether the magazines as such are obscene. . . .

Jacobellis v. Ohio (1964)

In this case U.S. Supreme Court Associate Justice Potter Stewart penned his famous statement on obscenity, "I know it when I see it"—one of the troublesome truisms of obscenity. Like Manual Enterprises, *this case elicited numerous opinions as the justices (like the larger culture of the United States) struggled to come to some understanding of the issues and problems of defining obscenity. In particular, Justice Brennan pressed his argument in favor of a single, national standard defining obscenity. This "one-size-fits-all" approach proved controversial.*

MR. JUSTICE BRENNAN announced the judgment of the Court.

Appellant, Nico Jacobellis, manager of a motion picture theater in Cleveland Heights, Ohio, was convicted on two counts of possessing and exhibiting an obscene film in violation of the Ohio Revised Code.

He was fined $500 on the first count and $2,000 on the second, and was sentenced to the workhouse if the fines were not paid. His conviction, by a court of three judges upon waiver of trial by jury, was affirmed by an intermediate appellate court and by the Supreme Court of Ohio. We noted probable jurisdiction of the appeal, and subsequently restored the case to the calendar for reargument. The dispositive question is whether the state courts properly found that the motion picture involved a French film called "Les Amants" ("The Lovers"), was obscene and hence not entitled to the protection for free expression that is guaranteed by the First and Fourteenth Amendments. We conclude that the film is not obscene and that the judgment must accordingly be reversed.

Motion pictures are within the ambit of the constitutional guarantees of freedom of speech and of the press. But in *Roth v. United States* and *Alberts v. California,* we held that obscenity is not subject to those guarantees. Application of an obscenity law to suppress a motion picture thus requires ascertainment of the "dim and uncertain line" that often separates obscenity from constitutionally protected expression. It has been suggested that this is a task in which our Court need not involve itself. We are told that the determination whether a particular motion picture, book, or other work of expression is obscene can be treated as a purely factual judgment on which a jury's verdict is all but conclusive, or that in any event the decision can be left essentially to state and lower federal courts, with this Court exercising only a limited review such as that needed to determine whether the ruling below is supported by "sufficient evidence." The suggestion is appealing, since it would lift from our shoulders a difficult, recurring, and unpleasant task. But we cannot accept it. Such an abnegation of judicial supervision in this field would be inconsistent with our duty to uphold the constitutional guarantees. Since it is only "obscenity" that is excluded from the constitutional protection, the question whether a particular work is obscene necessarily implicates an issue of constitutional law. Such an issue we think, must ultimately be decided by this Court. Our duty admits of no "substitute for facing up to the tough individual problems of constitutional judgment involved in every obscenity case."

. . . We cannot understand why the Court's duty should be any different in the present case, where Jacobellis has been subjected to a criminal conviction for disseminating a work of expression and is challenging that conviction as a deprivation of rights guaranteed by the First and Fourteenth Amendments. Nor can we understand why the Court's performance of its constitutional and judicial function in this sort of case should be denigrated by such epithets as "censor" or "super-censor." In judging alleged obscenity the Court is no more "censoring" expression than it has in other cases "censored" criticism of judges and public officials, advocacy of governmental overthrow, or speech alleged to constitute a breach of the peace. Use of an opprobrious label can neither obscure nor impugn the Court's performance of its obligation to test challenged judgments against the guarantees of the First and Fourteenth Amendments and, in doing so, to delineate the scope of constitutionally protected speech. Hence we reaffirm the principle that, in "obscenity" cases as in all others involving rights derived from the First Amendment guarantees of free expression, this Court cannot avoid making an independent constitutional judgment on the facts of the case as to whether the material involved is constitutionally protected.

The question of the proper standard for making this determination has been the subject of much discussion and controversy since our decision in *Roth* seven years ago. Recognizing that the test for obscenity enunciated there—"whether to the average person, applying contemporary community standards, the dominant theme of the material taken as a whole appeals to prurient interest"—is not perfect, we think any substitute would raise equally difficult problems, and we therefore adhere to that standard. We would reiterate, however, our recognition in *Roth* that obscenity is excluded from the constitutional protection only because it is "utterly without redeeming social importance," and that "the portrayal of sex, e.g., in art, literature and scientific works, is not itself sufficient reason to deny material the constitutional protection of freedom of speech and press." It follows that material dealing with sex in a manner that advocates ideas that has literary or scientific or artistic value or any other form of social importance, and may not be branded as obscenity and denied the constitutional protection. Nor may the constitutional status of the material be made to turn on a "weighing" of its social importance against its prurient appeal, for a work cannot be proscribed unless it is "utterly" without social importance. . . .

It has been suggested that the "contemporary community standards" aspect of the *Roth* test implies a determination of the constitutional question of obscenity in each case by the standards of the particular local community from which the case arises. This is an incorrect reading of *Roth*. The concept of "contemporary community standards" was first expressed by Judge Learned Hand in *United States v. Kennerley*. . . . Judge Hand was referring not to state and local "communities," but rather to "the community" in the sense of "society at large; . . . the public, or people in general." Thus, he recognized that under his standard the concept of obscenity would have "a varying meaning from time to time"—not from county to county, or town to town.

We do not see how any "local" definition of the "community" could properly be employed in delineating the area of expression that is protected by the Federal Constitution. . . . Furthermore, to sustain the suppression of a particular book or film in one locality would deter its dissemination in other localities where it might be held not obscene, since sellers and exhibitors would be reluctant to risk criminal conviction in testing the variation between the two places. It would be a hardy person who would sell a book or exhibit a film anywhere in the land after this Court had sustained the judgment of one "community" holding it to be outside the constitutional protection. The result would thus be "to restrict the public's access to forms of the printed word which the State could not constitutionally suppress directly."

It is true that local communities throughout the land are in fact diverse, and that in cases such as this one the Court is confronted with the task of reconciling the rights of such communities with the rights of individuals. Communities vary, however, in many respects other than their toleration of alleged obscenity, and such variances have never been considered to require or justify a varying standard for application of the Federal Constitution. . . . We thus reaffirm the position taken in *Roth* to the effect that the constitutional status of an allegedly obscene work must be determined on the basis of a national standard. It is, after all, a national Constitution we are expounding.

We recognize the legitimate and indeed exigent interest of States and localities throughout the Nation in preventing the dissemination of material deemed harmful to children. But that interest does not justify a total suppression of such material, the effect of which would be to "reduce the adult population . . . to reading only what is fit for children."

. . . We have applied that standard to the motion picture in question. "The Lovers" involves a woman bored with her life and marriage who abandons her husband and family for a young archaeologist with whom she has suddenly fallen in love. There is an explicit love scene in the last reel of the film, and the State's objections are based almost entirely upon that scene. The film was favorably reviewed in a number of national publications, although disparaged in others, and was rated by at least two critics of national stature among the best films of the year in which it was produced. It was shown in approximately 100 of the larger cities in the United States, including Columbus and Toledo, Ohio. We have viewed the film, in the light of the record made in the trial court, and we conclude that it is not obscene within the standards enunciated in *Roth v. United States* and *Alberts v. California,* which we reaffirm here.

Reversed.

MR. JUSTICE STEWART, concurring.

It is possible to read the Court's opinion in *Roth v. United States* and *Alberts v. California* in a variety of ways. In saying this, I imply no criticism of the Court, which in those cases was faced with the task of trying to define what may be indefinable. I have reached the conclusion, which I think is confirmed at least by negative implication in the Court's decisions since *Roth* and *Alberts,* that under the First and Fourteenth Amendments criminal laws in this area are constitutionally limited to hard-core pornography. I shall not today attempt further to define the kinds of material I understand to be embraced within that shorthand description; and perhaps I could never succeed in intelligibly doing so. But I know it when I see it, and the motion picture involved in this case is not that.

THE CHIEF JUSTICE, with whom MR. JUSTICE CLARK joins, dissenting.

In this and other cases in this area of the law, which are coming to us in ever-increasing numbers, we are faced with the resolution of rights basic both to individuals and to society as a whole. Specifically, we are called upon to reconcile the right of the Nation and of the States to maintain a decent society and, on the other hand, the right of individuals to express themselves freely in accordance with the guarantees of the First and Fourteenth Amendments. Although the Federal Government and virtually every State has had laws proscribing obscenity since the Union was formed, and although this Court has recently decided that obscenity is not within the protection of the First Amendment, neither courts nor legislatures have been able to evolve a truly satisfactory definition of obscenity. In other areas of the law, terms like "negligence," although in common use for centuries, have been difficult to define except in the most general manner. Yet the courts have been able to function in such areas with a reasonable degree of efficiency. The obscenity problem, however, is aggravated by the fact that it involves the area of public expression, an area in which a broad range of freedom is vital to our society and is constitutionally protected.

Recently this Court put its hand to the task of defining the term "obscenity" in *Roth v. United States.* The definition enunciated in that case has generated much legal speculation as well as further judicial interpretation by state and federal courts. It has also been relied upon by legislatures. Yet obscenity cases continue to come to this Court, and it becomes increasingly apparent that we must settle as well as we can the question of what constitutes "obscenity" and the question of what standards are permissible in enforcing proscriptions against obscene matter. This Court hears cases such as the instant one not merely to rule upon the alleged obscenity of a specific film or book but to establish principles for the guidance of lower courts and legislatures.

. . . For all the sound and fury that the *Roth* test has generated, it has not been proved unsound, and I believe that we should try to live with it—at least until a more satisfactory definition is evolved. No government—be it federal, state, or local—should be forced to choose between repressing all material, including that within the realm of decency, and allowing unrestrained license to publish any material, no matter how vile. There must be a rule of reason in this as in other areas of the law, and we have attempted in the *Roth* case to provide such a rule.

It is my belief that when the Court said in *Roth* that obscenity is to be defined by reference to "community standards," it meant community standards—not a national standard, as is sometimes argued. I believe that there is no provable "national standard," and perhaps there should be none. At all events, this Court has not been able to enunciate one, and it would be unreasonable to expect local courts to divine one. It is said that such a "community" approach may well result in material being proscribed as obscene in one community but not in another, and, in all probability, that is true. But communities throughout the Nation are in fact diverse, and it must be remembered that, in cases such as this one, the Court is confronted with the task of reconciling conflicting rights of the diverse communities within our society and of individuals. . . .

In light of the foregoing, I would reiterate my acceptance of the rule of the *Roth* case: Material is obscene and not constitutionally protected against regulation and proscription if "to the average person, applying contemporary community standards, the dominant theme of the material taken as a whole appeals to prurient interest." I would commit the enforcement of this rule to the appropriate state and federal courts, and I would accept their judgments made pursuant to the *Roth* rule, limiting myself to a consideration only of whether there is sufficient evidence in the record upon which a finding of obscenity could be made. If there is no evidence in the record upon which such a finding could be made, obviously the material involved cannot be held obscene. But since a mere modicum of evidence may satisfy a "no evidence" standard, I am unwilling to give the important constitutional right of free expression such limited protection. However, protection of society's right to maintain its moral fiber and the effective administration of justice require that this Court not establish itself as an ultimate censor, in each case reading the entire record, viewing the accused material, and making an independent judgment on the question of obscenity. Therefore, once a finding of obscenity has been made below under a proper application of the *Roth* test, I would apply a "sufficient evidence" standard of review—requiring something more than merely any evidence but something less than "substantial evidence on the record [including the allegedly obscene material] as a whole." This is the only reasonable way I can see to obviate the necessity of this Court's sitting as the Super-Censor of all the obscenity purveyed throughout the Nation. . . .

Therefore, I would affirm the judgment.

MR. JUSTICE HARLAN, dissenting.

While agreeing with my Brother BRENNAN'S opinion that the responsibilities of the Court in this area are no different from those which attend the adjudication of kindred constitutional questions, I have heretofore expressed the view that the States are constitutionally permitted greater latitude in determining what is bannable on the score of obscenity than is so with the Federal Government. While, as correctly said in MR. JUSTICE BRENNAN'S opinion, the Court has not accepted that view, I nonetheless feel free to adhere to it in this still developing aspect of constitutional law.

The more I see of these obscenity cases the more convinced I become that in permitting the States wide, but not federally unrestricted, scope in this field, while holding the Federal Government with a tight rein, lies the best promise for achieving a sensible accommodation between the public interest sought to be served by obscenity laws and protection of genuine rights of free expression. . . .

On this basis, having viewed the motion picture in question, I think the State acted within permissible limits in condemning the film and would affirm the judgment of the Ohio Supreme Court.

Memoirs v. Massachusetts (1966)

Justice Brennan continued his quest for precision in the definition of "obscenity" and his quest to build a consensus in the Supreme Court and in the country for his definition and understanding of obscenity. In his decision, Brennan proposed new language that amended and changed his original obscenity standard established in the 1957 Roth *case. Yet, no matter what language he proposed, some of his brethren on the Court opposed his efforts. The justices could not agree on a working definition of obscenity or on who should decide; it is therefore not surprising that the general public in the United States also could not reach a consensus.*

MR. JUSTICE BRENNAN announced the judgment of the Court.

This is an obscenity case in which *Memoirs of a Woman of Pleasure* (commonly known as *Fanny Hill*), written by John Cleland in about 1750, was adjudged obscene in a proceeding that put on trial the book itself, and not its publisher or distributor. The proceeding was a civil equity suit brought by the Attorney General of Massachusetts . . . to have the book declared obscene. Section 28C requires that the petition commencing the suit be "directed against [the] book by name" and that an order to show cause "why said book should not be judicially determined to be obscene" be published in a daily newspaper and sent by registered mail "to all persons interested in the publication." Publication of the order in this case occurred in a Boston daily newspaper, and a copy of the order was sent by registered mail to G. P. Putnam's Sons, alleged to be the publisher and copyright holder of the book.

As authorized by 28D, G. P. Putnam's Sons intervened in the proceedings in behalf of the book, but it did not claim the right provided by that section to have the issue of obscenity tried by a jury. At the hearing before a justice of the Superior Court, . . . the court received the book in evidence and also, as allowed by the section, heard the testimony of experts and accepted other evidence, such as book reviews, in order to assess the literary, cultural, or educational character of the book. . . . The trial justice entered a final decree, which adjudged *Memoirs* obscene and declared that the book "is not entitled to the protection of the First and Fourteenth Amendments to the Constitution of the United States against action by the Attorney General or other law enforcement officer pursuant to the provisions of . . . 28B, or otherwise." The Massachusetts Supreme Judicial Court affirmed the decree. We reverse.

The term "obscene" appearing in the Massachusetts statute has been interpreted by the Supreme Judicial Court to be as expansive as the Constitution permits: the "statute covers all material that is obscene in the constitutional sense." . . . Thus the sole question before the state courts was whether *Memoirs* satisfies the test of obscenity established in *Roth v. United States.*

We defined obscenity in *Roth* in the following terms: "[W]hether to the average person, applying contemporary community standards, the dominant theme of the material taken as a whole appeals to prurient interest." Under this definition, as elaborated in subsequent cases, three elements must coalesce: it must be established that (a) the dominant theme of the material taken as a whole appeals to a prurient interest in sex; (b) the material is patently offensive because it affronts contemporary community standards relating to the description or representation of sexual matters; and (c) the material is utterly without redeeming social value. . . .

The Supreme Judicial Court erred in holding that a book need not be "unqualifiedly worthless before it can be deemed obscene." A book cannot be proscribed unless it is found to be utterly without redeeming social value. This is so even though the book is found to possess the requisite prurient appeal and to be patently offensive. Each of the three federal constitutional criteria is to be applied independently; the social value of the book can neither be weighed against nor canceled by its prurient appeal or patent offensiveness. Hence, even on the view of the court below that *Memoirs* possessed only a modicum of social value, its judgment must be reversed as being founded on an erroneous interpretation of a federal constitutional standard.

It does not necessarily follow from this reversal that a determination that *Memoirs* is obscene in the constitutional sense would be improper under all circumstances. On the premise, which we have no occasion to assess, that *Memoirs* has the requisite prurient appeal and is patently offensive, but has only a minimum of social value, the circumstances of production, sale, and publicity are relevant in determining whether or not the publication or distribution of the book is constitutionally protected. Evidence that the book was commercially exploited for the sake of prurient appeal, to the exclusion of all other values, might justify the conclusion that the book was utterly without redeeming social importance. . . . In this proceeding, however, the courts were asked to judge the obscenity of *Memoirs* in the abstract, and the declaration of obscenity was neither aided nor limited by a specific set of circumstances of production, sale, and publicity. All possible uses of the book must therefore be considered, and the mere risk that the book might be exploited by panderers because it so pervasively treats sexual matters cannot alter the fact—given the view of the Massachusetts court attributing to *Memoirs* a modicum of literary and historical value—that the book will have redeeming social importance in the hands of those who publish or distribute it on the basis of that value.

Reversed.

MR. JUSTICE CLARK, dissenting.

It is with regret that I write this dissenting opinion. However, the public should know of the continuous flow of pornographic material reaching this Court and the increasing problem States have in controlling it. *Memoirs of a Woman of Pleasure,* the book involved here, is typical. I have "stomached" past cases for almost 10 years without much outcry. Though I am not known to be a purist—or a shrinking violet—this book is too much even for me. It is important that the Court has refused to declare it obscene and thus affords it further circulation. In order to give my remarks the proper setting I have been obliged to portray the book's contents, which causes me embarrassment. However, quotations from typical episodes would so debase our Reports that I will not follow that course.

Let me first pinpoint the effect of today's holding in the obscenity field. While there is no majority opinion in this case, there are three Justices who import a new test into that laid down in *Roth v. United States,* namely, that "[a] book cannot be proscribed unless it is found to be utterly without redeeming social value." I agree with my Brother WHITE that such a condition rejects the basic holding of *Roth* and gives the smut artist free rein to carry on his dirty business. My vote in that case—which was the deciding one for the majority opinion—was cast solely because the Court declared the test of obscenity to be: "whether to the average person, applying contemporary community standards, the dominant theme of the material taken as a whole appeals to prurient interest." I understood that test to include only two constitutional requirements: (1) the book must be judged as a whole, not by its parts; and (2) it must be judged in terms of its appeal to the prurient interest of the average person, applying contemporary community standards. . . .

Ginsberg v. New York (1968)

Differences continued to deepen among the justices of the Supreme Court regarding the proper role of the Court, Congress, and the states in the definition and control of obscenity. Although Brennan had started to push for a single, national standard of obscenity, in this case he deferred to the state and to the statute it had instituted to keep allegedly obscene materials away from children. Other justices were divided. Justice Douglas continued his campaign against all restrictions on the distribution of obscenity. Justice Fortas tried his hand at redefining obscenity more narrowly—an effort that brought him public opprobrium for being too permissive.

MR. JUSTICE BRENNAN delivered the opinion of the Court.

This case presents the question of the constitutionality on its face of a New York criminal obscenity statute which prohibits the sale to minors under 17 years of age of material defined to be obscene on the basis of its appeal to them whether or not it would be obscene to adults.

Appellant and his wife operate "Sam's Stationery and Luncheonette" in Bellmore, Long Island. They have a lunch counter, and, among other things, also sell magazines including some so-called "girlie" magazines. Appellant was prosecuted under two informations, each in two counts, which charged that he personally sold a 16-year-old boy two "girlie" magazines on each of two dates in October 1965, in violation of 484-h of the New York Penal Law. He was tried before a judge without a jury in Nassau County District Court and was found guilty on both counts. The judge found (1) that the magazines contained pictures which depicted female "nudity" in a manner defined in subsection 1 (b), that is "the showing of . . . female . . . buttocks with less than a full opaque covering, or the showing of the female breast with less than a fully opaque covering of any portion thereof below the top of the nipple . . . ," and (2) that the pictures were "harmful to minors" in that they had, within the meaning of subsection 1 (f) "that quality of . . . representation . . . of nudity . . . [which] . . . (i) predominantly appeals to the prurient, shameful or morbid interest of minors, and (ii) is patently offensive to prevailing standards in the adult community as a whole with respect to what is suitable material for minors, and (iii) is utterly without redeeming social importance for minors." He held that both sales to the 16-year-old boy therefore constituted the violation under 484-h of "knowingly to sell . . . to a minor" under 17 of "(a) any picture . . . which depicts nudity . . . and which is harmful to minors," and "(b) any . . . magazine . . . which contains . . . [such pictures] . . . and which, taken as a whole, is harmful to minors." The conviction was affirmed without opinion by the Appellate Term, Second Department, of the Supreme Court. Appellant was denied leave to appeal to the New York Court of Appeals and then appealed to this Court. We noted probable jurisdiction. We affirm.

The "girlie" picture magazines involved in the sales here are not obscene for adults. But 484-h does not bar the appellant from stocking the magazines and selling them to persons 17 years of age or older, and therefore the conviction is not invalid under our decision in *Butler v. Michigan.*

Obscenity is not within the area of protected speech or press. The three-pronged test of subsection 1 (f) for judging the obscenity of material sold to minors under 17 is a variable from the formulation for determining obscenity under *Roth* stated in the plurality opinion in *Memoirs v. Massachusetts.* Appellant's primary attack upon 484-h is leveled at the power of the State to adapt this *Memoirs* formulation to define the material's obscenity on the basis of its appeal to minors, and thus exclude material so defined from the area of protected expression. He makes no argument that the magazines are not "harmful to minors" within the definition in subsection 1 (f). Thus "[n]o issue is presented . . . concerning the obscenity of the material involved."

. . . We have no occasion in this case to consider the impact of the guarantees of freedom of expression upon the totality of the relationship of the minor and the State. It is enough for the purposes of this case that we inquire whether it was constitutionally impermissible for New York to accord minors under 17 a more restricted right than that assured to adults to judge and determine for themselves what sex material they may read or see. We conclude that we cannot say that the statute invades the area of freedom of expression constitutionally secured to minors. . . .

The well-being of its children is of course a subject within the State's constitutional power to regulate, and, in our view, two interests justify the limitations in 484-h upon the availability of sex material to minors under 17, at least if it was rational for the legislature to find that the minors' exposure to such material might be harmful. First of all, constitutional interpretation has consistently recognized that the parents' claim to authority in their own household to direct the rearing of their children is basic in the structure of our society. . . . The legislature could properly conclude that parents and others, teachers for example, who have this primary responsibility for children's well-being are entitled to the support of laws designed to aid discharge of that responsibility. Indeed, subsection 1 (f) (ii) of 484-h expressly recognizes the parental role in assessing sex-related material harmful to minors according "to prevailing standards in the adult community as a whole with respect to what is suitable material for minors." Moreover, the prohibition against sales to minors does not bar parents who so desire from purchasing the magazines for their children. . . .

Section 484-e of the law states a legislative finding that the material condemned by 484-h is "a basic factor in impairing the ethical and moral development of our youth and a clear and present danger to the people of the state." It is very doubtful that this finding expresses an accepted scientific fact. But obscenity is not protected expression and may be suppressed without a showing of the circumstances which lie behind the phrase "clear and present danger" in its application to protected speech. To sustain state power to exclude material defined as obscenity by 484-h requires only that we be able to say that it was not irrational for the legislature to find that exposure to material condemned by the statute is harmful to minors. . . . But the growing consensus of commentators is that "while these studies all agree that a causal link has not been demonstrated, they are equally agreed that a causal link has not been disproved either." We do not demand of legislatures "scientifically certain criteria of legislation." We therefore cannot say that 484-h, in defining the obscenity of material on the basis of its appeal to minors under 17, has no rational relation to the objective of safeguarding such minors from harm. . . .

Affirmed.

MR. JUSTICE STEWART, concurring in the result.

A doctrinaire, knee-jerk application of the First Amendment would, of course, dictate the nullification of this New York statute. But that result is not required, I think, if we bear in mind what it is that the First Amendment protects.

The First Amendment guarantees liberty of human expression in order to preserve in our Nation what Mr. Justice Holmes called a "free trade in ideas." To that end, the Constitution protects more than just a man's freedom to say or write or publish what he wants. It secures as well the liberty of each man to decide for himself what he will read and to what he will listen. The Constitution guarantees, in short, a society of free choice. Such a society presupposes the capacity of its members to choose. . . .

I think a State may permissibly determine that, at least in some precisely delineated areas, a child—like someone in a captive audience—is not possessed of that full capacity for individual choice which is the presupposition of First Amendment guarantees. It is only upon such a premise, I should suppose, that a State may deprive children of other rights—the right to marry, for example, or the right to vote—deprivations that would be constitutionally intolerable for adults.

I cannot hold that this state law, on its face, violates the First and Fourteenth Amendments.

MR. JUSTICE DOUGLAS, with whom MR. JUSTICE BLACK concurs, dissenting.

. . . [T]here is a view held by many that the so-called "obscene" book or tract or magazine has a deleterious effect upon the young, although I seriously doubt the wisdom of trying by law to put the fresh, evanescent, natural blossoming of sex in the category of "sin."

That, however, was the view of our preceptor in this field, Anthony Comstock, who waged his war against "obscenity" from the year 1872 until his death in 1915. . . .

It was Comstock who was responsible for the Federal Anti-Obscenity Act of March 3, 1873. It was he who was also responsible for the New York Act which soon followed. He was responsible for the organization of the New York Society for the Suppression of Vice, which by its act of incorporation was granted one half of the fines levied on people successfully prosecuted by the Society or its agents.

The problem under the First Amendment, however, has always seemed to me to be quite different. For its mandate (originally applicable only to the Federal Government but now applicable to the States as well by reason of the Fourteenth Amendment) is directed to any law "abridging the freedom of speech, or of the press." I appreciate that there are those who think that "obscenity" is impliedly excluded; but I have indicated on prior occasions why I have been unable to reach that conclusion. And the corollary of that view is that Big Brother can no more say what a person shall listen to or read than he can say what shall be published.

This is not to say that the Court and Anthony Comstock are wrong in concluding that the kind of literature New York condemns does harm. As a matter of fact, the notion of censorship is founded on the belief that speech and press sometimes do harm and therefore can be regulated. I once visited a foreign nation where the regime of censorship was so strict that all I could find in the bookstalls were tracts on religion and tracts on mathematics. . . . If rationality is the measure of the validity of this law, then I can see how modern Anthony Comstocks could make out a case for "protecting" many groups in our society, not merely children.

While I find the literature and movies which come to us for clearance exceedingly dull and boring, I understand how some can and do become very excited and alarmed and think that something should be done to stop the flow. It is one thing for parents and the religious organizations to be active and involved. It is quite a different matter for the state to become implicated as a censor. As I read the First Amendment, it was designed to keep the state and the hands of all state officials off the printing presses of America and off the distribution systems for all printed literature. Anthony Comstock wanted it the other way; he indeed put the police and prosecutor in the middle of this publishing business.

I think it would require a constitutional amendment to achieve that result. If there were a constitutional amendment, perhaps the people of the country would come up with some national board of censorship. Censors are, of course, propelled by their own neuroses. That is why a universally accepted definition of obscenity is impossible. Any definition is indeed highly subjective, turning on the neurosis of the censor. Those who have a deep-seated, subconscious conflict may well become either great crusaders against a particular kind of literature or avid customers of it. That, of course, is the danger of letting any group of citizens be the judges of what other people, young or old, should read. . . .

Today this Court sits as the Nation's board of censors. With all respect, I do not know of any group in the country less qualified first, to know what obscenity is when they see it, and second, to have any considered judgment as to what the deleterious or beneficial impact of a particular publication may be on minds either young or old.

I would await a constitutional amendment that authorized the modern Anthony Comstocks to censor literature before publishers, authors, or distributors can be fined or jailed for what they print or sell.

MR. JUSTICE FORTAS, dissenting.

. . . The Court avoids facing the problem whether the magazines in the present case are "obscene" when viewed by a 16-year-old boy, although not "obscene" when viewed by someone 17 years of age or older. It says that Ginsberg's lawyer did not choose to challenge the conviction on the ground that the magazines are not "obscene." He chose only to attack the statute on its face. Therefore, the Court reasons, we need not look at the magazines and determine whether they may be excluded from the ambit of the First Amendment as "obscene" for purposes of this case. But this Court has made strong and comprehensive statements about its duty in First Amendment cases—statements with which I agree. . . .

The Court certainly cannot mean that the States and cities and counties and villages have unlimited power to withhold anything and everything that is written or pictorial from younger people. But it here justifies the conviction of Sam Ginsberg because the impact of the Constitution, it says, is variable, and what is not obscene for an adult may be obscene for a child. This it calls "variable obscenity." I do not disagree with this, but I insist that to assess the principle—certainly to apply it—the Court must define it. We must know the extent to which literature or pictures may be less offensive than *Roth* requires in order to be "obscene" for purposes of a statute confined to youth.

I agree that the State in the exercise of its police power—even in the First Amendment domain—may make proper and careful differentiation between adults and children. But I do not agree that this power may be used on an arbitrary, free-wheeling basis. This is not a case where, on any standard enunciated by the Court, the magazines are obscene, nor one where the seller is at fault. Petitioner is being prosecuted for the sale of magazines which he had a right under the decisions of this Court to offer for sale, and he is being prosecuted without proof of "fault"—without even a claim that he deliberately, calculatedly sought to induce children to buy "obscene" material. Bookselling should not be a hazardous profession.

The conviction of Ginsberg on the present facts is a serious invasion of freedom. To sustain the conviction without inquiry as to whether the material is "obscene" and without any evidence of pushing or pandering, in face of this Court's asserted solicitude for First Amendment values, is to give the State a role in the rearing of children which is contrary to our traditions and to our conception of family responsibility. It begs the question to present this undefined, unlimited censorship as an aid to parents in the rearing of their children. This decision does not merely protect children from activities which all sensible parents would condemn. Rather, its undefined and unlimited approval of state censorship in this area denies to children free access to books and works of art to which many parents may wish their children to have uninhibited access. For denial of access to these magazines, without any standard or definition of their allegedly distinguishing characteristics, is also denial of access to great works of art and literature.

If this statute were confined to the punishment of pushers or panderers of vulgar literature I would not be so concerned by the Court's failure to circumscribe state power by defining its limits in terms of the meaning of "obscenity" in this field. The State's police power may, within very broad limits, protect the parents and their children from public aggression of panderers and pushers. This is defensible on the theory that they cannot protect themselves from such assaults. But it does not follow that the State may convict a passive luncheonette operator of a crime because a 16-year-old boy maliciously and designedly picks up and pays for two girlie magazines which are presumably not obscene.

I would therefore reverse the conviction.

Stanley v. Georgia (1969)

This litigation confronted the U.S. Supreme Court with the issue of whether the mere possession of obscene materials was a crime. The justices decided that it was not. This decision was the first time the Supreme Court had made such a sweeping statement, and it reflects just how far the support for strict restrictions on obscenity had been eroded. The excerpt below reflects the justices' thinking about a broad right to privacy for adults to view or read whatever they choose in the privacy of their homes. This case is unusual in obscenity jurisprudence in that the justices were unanimous in their decision.

MR. JUSTICE MARSHALL delivered the opinion of the Court.

An investigation of appellant's alleged bookmaking activities led to the issuance of a search warrant for appellant's home. Under authority of this warrant, federal and state agents secured entrance. They found very little evidence of bookmaking activity, but while looking through a desk drawer in an upstairs bedroom, one of the federal agents, accompanied by a state officer, found three reels of eight-millimeter film. Using a projector and screen found in an upstairs living room, they viewed the films. The state officer concluded that they were obscene and seized them. Since a further examination of the bedroom indicated that appellant occupied it, he was charged with possession of obscene matter and placed under arrest. He was later indicted for "knowingly hav[ing] possession of . . . obscene matter" in violation of Georgia law. Appellant was tried before a jury and convicted. The Supreme Court of Georgia affirmed. We noted probable jurisdiction of an appeal.

Appellant raises several challenges to the validity of his conviction. We find it necessary to consider only one. Appellant argues here that the Georgia obscenity statute, insofar as it punishes mere private possession of obscene matter, violates the First Amendment, as made applicable to the States by the Fourteenth Amendment. For reasons set forth below, we agree that the mere private possession of obscene matter cannot constitutionally be made a crime.

. . . The State and appellant both agree that the question here before us is whether "a statute imposing criminal sanctions upon the mere [knowing] possession of obscene matter" is constitutional. In this context, Georgia concedes that the present case appears to be one of "first impression . . . on this exact point," but contends that since "obscenity is not within the area of constitutionally protected speech or press," the States are free, subject to the limits of other provisions of the Constitution to deal with it any way deemed necessary, just as they may deal with possession of other things thought to be detrimental to the welfare of their citizens. If the State can protect the body of a citizen, may it not, argues Georgia, protect his mind?

... It is now well established that the Constitution protects the right to receive information and ideas. "This freedom [of speech and press] ... necessarily protects the right to receive...." This right to receive information and ideas, regardless of their social worth is fundamental to our free society. Moreover, in the context of this case—a prosecution for mere possession of printed or filmed matter in the privacy of a person's own home—that right takes on an added dimension. For also fundamental is the right to be free, except in very limited circumstances, from unwanted governmental intrusions into one's privacy....

These are the rights that appellant is asserting in the case before us. He is asserting the right to read or observe what he pleases—the right to satisfy his intellectual and emotional needs in the privacy of his own home. He is asserting the right to be free from state inquiry into the contents of his library. Georgia contends that appellant does not have these rights, that there are certain types of materials that the individual may not read or even possess. Georgia justifies this assertion by arguing that the films in the present case are obscene. But we think that mere categorization of these films as "obscene" is insufficient justification for such a drastic invasion of personal liberties guaranteed by the First and Fourteenth Amendments. Whatever may be the justifications for other statutes regulating obscenity, we do not think they reach into the privacy of one's own home. If the First Amendment means anything, it means that a State has no business telling a man, sitting alone in his own house, what books he may read or what films he may watch. Our whole constitutional heritage rebels at the thought of giving government the power to control men's minds.

And yet, in the face of these traditional notions of individual liberty, Georgia asserts the right to protect the individual's mind from the effects of obscenity. We are not certain that this argument amounts to anything more than the assertion that the State has the right to control the moral content of a person's thoughts. To some, this may be a noble purpose, but it is wholly inconsistent with the philosophy of the First Amendment....

Perhaps recognizing this, Georgia asserts that exposure to obscene materials may lead to deviant sexual behavior or crimes of sexual violence. There appears to be little empirical basis for that assertion. But more important, if the State is only concerned about printed or filmed materials inducing antisocial conduct, we believe that in the context of private consumption of ideas and information we should adhere to the view that "[a]mong free men, the deterrents ordinarily to be applied to prevent crime are education and punishment for violations of the law. . . ." Given the present state of knowledge, the State may no more prohibit mere possession of obscene matter on the ground that it may lead to antisocial conduct than it may prohibit possession of chemistry books on the ground that they may lead to the manufacture of home-made spirits. . . .

We hold that the First and Fourteenth Amendments prohibit making mere private possession of obscene material a crime. *Roth* and the cases following that decision are not impaired by today's holding. As we have said, the States retain broad power to regulate obscenity; that power simply does not extend to mere possession by the individual in the privacy of his own home. Accordingly, the judgment of the court below is reversed and the case is remanded for proceedings not inconsistent with this opinion.

It is so ordered.

United States v. Reidel (1971)

Not long after the Stanley v. Georgia *(1969) decision, came a case that challenged Congress's power to regulate the distribution of obscene materials through the mails. If according to* Stanley *it was not a crime to possess such materials, then did Congress still have the power to limit or prohibit their distribution to people who claimed to be 21 years old or older? Justice White upheld the power of Congress to control the mails and thereby control the distribution of obscenity, but he and most of the rest of the justices had begun to tire of the obscenity issue and its seemingly endless permutations.*

MR. JUSTICE WHITE delivered the opinion of the Court.

Section 1461 of Title 18, U.S.C., prohibits the knowing use of the mails for the delivery of obscene matter. The issue presented by the jurisdictional statement in this case is whether 1461 is constitutional as applied to the distribution of obscene materials to willing recipients who state that they are adults. The District Court held that it was not. We disagree and reverse the judgment.

On April 15, 1970, the appellee, Norman Reidel, was indicted on three counts, each count charging him with having mailed a single copy of an illustrated booklet entitled *The True Facts About Imported Pornography.* One of the copies had been mailed to a postal inspector stipulated to be over the age of 21, who had responded to a newspaper advertisement. The other two copies had been seized during a search of appellee's business premises; both of them had been deposited in the mail by Reidel but had been returned to him in their original mailing envelopes bearing the mark "undelivered." As to these two booklets, the Government conceded that it had no evidence as to the identity or age of the addressees or as to their willingness to receive the booklets. Nor does the record indicate why the booklets were returned undelivered.

Reidel moved in the District Court before trial to dismiss the indictment, contending, among other things, that 1461 was unconstitutional. Assuming for the purpose of the motion that the booklets were obscene, the trial judge granted the motion to dismiss on the ground that Reidel had made a constitutionally protected delivery and hence that 1461 was unconstitutional as applied to him. The Government's direct appeal is here under 18 U.S.C. 3731.

In *Roth v. United States* (1957), Roth was convicted under 1461 for mailing obscene circulars and advertising. The Court affirmed the conviction, holding that "obscenity is not within the area of constitutionally protected speech or press," and that 1461, "applied according to the proper standard for judging obscenity, do[es] not offend constitutional safeguards against convictions based upon protected material, or fail to give men in acting adequate notice of what is prohibited." *Roth* has not been overruled. . . .

Stanley v. Georgia (1969) compels no different result. There, pornographic films were found in Stanley's home and he was convicted under Georgia statutes for possessing obscene material. This Court reversed the conviction, holding that the mere private possession of obscene matter cannot constitutionally be made a crime. But it neither overruled nor disturbed the holding in *Roth*. Indeed, in the Court's view, the constitutionality of proscribing private possession of obscenity was a matter of first impression in this Court, a question neither involved nor decided in *Roth*. . . . Clearly the Court had no thought of questioning the validity of 1461 as applied to those who, like Reidel, are routinely disseminating obscenity through the mails and who have no claim, and could make none, about unwanted governmental intrusions into the privacy of their home. The Court considered this sufficiently clear to warrant summary affirmance of the judgment of the United States District Court for the Northern District of Georgia rejecting claims that under *Stanley v. Georgia,* Georgia's obscenity statute could not be applied to booksellers. . . .

The right Stanley asserted was "the right to read or observe what he pleases—the right to satisfy his intellectual and emotional needs in the privacy of his own home." The Court's response was that "a State has no business telling a man, sitting alone in his own house, what books he may read or what films he may watch. Our whole constitutional heritage rebels at the thought of giving government the power to control men's minds." The focus of this language was on freedom of mind and thought and on the privacy of one's home. It does not require that we fashion or recognize a constitutional right in people like Reidel to distribute or sell obscene materials. The personal constitutional rights of those like Stanley to possess and read obscenity in their homes and their freedom of mind and thought do not depend on whether the materials are obscene or whether obscenity is constitutionally protected. Their rights to have and view that material in private are independently saved by the Constitution.

Reidel is in a wholly different position. He has no complaints about governmental violations of his private thoughts or fantasies, but stands squarely on a claimed First Amendment right to do business in obscenity and use the mails in the process. But *Roth* has squarely placed obscenity and its distribution outside the reach of the First Amendment and they remain there today. *Stanley* did not overrule *Roth* and we decline to do so now. . . .

It is urged that there is developing sentiment that adults should have complete freedom to produce, deal in, possess, and consume whatever communicative materials may appeal to them and that the law's involvement with obscenity should be limited to those situations where children are involved or where it is necessary to prevent imposition on unwilling recipients of whatever age. The concepts involved are said to be so elusive and the laws so inherently unenforceable without extravagant expenditures of time and effort by enforcement officers and the courts that basic reassessment is not only wise but essential. This may prove to be the desirable and eventual legislative course. But if it is, the task of restructuring the obscenity laws lies with those who pass, repeal, and amend statutes and ordinances. *Roth* and like cases pose no obstacle to such developments.

The judgment of the District Court is reversed.

United States v. Thirty-Seven Photographs (1971)

Another offspring from the decision in Stanley v. Georgia *(1969), this case posed the following question to the justices of the Supreme Court: If it is no longer a crime to possess obscene materials, then may they be brought into the country in a traveler's luggage, presumably for that person's private use? The justices decided that* Stanley *had not altered Congress's power to prevent the importation of obscene materials into the country; but not all of them were comfortable with the assumptions on which this decision was based. The excerpt from Justice Stewart's opinion shows that he did not agree with the assumption about the defendant's intentions and that he therefore perceived a contradiction between the decision in this case and the decision in* Stanley.

MR. JUSTICE WHITE delivered the opinion of the Court.

When Milton Luros returned to the United States from Europe on October 24, 1969, he brought with him in his luggage the 37 photographs here involved. United States customs agents, acting pursuant to 305 of the Tariff Act of 1930, as amended, 46 Stat. 688, 19 U.S.C. 1305 (a) seized the photographs as obscene. They referred the matter to the United States Attorney, who on November 6 instituted proceedings in the United States District Court for forfeiture of the material. Luros, as claimant, answered, denying the photographs were obscene and setting up a counterclaim alleging the unconstitutionality of 1305 (a) on its face and as applied to him. . . . Hearing was held as scheduled on January 9, and on January 27 the three-judge court filed its judgment and opinion declaring 1305 (a) unconstitutional and enjoining its enforcement against the 37 photographs, which were ordered returned to Luros. . . . [White then reviewed the relevant case law and statutes.]

. . . On the authority of *Stanley,* Luros urged the trial court to construe the First Amendment as forbidding any restraints on obscenity except where necessary to protect children or where it intruded itself upon the sensitivity or privacy of an unwilling adult. Without rejecting this position, the trial court read *Stanley* as protecting, at the very least, the right to read obscene material in the privacy of one's own home and to receive it for that purpose. It therefore held that 1305 (a), which bars the importation of obscenity for private use as well as for commercial distribution, is overbroad and hence unconstitutional.

The trial court erred in reading *Stanley* as immunizing from seizure obscene materials possessed at a port of entry for the purpose of importation for private use. In *United States v. Reidel,* we have today held that Congress may constitutionally prevent the mails from being used for distributing pornography. In this case, neither Luros nor his putative buyers have rights that are infringed by the exclusion of obscenity from incoming foreign commerce. By the same token, obscene materials may be removed from the channels of commerce when discovered in the luggage of a returning foreign traveler even though intended solely for his private use. That the private user under *Stanley* may not be prosecuted for possession of obscenity in his home does not mean that he is entitled to import it from abroad free from the power of Congress to exclude noxious articles from commerce. *Stanley*'s emphasis was on the freedom of thought and mind in the privacy of the home. But a port of entry is not a traveler's home. His right to be let alone neither prevents the search of his luggage nor the seizure of unprotected, but illegal, materials when his possession of them is discovered during such a search. Customs officers characteristically inspect luggage and their power to do so is not questioned in this case; it is an old practice and is intimately associated with excluding illegal articles from the country. Whatever the scope of the right to receive obscenity adumbrated in *Stanley,* that right, as we said in *Reidel,* does not extend to one who is seeking, as was Luros here, to distribute obscene materials to the public, nor does it extend to one seeking to import obscene materials from abroad, whether for private use or public distribution. As we held in *Roth v. United States* and reiterated today in *Reidel,* obscenity is not within the scope of First Amendment protection. Hence Congress may declare it contraband and prohibit its importation, as it has elected in 1305 (a) to do.

The judgment of the District Court is reversed and the case is remanded for further proceedings consistent with this opinion.

It is so ordered.

MR. JUSTICE STEWART, concurring.

I agree that the First Amendment does not prevent the border seizure of obscene materials sought to be imported for commercial dissemination. . . .

But I would not in this case decide, even by way of dicta, that the Government may lawfully seize literary material intended for the purely private use of the importer. The terms of the statute appear to apply to an American tourist who, after exercising his constitutionally protected liberty to travel abroad, returns home with a single book in his luggage, with no intention of selling it or otherwise using it, except to read it. If the Government can constitutionally take the book away from him as he passes through customs, then I do not understand the meaning of *Stanley v. Georgia*. . . .

Miller v. California (1973)

With the resignation of Chief Justice Earl Warren and the appointment of Warren Burger as chief justice in 1969, the trend in Supreme Court decisions on obscenity changed. In Miller v. California, *the Court abandoned Brennan's goal of establishing a national standard of obscenity and instead sought to bring localities and states back into decisionmaking. Its new, tripartite standard brought clarity to the obscenity issue; but like any definition, it also brought its share of controversy and confusion.*

MR. CHIEF JUSTICE BURGER delivered the opinion of the Court.

This is one of a group of "obscenity-pornography" cases being reviewed by the Court in a re-examination of standards enunciated in earlier cases involving what Mr. Justice Harlan called "the intractable obscenity problem."

Appellant conducted a mass mailing campaign to advertise the sale of illustrated books, euphemistically called "adult" material. After a jury trial, he was convicted of violating California Penal Code 311.2 (a), a misdemeanor, by knowingly distributing obscene matter and the Appellate Department, Superior Court of California, County of Orange, summarily affirmed the judgment without opinion. Appellant's conviction was specifically based on his conduct in causing five unsolicited advertising brochures to be sent through the mail in an envelope addressed to a restaurant in Newport Beach, California. The envelope was opened by the manager of the restaurant and his mother. They had not requested the brochures; they complained to the police. . . .

This case involves the application of a State's criminal obscenity statute to a situation in which sexually explicit materials have been thrust by aggressive sales action upon unwilling recipients who had in no way indicated any desire to receive such materials. This Court has recognized that the States have a legitimate interest in prohibiting dissemination or exhibition of obscene material when the mode of dissemination carries with it a significant danger of offending the sensibilities of unwilling recipients or of exposure to juveniles. It is in this context that we are called on to define the standards which must be used to identify obscene material that a State may regulate without infringing on the First Amendment as applicable to the States through the Fourteenth Amendment. . . .

The case we now review was tried on the theory that the California Penal Code 311 approximately incorporates the three-stage *Memoirs* test. But now the *Memoirs* test has been abandoned as unworkable by its author and no Member of the Court today supports the *Memoirs* formulation.

This much has been categorically settled by the Court, that obscene material is unprotected by the First Amendment. We acknowledge, however, the inherent dangers of undertaking to regulate any form of expression. State statutes designed to regulate obscene materials must be carefully limited. As a result, we now confine the permissible scope of such regulation to works which depict or describe sexual conduct. That conduct must be specifically defined by the applicable state law, as written or authoritatively construed. A state offense must also be limited to works which, taken as a whole, appeal to the prurient interest in sex, which portray sexual conduct in a patently offensive way, and which, taken as a whole, do not have serious literary, artistic, political, or scientific value.

The basic guidelines for the trier of fact must be: (a) whether "the average person, applying contemporary community standards" would find that the work, taken as a whole, appeals to the prurient interest; (b) whether the work depicts or describes, in a patently offensive way, sexual conduct specifically defined by the applicable state law; and (c) whether the work, taken as a whole, lacks serious literary, artistic, political, or scientific value. We do not adopt as a constitutional standard the "utterly without redeeming social value" test of *Memoirs v. Massachusetts;* that concept has never commanded the adherence of more than three Justices at one time. If a state law that regulates obscene material is thus limited, as written or construed, the First Amendment values applicable to the States through the Fourteenth Amendment are adequately protected by the ultimate power of appellate courts to conduct an independent review of constitutional claims when necessary. We emphasize that it is not our function to propose regulatory schemes for the States. That must await their concrete legislative efforts. It is possible, however, to give a few plain examples of what a state statute could define for regulation under part (b) of the standard announced in this opinion:

(a) Patently offensive representations or descriptions of ultimate sexual acts, normal or perverted, actual or simulated.

(b) Patently offensive representations or descriptions of masturbation, excretory functions, and lewd exhibition of the genitals.

Sex and nudity may not be exploited without limit by films or pictures exhibited or sold in places of public accommodation any more than live sex and nudity can be exhibited or sold without limit in such public places. At a minimum, prurient, patently offensive depiction or description of sexual conduct must have serious literary, artistic, political, or scientific value to merit First Amendment protection. For example, medical books for the education of physicians and related personnel necessarily use graphic illustrations and descriptions of human anatomy. In resolving the inevitably sensitive questions of fact and law, we must continue to rely on the jury system, accompanied by the safeguards that judges, rules of evidence, presumption of innocence, and other protective features provide, as we do with rape, murder, and a host of other offenses against society and its individual members. . . .

Under the holdings announced today, no one will be subject to prosecution for the sale or exposure of obscene materials unless these materials depict or describe patently offensive "hard core" sexual conduct specifically defined by the regulating state law, as written or construed. We are satisfied that these specific prerequisites will provide fair notice to a dealer in such materials that his public and commercial activities may bring prosecution. If the inability to define regulated materials with ultimate, god-like precision altogether removes the power of the States or the Congress to regulate, then "hard core" pornography may be exposed without limit to the juvenile, the passerby, and the consenting adult alike, as, indeed, MR. JUSTICE DOUGLAS contends. . . .

It is certainly true that the absence, since *Roth,* of a single majority view of this Court as to proper standards for testing obscenity has placed a strain on both state and federal courts. But today, for the first time since *Roth* was decided in 1957, a majority of this Court has agreed on concrete guidelines to isolate "hard core" pornography from expression protected by the First Amendment. Now we may abandon the casual practice of *Redrup v. New York* (1967), and attempt to provide positive guidance to federal and state courts alike.

This may not be an easy road, free from difficulty. But no amount of "fatigue" should lead us to adopt a convenient "institutional" rationale—an absolutist, "anything goes" view of the First Amendment—because it will lighten our burdens. "Such an abnegation of judicial supervision in this field would be inconsistent with our duty to uphold the constitutional guarantees." Nor should we remedy "tension between state and federal courts" by arbitrarily depriving the States of a power reserved to them under the Constitution, a power which they have enjoyed and exercised continuously from before the adoption of the First Amendment to this day. "Our duty admits of no 'substitute for facing up to the tough individual problems of constitutional judgment involved in every obscenity case.'"

Under a National Constitution, fundamental First Amendment limitations on the powers of the States do not vary from community to community, but this does not mean that there are, or should or can be, fixed, uniform national standards of precisely what appeals to the "prurient interest" or is "patently offensive." These are essentially questions of fact, and our Nation is simply too big and too diverse for this Court to reasonably expect that such standards could be articulated for all 50 States in a single formulation, even assuming the prerequisite consensus exists. When triers of fact are asked to decide whether "the average person, applying contemporary community standards" would consider certain materials "prurient," it would be unrealistic to require that the answer be based on some abstract formulation. The adversary system, with lay jurors as the usual ultimate factfinders in criminal prosecutions, has historically permitted triers of fact to draw on the standards of their community, guided always by limiting instructions on the law. To require a State to structure obscenity proceedings around evidence of a national "community standard" would be an exercise in futility.

As noted before, this case was tried on the theory that the California obscenity statute sought to incorporate the tripartite test of *Memoirs*. This, a "national" standard of First Amendment protection enumerated by a plurality of this Court, was correctly regarded at the time of trial as limiting state prosecution under the controlling case law. The jury, however, was explicitly instructed that, in determining whether the "dominant theme of the material as a whole . . . appeals to the prurient interest" and in determining whether the material "goes substantially beyond customary limits of candor and affronts contemporary community standards of decency," it was to apply "contemporary community standards of the State of California."

. . . We conclude that neither the State's alleged failure to offer evidence of "national standards," nor the trial court's charge that the jury consider state community standards, were constitutional errors. Nothing in the First Amendment requires that a jury must consider hypothetical and unascertainable "national standards" when attempting to determine whether certain materials are obscene as a matter of fact. . . .

It is neither realistic nor constitutionally sound to read the First Amendment as requiring that the people of Maine or Mississippi accept public depiction of conduct found tolerable in Las Vegas, or New York City. People in different States vary in their tastes and attitudes, and this diversity is not to be strangled by the absolutism of imposed uniformity. . . .

[T]he primary concern with requiring a jury to apply the standard of "the average person, applying contemporary community standards" is to be certain that, so far as material is not aimed at a deviant group, it will be judged by its impact on an average person, rather than a particularly susceptible or sensitive person—or indeed a totally insensitive one. We hold that the requirement that the jury evaluate the materials with reference to "contemporary standards of the State of California" serves this protective purpose and is constitutionally adequate.

The dissenting Justices sound the alarm of repression. But, in our view, to equate the free and robust exchange of ideas and political debate with commercial exploitation of obscene material demeans the grand conception of the First Amendment and its high purposes in the historic struggle for freedom. It is a "misuse of the great guarantees of free speech and free press. . . ." The First Amendment protects works which, taken as a whole, have serious literary, artistic, political, or scientific value, regardless of whether the government or a majority of the people approve of the ideas these works represent. "The protection given speech and press was fashioned to assure unfettered interchange of ideas for the bringing about of political and social changes desired by the people." But the public portrayal of hard-core sexual conduct for its own sake, and for the ensuing commercial gain, is a different matter.

There is no evidence, empirical or historical, that the stern 19th century American censorship of public distribution and display of material relating to sex, in any way limited or affected expression of serious literary, artistic, political, or scientific ideas. On the contrary, it is beyond any question that the era following Thomas Jefferson to Theodore Roosevelt was an "extraordinarily vigorous period," not just in economics and politics, but in belles lettres and in "the outlying fields of social and political philosophies." We do not see the harsh hand of censorship of ideas—good or bad, sound or unsound—and "repression" of political liberty lurking in every state regulation of commercial exploitation of human interest in sex.

MR. JUSTICE BRENNAN finds "it is hard to see how state-ordered regimentation of our minds can ever be forestalled. These doleful anticipations assume that courts cannot distinguish commerce in ideas, protected by the First Amendment, from commercial exploitation of obscene material. Moreover, state regulation of hard-core pornography so as to make it unavailable to nonadults, a regulation which MR. JUSTICE BRENNAN finds constitutionally permissible, has all the elements of "censorship" for adults; indeed even more rigid enforcement techniques may be called for with such dichotomy of regulation. One can concede that the "sexual revolution" of recent years may have had useful byproducts in striking layers of prudery from a subject long irrationally kept from needed ventilation. But it does not follow that no regulation of patently offensive "hard core" materials is needed or permissible; civilized people do not allow unregulated access to heroin because it is a derivative of medicinal morphine.

In sum, we (a) reaffirm the *Roth* holding that obscene material is not protected by the First Amendment; (b) hold that such material can be regulated by the States, subject to the specific safeguards enunciated above, without a showing that the material is "utterly without redeeming social value"; and (c) hold that obscenity is to be determined by applying "contemporary community standards." The judgment of the Appellate Department of the Superior Court, Orange County, California, is vacated and the case remanded to that court for further proceedings not inconsistent with the First Amendment standards established by this opinion.

Vacated and remanded.

MR. JUSTICE DOUGLAS, dissenting.

Today we leave open the way for California to send a man to prison for distributing brochures that advertise books and a movie under freshly written standards defining obscenity which until today's decision were never the part of any law.

The Court has worked hard to define obscenity and concededly has failed. [Douglas reviewed the relevant case law of obscenity.]

. . . Obscenity—which even we cannot define with precision—is a hodge-podge. To send men to jail for violating standards they cannot understand, construe, and apply is a monstrous thing to do in a Nation dedicated to fair trials and due process. . . .

The idea that the First Amendment permits government to ban publications that are "offensive" to some people puts an ominous gloss on freedom of the press. That test would make it possible to ban any paper or any journal or magazine in some benighted place. The First Amendment was designed "to invite dispute," to induce "a condition of unrest," to "create dissatisfaction with conditions as they are," and even to stir "people to anger." The idea that the First Amendment permits punishment for ideas that are "offensive" to the particular judge or jury sitting in judgment is astounding. No greater leveler of speech or literature has ever been designed. To give the power to the censor, as we do today, is to make a sharp and radical break with the traditions of a free society. The First Amendment was not fashioned as a vehicle for dispensing tranquilizers to the people. Its prime function was to keep debate open to "offensive" as well as to "staid" people. The tendency throughout history has been to subdue the individual and to exalt the power of government. The use of the standard "offensive" gives authority to government that cuts the very vitals out of the First Amendment. As is intimated by the Court's opinion, the materials before us may be garbage. But so is much of what is said in political campaigns, in the daily press, on TV, or over the radio. By reason of the First Amendment—and solely because of it—speakers and publishers have not been threatened or subdued because their thoughts and ideas may be "offensive" to some. . . .

We deal with highly emotional, not rational, questions. To many the Song of Solomon is obscene. I do not think we, the judges, were ever given the constitutional power to make definitions of obscenity. If it is to be defined, let the people debate and decide by a constitutional amendment what they want to ban as obscene and what standards they want the legislatures and the courts to apply. Perhaps the people will decide that the path towards a mature, integrated society requires that all ideas competing for acceptance must have no censor.

Perhaps they will decide otherwise. Whatever the choice, the courts will have some guidelines. Now we have none except our own predilections.

Paris Adult Theatre I v. Slaton (1973)

Handed down the same day as Miller v. California, *the Supreme Court's decision in this case applied the three criteria established in* Miller *for defining obscenity. The case involved an "adult" theater that showed allegedly obscene films to adults. The theater owners argued that because they prohibited minors from seeing the films, their business was protected by the* Stanley v. Georgia *(1969) decision. This decision clarified the issue of whether the states could adopt guidelines for the control of obscenity in addition to the guidelines established by the Supreme Court. Justices Douglas and Brennan dissented, and continued to oppose the change in doctrinal direction.*

MR. CHIEF JUSTICE BURGER delivered the opinion of the Court.

Petitioners are two Atlanta, Georgia, movie theaters and their owners and managers, operating in the style of "adult" theaters. On December 28, 1970, respondents, the local state district attorney and the solicitor for the local state trial court, filed civil complaints in that court alleging that petitioners were exhibiting to the public for paid admission two allegedly obscene films, contrary to Georgia Code Ann. 26–2101. The two films in question, "Magic Mirror" and "It All Comes Out in the End," depict sexual conduct characterized by the Georgia Supreme Court as "hard core pornography" leaving "little to the imagination."

. . . On January 13, 1971, 15 days after the proceedings began, the films were produced by petitioners at a jury-waived trial. Certain photographs, also produced at trial, were stipulated to portray the single entrance to both Paris Adult Theatre I and Paris Adult Theatre II as it appeared at the time of the complaints. These photographs show a conventional, inoffensive theater entrance, without any pictures, but with signs indicating that the theaters exhibit "Atlanta's Finest Mature Feature Films." On the door itself is a sign saying: "Adult Theater—You must be 21 and able to prove it. If viewing the nude body offends you, Please Do Not Enter."

The two films were exhibited to the trial court. The only other state evidence was testimony by criminal investigators that they had paid admission to see the films and that nothing on the outside of the theater indicated the full nature of what was shown. . . . There was no evidence presented that minors had ever entered the theaters. Nor was there evidence presented that petitioners had a systematic policy of barring minors, apart from posting signs at the entrance. On April 12, 1971, the trial judge dismissed respondents' complaints. . . .

On appeal, the Georgia Supreme Court unanimously reversed. It assumed that the adult theaters in question barred minors and gave a full warning to the general public of the nature of the films shown, but held that the films were without protection under the First Amendment. . . . After viewing the films, the Georgia Supreme Court held that their exhibition should have been enjoined. . . .

It should be clear from the outset that we do not undertake to tell the States what they must do, but rather to define the area in which they may chart their own course in dealing with obscene material. This Court has consistently held that obscene material is not protected by the First Amendment as a limitation on the state police power by virtue of the Fourteenth Amendment.

Georgia case law permits a civil injunction of the exhibition of obscene materials. While this procedure is civil in nature, and does not directly involve the state criminal statute proscribing exhibition of obscene material, the Georgia case law permitting civil injunction does adopt the definition of "obscene materials" used by the criminal statute. Today, in *Miller v. California,* we have sought to clarify the constitutional definition of obscene material subject to regulation by the States, and we vacate and remand this case for reconsideration in light of *Miller.* . . .

We categorically disapprove the theory, apparently adopted by the trial judge, that obscene, pornographic films acquire constitutional immunity from state regulation simply because they are exhibited for consenting adults only. This holding was properly rejected by the Georgia Supreme Court. Although we have often pointedly recognized the high importance of the state interest in regulating the exposure of obscene materials to juveniles and unconsenting adults, this Court has never declared these to be the only legitimate state interests permitting regulation of obscene material. The States have a long-recognized legitimate interest in regulating the use of obscene material in local commerce and in all places of public accommodation, as long as these regulations do not run afoul of specific constitutional prohibitions. In particular, we hold that there are legitimate state interests at stake in stemming the tide of commercialized obscenity, even assuming it is feasible to enforce effective safeguards against exposure to juveniles and to passersby. These include the interest of the public in the quality of life and the total community environment, the tone of commerce in the great city centers, and, possibly, the public safety itself. . . .

As Mr. Chief Justice Warren stated, there is a "right of the Nation and of the States to maintain a decent society. . . ."

But, it is argued, there are no scientific data which conclusively demonstrate that exposure to obscene material adversely affects men and women or their society. It is urged on behalf of the petitioners that, absent such a demonstration, any kind of state regulation is "impermissible." We reject this argument. It is not for us to resolve empirical uncertainties underlying state legislation, save in the exceptional case where that legislation plainly impinges upon rights protected by the Constitution itself. Although there is no conclusive proof of a connection between antisocial behavior and obscene material, the legislature of Georgia could quite reasonably determine that such a connection does or might exist. In deciding *Roth,* this Court implicitly accepted that a legislature could legitimately act on such a conclusion to protect "the social interest in order and morality."

. . . If we accept the unprovable assumption that a complete education requires the reading of certain books, and the well nigh universal belief that good books, plays, and art lift the spirit, improve the mind, enrich the human personality, and develop character, can we then say that a state legislature may not act on the corollary assumption that commerce in obscene books, or public exhibitions focused on obscene conduct, have a tendency to exert a corrupting and debasing impact leading to antisocial behavior? . . . The sum of experience, including that of the past two decades, affords an ample basis for legislatures to conclude that a sensitive, key relationship of human existence, central to family life, community welfare, and the development of human personality, can be debased and distorted by crass commercial exploitation of sex. Nothing in the Constitution prohibits a State from reaching such a conclusion and acting on it legislatively simply because there is no conclusive evidence or empirical data.

. . . The States, of course, may follow such a "laissez-faire" policy and drop all controls on commercialized obscenity, if that is what they prefer, just as they can ignore consumer protection in the marketplace, but nothing in the Constitution compels the States to do so with regard to matters falling within state jurisdiction. . . .

Our prior decisions recognizing a right to privacy guaranteed by the Fourteenth Amendment included "only personal rights that can be deemed 'fundamental' or 'implicit in the concept of ordered liberty.'" This privacy right encompasses and protects the personal intimacies of the home, the family, marriage, motherhood, procreation, and child rearing. Nothing, however, in this Court's decisions intimates that there is any "fundamental" privacy right "implicit in the concept of ordered liberty" to watch obscene movies in places of public accommodation.

If obscene material unprotected by the First Amendment in itself carried with it a "penumbra" of constitutionally protected privacy, this Court would not have found it necessary to decide *Stanley* on the narrow basis of the "privacy of the home," which was hardly more than a reaffirmation that "a man's home is his castle." Moreover, we have declined to equate the privacy of the home relied on in *Stanley* with a "zone" of "privacy" that follows a distributor or a consumer of obscene materials wherever he goes. The idea of a "privacy" right and a place of public accommodation are, in this context, mutually exclusive. Conduct or depictions of conduct that the state police power can prohibit on a public street do not become automatically protected by the Constitution merely because the conduct is moved to a bar or a "live" theater stage, any more than a "live" performance of a man and woman locked in a sexual embrace at high noon in Times Square is protected by the Constitution because they simultaneously engage in a valid political dialogue.

It is also argued that the State has no legitimate interest in "control [of] the moral content of a person's thoughts," and we need not quarrel with this. But we reject the claim that the State of Georgia is here attempting to control the minds or thoughts of those who patronize theaters. Preventing unlimited display or distribution of obscene material, which by definition lacks any serious literary, artistic, political, or scientific value as communication, *Miller v. California* is distinct from a control of reason and the intellect. Where communication of ideas, protected by the First Amendment, is not involved, or the particular privacy of the home protected by *Stanley,* or any of the other "areas or zones" of constitutionally protected privacy, the mere fact that, as a consequence, some human "utterances" or "thoughts" may be incidentally affected does not bar the State from acting to protect legitimate state interests. The fantasies of a drug addict are his own and beyond the reach of government, but government regulation of drug sales is not prohibited by the Constitution. . . .

To summarize, we have today reaffirmed the basic holding of *Roth v. United States* that obscene material has no protection under the First Amendment. We have directed our holdings, not at thoughts or speech, but at depiction and description of specifically defined sexual conduct that States may regulate within limits designed to prevent infringement of First Amendment rights. . . . Nothing precludes the State of Georgia from the regulation of the allegedly obscene material exhibited in Paris Adult Theatre I or II, provided that the applicable Georgia law, as written or authoritatively interpreted by the Georgia courts, meets the First Amendment standards set forth in *Miller v. California*. The judgment is vacated and the case remanded to the Georgia Supreme Court for further proceedings not inconsistent with this opinion and *Miller v. California*.

MR. JUSTICE DOUGLAS, dissenting.

My Brother BRENNAN is to be commended for seeking a new path through the thicket which the Court entered when it undertook to sustain the constitutionality of obscenity laws and to place limits on their application. I have expressed on numerous occasions my disagreement with the basic decision that held that "obscenity" was not protected by the First Amendment. I disagreed also with the definitions that evolved. Art and literature reflect tastes; and tastes, like musical appreciation, are hardly reducible to precise definitions. That is one reason I have always felt that "obscenity" was not an exception to the First Amendment. For matters of taste, like matters of belief, turn on the idiosyncrasies of individuals. They are too personal to define and too emotional and vague to apply. . . .

The other reason I could not bring myself to conclude that "obscenity" was not covered by the First Amendment was that prior to the adoption of our Constitution and Bill of Rights the Colonies had no law excluding "obscenity" from the regime of freedom of expression and press that then existed. I could find no such laws; and more important, our leading colonial expert, Julius Goebel, could find none. So I became convinced that the creation of the "obscenity" exception to the First Amendment was a legislative and judicial tour de force; that if we were to have such a regime of censorship and punishment, it should be done by constitutional amendment.

People are, of course, offended by many offerings made by merchants in this area. They are also offended by political pronouncements, sociological themes, and by stories of official misconduct. The list of activities and publications and pronouncements that offend someone is endless. Some of it goes on in private; some of it is inescapably public, as when a government official generates crime, becomes a blatant offender of the moral sensibilities of the people, engages in burglary, or breaches the privacy of the telephone, the conference room or the home. Life in this crowded modern technological world creates many offensive statements and many offensive deeds. There is no protection against offensive ideas, only against offensive conduct.

"Obscenity" at most is the expression of offensive ideas. There are regimes in the world where ideas "offensive" to the majority (or at least to those who control the majority) are suppressed. There life proceeds at a monotonous pace. Most of us would find that world offensive. One of the most offensive experiences in my life was a visit to a nation where bookstalls were filled only with books on mathematics and books on religion. . . .

When man was first in the jungle he took care of himself. When he entered a societal group, controls were necessarily imposed. But our society—unlike most in the world—presupposes that freedom and liberty are in a frame of reference that makes the individual, not government, the keeper of his tastes, beliefs, and ideas. That is the philosophy of the First Amendment; and it is the article of faith that sets us apart from most nations in the world.

MR. JUSTICE BRENNAN, with whom MR. JUSTICE STEWART and MR. JUSTICE MARSHALL join, dissenting.

This case requires the Court to confront once again the vexing problem of reconciling state efforts to suppress sexually oriented expression with the protections of the First Amendment, as applied to the States through the Fourteenth Amendment. No other aspect of the First Amendment has, in recent years, demanded so substantial a commitment of our time, generated such disharmony of views, and remained so resistant to the formulation of stable and manageable standards. I am convinced that the approach initiated 16 years ago in *Roth v. United States* (1957), and culminating in the Court's decision today, cannot bring stability to this area of the law without jeopardizing fundamental First Amendment values, and I have concluded that the time has come to make a significant departure from that approach. [Brennan then reviewed the history of this case and the relevant case law.]

. . . Yet our efforts to implement that approach [of *Roth*] demonstrate that agreement on the existence of something called "obscenity" is still a long and painful step from agreement on a workable definition of the term. . . .

Of course, the vagueness problem would be largely of our own creation if it stemmed primarily from our failure to reach a consensus on any one standard. But after 16 years of experimentation and debate I am reluctantly forced to the conclusion that none of the available formulas, including the one announced today, can reduce the vagueness to a tolerable level while at the same time striking an acceptable balance between the protections of the First and Fourteenth Amendments, on the one hand, and on the other the asserted state interest in regulating the dissemination of certain sexually oriented materials. Any effort to draw a constitutionally acceptable boundary on state power must resort to such indefinite concepts as "prurient interest," "patent offensiveness," "serious literary value," and the like. The meaning of these concepts necessarily varies with the experience, outlook, and even idiosyncrasies of the person defining them. Although we have assumed that obscenity does exist and that we "know it when [we] see it," we are manifestly unable to describe it in advance except by reference to concepts so elusive that they fail to distinguish clearly between protected and unprotected speech. . . .

The differences between this formulation and the three-pronged *Memoirs* test are, for the most part, academic. The first element of the Court's test is virtually identical to the *Memoirs* requirement that "the dominant theme of the material taken as a whole [must appeal] to a prurient interest in sex." Whereas the second prong of the *Memoirs* test demanded that the material be "patently offensive because it affronts contemporary community standards relating to the description or representation of sexual matters," the test adopted today requires that the material describe, "in a patently offensive way, sexual conduct specifically defined by the applicable state law." The third component of the *Memoirs* test is that the material must be "utterly without redeeming social value." The Court's rephrasing requires that the work, taken as a whole, must be proved to lack "serious literary, artistic, political, or scientific value."

The Court evidently recognizes that difficulties with the *Roth* approach necessitate a significant change of direction. But the Court does not describe its understanding of those difficulties, nor does it indicate how the restatement of the *Memoirs* test is in any way responsive to the problems that have arisen. In my view, the restatement leaves unresolved the very difficulties that compel our rejection of the underlying *Roth* approach, while at the same time contributing substantial difficulties of its own. The modification of the *Memoirs* test may prove sufficient to jeopardize the analytic underpinnings of the entire scheme. And today's restatement will likely have the effect, whether or not intended, of permitting far more sweeping suppression of sexually oriented expression, including expression that would almost surely be held protected under our current formulation. . . .

I have also considered the possibility of reducing our own role, and the role of appellate courts generally, in determining whether particular matter is obscene. Thus, we might conclude that juries are best suited to determine obscenity and that jury verdicts in this area should not be set aside except in cases of extreme departure from prevailing standards. Or, more generally, we might adopt the position that where a lower federal or state court has conscientiously applied the constitutional standard, its finding of obscenity will be no more vulnerable to reversal by this Court than any finding of fact. . . . In any event, even if the Constitution would permit us to refrain from judging for ourselves the alleged obscenity of particular materials, that approach would solve at best only a small part of our problem. For while it would mitigate the institutional stress produced by the *Roth* approach, it would neither offer nor produce any cure for the other vices of vagueness. Far from providing a clearer guide to permissible primary conduct, the approach would inevitably lead to even greater uncertainty and the consequent due process problems of fair notice. And the approach would expose much protected, sexually oriented expression to the vagaries of jury determinations. Plainly, the institutional gain would be more than offset by the unprecedented infringement of First Amendment rights.

Finally, I have considered the view, urged so forcefully since 1957 by our Brothers BLACK and DOUGLAS, that the First Amendment bars the suppression of any sexually oriented expression. That position would effect a sharp reduction, although perhaps not a total elimination, of the uncertainty that surrounds our current approach. Nevertheless, I am convinced that it would achieve that desirable goal only by stripping the States of power to an extent that cannot be justified by the commands of the Constitution, at least so long as there is available an alternative approach that strikes a better balance between the guarantee of free expression and the States' legitimate interests.

Our experience since *Roth* requires us not only to abandon the effort to pick out obscene materials on a case-by-case basis, but also to reconsider a fundamental postulate of *Roth:* that there exists a definable class of sexually oriented expression that may be totally suppressed by the Federal and State Governments. Assuming that such a class of expression does in fact exist, I am forced to conclude that the concept of "obscenity" cannot be defined with sufficient specificity and clarity to provide fair notice to persons who create and distribute sexually oriented materials, to prevent substantial erosion of protected speech as a byproduct of the attempt to suppress unprotected speech, and to avoid very costly institutional harms. . . .

Even a legitimate, sharply focused state concern for the morality of the community cannot, in other words, justify an assault on the protections of the First Amendment. Where the state interest in regulation of morality is vague and ill defined, interference with the guarantees of the First Amendment is even more difficult to justify.

In short, while I cannot say that the interests of the State—apart from the question of juveniles and unconsenting adults—are trivial or nonexistent, I am compelled to conclude that these interests cannot justify the substantial damage to constitutional rights and to this Nation's judicial machinery that inevitably results from state efforts to bar the distribution even of unprotected material to consenting adults. I would hold, therefore, that at least in the absence of distribution to juveniles or obtrusive exposure to unconsenting adults, the First and Fourteenth Amendments prohibit the State and Federal Governments from attempting wholly to suppress sexually oriented materials on the basis of their allegedly "obscene" contents. Nothing in this approach precludes those governments from taking action to serve what may be strong and legitimate interests through regulation of the manner of distribution of sexually oriented material.

Since the Supreme Court of Georgia erroneously concluded that the State has power to suppress sexually oriented material even in the absence of distribution to juveniles or exposure to unconsenting adults, I would reverse that judgment and remand the case to that court for further proceedings not inconsistent with this opinion.

Jenkins v. Georgia (1974)

A practical test of the 1973 Miller *standard for defining obscenity came the next year. Georgia had prosecuted and convicted a theater owner for showing a risqué film,* Carnal Knowledge. *The owner appealed, and the case became the first test of* Miller *before the U.S. Supreme Court. A majority of the justices found the* Miller *obscenity test useful, but the dissenters continued to fear its consequences.*

MR. JUSTICE REHNQUIST delivered the opinion of the Court.

Appellant was convicted in Georgia of the crime of distributing obscene material. His conviction, in March 1972, was for showing the film "Carnal Knowledge" in a movie theater in Albany, Georgia. The jury that found appellant guilty was instructed on obscenity pursuant to the Georgia statute, which defines obscene material in language similar to that of the definition of obscenity set forth in this Court's plurality opinion in *Memoirs v. Massachusetts* (1966). . . .

We hold today that defendants convicted prior to the announcement of our *Miller* decisions but whose convictions were on direct appeal at that time should receive any benefit available to them from those decisions. We conclude here that the film "Carnal Knowledge" is not obscene under the constitutional standards announced in *Miller v. California* (1973), and that the First and Fourteenth Amendments therefore require that the judgment of the Supreme Court of Georgia affirming appellant's conviction be reversed.

Appellant was the manager of the theater in which "Carnal Knowledge" was being shown. While he was exhibiting the film on January 13, 1972, local law enforcement officers seized it pursuant to a search warrant. Appellant was later charged by accusation with the offense of distributing obscene material. After his trial in the Superior Court of Dougherty County, the jury, having seen the film and heard testimony, returned a general verdict of guilty on March 23, 1972. Appellant was fined $750 and sentenced to 12 months' probation. He appealed to the Supreme Court of Georgia, which by a divided vote affirmed the judgment of conviction on July 2, 1973. . . .

We agree with the Supreme Court of Georgia's implicit ruling that the Constitution does not require that juries be instructed in state obscenity cases to apply the standards of a hypothetical statewide community. *Miller* approved the use of such instructions; it did not mandate their use. What *Miller* makes clear is that state juries need not be instructed to apply "national standards." We also agree with the Supreme Court of Georgia's implicit approval of the trial court's instructions directing jurors to apply "community standards" without specifying what "community." *Miller* held that it was constitutionally permissible to permit juries to rely on the understanding of the community from which they came as to contemporary community standards, and the States have considerable latitude in framing statutes under this element of the *Miller* decision. A State may choose to define an obscenity offense in terms of "contemporary community standards" as defined in *Miller* without further specification, as was done here, or it may choose to define the standards in more precise geographic terms, as was done by California in *Miller*. . . .

There is little to be found in the record about the film "Carnal Knowledge" other than the film itself. However, appellant has supplied a variety of information and critical commentary, the authenticity of which appellee does not dispute. The film appeared on many "Ten Best" lists for 1971, the year in which it was released. Many but not all of the reviews were favorable. . . .

Miller states that the questions of what appeals to the "prurient interest" and what is "patently offensive" under the obscenity test which it formulates are "essentially questions of fact." . . . We held in *Paris Adult Theatre I v. Slaton* decided on the same day, that expert testimony as to obscenity is not necessary when the films at issue are themselves placed in evidence.

But all of this does not lead us to agree with the Supreme Court of Georgia's apparent conclusion that the jury's verdict against appellant virtually precluded all further appellate review of appellant's assertion that his exhibition of the film was protected by the First and Fourteenth Amendments. Even though questions of appeal to the "prurient interest" or of patent offensiveness are "essentially questions of fact," it would be a serious misreading of *Miller* to conclude that juries have unbridled discretion in determining what is "patently offensive." Not only did we there say that "the First Amendment values applicable to the States through the Fourteenth Amendment are adequately protected by the ultimate power of appellate courts to conduct an independent review of constitutional claims when necessary," but we made it plain that under that holding "no one will be subject to prosecution for the sale or exposure of obscene materials unless these materials depict or describe patently offensive 'hard core' sexual conduct. . . ."

We also took pains in *Miller* to "give a few plain examples of what a state statute could define for regulation under part (b) of the standard announced," that is, the requirement of patent offensiveness.... While this did not purport to be an exhaustive catalog of what juries might find patently offensive, it was certainly intended to fix substantive constitutional limitations, deriving from the First Amendment, on the type of material subject to such a determination. It would be wholly at odds with this aspect of *Miller* to uphold an obscenity conviction based upon a defendant's depiction of a woman with a bare midriff, even though a properly charged jury unanimously agreed on a verdict of guilty.

Our own viewing of the film satisfies us that "Carnal Knowledge" could not be found under the *Miller* standards to depict sexual conduct in a patently offensive way. Nothing in the movie falls within either of the two examples given in *Miller* of material which may constitutionally be found to meet the "patently offensive" element of those standards, nor is there anything sufficiently similar to such material to justify similar treatment.... There are occasional scenes of nudity, but nudity alone is not enough to make material legally obscene under the *Miller* standards.

Appellant's showing of the film "Carnal Knowledge" is simply not the "public portrayal of hard core sexual conduct for its own sake, and for the ensuing commercial gain" which we said was punishable in *Miller.* We hold that the film could not, as a matter of constitutional law, be found to depict sexual conduct in a patently offensive way, and that it is therefore not outside the protection of the First and Fourteenth Amendments because it is obscene. No other basis appearing in the record upon which the judgment of conviction can be sustained, we reverse the judgment of the Supreme Court of Georgia.

Reversed.

MR. JUSTICE DOUGLAS, being of the view that any ban on obscenity is prohibited by the First Amendment, made applicable to the States through the Fourteenth, concurs in the reversal of this conviction.

MR. JUSTICE BRENNAN, with whom MR. JUSTICE STEWART and MR. JUSTICE MARSHALL join, concurring in the result.

Adopting a restatement of the *Roth-Memoirs* definition of "obscenity," the Court in *Miller v. California* held that obscene material could be regulated, provided that "(a)... 'the average person, applying contemporary community standards' would find that the work, taken as a whole, appeals to the prurient interest . . . ; (b) . . . the work depicts or describes, in a patently offensive way, sexual conduct specifically defined by the applicable state law; and (c) . . . the work, taken as a whole, lacks serious literary, artistic, political, or scientific value." It was my view then—and it remains so—that the Court's reformulation hardly represented a solution to what Mr. Justice Harlan called "the intractable obscenity problem." Today's decision confirms my observation in *Paris Adult Theatre I v. Slaton* that the Court's new formulation does not extricate us from the mire of case-by-case determinations of obscenity. . . .

After the Court's decision today, there can be no doubt that *Miller* requires appellate courts—including this Court—to review independently the constitutional fact of obscenity. Moreover, the Court's task is not limited to reviewing a jury finding under part (c) of the *Miller* test that "the work, taken as a whole, lack[ed] serious literary, artistic, political, or scientific value." *Miller* also requires independent review of a jury's determination under part (b) of the *Miller* test that "the work depicts or describes, in a patently offensive way, sexual conduct specifically defined by the applicable state law."

. . . In order to make the review mandated by *Miller*, the Court was required to screen the film "Carnal Knowledge" and make an independent determination of obscenity. . . . Following that review, the Court holds that "Carnal Knowledge" "could not, as a matter of constitutional law, be found to depict sexual conduct in a patently offensive way, and that it is therefore not outside the protection of the First and Fourteenth Amendments because it is obscene."

Thus, it is clear that as long as the *Miller* test remains in effect "one cannot say with certainty that material is obscene until at least five members of this Court, applying inevitably obscure standards, have pronounced it so." Because of the attendant uncertainty of such a process and its inevitable institutional stress upon the judiciary, I continue to adhere to my view that, "at least in the absence of distribution to juveniles or obtrusive exposure to unconsenting adults, the First and Fourteenth Amendments prohibit the State and Federal Governments from attempting wholly to suppress sexually oriented materials on the basis of their allegedly 'obscene' contents." It is clear that, tested by that constitutional standard, the Georgia obscenity statutes under which appellant Jenkins was convicted are constitutionally overbroad and therefore facially invalid. I therefore concur in the result in the Court's reversal of Jenkins' conviction.

Young v. American Mini Theatres (1976)

How to deal with the physical buildings that housed "adult" movie theaters or bookstores is a question that many if not most cities and towns have had to face. The Detroit city council decided to use its zoning powers and prohibit an adult theater within a certain number of feet of churches, schools, or residential neighborhoods. The goal was to scatter and isolate such businesses, to prevent them from becoming a blight in one particular area of the city. But the theaters challenged these zoning restrictions on the grounds that they were not, in reality, zoning restrictions, but restrictions on the First Amendment right of freedom of speech and press. The case was heard by the U.S. Supreme Court.

MR. JUSTICE STEVENS delivered the opinion of the Court.

Zoning ordinances adopted by the city of Detroit differentiate between motion picture theaters which exhibit sexually explicit "adult" movies and those which do not. The principal question presented by this case is whether that statutory classification is unconstitutional because it is based on the content of communication protected by the First Amendment.

Effective November 2, 1972, Detroit adopted the ordinances challenged in this litigation. Instead of concentrating "adult" theaters in limited zones, these ordinances require that such theaters be dispersed. Specifically, an adult theater may not be located within 1,000 feet of any two other "regulated uses" or within 500 feet of a residential area. The term "regulated uses" includes 10 different kinds of establishments in addition to adult theaters.

The classification of a theater as "adult" is expressly predicated on the character of the motion pictures which it exhibits. If the theater is used to present "material distinguished or characterized by an emphasis on matter depicting, describing or relating to 'Specified Sexual Activities' or 'Specified Anatomical Areas,'" it is an adult establishment.

The 1972 ordinances were amendments to an "Anti–Skid Row Ordinance" which had been adopted 10 years earlier. At that time the Detroit Common Council made a finding that some uses of property are especially injurious to a neighborhood when they are concentrated in limited areas. The decision to add adult motion picture theaters and adult book stores to the list of businesses which, apart from a special waiver, could not be located within 1,000 feet of two other "regulated uses," was, in part, a response to the significant growth in the number of such establishments. In the opinion of urban planners and real estate experts who supported the ordinances, the location of several such businesses in the same neighborhood tends to attract an undesirable quantity and quality of transients, adversely affects property values, causes an increase in crime, especially prostitution, and encourages residents and businesses to move elsewhere.

Respondents are the operators of two adult motion picture theaters. One, the Nortown, was an established theater which began to exhibit adult films in March 1973. The other, the Pussy Cat, was a corner gas station which was converted into a "mini theater," but denied a certificate of occupancy because of its plan to exhibit adult films. Both theaters were located within 1,000 feet of two other regulated uses and the Pussy Cat was less than 500 feet from a residential area. The respondents brought two separate actions against appropriate city officials, seeking a declaratory judgment that the ordinances were unconstitutional and an injunction against their enforcement. Federal jurisdiction was properly invoked and the two cases were consolidated for decision.

The District Court granted defendants' motion for summary judgment. . . .

The Court of Appeals reversed. . . .

Because of the importance of the decision, we granted certiorari.

As they did in the District Court, respondents contend (1) that the ordinances are so vague that they violate the Due Process Clause of the Fourteenth Amendment; (2) that they are invalid under the First Amendment as prior restraints on protected communication; and (3) that the classification of theaters on the basis of the content of their exhibitions violates the Equal Protection Clause of the Fourteenth Amendment. We consider their arguments in that order. . . .

We are not persuaded that the Detroit zoning ordinances will have a significant deterrent effect on the exhibition of films protected by the First Amendment. . . .

The only area of protected communication that may be deterred by these ordinances comprises films containing material falling within the specific definitions of "Specified Sexual Activities" or "Specified Anatomical Areas." The fact that the First Amendment protects some, though not necessarily all, of that material from total suppression does not warrant the further conclusion that an exhibitor's doubts as to whether a borderline film may be shown in his theater, as well as in theaters licensed for adult presentations, involves the kind of threat to the free market in ideas and expression that justifies the exceptional approach to constitutional adjudication. . . .

The application of the ordinances to respondents is plain; even if there is some area of uncertainty about their application in other situations, we agree with the District Court that respondents' due process argument must be rejected. . . .

It is true, however, that adult films may only be exhibited commercially in licensed theaters. But that is also true of all motion pictures. The city's general zoning laws require all motion picture theaters to satisfy certain locational as well as other requirements; we have no doubt that the municipality may control the location of theaters as well as the location of other commercial establishments, either by confining them to certain specified commercial zones or by requiring that they be dispersed throughout the city. The mere fact that the commercial exploitation of material protected by the First Amendment is subject to zoning and other licensing requirements is not a sufficient reason for invalidating these ordinances.

Putting to one side for the moment the fact that adult motion picture theaters must satisfy a locational restriction not applicable to other theaters, we are also persuaded that the 1,000-foot restriction does not, in itself, create an impermissible restraint on protected communication. The city's interest in planning and regulating the use of property for commercial purposes is clearly adequate to support that kind of restriction applicable to all theaters within the city limits. In short, apart from the fact that the ordinances treat adult theaters differently from other theaters and the fact that the classification is predicated on the content of material shown in the respective theaters, the regulation of the place where such films may be exhibited does not offend the First Amendment. We turn, therefore, to the question whether the classification is consistent with the Equal Protection Clause.

A remark attributed to Voltaire characterizes our zealous adherence to the principle that the government may not tell the citizen what he may or may not say. Referring to a suggestion that the violent overthrow of tyranny might be legitimate, he said: "I disapprove of what you say, but I will defend to the death your right to say it." The essence of that comment has been repeated time after time in our decisions invalidating attempts by the government to impose selective controls upon the dissemination of ideas.

Thus, the use of streets and parks for the free expression of views on national affairs may not be conditioned upon the sovereign's agreement with what a speaker may intend to say. Nor may speech be curtailed because it invites dispute, creates dissatisfaction with conditions the way they are, or even stirs people to anger. The sovereign's agreement or disagreement with the content of what a speaker has to say may not affect the regulation of the time, place, or manner of presenting the speech. . . .

More directly in point are opinions dealing with the question whether the First Amendment prohibits the State and Federal Governments from wholly suppressing sexually oriented materials on the basis of their "obscene character." In *Ginsberg v. New York,* the Court upheld a conviction for selling to a minor magazines which were concededly not "obscene" if shown to adults. Indeed, the Members of the Court who would accord the greatest protection to such materials have repeatedly indicated that the State could prohibit the distribution or exhibition of such materials to juveniles and unconsenting adults. Surely the First Amendment does not foreclose such a prohibition; yet it is equally clear that any such prohibition must rest squarely on an appraisal of the content of material otherwise within a constitutionally protected area.

Such a line may be drawn on the basis of content without violating the government's paramount obligation of neutrality in its regulation of protected communication. For the regulation of the places where sexually explicit films may be exhibited is unaffected by whatever social, political, or philosophical message a film may be intended to communicate; whether a motion picture ridicules or characterizes one point of view or another, the effect of the ordinances is exactly the same.

Moreover, even though we recognize that the First Amendment will not tolerate the total suppression of erotic materials that have some arguably artistic value, it is manifest that society's interest in protecting this type of expression is of a wholly different, and lesser, magnitude than the interest in untrammeled political debate that inspired Voltaire's immortal comment. Whether political oratory or philosophical discussion moves us to applaud or to despise what is said, every schoolchild can understand why our duty to defend the right to speak remains the same. But few of us would march our sons and daughters off to war to preserve the citizen's right to see "Specified Sexual Activities" exhibited in the theaters of our choice. Even though the First Amendment protects communication in this area from total suppression, we hold that the State may legitimately use the content of these materials as the basis for placing them in a different classification from other motion pictures.

The remaining question is whether the line drawn by these ordinances is justified by the city's interest in preserving the character of its neighborhoods. . . . The record discloses a factual basis for the Common Council's conclusion that this kind of restriction will have the desired effect. It is not our function to appraise the wisdom of its decision to require adult theaters to be separated rather than concentrated in the same areas. In either event, the city's interest in attempting to preserve the quality of urban life is one that must be accorded high respect. Moreover, the city must be allowed a reasonable opportunity to experiment with solutions to admittedly serious problems.

Since what is ultimately at stake is nothing more than a limitation on the place where adult films may be exhibited, even though the determination of whether a particular film fits that characterization turns on the nature of its content, we conclude that the city's interest in the present and future character of its neighborhoods adequately supports its classification of motion pictures. We hold that the zoning ordinances requiring that adult motion picture theaters not be located within 1,000 feet of two other regulated uses does not violate the Equal Protection Clause of the Fourteenth Amendment.

The judgment of the Court of Appeals is

Reversed.

Federal Communications Commission v. Pacifica Foundation (1978)

By the late twentieth century, most Americans were regularly tuning in to their favorite radio programs while at home or in their cars. They were accustomed to searching for news, weather, or music programming without concern about being confronted by obscene words or phrases. Yet, in 1973, a radio station broadcast a "humorous" monologue by the comic George Carlin that was an almost nonstop stream of obscenities. The federal regulatory agency, the Federal Communications Commission, had established guidelines for programming going out over the airwaves and this broadcast clearly violated those regulations. The FCC fined the radio station's owner. The owner appealed the fine and challenged the FCC's regulations. This was the first obscenity case heard by the U.S. Supreme Court that involved mass communications.

MR. JUSTICE STEVENS delivered the opinion of the Court.

This case requires that we decide whether the Federal Communications Commission has any power to regulate a radio broadcast that is indecent but not obscene.

A satiric humorist named George Carlin recorded a 12-minute monologue entitled "Filthy Words" before a live audience in a California theater. He began by referring to his thoughts about "the words you couldn't say on the public, ah, airwaves, um, the ones you definitely wouldn't say, ever." He proceeded to list those words and repeat them over and over again in a variety of colloquialisms. The transcript of the recording indicates frequent laughter from the audience.

At about 2 o'clock in the afternoon on Tuesday, October 30, 1973, a New York radio station, owned by respondent Pacifica Foundation, broadcast the "Filthy Words" monologue. A few weeks later a man, who stated that he had heard the broadcast while driving with his young son, wrote a letter complaining to the Commission. He stated that, although he could perhaps understand the "record's being sold for private use, I certainly cannot understand the broadcast of same over the air that, supposedly, you control."

The complaint was forwarded to the station for comment. In its response, Pacifica explained that the monologue had been played during a program about contemporary society's attitude toward language and that, immediately before its broadcast, listeners had been advised that it included "sensitive language which might be regarded as offensive to some." Pacifica characterized George Carlin as "a significant social satirist" who "like Twain and Sahl before him, examines the language of ordinary people. . . . Carlin is not mouthing obscenities, he is merely using words to satirize as harmless and essentially silly our attitudes towards those words." Pacifica stated that it was not aware of any other complaints about the broadcast. . . .

The Commission characterized the language used in the Carlin monologue as "patently offensive," though not necessarily obscene, and expressed the opinion that it should be regulated by principles analogous to those found in the law of nuisance where the "law generally speaks to channeling behavior more than actually prohibiting it. . . . [T]he concept of 'indecent' is intimately connected with the exposure of children to language that describes, in terms patently offensive as measured by contemporary community standards for the broadcast medium, sexual or excretory activities and organs, at times of the day when there is a reasonable risk that children may be in the audience."

Applying these considerations to the language used in the monologue as broadcast by respondent, the Commission concluded that certain words depicted sexual and excretory activities in a patently offensive manner, noted that they "were broadcast at a time when children were undoubtedly in the audience (i.e., in the early afternoon)," and that the prerecorded language, with these offensive words "repeated over and over," was "deliberately broadcast." In summary, the Commission stated: "We therefore hold that the language as broadcast was indecent and prohibited by 18 U.S.C. § 1464. . . ."

After the order issued, the Commission was asked to clarify its opinion by ruling that the broadcast of indecent words as part of a live newscast would not be prohibited. . . .

The relevant statutory questions are whether the Commission's action is forbidden "censorship" and whether speech that concededly is not obscene may be restricted as "indecent" under the authority of 18 U.S.C. 1464. . . .

Section 29 of the Radio Act of 1927 provided: "Nothing in this Act shall be understood or construed to give the licensing authority the power of censorship over the radio communications or signals transmitted by any radio station, and no regulation or condition shall be promulgated or fixed by the licensing authority which shall interfere with the right of free speech by means of radio communications. No person within the jurisdiction of the United States shall utter any obscene, indecent, or profane language by means of radio communication."

The prohibition against censorship unequivocally denies the Commission any power to edit proposed broadcasts in advance and to excise material considered inappropriate for the airwaves. The prohibition, however, has never been construed to deny the Commission the power to review the content of completed broadcasts in the performance of its regulatory duties.

During the period between the original enactment of the provision in 1927 and its re-enactment in the Communications Act of 1934, the courts and the Federal Radio Commission held that the section deprived the Commission of the power to subject "broadcasting matter to scrutiny prior to its release," but they concluded that the Commission's "undoubted right" to take note of past program content when considering a licensee's renewal application "is not censorship."

Not only did the Federal Radio Commission so construe the statute prior to 1934; its successor, the Federal Communications Commission, has consistently interpreted the provision in the same way ever since. . . .

We conclude, therefore, that 326 does not limit the Commission's authority to impose sanctions on licensees who engage in obscene, indecent, or profane broadcasting . . .

Pacifica makes two constitutional attacks on the Commission's order. First, it argues that the Commission's construction of the statutory language broadly encompasses so much constitutionally protected speech that reversal is required even if Pacifica's broadcast of the "Filthy Words" monologue is not itself protected by the First Amendment. Second, Pacifica argues that inasmuch as the recording is not obscene, the Constitution forbids any abridgment of the right to broadcast it on the radio.

The first argument fails because our review is limited to the question whether the Commission has the authority to proscribe this particular broadcast. As the Commission itself emphasized, its order was "issued in a specific factual context." That approach is appropriate for courts as well as the Commission when regulation of indecency is at stake, for indecency is largely a function of context—it cannot be adequately judged in the abstract. . . .

It is true that the Commission's order may lead some broadcasters to censor themselves. At most, however, the Commission's definition of indecency will deter only the broadcasting of patently offensive references to excretory and sexual organs and activities. While some of these references may be protected, they surely lie at the periphery of First Amendment concern. . . .

The words of the Carlin monologue are unquestionably "speech" within the meaning of the First Amendment. It is equally clear that the Commission's objections to the broadcast were based in part on its content. The order must therefore fall if, as Pacifica argues, the First Amendment prohibits all governmental regulation that depends on the content of speech. Our past cases demonstrate, however, that no such absolute rule is mandated by the Constitution.

The question in this case is whether a broadcast of patently offensive words dealing with sex and excretion may be regulated because of its content. Obscene materials have been denied the protection of the

First Amendment because their content is so offensive to contemporary moral standards. But the fact that society may find speech offensive is not a sufficient reason for suppressing it. Indeed, if it is the speaker's opinion that gives offense, that consequence is a reason for according it constitutional protection. For it is a central tenet of the First Amendment that the government must remain neutral in the marketplace of ideas. If there were any reason to believe that the Commission's characterization of the Carlin monologue as offensive could be traced to its political content—or even to the fact that it satirized contemporary attitudes about four-letter words—First Amendment protection might be required. But that is simply not this case. These words offend for the same reasons that obscenity offends. . . .

Although these words ordinarily lack literary, political, or scientific value, they are not entirely outside the protection of the First Amendment. Some uses of even the most offensive words are unquestionably protected. Indeed, we may assume that this monologue would be protected in other contexts. Nonetheless, the constitutional protection accorded to a communication containing such patently offensive sexual and excretory language need not be the same in every context. It is a characteristic of speech such as this that both its capacity to offend and its "social value," to use Mr. Justice Murphy's term, vary with the circumstances. Words that are commonplace in one setting are shocking in another. To paraphrase Mr. Justice Harlan, one occasion's lyric is another's vulgarity.

We have long recognized that each medium of expression presents special First Amendment problems. And of all forms of communication, it is broadcasting that has received the most limited First Amendment protection. . . .

[B]roadcasting is uniquely accessible to children, even those too young to read. Although Carlin's written message might have been incomprehensible to a first grader, Pacifica's broadcast could have enlarged a child's vocabulary in an instant. Other forms of offensive expression may be withheld from the young without restricting the expression at its source. Bookstores and motion picture theaters, for example, may be prohibited from making indecent material available to children. . . .

It is appropriate, in conclusion, to emphasize the narrowness of our holding. This case does not involve a two-way radio conversation between a cab driver and a dispatcher, or a telecast of an Elizabethan comedy. We have not decided that an occasional expletive in either setting would justify any sanction or, indeed, that this broadcast would justify a criminal prosecution. The Commission's decision rested entirely on a nuisance rationale under which context is all-important. The concept requires consideration of a host of variables. The time of day was emphasized by the Commission. The content of the program in which the language is used will also affect the composition of the audience, and differences between radio, television, and perhaps closed-circuit transmissions, may also be relevant. As Mr. Justice Sutherland wrote, a "nuisance may be merely a right thing in the wrong place—like a pig in the parlor instead of the barnyard." We simply hold that when the Commission finds that a pig has entered the parlor, the exercise of its regulatory power does not depend on proof that the pig is obscene.

The judgment of the Court of Appeals is reversed.

MR. JUSTICE POWELL, with whom MR. JUSTICE BLACK-MUN joins, concurring in part and concurring in the judgment.

It is conceded that the monologue at issue here is not obscene in the constitutional sense. . . . I do not think Carlin, consistently with the First Amendment, could be punished for delivering the same monologue to a live audience composed of adults who, knowing what to expect, chose to attend his performance. And I would assume that an adult could not constitutionally be prohibited from purchasing a recording or transcript of the monologue and playing or reading it in the privacy of his own home.

But it also is true that the language employed is, to most people, vulgar and offensive. It was chosen specifically for this quality, and it was repeated over and over as a sort of verbal shock treatment. The Commission did not err in characterizing the narrow category of language used here as "patently offensive" to most people regardless of age.

The issue, however, is whether the Commission may impose civil sanctions on a licensee radio station for broadcasting the monologue at two o'clock in the afternoon. The Commission's primary concern was to prevent the broadcast from reaching the ears of unsupervised children who were likely to be in the audience at that hour. In essence, the Commission sought to "channel" the monologue to hours when the fewest unsupervised children would be exposed to it. In my view, this consideration provides strong support for the Commission's holding. . . .

The Commission properly held that the speech from which society may attempt to shield its children is not limited to that which appeals to the youthful prurient interest. The language involved in this case is as potentially degrading and harmful to children as representations of many erotic acts.

In most instances, the dissemination of this kind of speech to children may be limited without also limiting willing adults' access to it. Sellers of printed and recorded matter and exhibitors of motion pictures and live performances may be required to shut their doors to children, but such a requirement has no effect on adults' access. The difficulty is that such a physical separation of the audience cannot be accomplished in the broadcast media. During most of the broadcast hours, both adults and unsupervised children are likely to be in the broadcast audience, and the broadcaster cannot reach willing adults without also reaching children. This, as the Court emphasizes, is one of the distinctions between the broadcast and other media to which we often have adverted as justifying a different treatment of the broadcast media for First Amendment purposes. In my view, the Commission was entitled to give substantial weight to this difference in reaching its decision in this case. . . .

It is argued that despite society's right to protect its children from this kind of speech, and despite everyone's interest in not being assaulted by offensive speech in the home, the Commission's holding in this case is impermissible because it prevents willing adults from listening to Carlin's monologue over the radio in the early afternoon hours. . . . This argument is not without force. The Commission certainly should consider it as it develops standards in this area. But it is not sufficiently strong to leave the Commission powerless to act in circumstances such as those in this case.

The Commission's holding does not prevent willing adults from purchasing Carlin's record, from attending his performances. . . . On its face, it does not prevent respondent Pacifica Foundation from broadcasting the monologue during late evening hours when fewer children are likely to be in the audience, nor from broadcasting discussions of the contemporary use of language at any time during the day. . . . In short, I agree that on the facts of this case, the Commission's order did not violate respondent's First Amendment rights.

MR. JUSTICE BRENNAN, with whom MR. JUSTICE MARSHALL joins, dissenting.

. . . I would, therefore, normally refrain from expressing my views on any constitutional issues implicated in this case. However, I find

the Court's misapplication of fundamental First Amendment principles so patent, and its attempt to impose its notions of propriety on
the whole of the American people so misguided, that I am unable to
remain silent. . . .

The Court's balance, of necessity, fails to accord proper weight to
the interests of listeners who wish to hear broadcasts the FCC deems
offensive. It permits majoritarian tastes completely to preclude a protected message from entering the homes of a receptive, unoffended
minority. No decision of this Court supports such a result. Where the
individuals constituting the offended majority may freely choose to
reject the material being offered, we have never found their privacy
interests of such moment to warrant the suppression of speech on privacy grounds. In *Rowan,* the Court upheld a statute, permitting
householders to require that mail advertisers stop sending them lewd
or offensive materials and remove their names from mailing lists. . . .
In contrast, the visage of the censor is all too discernible here.

Most parents will undoubtedly find understandable as well as commendable the Court's sympathy with the FCC's desire to prevent
offensive broadcasts from reaching the ears of unsupervised children.
Unfortunately, the facial appeal of this justification for radio censorship masks its constitutional insufficiency. Although the government
unquestionably has a special interest in the well-being of children and
consequently "can adopt more stringent controls on communicative
materials available to youths than on those available to adults," the
Court has accounted for this societal interest by adopting a "variable
obscenity" standard that permits the prurient appeal of material available to children to be assessed in terms of the sexual interests of
minors. . . .

In concluding that the presence of children in the listening audience
provides an adequate basis for the FCC to impose sanctions for Pacifica's broadcast of the Carlin monologue, the opinions of my Brother
POWELL, and my Brother STEVENS, both stress the time-honored
right of a parent to raise his child as he sees fit—a right this Court has
consistently been vigilant to protect. . . . As surprising as it may be to
individual Members of this Court, some parents may actually find Mr.
Carlin's unabashed attitude towards the seven "dirty words" healthy,
and deem it desirable to expose their children to the manner in which
Mr. Carlin defuses the taboo surrounding the words. Such parents
may constitute a minority of the American public, but the absence of
great numbers willing to exercise the right to raise their children in

this fashion does not alter the right's nature or its existence. Only the Court's regrettable decision does that.

. . . Taken to their logical extreme, these rationales would support the cleansing of public radio of any "four-letter words" whatsoever, regardless of their context. The rationales could justify the banning from radio of a myriad of literary works, novels, poems, and plays by the likes of Shakespeare, Joyce, Hemingway, Ben Jonson, Henry Fielding, Robert Burns, and Chaucer; they could support the suppression of a good deal of political speech, such as the Nixon tapes; and they could even provide the basis for imposing sanctions for the broadcast of certain portions of the Bible.

It is quite evident that I find the Court's attempt to unstitch the warp and woof of First Amendment law in an effort to reshape its fabric to cover the patently wrong result the Court reaches in this case dangerous as well as lamentable. Yet there runs throughout the opinions of my Brothers POWELL and STEVENS another vein I find equally disturbing: a depressing inability to appreciate that in our land of cultural pluralism, there are many who think, act, and talk differently from the Members of this Court, and who do not share their fragile sensibilities. It is only an acute ethnocentric myopia that enables the Court to approve the censorship of communications solely because of the words they contain. . . .

Today's decision will thus have its greatest impact on broadcasters desiring to reach, and listening audiences composed of, persons who do not share the Court's view as to which words or expressions are acceptable and who, for a variety of reasons, including a conscious desire to flout majoritarian conventions, express themselves using words that may be regarded as offensive by those from different socio-economic backgrounds. In this context, the Court's decision may be seen for what, in the broader perspective, it really is: another of the dominant culture's inevitable efforts to force those groups who do not share its mores to conform to its way of thinking, acting, and speaking.

Pacifica, in response to an FCC inquiry about its broadcast of Carlin's satire on "'the words you couldn't say on the public . . . airways,'" explained that "Carlin is not mouthing obscenities, he is merely using words to satirize as harmless and essentially silly our attitudes towards those words." In confirming Carlin's prescience as a social commentator by the result it reaches today, the Court evinces an attitude toward the "seven dirty words" that many others besides Mr. Carlin and Pacifica might describe as "silly." Whether today's decision

will similarly prove "harmless" remains to be seen. One can only hope
that it will.

American Booksellers Association v. Hudnut (1985)

In the 1980s, feminism reached the law schools, and feminist law pro-
fessors began to consider creative methods of attack against obscenity
and pornography in American culture. One group of feminists and
feminist lawyers believed that obscenity was a threat to women's
civil rights and that women had a civil right to live in a culture that
did not degrade women. Since pornography and obscenity degraded
women, in this group's view, the law could suppress obscenity. The
group pressed for change. In Minneapolis, Minnesota, and Indi-
anapolis, Indiana, the city councils adopted city ordinances that
defined pornography as a violation of the civil rights of women. This
potential threat to the freedom of expression caused a coalition of
booksellers and other concerned citizens to file suit to prevent the
implementation of the Indianapolis ordinance. Although this litiga-
tion did not reach the U.S. Supreme Court, the issues received a full
examination by noted federal circuit court judge Frank H. Easter-
brook.

JUDGE EASTERBROOK delivered the opinion of the Court.
    Indianapolis enacted an ordinance defining "pornography" as a
practice that discriminates against women. "Pornography" is to be
redressed through the administrative and judicial methods used for
other discrimination. The City's definition of "pornography" is considerably different from "obscenity," which the Supreme Court has
held is not protected by the First Amendment.
    To be "obscene" under *Miller v. California*, "a publication must,
taken as a whole, appeal to the prurient interest, must contain patently
offensive depictions or descriptions of specified sexual conduct, and
on the whole have no serious literary, artistic, political, or scientific
value." Offensiveness must be assessed under the standards of the
community. Both offensiveness and an appeal to something other than
"normal, healthy sexual desires" are essential elements of "obscenity."
"Pornography" under the ordinance is "the graphic sexually explicit
subordination of women, whether in pictures or in words, that also
includes one or more of the following:

1. Women are presented as sexual objects who enjoy pain or humiliation; or
2. Women are presented as sexual objects who experience sexual pleasure in being raped;
3. Women are presented as sexual objects tied up or cut up or mutilated or bruised or physically hurt, or as dismembered or truncated or fragmented or severed into body parts; or
4. Women are presented as being penetrated by objects or animals; or
5. Women are presented in scenarios of degradation, injury, abasement, torture, shown as filthy or inferior, bleeding, bruised, or hurt in a context that makes these conditions sexual; or
6. Women are presented as sexual objects for domination, conquest, violation, exploitation, possession, or use, or through postures or positions of servility or submission or display."

. . . The Indianapolis ordinance does not refer to the prurient interest, to offensiveness, or to the standards of the community. It demands attention to particular depictions, not to the work judged as a whole. It is irrelevant under the ordinance whether the work has literary, artistic, political, or scientific value. The City and many amici point to these omissions as virtues. They maintain that pornography influences attitudes, and the statute is a way to alter the socialization of men and women rather than to vindicate community standards of offensiveness. And as one of the principal drafters of the ordinance has asserted, "if a woman is subjected, why should it matter that the work has other value?"

Civil rights groups and feminists have entered this case as amici on both sides. Those supporting the ordinance say that it will play an important role in reducing the tendency of men to view women as sexual objects, a tendency that leads to both unacceptable attitudes and discrimination in the workplace and violence away from it. Those opposing the ordinance point out that much radical feminist literature is explicit and depicts women in ways forbidden by the ordinance and that the ordinance would reopen old battles. It is unclear how Indianapolis would treat works from James Joyce's *Ulysses* to Homer's *Iliad;* both depict women as submissive objects for conquest and domination.

We do not try to balance the arguments for and against an ordinance such as this. The ordinance discriminates on the ground of the content of the speech. Speech treating women in the approved way—in sexual encounters "premised on equality"—is lawful no matter how sexually explicit. Speech treating women in the disapproved way—as submissive in matters sexual or as enjoying humiliation—is unlawful no matter how significant the literary, artistic, or political qualities of the work taken as a whole. The state may not ordain preferred viewpoints in this way. The Constitution forbids the state to declare one perspective right and silence opponents.

The district court held the ordinance unconstitutional. The court concluded that the ordinance regulates speech rather than the conduct involved in making pornography. The regulation of speech could be justified, the court thought, only by a compelling interest in reducing sex discrimination, an interest Indianapolis had not established. The ordinance is also vague and overbroad, the court believed, and establishes a prior restraint of speech.

The plaintiffs are a congeries of distributors and readers of books, magazines, and films. The American Booksellers Association comprises about 5,200 bookstores and chains. The Association for American Publishers includes most of the country's publishers. Video Shack, Inc., sells and rents videocassettes in Indianapolis. Kelly Bentley, a resident of Indianapolis, reads books and watches films. There are many more plaintiffs. Collectively the plaintiffs (or their members, whose interests they represent) make, sell, or read just about every kind of material that could be affected by the ordinance, from hard-core films to W. B. Yeats's poem "Leda and the Swan" (from the myth of Zeus in the form of a swan impregnating an apparently subordinate Leda), to the collected works of James Joyce, D. H. Lawrence, and John Cleland. . . .

"If there is any fixed star in our constitutional constellation, it is that no official, high or petty, can prescribe what shall be orthodox in politics, nationalism, religion, or other matters of opinion or force citizens to confess by word or act their faith therein." Under the First Amendment the government must leave to the people the evaluation of ideas. Bald or subtle, an idea is as powerful as the audience allows it to be. A belief may be pernicious—the beliefs of Nazis led to the death of millions, those of the Klan to the repression of millions. A pernicious belief may prevail. Totalitarian governments today rule much of the planet, practicing suppression of billions and spreading dogma that may enslave others. One of the things that separates our society from theirs is our absolute right to propagate opinions that the government finds wrong or even hateful.

The ideas of the Klan may be propagated. Communists may speak freely and run for office. The Nazi Party may march through a city with a large Jewish population. People may criticize the President by misrepresenting his positions, and they have a right to post their misrepresentations on public property. People may seek to repeal laws guaranteeing equal opportunity in employment or to revoke the constitutional amendments granting the vote to blacks and women. They may do this because "above all else, the First Amendment means that government has no power to restrict expression because of its message [or] its ideas. . . ."

Under the ordinance graphic sexually explicit speech is "pornography" or not, depending on the perspective the author adopts. Speech that "subordinates" women and also, for example, presents women as enjoying pain, humiliation, or rape, or even simply presents women in "positions of servility or submission or display" is forbidden, no matter how great the literary or political value of the work taken as a whole. Speech that portrays women in positions of equality is lawful, no matter how graphic the sexual content. This is thought control. It establishes an "approved" view of women, of how they may react to sexual encounters, of how the sexes may relate to each other. Those who espouse the approved view may use sexual images; those who do not, may not.

Indianapolis justifies the ordinance on the ground that pornography affects thoughts. Men who see women depicted as subordinate are more likely to treat them so. Pornography is an aspect of dominance. It does not persuade people so much as change them. It works by socializing, by establishing the expected and the permissible. In this view pornography is not an idea; pornography is the injury.

There is much to this perspective. Beliefs are also facts. People often act in accordance with the images and patterns they find around them. People raised in a religion tend to accept the tenets of that religion, often without independent examination. People taught from birth that black people are fit only for slavery rarely rebelled against that creed; beliefs coupled with the self-interest of the masters established a social structure that inflicted great harm while enduring for centuries. Words and images act at the level of the subconscious before they persuade at the level of the conscious. Even the truth has little chance unless a statement fits within the framework of beliefs that may never have been subjected to rational study.

Therefore we accept the premises of this legislation. Depictions of subordination tend to perpetuate subordination. The subordinate status of women in turn leads to affront and lower pay at work, insult and injury at home, battery and rape on the streets. In the language of the legislature, "pornography is central in creating and maintaining sex as a basis of discrimination. Pornography is systematic practice of exploitation and subordination based on sex which differentially harms women. The bigotry and contempt it produces, with the acts of aggression it fosters, harm women's opportunities for equality and rights [of all kinds]."

Yet this simply demonstrates the power of pornography as speech. All of these unhappy effects depend on mental intermediation. Pornography affects how people see the world, their fellows, and social relations. If pornography is what pornography does, so is other speech. Hitler's orations affected how some Germans saw Jews. Communism is a worldview, not simply a Manifesto by Marx and Engels or a set of speeches. Efforts to suppress communist speech in the United States were based on the belief that the public acceptability of such ideas would increase the likelihood of totalitarian government. Religions affect socialization in the most pervasive way. . . . Many people believe that the existence of television, apart from the content of specific programs, leads to intellectual laziness, to a penchant for violence, to many other ills. The Alien and Sedition Acts passed during the administration of John Adams rested on a sincerely held belief that disrespect for the government leads to social collapse and revolution—a belief with support in the history of many nations. Most governments of the world act on this empirical regularity, suppressing critical speech. In the United States, however, the strength of the support for this belief is irrelevant. Seditious libel is protected speech unless the danger is not only grave but also imminent.

Racial bigotry, anti-Semitism, violence on television, reporters' biases—these and many more influence the culture and shape our socialization. None is directly answerable by more speech, unless that speech too finds its place in the popular culture. Yet all is protected as speech, however insidious. Any other answer leaves the government in control of all of the institutions of culture, the great censor and director of which thoughts are good for us. . . .

Much of Indianapolis's argument rests on the belief that when speech is "unanswerable," and the metaphor that there is a "marketplace of ideas" does not apply, the First Amendment does not apply either. The metaphor is honored; Milton's *Aeropagitica* and John Stuart Mill's *On Liberty* defend freedom of speech on the ground that the truth will prevail, and many of the most important cases under the First Amendment recite this position. The Framers undoubtedly believed it. As a general matter it is true. But the Constitution does not make the dominance of truth a necessary condition of freedom of speech. To say that it does would be to confuse an outcome of free speech with a necessary condition for the application of the amendment. . . .

Any rationale we could imagine in support of this ordinance could not be limited to sex discrimination. Free speech has been on balance an ally of those seeking change. Governments that want stasis start by restricting speech. Culture is a powerful force of continuity; Indianapolis paints pornography as part of the culture of power. Change in any complex system ultimately depends on the ability of outsiders to challenge accepted views and the reigning institutions. Without a strong guarantee of freedom of speech, there is no effective right to challenge what is.

The definition of "pornography" is unconstitutional. No construction or excision of particular terms could save it. . . .

Much speech is dangerous. Chemists whose work might help someone build a bomb, political theorists whose papers might start political movements that lead to riots, speakers whose ideas attract violent protesters, all these and more leave loss in their wake. Unless the remedy is very closely confined, it could be more dangerous to speech than all the libel judgments in history. The constitutional requirements for a valid recovery for assault caused by speech might turn out to be too rigorous for any plaintiff to meet. . . .

No amount of struggle with particular words and phrases in this ordinance can leave anything in effect. The district court came to the same conclusion. Its judgment is therefore

Affirmed.

City of Renton v. Playtime Theatres (1986)

Unlike Detroit, which sought to scatter "adult" businesses, the city of Renton, Washington, passed a zoning ordinance aimed at concentrat-

ing such businesses in one specific area. Like those in Detroit, the adult businesses in Renton challenged the city's zoning ordinance, arguing that the regulation restricted their First Amendment free speech and press rights.

JUSTICE REHNQUIST delivered the opinion of the Court.

This case involves a constitutional challenge to a zoning ordinance, enacted by appellant city of Renton, Washington, that prohibits adult motion picture theaters from locating within 1,000 feet of any residential zone, single- or multiple-family dwelling, church, park, or school. Appellees, Playtime Theatres, Inc., and Sea-First Properties, Inc., filed an action in the United States District Court for the Western District of Washington seeking a declaratory judgment that the Renton ordinance violated the First and Fourteenth Amendments and a permanent injunction against its enforcement. The District Court ruled in favor of Renton and denied the permanent injunction, but the Court of Appeals for the Ninth Circuit reversed and remanded for reconsideration. We noted probable jurisdiction and now reverse the judgment of the Ninth Circuit.

In May 1980, the Mayor of Renton, a city of approximately 32,000 people located just south of Seattle, suggested to the Renton City Council that it consider the advisability of enacting zoning legislation dealing with adult entertainment uses. . . .

In April 1981, acting on the basis of the Planning and Development Committee's recommendation, the City Council enacted Ordinance No. 3526. The ordinance prohibited any "adult motion picture theater" from locating within 1,000 feet of any residential zone, single- or multiple-family dwelling, church, or park, and within one mile of any school. The term "adult motion picture theater" was defined as "[a]n enclosed building used for presenting motion picture films, video cassettes, cable television, or any other such visual media, distinguished or characteri[zed] by an emphasis on matter depicting, describing or relating to 'specified sexual activities' or 'specified anatomical areas' . . . for observation by patrons therein."

In our view, the resolution of this case is largely dictated by our decision in *Young v. American Mini Theatres, Inc.* There, although five Members of the Court did not agree on a single rationale for the decision, we held that the city of Detroit's zoning ordinance, which prohibited locating an adult theater within 1,000 feet of any two other "regulated uses" or within 500 feet of any residential zone, did not violate the First and Fourteenth Amendments. The Renton ordinance, like the one in *American Mini Theatres,* does not ban adult theaters altogether, but merely provides that such theaters may not be located within 1,000 feet of any residential zone, single- or multiple-family dwelling, church, park, or school. The ordinance is therefore properly analyzed as a form of time, place, and manner regulation.

Describing the ordinance as a time, place, and manner regulation is, of course, only the first step in our inquiry. This Court has long held that regulations enacted for the purpose of restraining speech on the basis of its content presumptively violate the First Amendment. On the other hand, so-called "content-neutral" time, place, and manner regulations are acceptable so long as they are designed to serve a substantial governmental interest and do not unreasonably limit alternative avenues of communication.

At first glance, the Renton ordinance, like the ordinance in *American Mini Theatres,* does not appear to fit neatly into either the "content-based" or the "content-neutral" category. To be sure, the ordinance treats theaters that specialize in adult films differently from other kinds of theaters. Nevertheless, as the District Court concluded, the Renton ordinance is aimed not at the content of the films shown at "adult motion picture theatres," but rather at the secondary effects of such theaters on the surrounding community. The District Court found that the City Council's "predominate concerns" were with the secondary effects of adult theaters, and not with the content of adult films themselves. But the Court of Appeals . . . held that this was not enough to sustain the ordinance. According to the Court of Appeals, if "a motivating factor" in enacting the ordinance was to restrict respondents' exercise of First Amendment rights the ordinance would be invalid, apparently no matter how small a part this motivating factor may have played in the City Council's decision. . . .

The District Court's finding as to "predominate" intent, left undisturbed by the Court of Appeals, is more than adequate to establish that the city's pursuit of its zoning interests here was unrelated to the suppression of free expression. The ordinance by its terms is designed to prevent crime, protect the city's retail trade, maintain property values, and generally "protec[t] and preserv[e] the quality of [the city's] neighborhoods, commercial districts, and the quality of urban life, not to suppress the expression of unpopular views."

. . . In short, the Renton ordinance is completely consistent with our definition of "content-neutral" speech regulations as those that "are justified without reference to the content of the regulated speech." The ordinance does not contravene the fundamental principle that underlies our concern about "content-based" speech regulations: that "government may not grant the use of a forum to people whose views it finds acceptable, but deny use to those wishing to express less favored or more controversial views."

. . . The appropriate inquiry in this case, then, is whether the Renton ordinance is designed to serve a substantial governmental interest and allows for reasonable alternative avenues of communication. It is clear that the ordinance meets such a standard. As a majority of this Court recognized in *American Mini Theatres,* a city's "interest in attempting to preserve the quality of urban life is one that must be accorded high respect." Exactly the same vital governmental interests are at stake here. . . .

We also find no constitutional defect in the method chosen by Renton to further its substantial interests. Cities may regulate adult theaters by dispersing them, as in Detroit, or by effectively concentrating them, as in Renton. "It is not our function to appraise the wisdom of [the city's] decision to require adult theaters to be separated rather than concentrated in the same areas. . . . [T]he city must be allowed a reasonable opportunity to experiment with solutions to admittedly serious problems." Moreover, the Renton ordinance is "narrowly tailored" to affect only that category of theaters shown to produce the unwanted secondary effects, thus avoiding the flaw that proved fatal to the regulations. . . .

Finally, turning to the question whether the Renton ordinance allows for reasonable alternative avenues of communication, we note that the ordinance leaves some 520 acres, or more than five percent of the entire land area of Renton, open to use as adult theater sites. The District Court found, and the Court of Appeals did not dispute the finding, that the 520 acres of land consists of "[a]mple, accessible real estate," including "acreage in all stages of development from raw land to developed, industrial, warehouse, office, and shopping space that is crisscrossed by freeways, highways, and roads."

Respondents argue, however, that some of the land in question is already occupied by existing businesses, that "practically none" of the undeveloped land is currently for sale or lease, and that in general there are no "commercially viable" adult theater sites within the 520 acres left open by the Renton ordinance. The Court of Appeals accepted these arguments, concluded that the 520 acres was not truly "available" land, and therefore held that the Renton ordinance "would result in a substantial restriction" on speech. . . .

In sum, we find that the Renton ordinance represents a valid governmental response to the "admittedly serious problems" created by adult theaters. Renton has not used "the power to zone as a pretext for suppressing expression," but rather has sought to make some areas available for adult theaters and their patrons, while at the same time preserving the quality of life in the community at large by preventing those theaters from locating in other areas. This, after all, is the essence of zoning. Here, as in *American Mini Theatres,* the city has enacted a zoning ordinance that meets these goals while also satisfying the dictates of the First Amendment. The judgment of the Court of Appeals is therefore

Reversed.

JUSTICE BRENNAN, with whom JUSTICE MARSHALL joins, dissenting.

Renton's zoning ordinance selectively imposes limitations on the location of a movie theater based exclusively on the content of the films shown there. The constitutionality of the ordinance is therefore not correctly analyzed under standards applied to content-neutral time, place, and manner restrictions. But even assuming that the ordinance may fairly be characterized as content neutral, it is plainly unconstitutional under the standards established by the decisions of this Court. Although the Court's analysis is limited to cases involving "businesses that purvey sexually explicit materials," and thus does not affect our holdings in cases involving state regulation of other kinds of speech, I dissent.

The fact that adult movie theaters may cause harmful "secondary" land-use effects may arguably give Renton a compelling reason to regulate such establishments; it does not mean, however, that such regulations are content neutral. Because the ordinance imposes special restrictions on certain kinds of speech on the basis of content, I cannot simply accept, as the Court does, Renton's claim that the ordinance was not designed to suppress the content of adult movies. . . .

The ordinance discriminates on its face against certain forms of speech based on content. Movie theaters specializing in "adult motion pictures" may not be located within 1,000 feet of any residential zone, single- or multiple-family dwelling, church, park, or school. Other motion picture theaters, and other forms of "adult entertainment," such as bars, massage parlors, and adult bookstores, are not subject to the same restrictions. This selective treatment strongly suggests that Renton was interested not in controlling the "secondary effects" associated with adult businesses, but in discriminating against adult theaters based on the content of the films they exhibit. The Court ignores this discriminatory treatment, declaring that Renton is free "to address the potential problems created by one particular kind of adult business," and to amend the ordinance in the future to include other adult enterprises. However, because of the First Amendment interests at stake here, this one-step-at-a-time analysis is wholly inappropriate. . . .

The Court holds that Renton was entitled to rely on the experiences of cities like Detroit and Seattle, which had enacted special zoning regulations for adult entertainment businesses after studying the adverse effects caused by such establishments. However, even assuming that Renton was concerned with the same problems as Seattle and Detroit, it never actually reviewed any of the studies conducted by those cities. Renton had no basis for determining if any of the "findings" made by these cities were relevant to Renton's problems or needs. Moreover, since Renton ultimately adopted zoning regulations different from either Detroit or Seattle, these "studies" provide no basis for assessing the effectiveness of the particular restrictions adopted under the ordinance. Renton cannot merely rely on the general experiences of Seattle or Detroit, for it must "justify its ordinance in the context of Renton's problems—not Seattle's or Detroit's problems."

In sum, the circumstances here strongly suggest that the ordinance was designed to suppress expression, even that constitutionally protected, and thus was not to be analyzed as a content-neutral time, place, and manner restriction. The Court allows Renton to conceal its illicit motives, however, by reliance on the fact that other communities adopted similar restrictions. The Court's approach largely immunizes such measures from judicial scrutiny, since a municipality can readily find other municipal ordinances to rely upon, thus always retrospectively justifying special zoning regulations for adult theaters. Rather than speculate about Renton's motives for adopting such measures, our cases require the conclusion that the ordinance, like any other content-based restriction on speech, is constitutional "only if the [city] can show that [it] is a precisely drawn means of serving a compelling [governmental] interest." Only this strict approach can insure that cities will not use their zoning powers as a pretext for suppressing constitutionally protected expression.

Applying this standard to the facts of this case, the ordinance is patently unconstitutional. Renton has not shown that locating adult movie theaters in proximity to its churches, schools, parks, and residences will necessarily result in undesirable "secondary effects," or that these problems could not be effectively addressed by less intrusive restrictions.

Even assuming that the ordinance should be treated like a content-neutral time, place, and manner restriction, I would still find it unconstitutional. . . . In applying this standard, the Court "fails to subject the alleged interests of the [city] to the degree of scrutiny required to ensure that expressive activity protected by the First Amendment remains free of unnecessary limitations." The Court "evidently [and wrongly] assumes that the balance struck by [Renton] officials is deserving of deference so long as it does not appear to be tainted by content discrimination." Under a proper application of the relevant standards, the ordinance is clearly unconstitutional.

The Court finds that the ordinance was designed to further Renton's substantial interest in "preserv[ing] the quality of urban life." As explained above, the record here is simply insufficient to support this assertion. The city made no showing as to how uses "protected" by the ordinance would be affected by the presence of an adult movie theater. Thus, the Renton ordinance is clearly distinguishable from the Detroit zoning ordinance upheld in *Young v. American Mini Theatres, Inc.* The Detroit ordinance, which was designed to disperse adult theaters throughout the city, was supported by the testimony of urban planners and real estate experts regarding the adverse effects of locating several such businesses in the same neighborhood. Here, the Renton Council was aware only that some residents had complained about adult movie theaters, and that other localities had adopted special zoning restrictions for such establishments. These are not "facts" sufficient to justify the burdens the ordinance imposed upon constitutionally protected expression. . . .

Despite the evidence in the record, the Court reasons that the fact "[t]hat respondents must fend for themselves in the real estate market, on an equal footing with other prospective purchasers and lessees, does not give rise to a First Amendment violation." However, respondents are not on equal footing with other prospective purchasers and lessees, but must conduct business under severe restrictions not imposed upon other establishments. The Court also argues that the First Amendment does not compel "the government to ensure that adult theaters, or any other kinds of speech-related businesses for that matter, will be able to obtain sites at bargain prices." However, respondents do not ask Renton to guarantee low-price sites for their businesses, but seek only a reasonable opportunity to operate adult theaters in the city. By denying them this opportunity, Renton can effectively ban a form of protected speech from its borders. The ordinance "greatly restrict[s] access to . . . lawful speech," and is plainly unconstitutional.

Sable Communications v. Federal Communications Commission (1989)

Litigation involving technology and obscenity continued to come before the U.S. Supreme Court. In this instance, companies had developed what is popularly called a "dial-a-porn" service. At issue was whether Congress's and the Federal Communications Commission's regulations could regulate "indecent" speech versus "obscene" speech without running afoul of First Amendment problems. In this case the Court faced the question of whether Congress and the FCC could totally prohibit "indecent" or "obscene" speech delivered through the telephone. The Court's decision drew the expected dissent from Justice Brennan.

JUSTICE WHITE delivered the opinion of the Court.

The issue before us is the constitutionality of 223(b) of the Communications Act of 1934. The statute, as amended in 1988, imposes an outright ban on indecent as well as obscene interstate commercial telephone messages. The District Court upheld the prohibition against obscene interstate telephone communications for commercial purposes, but enjoined the enforcement of the statute insofar as it applied to indecent messages. We affirm the District Court in both respects.

In 1983, Sable Communications, Inc., a Los Angeles–based affiliate of Carlin Communications, Inc., began offering sexually oriented prerecorded telephone messages (popularly known as "dial-a-porn") through the Pacific Bell telephone network. In order to provide the messages, Sable arranged with Pacific Bell to use special telephone lines, designed to handle large volumes of calls simultaneously. Those who called the adult message number were charged a special fee. The fee was collected by Pacific Bell and divided between the phone company and the message provider. Callers outside the Los Angeles metropolitan area could reach the number by means of a long-distance toll call to the Los Angeles area code.

In 1988, Sable brought suit in District Court seeking declaratory and injunctive relief against enforcement of the recently amended 223(b). The 1988 amendments to the statute imposed a blanket prohibition on indecent as well as obscene interstate commercial telephone messages. Sable brought this action to enjoin the Federal Communications Commission (FCC) and the Justice Department from initiating any criminal investigation or prosecution, civil action or administrative proceeding under the statute. Sable also sought a declaratory judgment, challenging the indecency and the obscenity provisions of the amended 223(b) as unconstitutional, chiefly under the First and Fourteenth Amendments to the Constitution.

The District Court found that a concrete controversy existed and that Sable met the irreparable injury requirement for issuance of a preliminary injunction. . . . The District Court denied Sable's request for a preliminary injunction against enforcement of the statute's ban on obscene telephone messages, rejecting the argument that the statute was unconstitutional because it created a national standard of obscenity. The District Court, however, struck down the "indecent speech" provision of 223(b), holding that in this respect the statute was overbroad and unconstitutional and that this result was consistent with *FCC v. Pacifica Foundation* (1978). . . .

We noted probable jurisdiction on Sable's appeal of the obscenity ruling. . . .

Congress made its first effort explicitly to address "dial-a-porn" when it added a subsection 223(b) to the 1934 Communications Act. The provision, which was the predecessor to the amendment at issue in this case, pertained directly to sexually oriented commercial telephone messages and sought to restrict the access of minors to dial-a-porn. The relevant provision of the Act, Federal Communications Commission Authorization Act of 1983 made it a crime to use telephone facilities to make "obscene or indecent" interstate telephone communications "for commercial purposes to any person under eighteen years of age or to any other person without that person's consent." The statute criminalized commercial transmission of sexually

oriented communications to minors and required the FCC to promulgate regulations laying out the means by which dial-a-porn sponsors
could screen out underaged callers. The enactment provided that it
would be a defense to prosecution that the defendant restricted access
to adults only, in accordance with procedures established by the FCC.
The statute did not criminalize sexually oriented messages to adults,
whether the messages were obscene or indecent.

The FCC initially promulgated regulations that would have established a defense to message providers operating only between the
hours of 9 p.m. and 8 a.m. eastern time (time channeling) and to
providers requiring payment by credit card (screening) before transmission of the dial-a-porn message. . . .

In 1985, the FCC promulgated new regulations which continued to
permit credit card payment as a defense to prosecution. Instead of
time restrictions, however, the Commission added a defense based on
use of access codes (user identification codes). . . . Callers would be
required to provide an access number for identification (or a credit
card) before receiving the message. The access code would be received
through the mail after the message provider reviewed the application
and concluded through a written age ascertainment procedure that the
applicant was at least 18 years of age. . . .

The FCC then promulgated a third set of regulations, which again
rejected customer premises blocking but added to the prior defenses of
credit card payment and access code use a third defense: message
scrambling. Under this system, providers would scramble the message, which would then be unintelligible without the use of a descrambler, the sale of which would be limited to adults. On January 15,
1988, the Court of Appeals for the Second Circuit held that the new
regulations, which made access codes, along with credit card payments
and scrambled messages, defenses to prosecution under 223(b) for
dial-a-porn providers, were supported by the evidence, had been
properly arrived at, and were a "feasible and effective way to serve"
the "compelling state interest" in protecting minors, the Court
directed the FCC to reopen proceedings if a less restrictive technology
became available. The Court of Appeals, however, this time reaching
the constitutionality of the statute, invalidated 223(b) insofar as it
sought to apply to nonobscene speech.

Thereafter, in April 1988, Congress amended 223(b) of the Communications Act to prohibit indecent as well as obscene interstate
commercial telephone communications directed to any person regard-

less of age. The amended statute, which took effect on July 1, 1988, also eliminated the requirement that the FCC promulgate regulations for restricting access to minors since a total ban was imposed on dial-a-porn, making it illegal for adults, as well as children, to have access to the sexually explicit messages. It was this version of the statute that was in effect when Sable commenced this action.

In the ruling at issue in No. 88–515, the District Court upheld 223(b)'s prohibition of obscene telephone messages as constitutional. We agree with that judgment. In contrast to the prohibition on indecent communications, there is no constitutional barrier to the ban on obscene dial-a-porn recordings. We have repeatedly held that the protection of the First Amendment does not extend to obscene speech. The cases before us today do not require us to decide what is obscene or what is indecent but rather to determine whether Congress is empowered to prohibit transmission of obscene telephonic communications. . . .

We do not read 223(b) as contravening the "contemporary community standards" requirement of *Miller v. California* (1973). Section 223(b) no more establishes a "national standard" of obscenity than do federal statutes prohibiting the mailing of obscene material or the broadcasting of obscene messages. . . . Similarly, we hold today that there is no constitutional stricture against Congress' prohibiting the interstate transmission of obscene commercial telephone recordings. . . .

In No. 88–525, the District Court concluded that while the Government has a legitimate interest in protecting children from exposure to indecent dial-a-porn messages, 223(b) was not sufficiently narrowly drawn to serve that purpose and thus violated the First Amendment. We agree.

Sexual expression which is indecent but not obscene is protected by the First Amendment; and the federal parties do not submit that the sale of such materials to adults could be criminalized solely because they are indecent. The Government may, however, regulate the content of constitutionally protected speech in order to promote a compelling interest if it chooses the least restrictive means to further the articulated interest. We have recognized that there is a compelling interest in protecting the physical and psychological well-being of minors. This interest extends to shielding minors from the influence of literature that is not obscene by adult standards. The Government may serve this legitimate interest, but to withstand constitutional scrutiny, "it must do so by narrowly drawn regulations designed to serve those interests without unnecessarily interfering with First Amendment freedoms." It is not enough to show that the Government's ends are compelling; the means must be carefully tailored to achieve those ends.

In *Butler v. Michigan* (1957), a unanimous Court reversed a conviction under a statute which made it an offense to make available to the general public materials found to have a potentially harmful influence on minors. The Court found the law to be insufficiently tailored since it denied adults their free speech rights by allowing them to read only what was acceptable for children. As Justice Frankfurter said in that case, "[s]urely this is to burn the house to roast the pig." In our judgment, this case, like *Butler*, presents us with "legislation not reasonably restricted to the evil with which it is said to deal."

In attempting to justify the complete ban and criminalization of the indecent commercial telephone communications with adults as well as minors, the federal parties rely on *FCC v. Pacifica Foundation* (1978), a case in which the Court considered whether the FCC has the power to regulate a radio broadcast that is indecent but not obscene. In an emphatically narrow holding, the *Pacifica* Court concluded that special treatment of indecent broadcasting was justified.

Pacifica is readily distinguishable from these cases, most obviously because it did not involve a total ban on broadcasting indecent material. The FCC rule was not "intended to place an absolute prohibition on the broadcast of this type of language, but rather sought to channel it to times of day when children most likely would not be exposed to it." The issue of a total ban was not before the Court.

The *Pacifica* opinion also relied on the "unique" attributes of broadcasting, noting that broadcasting is "uniquely pervasive," can intrude on the privacy of the home without prior warning as to program content, and is "uniquely accessible to children, even those too young to read." The private commercial telephone communications at issue here are substantially different from the public radio broadcast at issue in Pacifica. . . . There is no "captive audience" problem here; callers will generally not be unwilling listeners. The context of dial-in services, where a caller seeks and is willing to pay for the communication, is manifestly different from a situation in which a listener does not want the received message. Placing a telephone call is not the same as turning on a radio and being taken by surprise by an indecent message. Unlike an unexpected outburst on a radio broadcast, the message received by one who places a call to a dial-a-porn service is not so invasive or surprising that it prevents an unwilling listener from avoiding exposure to it. . . .

The federal parties nevertheless argue that the total ban on indecent commercial telephone communications is justified because nothing less could prevent children from gaining access to such messages. We find the argument quite unpersuasive. The FCC, after lengthy proceedings, determined that its credit card, access code, and scrambling rules were a satisfactory solution to the problem of keeping indecent dial-a-porn messages out of the reach of minors. The Court of Appeals, after careful consideration, agreed that these rules represented a "feasible and effective" way to serve the Government's compelling interest in protecting children. . . .

For all we know from this record, the FCC's technological approach to restricting dial-a-porn messages to adults who seek them would be extremely effective, and only a few of the most enterprising and disobedient young people would manage to secure access to such messages. If this is the case, it seems to us that 223(b) is not a narrowly tailored effort to serve the compelling interest of preventing minors from being exposed to indecent telephone messages. Under our precedents, 223(b), in its present form, has the invalid effect of limiting the content of adult telephone conversations to that which is suitable for children to hear. It is another case of "burn[ing] the house to roast the pig."

Because the statute's denial of adult access to telephone messages which are indecent but not obscene far exceeds that which is necessary to limit the access of minors to such messages, we hold that the ban does not survive constitutional scrutiny.

Accordingly, we affirm the judgment. . . .

It is so ordered.

JUSTICE BRENNAN, with whom JUSTICE MARSHALL and JUSTICE STEVENS join, concurring in part and dissenting in part.

I agree that a statute imposing criminal penalties for making, or for allowing others to use a telephone under one's control to make, any indecent telephonic communication for a commercial purpose is patently unconstitutional. . . .

In my view, however, . . . parallel criminal prohibition with regard to obscene commercial communications . . . violates the First Amendment. I have long been convinced that the exaction of criminal penalties for the distribution of obscene materials to consenting adults is constitutionally intolerable. In my judgment, "the concept of 'obscenity' cannot be defined with sufficient specificity and clarity to provide fair notice to persons who create and distribute sexually oriented materials, to prevent substantial erosion of protected speech as a byproduct of the attempt to suppress unprotected speech, and to avoid very costly institutional harms." To be sure, the Government has a strong interest in protecting children against exposure to pornographic material that might be harmful to them. But a complete criminal ban on obscene telephonic messages for profit is "unconstitutionally overbroad, and therefore invalid on its face," as a means for achieving this end.

The very evidence the Court adduces to show that denying adults access to all indecent commercial messages "far exceeds that which is necessary to limit the access of minors to such messages," also demonstrates that forbidding the transmission of all obscene messages is unduly heavyhanded. After painstaking scrutiny, both the FCC and the Second Circuit found that "a scheme involving access codes, scrambling, and credit card payment is a feasible and effective way to serve this compelling state interest" in safeguarding children. And during the 1987 hearings on H. R. 1786, a United States attorney speaking on behalf of the Justice Department described the FCC's proposed regulations as "very effective," because they would "dramatically reduc[e] the number of calls from minors in the United States, almost eliminating them. . . ."

Section 223(b)(1)(A) unambiguously proscribes all obscene commercial messages, and thus admits of no construction that would render it constitutionally permissible. Because this criminal statute curtails freedom of speech far more radically than the Government's interest in preventing harm to minors could possibly license on the record before us, I would reverse the District Court's decision in No. 88–515 and strike down the statute on its face. Accordingly, I dissent. . . .

Denver Area Educational Telecommunications Consortium v. Federal Communications Commission (1996)

Advances in the technology of cable television forged ahead in the 1980s. These advances brought more and more consumers into the cable television networks, attracted by the greater variety of pro-

*gramming than was available through broadcast television. Some of
the cable networks carried "adults only" programming. The potential
exposure of children to this material caused Congress to respond. In
1992, Congress passed the Cable Television Consumer Protection and
Competition Act (CTCPCA). A coalition of concerned citizens and
groups then filed suit, challenging three sections of the Act on the
grounds that the restrictions on "adult" programming were unreasonable. The Court splintered again on this case, and six justices wrote
separate opinions. The Court's response clearly reflected the lack of a
general consensus among Americans about how best to regulate and
control adult programming in the public medium of cable television.*

JUSTICE BREYER announced the judgment of the Court.

These cases present First Amendment challenges to three statutory
provisions that seek to regulate the broadcasting of "patently offensive" sex-related material on cable television. Cable Television Consumer Protection and Competition Act of 1992 (1992 Act or Act), 106
Stat. 1486, Section(s) 10(a), 10(b), and 10(c), 47 U. S. C. Section(s)
532(h), 532(j), and note following Section(s) 531. The provisions apply
to programs broadcast over cable on what are known as "leased access
channels" and "public, educational, or governmental channels." Two
of the provisions essentially permit a cable system operator to prohibit
the broadcasting of "programming" that the "operator reasonably
believes describes or depicts sexual or excretory activities or organs in
a patently offensive manner." The remaining provision requires cable
system operators to segregate certain "patently offensive" programming, to place it on a single channel, and to block that channel from
viewer access unless the viewer requests access in advance and in writing.

We conclude that the first provision—that permits the operator to
decide whether or not to broadcast such programs on leased access
channels—is consistent with the First Amendment. The second provision, that requires leased channel operators to segregate and to block
that programming, and the third provision, applicable to public, educational, and governmental channels, violate the First Amendment, for
they are not appropriately tailored to achieve the basic, legitimate
objective of protecting children from exposure to "patently offensive"
material.

Cable operators typically own a physical cable network used to
convey programming over several dozen cable channels into sub-

scribers' houses. Program sources vary from channel to channel. Most channels carry programming produced by independent firms, including "many national and regional cable programming networks that have emerged in recent years," as well as some programming that the system operator itself (or an operator affiliate) may provide. Other channels may simply retransmit through cable the signals of over-the-air broadcast stations. Certain special channels here at issue, called "leased channels" and "public, educational, or governmental channels," carry programs provided by those to whom the law gives special cable system access rights.

A "leased channel" is a channel that federal law requires a cable system operator to reserve for commercial lease by unaffiliated third parties. About 10 to 15 percent of a cable system's channels would typically fall into this category. . . .

The upshot is, as we said at the beginning, that the federal law before us (the statute as implemented through regulations) now permits cable operators either to allow or to forbid the transmission of "patently offensive" sex-related materials over both leased and public access channels, and requires those operators, at a minimum, to segregate and to block transmission of that same material on leased channels.

Petitioners, claiming that the three statutory provisions, as implemented by the Commission regulations, violate the First Amendment, sought judicial review of the Commission's First Report and Order and its Second Report and Order in the United States Court of Appeals for the District of Columbia Circuit. A panel of that Circuit agreed with petitioners that the provisions violated the First Amendment. The entire Court of Appeals, however, heard the case en banc and reached the opposite conclusion. . . .

We turn initially to the provision that permits cable system operators to prohibit "patently offensive" (or "indecent") programming transmitted over leased access channels. The Court of Appeals held that this provision did not violate the First Amendment because the First Amendment prohibits only "Congress" (and, through the Fourteenth Amendment, a "State"), not private individuals, from "abridging the freedom of speech." Although the court said that it found no "state action," it could not have meant that phrase literally, for, of course, petitioners attack (as "abridg[ing] . . . speech") a congressional statute—which, by definition, is an Act of "Congress. . . ."

We recognize that the First Amendment, the terms of which apply to governmental action, ordinarily does not itself throw into constitutional doubt the decisions of private citizens to permit, or to restrict, speech—and this is so ordinarily even where those decisions take place within the framework of a regulatory regime such as broadcasting. Were that not so, courts might have to face the difficult, and potentially restrictive, practical task of deciding which, among any number of private parties involved in providing a program (for example, networks, station owners, program editors, and program producers), is the "speaker" whose rights may not be abridged, and who is the speech-restricting "censor. . . ."

The history of this Court's First Amendment jurisprudence, however, is one of continual development, as the Constitution's general command that "Congress shall make no law . . . abridging the freedom of speech, or of the press," has been applied to new circumstances requiring different adaptations of prior principles and precedents. The essence of that protection is that Congress may not regulate speech except in cases of extraordinary need and with the exercise of a degree of care that we have not elsewhere required At the same time, our cases have not left Congress or the States powerless to address the most serious problems.

Over the years, this Court has restated and refined these basic First Amendment principles, adapting them more particularly to the balance of competing interests and the special circumstances of each field of application.

This tradition teaches that the First Amendment embodies an overarching commitment to protect speech from Government regulation through close judicial scrutiny, thereby enforcing the Constitution's constraints, but without imposing judicial formulae so rigid that they become a straightjacket that disables Government from responding to serious problems. This Court, in different contexts, has consistently held that the Government may directly regulate speech to address extraordinary problems, where its regulations are appropriately tailored to resolve those problems without imposing an unnecessarily great restriction on speech. . . .

We can decide this case more narrowly, by closely scrutinizing Section(s) 10(a) to assure that it properly addresses an extremely important problem, without imposing, in light of the relevant interests, an unnecessarily great restriction on speech. The importance of the interest at stake here—protecting children from exposure to patently offensive depictions of sex; the accommodation of the interests of programmers in maintaining access channels and of cable operators in editing the contents of their channels; the similarity of the problem and its solution to those at issue in *Pacifica*; and the flexibility inherent in an approach that permits private cable operators to make editorial decisions—lead us to conclude that Section(s) 10(a) is a sufficiently tailored response to an extraordinarily important problem.

First, the provision before us comes accompanied with an extremely important justification, one that this Court has often found compelling—the need to protect children from exposure to patently offensive sex-related material.

Second, the provision arises in a very particular context—congressional permission for cable operators to regulate programming that, but for a previous Act of Congress, would have had no path of access to cable channels free of an operator's control. The First Amendment interests involved are therefore complex, and involve a balance between those interests served by the access requirements themselves (increasing the availability of avenues of expression to programmers who otherwise would not have them) and the disadvantage to the First Amendment interests of cable operators and other programmers (those to whom the cable operator would have assigned the channels devoted to access).

Third, the problem Congress addressed here is remarkably similar to the problem addressed by the FCC in *Pacifica,* and the balance Congress struck is commensurate with the balance we approved there. In *Pacifica* this Court considered a governmental ban of a radio broadcast of "indecent" materials, defined in part, like the provisions before us, to include "'language that describes, in terms patently offensive as measured by contemporary community standards for the broadcast medium, sexual or excretory activities and organs, at times of the day when there is a reasonable risk that children may be in the audience.'"

The Court found this ban constitutionally permissible primarily because "broadcasting is uniquely accessible to children" and children were likely listeners to the program there at issue—an afternoon radio broadcast. In addition, the Court wrote, "the broadcast media have established a uniquely pervasive presence in the lives of all Americans," "[p]atently offensive, indecent material . . . confronts the citizen, not only in public, but also in the privacy of the home," generally without sufficient prior warning to allow the recipient to avert his or her eyes or ears; and "[a]dults who feel the need may purchase tapes and records or go to theaters and nightclubs" to hear similar performances.

All these factors are present here. Cable television broadcasting, including access channel broadcasting, is as "accessible to children" as over-the-air broadcasting, if not more so . . . (cable subscribers tended to sample more channels before settling on a program, thereby making them more, not less susceptible to random exposure to unwanted materials). There is nothing to stop "adults who feel the need" from finding similar programming elsewhere, say, on tape or in theaters. In fact, the power of cable systems to control home program viewing is not absolute. Over-the-air broadcasting and direct broadcast satellites already provide alternative ways for programmers to reach the home, and are likely to do so to a greater extent in the near future.

Fourth, the permissive nature of Section(s) 10(a) means that it likely restricts speech less than, not more than, the ban at issue in *Pacifica.* The provision removes a restriction as to some speakers—namely, cable operators. Moreover, although the provision does create a risk that a program will not appear, that risk is not the same as the certainty that accompanies a governmental ban. In fact, a glance at the programming that cable operators allow on their own (nonaccess) channels suggests that this distinction is not theoretical, but real. Finally, the provision's permissive nature brings with it a flexibility that allows cable operators, for example, not to ban broadcasts, but, say, to rearrange broadcast times, better to fit the desires of adult audiences while lessening the risks of harm to children. In all these respects, the permissive nature of the approach taken by Congress renders this measure appropriate as a means of achieving the underlying purpose of protecting children. . . .

For the reasons discussed, we conclude that Section(s) 10(a) is consistent with the First Amendment.

The statute's second provision significantly differs from the first, for it does not simply permit, but rather requires, cable system operators to restrict speech—by segregating and blocking "patently offensive" sex-related material appearing on leased channels (but not on other channels). In particular, as previously mentioned, this provision and its implementing regulations require cable system operators to place "patently offensive" leased channel programming on a separate channel; to block that channel; to unblock the channel within 30 days of a subscriber's written request for access; and to reblock the channel within 30 days of a subscriber's request for reblocking. Also, leased channel programmers must notify cable operators of an intended "patently offensive" broadcast up to 30 days before its scheduled broadcast date.

These requirements have obvious restrictive effects. The several up-to-30-day delays, along with single channel segregation, mean that a subscriber cannot decide to watch a single program without consider-able advance planning and without letting the "patently offensive" channel in its entirety invade his household for days, perhaps weeks, at a time. These restrictions will prevent programmers from broad-casting to viewers who select programs day by day (or, through "surf-ing," minute by minute); to viewers who would like occasionally to watch a few, but not many, of the programs on the "patently offen-sive" channel; and to viewers who simply tend to judge a program's value through channel reputation, i.e., by the company it keeps. More-over, the "written notice" requirement will further restrict viewing by subscribers who fear for their reputations should the operator, adver-tently or inadvertently, disclose the list of those who wish to watch the "patently offensive" channel. Further, the added costs and burdens that these requirements impose upon a cable system operator may encourage that operator to ban programming that the operator would otherwise permit to run, even if only late at night. . . .

We agree with the Government that protection of children is a "compelling interest." But we do not agree that the "segregate and block" requirements properly accommodate the speech restrictions they impose and the legitimate objective they seek to attain. Nor need we here determine whether, or the extent to which, *Pacifica* does, or does not, impose some lesser standard of review where indecent speech is at issue. That is because once one examines this governmen-tal restriction, it becomes apparent that, not only is it not a "least restrictive alternative," and is not "narrowly tailored" to meet its legit-imate objective, it also seems considerably "more extensive than nec-essary." That is to say, it fails to satisfy this Court's formulations of the First Amendment's "strictest," as well as its somewhat less "strict," requirements. The provision before us does not reveal the caution and care that the standards underlying these various verbal formulas impose upon laws that seek to reconcile the critically important inter-est in protecting free speech with very important, or even compelling, interests that sometimes warrant restrictions. . . .

No provision, we concede, short of an absolute ban, can offer cer-tain protection against assault by a determined child. We have not, however, generally allowed this fact alone to justify "reduc[ing] the adult population . . . to . . . only what is fit for children." But, leaving that problem aside, the Solicitor General's list of practical difficulties would seem to call, not for "segregate and block" requirements, but, rather, for informational requirements, for a simple coding system, for readily available blocking equipment (perhaps accessible by telephone), for imposing cost burdens upon system operators (who may spread them through subscription fees), or perhaps even for a system that requires lockbox defaults to be set to block certain channels (say, sex-dedicated channels). . . .

Consequently, we cannot find that the "segregate and block" restrictions on speech are a narrowly, or reasonably, tailored effort to protect children. Rather, they are overly restrictive, "sacrific[ing]" important First Amendment interests for too "speculative a gain." For that reason they are not consistent with the First Amendment. . . .

The upshot, in respect to the public access channels, is a law that could radically change present programming-related relationships among local community and nonprofit supervising boards and access managers, which relationships are established through municipal law, regulation, and contract. In doing so, it would not significantly restore editorial rights of cable operators, but would greatly increase the risk that certain categories of programming (say, borderline offensive programs) will not appear. At the same time, given present supervisory mechanisms, the need for this particular provision, aimed directly at public access channels, is not obvious. Having carefully reviewed the legislative history of the Act, the proceedings before the FCC, the record below, and the submissions of the parties and amici here, we conclude that the Government cannot sustain its burden of showing that Section(s) 10(c) is necessary to protect children or that it is appropriately tailored to secure that end. Consequently, we find that this third provision violates the First Amendment. . . .

For these reasons, the judgment of the Court of Appeals is affirmed insofar as it upheld Section(s) 10(a); the judgment of the Court of Appeals is reversed insofar as it upheld Section(s) 10(b) and it is so ordered.

Reno v. American Civil Liberties Union (1997)

Obscenity eventually touches all of the newest technologies, and personal computers and the Internet are no exception. In the early 1990s, private computer ownership skyrocketed and numerous companies developed to fulfill the demand for computers and information. Some of those companies delivered allegedly obscene images and texts. As it had with regard to cable television, Congress became concerned about the threat to children from obscene Internet sites, and it passed legislation regulating such sites. In 1996, Congress enacted the Telecommunications Act, Title V of which was the controversial Communications Decency Act (CDA). Sections of the CDA made it a federal crime to knowingly send obscene or indecent images to minors. The Act established other crimes as well. Arising from this thicket of regulations and obscenity doctrines came the case that challenged the constitutionality of sections of the CDA, which found that parts of the Act indeed went too far.

JUSTICE STEVENS delivered the opinion of the Court.

At issue is the constitutionality of two statutory provisions enacted to protect minors from "indecent" and "patently offensive" communications on the Internet. Notwithstanding the legitimacy and importance of the congressional goal of protecting children from harmful materials, we agree with the three-judge District Court that the statute abridges "the freedom of speech" protected by the First Amendment.

The District Court made extensive findings of fact, most of which were based on a detailed stipulation prepared by the parties. The findings describe the character and the dimensions of the Internet, the availability of sexually explicit material in that medium, and the problems confronting age verification for recipients of Internet communications. Because those findings provide the underpinnings for the legal issues, we begin with a summary of the undisputed facts.

The Internet

The Internet is an international network of interconnected computers. It is the outgrowth of what began in 1969 as a military program called "ARPANET," which was designed to enable computers operated by the military, defense contractors, and universities conducting defense-related research to communicate with one another by redundant channels even if some portions of the network were damaged in a war. . . . The Internet is "a unique and wholly new medium of worldwide human communication."

The Internet has experienced "extraordinary growth." The number of "host" computers—those that store information and relay communications—increased from about 300 in 1981 to approximately 9,400,000 by the time of the trial in 1996. Roughly 60% of these hosts are located in the United States. About 40 million people used the

Internet at the time of trial, a number that is expected to mushroom to 200 million by 1999. . . .

Anyone with access to the Internet may take advantage of a wide variety of communication and information retrieval methods. These methods are constantly evolving and difficult to categorize precisely. But, as presently constituted, those most relevant to this case are electronic mail ("e-mail"), automatic mailing list services ("mail exploders," sometimes referred to as "listservs"), "newsgroups," "chat rooms," and the "World Wide Web." All of these methods can be used to transmit text; most can transmit sound, pictures, and moving video images. Taken together, these tools constitute a unique medium—known to its users as "cyberspace"—located in no particular geographical location but available to anyone, anywhere in the world, with access to the Internet.

E-mail enables an individual to send an electronic message—generally akin to a note or letter—to another individual or to a group of addressees. The message is generally stored electronically, sometimes waiting for the recipient to check her "mailbox" and sometimes making its receipt known through some type of prompt. . . . Newsgroups also serve groups of regular participants, but these postings may be read by others as well. There are thousands of such groups, each serving to foster an exchange of information or opinion on a particular topic running the gamut from, say, the music of Wagner to Balkan politics to AIDS prevention to the Chicago Bulls. About 100,000 new messages are posted every day. . . . The District Court found that at any given time "tens of thousands of users are engaging in conversations on a huge range of subjects." It is "no exaggeration to conclude that the content on the Internet is as diverse as human thought."

The best known category of communication over the Internet is the World Wide Web, which allows users to search for and retrieve information stored in remote computers, as well as, in some cases, to communicate back to designated sites. . . .

Navigating the Web is relatively straightforward. A user may either type the address of a known page or enter one or more keywords into a commercial "search engine" in an effort to locate sites on a subject of interest. . . .

From the publishers' point of view, it constitutes a vast platform from which to address and hear from a world-wide audience of millions of readers, viewers, researchers, and buyers. Any person or organization with a computer connected to the Internet can "publish" information. Publishers include government agencies, educational institutions, commercial entities, advocacy groups, and individuals. Publishers may either make their material available to the entire pool of Internet users, or confine access to a selected group, such as those willing to pay for the privilege.

Sexually Explicit Material

Sexually explicit material on the Internet includes text, pictures, and chat and "extends from the modestly titillating to the hardest-core. . . ."

Though such material is widely available, users seldom encounter such content accidentally. "A document's title or a description of the document will usually appear before the document itself" . . . and in many cases the user will receive detailed information about a site's content before he or she need take the step to access the document. Almost all sexually explicit images are preceded by warnings as to the content. For that reason, the "odds are slim" that a user would enter a sexually explicit site by accident. Unlike communications received by radio or television, "the receipt of information on the Internet requires a series of affirmative steps more deliberate and directed than merely turning a dial. A child requires some sophistication and some ability to read to retrieve material and thereby to use the Internet unattended."

Systems have been developed to help parents control the material that may be available on a home computer with Internet access. . . .

Age Verification

The problem of age verification differs for different uses of the Internet. . . . The Government offered no evidence that there was a reliable way to screen recipients and participants in such for age. . . .

In sum, the District Court found:

"Even if credit card verification or adult password verification were implemented, the Government presented no testimony as to how such systems could ensure that the user of the password or credit card is in fact over 18." . . .

The Telecommunications Act of 1996, was an unusually important legislative enactment. As stated on the first of its 103 pages, its primary purpose was to reduce regulation and encourage "the rapid deployment of new telecommunications technologies." The major components of the statute have nothing to do with the Internet; they were designed to promote competition in the local telephone service market, the multichannel video market, and the market for over-the-air broadcasting. The Act includes seven Titles, six of which are the product of extensive committee hearings and the subject of discussion in Reports prepared by Committees of the Senate and the House of Representatives. By contrast, Title V—known as the "Communications Decency Act of 1996" (CDA)—contains provisions that were either added in executive committee after the hearings were concluded or as amendments offered during floor debate on the legislation. An amendment offered in the Senate was the source of the two statutory provisions challenged in this case. They are informally described as the "indecent transmission" provision and the "patently offensive display" provision.

The first prohibits the knowing transmission of obscene or indecent messages to any recipient under 18 years of age. It provides in pertinent part:

"(a) Whoever—

"(1) in interstate or foreign communications—. . . .

"(B) by means of a telecommunications device knowingly—

"(i) makes, creates, or solicits, and

"(ii) initiates the transmission of,

"any comment, request, suggestion, proposal, image, or other communication which is obscene or indecent, knowing that the recipient of the communication is under 18 years of age, regardless of whether the maker of such communication placed the call or initiated the communication; . . .

"(2) knowingly permits any telecommunications facility under his control to be used for any activity prohibited by paragraph (1) with the intent that it be used for such activity, shall be fined under Title 18, or imprisoned not more than two years, or both."

The second provision, § 223(d), prohibits the knowing sending or displaying of patently offensive messages in a manner that is available to a person under 18 years of age. It provides:

"(d) Whoever—

"(1) in interstate or foreign communications knowingly—

"(A) uses an interactive computer service to send to a specific person or persons under 18 years of age, or

"(B) uses any interactive computer service to display in a manner available to a person under 18 years of age, any comment, request, suggestion, proposal, image, or other communication that, in context, depicts or describes, in terms patently offensive as measured by contemporary community standards, sexual or excretory activities or organs, regardless of whether the user of such service placed the call or initiated the communication; or

"(2) knowingly permits any telecommunications facility under such person's control to be used for an activity prohibited by paragraph (1) with the intent that it be used for such activity, shall be fined under Title 18, or imprisoned not more than two years, or both."

The breadth of these prohibitions is qualified by two affirmative defenses. One covers those who take "good faith, reasonable, effective, and appropriate actions" to restrict access by minors to the prohibited communications. The other covers those who restrict access to covered material by requiring certain designated forms of age proof, such as a verified credit card or an adult identification number or code.

On February 8, 1996, immediately after the President signed the statute, 20 plaintiffs filed suit against the Attorney General of the United States and the Department of Justice challenging the constitutionality of §§ 223(a)(1) and 223(d). A week later, based on his conclusion that the term "indecent" was too vague to provide the basis for a criminal prosecution, District Judge Buckwalter entered a temporary restraining order against enforcement of § 223(a)(1)(B)(ii) insofar as it applies to indecent communications. A second suit was then filed by 27 additional plaintiffs, the two cases were consolidated, and a three-judge District Court was convened pursuant to § 561 of the Act. After an evidentiary hearing, that Court entered a preliminary injunction against enforcement of both of the challenged provisions. Each of the three judges wrote a separate opinion, but their judgment was unanimous. . . .

The judgment of the District Court enjoins the Government from enforcing the prohibitions in § 223(a)(1)(B) insofar as they relate to "indecent" communications, but expressly preserves the Government's right to investigate and prosecute the obscenity or child pornography activities prohibited therein. The injunction against enforcement of §§ 223(d)(1) and (2) is unqualified because those provisions contain no separate reference to obscenity or child pornography.

The Government appealed under the Act's special review provisions and we noted probable jurisdiction. In its appeal, the Government argues that the District Court erred in holding that the CDA violated both the First Amendment because it is overbroad and the Fifth Amendment because it is vague. While we discuss the vagueness of the CDA because of its relevance to the First Amendment over-breadth inquiry, we conclude that the judgment should be affirmed without reaching the Fifth Amendment issue. We begin our analysis by reviewing the principal authorities on which the Government relies. Then, after describing the overbreadth of the CDA, we consider the Government's specific contentions, including its submission that we save portions of the statute either by severance or by fashioning judicial limitations on the scope of its coverage. . . .

Regardless of whether the CDA is so vague that it violates the Fifth Amendment, the many ambiguities concerning the scope of its coverage render it problematic for purposes of the First Amendment. For instance, each of the two parts of the CDA uses a different linguistic form. The first uses the word "indecent," while the second speaks of material that "in context, depicts or describes, in terms patently offensive as measured by contemporary community standards, sexual or excretory activities or organs." Given the absence of a definition of either term, this difference in language will provoke uncertainty among speakers about how the two standards relate to each other and just what they mean. Could a speaker confidently assume that a serious discussion about birth control practices, homosexuality, the First Amendment issues raised by the Appendix to our *Pacifica* opinion, or the consequences of prison rape would not violate the CDA? This uncertainty undermines the likelihood that the CDA has been carefully tailored to the congressional goal of protecting minors from potentially harmful materials.

The vagueness of the CDA is a matter of special concern for two reasons. First, the CDA is a content-based regulation of speech. The vagueness of such a regulation raises special First Amendment concerns because of its obvious chilling effect on free speech. Second, the CDA is a criminal statute. In addition to the opprobrium and stigma of a criminal conviction, the CDA threatens violators with penalties including up to two years in prison for each act of violation. The severity of criminal sanctions may well cause speakers to remain silent rather than communicate even arguably unlawful words, ideas, and images. . . .

The Government argues that the statute is no more vague than the obscenity standard this Court established in *Miller* v. *California*. But that is not so. In *Miller,* this Court reviewed a criminal conviction against a commercial vendor who mailed brochures containing pictures of sexually explicit activities to individuals who had not requested such materials. Having struggled for some time to establish a definition of obscenity, we set forth in *Miller* the test for obscenity that controls to this day:

"(a) whether the average person, applying contemporary community standards would find that the work, taken as a whole, appeals to the prurient interest; (b) whether the work depicts or describes, in a patently offensive way, sexual conduct specifically defined by the applicable state law; and (c) whether the work, taken as a whole, lacks serious literary, artistic, political, or scientific value."

Because the CDA's "patently offensive" standard (and, we assume *arguendo*, its synonymous "indecent" standard) is one part of the three-prong *Miller* test, the Government reasons, it cannot be unconstitutionally vague. . . .

In contrast to *Miller* and our other previous cases, the CDA thus presents a greater threat of censoring speech that, in fact, falls outside the statute's scope. Given the vague contours of the coverage of the statute, it unquestionably silences some speakers whose messages would be entitled to constitutional protection. That danger provides further reason for insisting that the statute not be overly broad. The CDA's burden on protected speech cannot be justified if it could be avoided by a more carefully drafted statute.

We are persuaded that the CDA lacks the precision that the First Amendment requires when a statute regulates the content of speech. In order to deny minors access to potentially harmful speech, the CDA effectively suppresses a large amount of speech that adults have a constitutional right to receive and to address to one another. That burden on adult speech is unacceptable if less restrictive alternatives would be at least as effective in achieving the legitimate purpose that the statute was enacted to serve.

In evaluating the free speech rights of adults, we have made it perfectly clear that "sexual expression which is indecent but not obscene is protected by the First Amendment." Indeed, *Pacifica* itself admonished that "the fact that society may find speech offensive is not a sufficient reason for suppressing it. . . ."

The District Court found that at the time of trial existing technology did not include any effective method for a sender to prevent minors from obtaining access to its communications on the Internet without also denying access to adults. The Court found no effective way to determine the age of a user who is accessing material through e-mail,

mail exploders, newsgroups, or chat rooms. As a practical matter, the Court also found that it would be prohibitively expensive for noncommercial—as well as some commercial—speakers who have Web sites to verify that their users are adults. These limitations must inevitably curtail a significant amount of adult communication on the Internet. By contrast, the District Court found that "despite its limitations, currently available *user-based* software suggests that a reasonably effective method by which *parents* can prevent their children from accessing sexually explicit and other material which *parents* may believe is inappropriate for their children will soon be widely available."

The breadth of the CDA's coverage is wholly unprecedented. Unlike the regulations upheld in *Ginsberg* and *Pacifica*, the scope of the CDA is not limited to commercial speech or commercial entities. Its open-ended prohibitions embrace all nonprofit entities and individuals posting indecent messages or displaying them on their own computers in the presence of minors. . . . The regulated subject matter includes any of the seven "dirty words" used in the Pacifica monologue, the use of which the Government's expert acknowledged could constitute a felony. It may also extend to discussions about prison rape or safe sexual practices, artistic images that include nude subjects, and arguably the card catalogue of the Carnegie Library . . .

We agree with the District Court's conclusion that the CDA places an unacceptably heavy burden on protected speech, and that the defenses do not constitute the sort of "narrow tailoring" that will save an otherwise patently invalid unconstitutional provision. In *Sable*, we remarked that the speech restriction at issue there amounted to "'burning the house to roast the pig.'" The CDA, casting a far darker shadow over free speech, threatens to torch a large segment of the Internet community. . . .

In this Court, though not in the District Court, the Government asserts that—in addition to its interest in protecting children—its "equally significant" interest in fostering the growth of the Internet provides an independent basis for upholding the constitutionality of the CDA. The Government apparently assumes that the unregulated availability of "indecent" and "patently offensive" material on the Internet is driving countless citizens away from the medium because of the risk of exposing themselves or their children to harmful material.

We find this argument singularly unpersuasive. The dramatic expansion of this new marketplace of ideas contradicts the factual basis of this contention. The record demonstrates that the growth of the Internet has been and continues to be phenomenal. As a matter of constitutional tradition, in the absence of evidence to the contrary, we presume that governmental regulation of the content of speech is more likely to interfere with the free exchange of ideas than to encourage it. The interest in encouraging freedom of expression in a democratic society outweighs any theoretical but unproven benefit of censorship.

For the foregoing reasons, the judgment of the district court is affirmed.

It is so ordered.

JUSTICE O'CONNOR, with whom THE CHIEF JUSTICE joins, concurring in the judgment in part and dissenting in part.

I write separately to explain why I view the Communications Decency Act of 1996 (CDA) as little more than an attempt by Congress to create "adult zones" on the Internet. Our precedent indicates that the creation of such zones can be constitutionally sound. Despite the soundness of its purpose, however, portions of the CDA are unconstitutional because they stray from the blueprint our prior cases have developed for constructing a "zoning law" that passes constitutional muster.

Appellees bring a facial challenge to three provisions of the CDA. The first, which the Court describes as the "indecency transmission" provision, makes it a crime to knowingly transmit an obscene or indecent message or image to a person the sender knows is under 18 years old. What the Court classifies as a single "'patently offensive display'" provision is in reality two separate provisions. The first of these makes it a crime to knowingly send a patently offensive message or image to a specific person under the age of 18. The second criminalizes the display of patently offensive messages or images "in any manner available" to minors. None of these provisions purports to keep indecent (or patently offensive) material away from adults, who have a First Amendment right to obtain this speech. Thus, the undeniable purpose of the CDA is to segregate indecent material on the Internet into certain areas that minors cannot access.

The creation of "adult zones" is by no means a novel concept. States have long denied minors access to certain establishments frequented by adults. States have also denied minors access to speech deemed to be "harmful to minors." The Court has previously sustained such zoning laws, but only if they respect the First Amendment rights of adults and minors. That is to say, a zoning law is valid if (i) it does not unduly restrict adult access to the material; and (ii) minors have no First Amendment right to read or view the banned material. As applied to the Internet as it exists in 1997, the "display" provision and some applications of the "indecency transmission" and "specific person" provisions fail to adhere to the first of these limiting principles by restricting adults' access to protected materials in certain circumstances. Unlike the Court, however, I would invalidate the provisions only in those circumstances. . . .

United States v. Playboy Entertainment Group (2000)

Problems unique to cable television were brought to the attention of the U.S. Supreme Court once more in an obscenity case that dealt with the Telecommunications Act of 1996 and the cable problem of "signal bleed." Occasionally in cable television, one channel's programming will "bleed" through to another channel. As a result, it might be possible for children or nonconsenting adults to be confronted with allegedly obscene images and/or audio. Scrambling technology has proven imperfect. Under the Telecommunications Act, cable operators had to either scramble "adult" programming or "time channel" such programming to hours when children and nonconsenting adults would be least likely to be affected by "signal bleed." Cable operators challenged these regulations on First Amendment grounds. The Court split in a 5–4 decision finding such regulations too restrictive of cable operators' First Amendment rights, with the dissenting justices strongly disagreeing.

JUSTICE KENNEDY delivered the opinion of the Court.

This case presents a challenge to §505 of the Telecommunications Act of 1996, Pub. L. 104–104, 110 Stat. 136, 47 U. S. C. §561 (1994 ed., Supp. III). Section 505 requires cable television operators who provide channels "primarily dedicated to sexually oriented programming" either to "fully scramble or otherwise fully block" those channels or to limit their transmission to hours when children are unlikely to be viewing, set by administrative regulation as the time between 10 p.m. and 6 a.m. Even before enactment of the statute, signal scrambling was already in use. Cable operators used scrambling in the regular course of business, so that only paying customers had access to certain programs. Scrambling could be imprecise, however; and either or both audio and visual portions of the scrambled programs might be heard or seen, a phenomenon known as "signal bleed." The purpose of §505 is to shield children from hearing or seeing images resulting from signal bleed.

To comply with the statute, the majority of cable operators adopted the second, or "time channeling," approach. The effect of the widespread adoption of time channeling was to eliminate altogether the transmission of the targeted programming outside the safe harbor period in affected cable service areas. In other words, for two-thirds of the day no household in those service areas could receive the programming, whether or not the household or the viewer wanted to do so.

Appellee Playboy Entertainment Group, Inc., challenged the statute as unnecessarily restrictive content-based legislation violative of the First Amendment. After a trial, a three-judge District Court concluded that a regime in which viewers could order signal blocking on a household-by-household basis presented an effective, less restrictive alternative to §505. Finding no error in this conclusion, we affirm.

Playboy Entertainment Group owns and prepares programs for adult television networks, including Playboy Television and Spice. Playboy transmits its programming to cable television operators, who retransmit it to their subscribers, either through monthly subscriptions to premium channels or on a so-called "pay-per-view" basis. Cable operators transmit Playboy's signal, like other premium channel signals, in scrambled form. The operators then provide paying subscribers with an "addressable converter," a box placed on the home television set. The converter permits the viewer to see and hear the descrambled signal. It is conceded that almost all of Playboy's programming consists of sexually explicit material as defined by the statute.

The statute was enacted because not all scrambling technology is perfect. Analog cable television systems may use either "RF" or "baseband" scrambling systems, which may not prevent signal bleed, so discernible pictures may appear from time to time on the scrambled screen. Furthermore, the listener might hear the audio portion of the program.

These imperfections are not inevitable. The problem is that at present it appears not to be economical to convert simpler RF or baseband scrambling systems to alternative scrambling technologies on a systemwide scale. Digital technology may one day provide another solution, as it presents no bleed problem at all. Indeed, digital systems are projected to become the technology of choice, which would eliminate the signal bleed problem. Digital technology is not yet in widespread use, however. . . .

Section 505 was enacted to address the signal bleed phenomenon. As noted, the statute and its implementing regulations require cable operators either to scramble a sexually explicit channel in full or to limit the channel's programming to the hours between 10 p.m. and 6 a.m. . . .

Two essential points should be understood concerning the speech at issue here. First, we shall assume that many adults themselves would find the material highly offensive; and when we consider the further circumstance that the material comes unwanted into homes where children might see or hear it against parental wishes or consent, there are legitimate reasons for regulating it. Second, all parties bring the case to us on the premise that Playboy's programming has First Amendment protection. As this case has been litigated, it is not alleged to be obscene; adults have a constitutional right to view it; the Government disclaims any interest in preventing children from seeing or hearing it with the consent of their parents; and Playboy has concomitant rights under the First Amendment to transmit it. These points are undisputed.

The speech in question is defined by its content; and the statute which seeks to restrict it is content based. Section 505 applies only to channels primarily dedicated to "sexually explicit adult programming or other programming that is indecent." The statute is unconcerned with signal bleed from any other channels. The overriding justification for the regulation is concern for the effect of the subject matter on young viewers. Section 505 is not "justified without reference to the content of the regulated speech." It "focuses *only* on the content of the speech and the direct impact that speech has on its listeners." This is the essence of content-based regulation.

Not only does §505 single out particular programming content for regulation, it also singles out particular programmers. The speech in question was not thought by Congress to be so harmful that all channels were subject to restriction. Instead, the statutory disability applies only to channels "primarily dedicated to sexually oriented programming." One sponsor of the measure even identified appellee by name. Laws designed or intended to suppress or restrict the expression of specific speakers contradict basic First Amendment principles. Section 505 limited Playboy's market as a penalty for its programming choice, though other channels capable of transmitting like material are altogether exempt.

The effect of the federal statute on the protected speech is now apparent. It is evident that the only reasonable way for a substantial number of cable operators to comply with the letter of §505 is to time channel, which silences the protected speech for two-thirds of the day in every home in a cable service area, regardless of the presence or likely presence of children or of the wishes of the viewers. According to the District Court, "30 to 50 percent of all adult programming is viewed by households prior to 10 p.m.," when the safe-harbor period begins. To prohibit this much speech is a significant restriction of communication between speakers and willing adult listeners, communication which enjoys First Amendment protection. It is of no moment that the statute does not impose a complete prohibition. The distinction between laws burdening and laws banning speech is but a matter of degree. The Government's content-based burdens must satisfy the same rigorous scrutiny as its content-based bans.

Since §505 is a content-based speech restriction, it can stand only if it satisfies strict scrutiny. If a statute regulates speech based on its content, it must be narrowly tailored to promote a compelling Government interest. If a less restrictive alternative would serve the Government's purpose, the legislature must use that alternative. To do otherwise would be to restrict speech without an adequate justification, a course the First Amendment does not permit.

Our precedents teach these principles. Where the designed benefit of a content-based speech restriction is to shield the sensibilities of listeners, the general rule is that the right of expression prevails, even where no less restrictive alternative exists.... Cable television, like broadcast media, presents unique problems, which inform our assessment of the interests at stake, and which may justify restrictions that would be unacceptable in other contexts. No one suggests the Government must be indifferent to unwanted, indecent speech that comes into the home without parental consent. The speech here, all agree, is protected speech; and the question is what standard the Government must meet in order to restrict it. As we consider a content-based regulation, the answer should be clear: The standard is strict scrutiny. This case involves speech alone; and even where speech is indecent and enters the home, the objective of shielding children does not suffice to support a blanket ban if the protection can be accomplished by a less restrictive alternative. ...

There is, moreover, a key difference between cable television and the broadcasting media, which is the point on which this case turns: Cable systems have the capacity to block unwanted channels on a household-by-household basis. The option to block reduces the likelihood, so concerning to the Court in *Pacifica* that traditional First Amendment scrutiny would deprive the Government of all authority to address this sort of problem. The corollary, of course, is that targeted blocking enables the Government to support parental authority without affecting the First Amendment interests of speakers and willing listeners—listeners for whom, if the speech is unpopular or indecent, the privacy of their own homes may be the optimal place of receipt. Simply put, targeted blocking is less restrictive than banning, and the Government cannot ban speech if targeted blocking is a feasible and effective means of furthering its compelling interests. This is not to say that the absence of an effective blocking mechanism will in all cases suffice to support a law restricting the speech in question; but if a less restrictive means is available for the Government to achieve its goals, the Government must use it.

The District Court concluded that a less restrictive alternative is available: §504, with adequate publicity. . . . The question is whether §504 can be effective.

When a plausible, less restrictive alternative is offered to a content-based speech restriction, it is the Government's obligation to prove that the alternative will be ineffective to achieve its goals. The Government has not met that burden here. In support of its position, the Government cites empirical evidence showing that §504, as promulgated and implemented before trial, generated few requests for household-by-household blocking. Between March 1996 and May 1997, while the Government was enjoined from enforcing §505, §504 remained in operation. A survey of cable operators determined that fewer than 0.5 percent of cable subscribers requested full blocking during that time. The uncomfortable fact is that §504 was the sole blocking regulation in effect for over a year; and the public greeted it with a collective yawn. . . .

It is through speech that our convictions and beliefs are influenced, expressed, and tested. It is through speech that we bring those beliefs to bear on Government and on society. It is through speech that our personalities are formed and expressed. The citizen is entitled to seek out or reject certain ideas or influences without Government interference or control.

When a student first encounters our free speech jurisprudence, he or she might think it is influenced by the philosophy that one idea is as good as any other, and that in art and literature objective standards of style, taste, decorum, beauty, and esthetics are deemed by the Constitution to be inappropriate, indeed unattainable. Quite the opposite is true. The Constitution no more enforces a relativistic philosophy or moral nihilism than it does any other point of view. The Constitution exists precisely so that opinions and judgments, including esthetic and moral judgments about art and literature, can be formed, tested, and expressed. What the Constitution says is that these judgments are for the individual to make, not for the Government to decree, even with the mandate or approval of a majority. Technology expands the capacity to choose; and it denies the potential of this revolution if we assume the Government is best positioned to make these choices for us.

It is rare that a regulation restricting speech because of its content will ever be permissible. Indeed, were we to give the Government the benefit of the doubt when it attempted to restrict speech, we would risk leaving regulations in place that sought to shape our unique personalities or to silence dissenting ideas. When First Amendment compliance is the point to be proved, the risk of non-persuasion—operative in all trials—must rest with the Government, not with the citizen.

With this burden in mind, the District Court explored three explanations for the lack of individual blocking requests. First, individual blocking might not be an effective alternative, due to technological or other limitations. Second, although an adequately advertised blocking provision might have been effective, §504 as written did not require sufficient notice to make it so. Third, the actual signal bleed problem might be far less of a concern than the Government at first had supposed.

To sustain its statute, the Government was required to show that the first was the right answer. According to the District Court, however, the first and third possibilities were "equally consistent" with the record before it. As for the second, the record was "not clear" as to whether enough notice had been issued to give §504 a fighting chance. The case, then, was at best a draw. Unless the District Court's findings are clearly erroneous, the tie goes to free expression. . . .

The whole point of a publicized §504 would be to advise parents that indecent material may be shown and to afford them an opportunity to block it at all times, even when they are not at home and even after 10 p.m. Time channeling does not offer this assistance. The regulatory alternative of a publicized §504, which has the real possibility of promoting more open disclosure and the choice of an effective blocking system, would provide parents the information needed to engage in active supervision. The Government has not shown that this alternative, a regime of added communication and support, would be insufficient to secure its objective, or that any overriding harm justifies its intervention.

Basic speech principles are at stake in this case. When the purpose and design of a statute is to regulate speech by reason of its content, special consideration or latitude is not accorded to the Government merely because the law can somehow be described as a burden rather than outright suppression. We cannot be influenced, moreover, by the perception that the regulation in question is not a major one because the speech is not very important. The history of the law of free expression is one of vindication in cases involving speech that many citizens may find shabby, offensive, or even ugly. It follows that all content-based restrictions on speech must give us more than a moment's pause. If television broadcasts can expose children to the real risk of harmful exposure to indecent materials, even in their own home and without parental consent, there is a problem the Government can address. It must do so, however, in a way consistent with First Amendment principles. Here the Government has not met the burden the First Amendment imposes.

The Government has failed to show that §505 is the least restrictive means for addressing a real problem; and the District Court did not err in holding the statute violative of the First Amendment. In light of our ruling, it is unnecessary to address the second question presented: whether the District Court was divested of jurisdiction to consider the Government's postjudgment motions after the Government filed a notice of appeal in this Court. The judgment of the District Court is affirmed.

It is so ordered.

JUSTICE SCALIA, dissenting.

I agree with the principal dissent in this case that §505 of the Telecommunications Act of 1996 is supported by a compelling state interest and is narrowly tailored. I write separately to express my view that §505 can be upheld in simpler fashion: by finding that it regulates the business of obscenity. . . .

We have recognized that commercial entities which engage in "the sordid business of pandering" by "deliberately emphasiz[ing] the sexually provocative aspects of [their nonobscene products], in order to catch the salaciously disposed," engage in constitutionally unprotected behavior. This is so whether or not the products in which the business traffics independently meet the high hurdle we have established for delineating the obscene, viz., that they contain no "serious literary, artistic, political, or scientific value. . . ."

Section 505 regulates just this sort of business. Its coverage is limited to programming that "describes or depicts sexual or excretory activities or organs *in a patently offensive manner* as measured by contemporary community standards [for cable television]." It furthermore applies only to those channels that are *"primarily dedicated* to sexually oriented programming" (emphasis added). It is conceivable, I suppose, that a channel which is primarily dedicated to sex might not *hold itself forth* as primarily dedicated to sex—in which case its productions which contain "serious literary, artistic, political, or scientific value" (if any) would be as entitled to First Amendment protection as the statuary rooms of the National Gallery. But in the competitive world of cable programming, the possibility that a channel devoted to sex would not advertise itself as such is sufficiently remote, and the number of such channels sufficiently small (if not indeed nonexistent), as not to render the provision substantially overbroad.

Playboy itself illustrates the type of business §505 is designed to reach. Playboy provides, through its networks—Playboy Television, AdulTVision, Adam & Eve, and Spice—"virtually 100 percent sexually explicit adult programming." For example, on its Spice network, Playboy describes its own programming as depicting such activities as "female masturbation/external," "girl/girl sex," and "oral sex/cunnilingus." As one would expect, given this content, Playboy advertises accordingly, with calls to "Enjoy the sexiest, hottest adult movies in the privacy of your own home." An example of the promotion for a particular movie is as follows: "Little miss country girls are aching for a quick roll in the hay! Watch southern hospitality pull out all the stops as these ravin' nymphos tear down the barn and light up the big country sky." One may doubt whether—or marvel that—this sort of embarrassingly juvenile promotion really attracts what Playboy assures us is an "adult" audience. But it is certainly marketing sex.

Thus, while I agree with *Justice Breyer's* child-protection analysis, it leaves me with the same feeling of true-but-inadequate as the conclusion that Al Capone did not accurately report his income. It is not only children who can be protected from occasional uninvited exposure to what appellee calls "adult-oriented programming"; we can all be. . . . In most contexts, contemporary American society has chosen to permit such commercial exploitation. That may be a wise democratic choice, if only because of the difficulty in many contexts (though not this one) of identifying the panderer to sex. It is, however, not a course compelled by the Constitution. Since the Government is entirely free to *block* these transmissions, it may certainly take the less drastic step of dictating how, and during what times, they may occur.

JUSTICE BREYER, with whom the Chief Justice, JUSTICE O'CONNOR, and JUSTICE SCALIA join, dissenting.

This case involves the application, not the elucidation, of First Amendment principles. We apply established First Amendment law to a statute that focuses upon the broadcast of "sexually explicit adult programming" on AdulTVision, Adam & Eve, Spice, and Playboy cable channels. These channels are, as the statute requires, "primarily dedicated to sexually oriented programming." Section 505 forbids cable operators from sending these adult channels into the homes of viewers who do not request them. In practice, it requires a significant number of cable operators either to upgrade their scrambling technology or to avoid broadcasting these channels during daylight and evening hours (6 a.m. to 10 p.m.). We must decide whether the First Amendment permits Congress to enact this statute. . . .

At the outset, I would describe the statutory scheme somewhat differently than does the majority. I would emphasize three background points. First, the statutory scheme reflects more than a congressional effort to control incomplete scrambling. Previously, federal law had left cable operators free to decide whether, when, and how to transmit adult channels. Most channel operators on their own had decided not to send adult channels into a subscriber's home except on request. But the operators then implemented that decision with inexpensive technology. Through signal "bleeding," the scrambling technology (either inadvertently or by way of enticement) allowed non subscribers to see and hear what was going on. That is why Congress decided to act. . . .

Second, the majority's characterization of this statutory scheme as "prohibit[ing] . . . speech" is an exaggeration. Rather, the statute places a *burden* on adult channel speech by requiring the relevant cable operator either to use better scrambling technology, or, if that technology is too expensive, to broadcast only between 10 p.m. and 6 a.m. Laws that burden speech, say, by making speech less profitable, may create serious First Amendment issues, but they are not the equivalent of an absolute ban on speech itself. Thus, this Court has upheld laws that do not ban the access of adults to sexually explicit speech, but burden that access through geographical or temporal zoning. This Court has also recognized that material the First Amendment guarantees adults the right to see may not be suitable for children. And it has consequently held that legislatures maintain a limited power to protect children by restricting access to, but not banning, adult material. The difference—between imposing a burden and enacting a ban—can matter even when strict First Amendment rules are at issue.

Third, this case concerns only the regulation of commercial actors who broadcast "virtually 100% sexually explicit" material. The channels do not broadcast more than trivial amounts of more serious material such as birth control information, artistic images, or the visual equivalents of classical or serious literature. This case therefore does not present the kind of narrow tailoring concerns seen in other cases. . . .

The majority first concludes that the Government failed to prove the seriousness of the problem—receipt of adult channels by children whose parents did not request their broadcast. This claim is flat-out wrong. For one thing, the parties concede that basic RF scrambling does not scramble the audio portion of the program. For another, Playboy itself conducted a survey of cable operators who were asked: "Is your system in full compliance with Section 505 (no discernible audio or video bleed)?" To this question, 75% of cable operators answered "no." Further, the Government's expert took the number of homes subscribing to Playboy or Spice, multiplied by the fraction of cable households with children and the average number of children per household, and found 29 million children are potentially exposed to audio and video bleed from adult programming. Even discounting by 25% for systems that might be considered in full compliance, this left 22 million children in homes with faulty scrambling systems. And, of course, the record contains additional anecdotal evidence and the concerns expressed by elected officials, probative of a larger problem. . . .

I turn then to the major point of disagreement. Unlike the majority, I believe the record makes clear that §504's opt-out is not a similarly effective alternative. Section 504 (opt-out) and §505 (opt-in) work differently in order to achieve very different legislative objectives. Section 504 gives parents the power to tell cable operators to keep any channel out of their home. Section 505 does more. Unless parents explicitly consent, it inhibits the transmission of adult cable channels to children whose parents may be unaware of what they are watching, whose parents cannot easily supervise television viewing habits, whose parents do not know of their §504 "opt-out" rights, or whose parents are simply unavailable at critical times. In this respect, §505 serves the same interests as the laws that deny children access to adult cabarets or X-rated movies.

This legislative objective is perfectly legitimate. Where over 28 million school age children have both parents or their only parent in the work force, where at least 5 million children are left alone at home without supervision each week, and where children may spend afternoons and evenings watching television outside of the home with friends, §505 offers independent protection for a large number of families. I could not disagree more when the majority implies that the Government's independent interest in offering such protection—preventing, say, an 8-year-old child from watching virulent pornography without parental consent—might not be "compelling." No previous case in which the protection of children was at issue has suggested any such thing. Indeed, they all say precisely the opposite. They make clear that Government has a compelling interest in helping parents by preventing minors from accessing sexually explicit materials in the absence of parental supervision. . . .

Nor is it a satisfactory answer to say that the Government remains free to prosecute under the obscenity laws. The obscenity exception permits censorship of communication even among *adults.* It must be kept narrow lest the Government improperly interfere with the communication choices that adults have freely made. To rely primarily upon law that bans speech for adults is to overlook the special need to protect children.

Congress has taken seriously the importance of maintaining adult access to the sexually explicit channels here at issue. It has tailored the restrictions to minimize their impact upon adults while offering parents help in keeping unwanted transmissions from their children. By finding "adequate alternatives" where there are none, the Court reduces Congress' protective power to the vanishing point. That is not what the First Amendment demands. I respectfully dissent.

Key People, Laws, and Concepts

Black, Hugo
(February 27, 1886–September 25, 1971)

Earned his law degree from the University of Alabama School of Law in 1906. He entered private practice in Ashland and Birmingham, Alabama, and continued in it until 1927. He served as a Birmingham, Alabama, police court judge in 1910–1911. He became prosecuting attorney in Birmingham in 1914, but stepped down from that position in 1917 in order to serve as a captain in the U.S. Army. He was elected to two terms as U.S. senator from Alabama, serving from 1927 to 1937. President Franklin D. Roosevelt nominated him to the U.S. Supreme Court in 1937.

Blackmun, Harry Andrew
(November 12, 1908–March 4, 1999)

Earned his law degree from the Harvard Law School in 1932. He clerked for Judge John B. Sanford on the Eighth Circuit of the U.S. Court of Appeals in 1932–1933. He then pursued private practice until 1950, when he became counsel for the Mayo Clinic. President Dwight D. Eisenhower appointed him to the Eighth Circuit of the U.S. Court of Appeals in 1959. In 1970, President Richard M. Nixon nominated him to the U.S. Supreme Court.

Blatchford, Samuel (March 9, 1820–July 7, 1893)

Read law with New York Governor William Seward and served as his private secretary before entering private practice in 1842. He practiced in Auburn, New York, and in New York City. In 1867, President Andrew Johnson appointed him to the federal district court for the Southern District of New York. In 1878, President Rutherford B. Hayes appointed him to the Second Circuit of the U.S. Court of Appeals. In 1882, President Chester A. Arthur appointed him to the U.S. Supreme Court.

Brennan, William Joseph, Jr. (April 25, 1906–July 24, 1997)

Earned his law degree from the Harvard Law School in 1931, and entered private practice in New Jersey. In World War II he joined the U.S. Army and served the undersecretary of war. After the war, he reentered private practice before becoming a judge on the Superior Court of New Jersey in 1949. In 1951, he became a judge on the Appellate Division, and in 1952, he became a judge on the New Jersey Supreme Court. President Dwight D. Eisenhower nominated him for the U. S. Supreme Court in 1956. He became one of the most influential of the liberal judges of the Warren Court. He retired from the Court in 1990.

Breyer, Steven G. (August 15, 1938–)

Earned his law degree from the Harvard Law School in 1963 and served as a law clerk to Associate Justice of the Supreme Court Arthur Goldberg during the 1964 term. He worked as a special assistant to the assistant U.S. attorney general for antitrust from 1965–1967. He joined the law faculty of the Harvard Law School in 1967 and remained there until 1994. In 1980, he was appointed to the First Circuit of the U.S. Court of Appeals, on which he served as chief judge from 1990 to 1994. President William Jefferson Clinton appointed him to the U.S. Supreme Court in 1994.

Burger, Warren Earl (September 17, 1907–June 25, 1995)

Earned his law degree from the St. Paul School of Law (now William Mitchell College of Law) in 1931. He entered private practice in St. Paul, Minnesota, and developed a thriving law business. In 1953, he became an assistant attorney general of the claims division. In 1956, President Dwight D. Eisenhower appointed him to the District of Columbia Court of the U.S. Court of Appeals, where he served until 1969. President Richard M. Nixon nominated him as chief justice of the U. S. Supreme Court in 1969. He was chosen because of his spotless record and his opposition to the judicial activism of the Warren Court. He retired from the Supreme Court in 1986.

Cable Television Consumer Protection and Competition Act of 1992

Congressional statute that sought to establish guidelines for the cable television industry, including restrictions on so-called "adult" programming.

Clark, Tom Campbell (September 23, 1899–June 13, 1977)

Earned his law degree from the University of Texas Law School in 1922. He entered private practice in Dallas, and was appointed civil district attorney in the late 1920s. In 1937, he joined the U.S. Justice Department as a special assistant. He also worked in the Department of Antitrust and Criminal Divisions. After World War II, in 1945, President Harry S. Truman appointed him U.S. attorney general. President Truman appointed him to the U.S. Supreme Court in 1949. He retired from the Supreme Court in 1967.

Cockburn, Sir Alexander James Edmund (December 24, 1802–November 20, 1880)

He completed his university training at Trinity Hall, Cambridge University, and then studied law at the Middle Temple. He entered the bar on February 6, 1829. He entered private practice and became interested in collecting, analyzing, and publishing election results in light of the changes brought about under the "Great Reform Bill" of 1832. His challenges of election results brought him renown, and his practice flourished. In 1841, he was made Queen's Counsel. In 1847, he entered Parliament for Southampton. For his work in Parliament, he was knighted in 1850 and made solicitor general. In 1851, he became attorney general. In 1856, he was appointed chief justice of the Court of Common Pleas. In 1859, he became lord chief justice of Queen's Bench. He presided over some of the most famous and infamous litigations during the reign of Queen Victoria. He was the tenth and last baron of Langston.

Common Law

The body of written and unwritten principles and rules of action derived from the customs and traditions inherited from English law and developed within the colonies and states of the United States.

Communications Decency Act of 1996

Title V of the Telecommunications Act of 1996, which was devised by the U.S. Congress to establish regulations, procedures, and standards for the transmission of "obscenity" over the Internet.

Comstock Act

Named for moral reformer Anthony Comstock. Congress passed this statute in 1873 to prohibit the use of the mails for the distribution of "obscenity." As a "special agent" of the Post Office, Comstock initiated numerous prosecutions against allegedly obscene publications, including those providing information about birth control.

Comstock, Anthony (1844–1915)

After service in the Union Army during the U.S. Civil War, he entered the grocery business; but he found his true calling in the social purity movement of the late nineteenth century. He became an advocate of antiabortion legislation, and broadened his efforts to focus on immoral literature and sexual information of all kinds. He was instrumental in the passage of an 1868 New York state statute forbidding immoral works, and he lobbied Congress for a similar federal statute, which was passed in 1873. He became a "Special Agent" of the U.S. Postal Service and spent the rest of his career purging the mail of allegedly obscene and offensive materials. He helped found the New York Society for the Suppression of Vice.

Douglas, William O.
(October 16, 1898–January 19, 1980)

Earned his law degree from Columbia University Law School in 1923. He pursued private practice for two years before accepting an appointment as professor of law at Columbia University, where he remained another two years. In 1929, he took a position at the Yale Law School. In 1936, he joined the recently created Securities and Exchange Commission, and in 1937, became its chairman. President Franklin D. Roosevelt appointed him to the U.S. Supreme Court in 1939. Then 41 years old, Douglas became the second-youngest justice to serve on the Supreme Court. His term also would be the longest served by any justice on the Court. It ended with his resignation in November 1975, in the aftermath of a stroke that took place the previous December.

Easterbrook, Frank H. (September 3, 1948–)

Earned his law degree from the University of Chicago School of Law in 1973. He then clerked for the First Circuit of the U.S. Court of Appeals before joining the U.S. Solicitor General's Office, where he worked as an assistant and deputy U.S. solicitor general. In 1979, he joined the law faculty of the University of Chicago, and in 1985, he accepted an appointment to the U.S. Court of Appeals, Seventh Circuit.

En banc

A legal term meaning that all of the judges on an appeals court, and not the usual three judges that decide routine matters, hear and dispose of the case.

Federalism

The division of powers, duties, and responsibilities of government among local, state or regional, and national levels of government.

Fortas, Abe (June 19, 1910–April 5, 1982)

Earned his law degree at the Yale Law School in 1933. He joined President Franklin D. Roosevelt's New Deal government, and served in the Agricultural Adjustment Administration. In 1939, he became undersecretary in the Department of the Interior. After World War II, he entered private practice in Washington, D.C., and established a name for himself as an opponent of the Red Scare of that era. Because of his long association with Lyndon B. Johnson, President Johnson appointed him to the U.S. Supreme Court in 1965. In 1969, Johnson nominated Fortas for chief justice, but the nomination was withdrawn when allegations of improper payments for speaking engagements emerged against Fortas. Fortas resigned from the Supreme Court in 1969.

Frankfurter, Felix
(November 15, 1882–February 21, 1965)

Earned his law degree from the Harvard Law School in 1906. He served as assistant federal district attorney for the Southern District of New York until 1909. He then worked in politics and as a law officer in the Bureau of Insular Affairs in the War Department. From 1914 to 1917, he taught at the Harvard Law School. In World War I, he served in the Judge Advocate-General's Corps. He resumed his law teaching in 1920, and served until 1939 as a law professor at the Harvard Law School, where he influenced many students who went on to notable careers. President Franklin D. Roosevelt nominated him to the U.S. Supreme Court in 1939.

Ginsburg, Ruth Bader
(March 15, 1933–)

Earned her law degree from Harvard University in 1958 and in 1959 served as a Kent Scholar at the Columbia Law Review. She served as a law clerk to the United States District Court for the Southern District of New York from 1959 to 1961. She became a research associate with the Columbia Law School Project on International Law in 1961–1962 and became the project's associate director in 1962–1963. She then entered law teaching becoming a law professor at Rutgers University School of Law where she served until 1972 when she moved to the Columbia Law School. In 1980, President James E. Carter appointed her to the United States District Court for the District of Columbia Circuit. President William J. Clinton appointed her to the United States Supreme Court and she took her seat on August 10, 1993.

Gitlow Assumption

Justice Edward T. Sanford's statement in *Gitlow v. New York* (1925) that the freedom of speech and press mentioned in the First Amendment limited not only the federal government but also the states. The *Gitlow* assumption was an important step in the incorporation of the Bill of Rights.

Goldberg, Arthur Joseph
(August 8, 1908–January 19, 1990)

Earned his law degree from Northwestern University School of Law in 1929. He entered private practice in Chicago, served in the U.S. Army in 1942–1944, and returned to private practice specializing in labor law. In 1948, he became general counsel of the United Steelworkers and the Congress of Industrial Relations (CIO). He oversaw the 1955 merger of the CIO and the American Federation of Labor into one organization. President John F. Kennedy appointed him secretary of labor in 1961, and in 1962, nominated him to the U.S. Supreme Court. He served on the Supreme Court until 1965.

Hand, Augustus Noble
(July 26, 1869–October 28, 1954)

Earned his law degree from the Harvard Law School in 1894 and then practiced law in New York City from 1897 to 1914. In 1914, President Woodrow Wilson appointed him to the U.S. District Court for the Southern District of New York. In 1927, President Calvin Coolidge appointed him to the Second Circuit of the U.S. Court of Appeals. He was one of the most influential judges of his era, and was noted for his impartiality.

Hand, Learned (January 27,1872–August 18, 1961)

Earned his law degree from the Harvard Law School in 1896 and then practiced law in Albany, New York, and in New York City. President William Howard Taft appointed him to the federal bench in 1909. In 1924, President Calvin Coolidge appointed him to the Second Circuit of the U.S. Court of Appeals. Scholars consider his contributions to U.S. law in the twentieth century comparable to those of such luminaries of the bench as Oliver Wendell Holmes, Louis Brandeis, and Benjamin N. Cardozo.

Harlan, John Marshall (June 1, 1833–October 14, 1911)

Studied law at Transylvania University and in his father's law office. He was admitted to the bar in 1853. He entered private practice, and in 1858 he was elected county judge. He joined the Union Army at the start of the U.S. Civil War and served until 1863. He then resumed his private practice and was elected Kentucky's attorney general. He twice ran unsuccessfully for the governorship of Kentucky. In 1876, he served on a commission appointed by President Rutherford B. Hayes to determine which rival state government in Louisiana was legitimate. Hayes wished to appoint a southerner to the U.S. Supreme Court, and his first choice in 1877 was Harlan, who served on the Court for the next thirty-four years. His grandson also served on the Supreme Court.

Harlan, John Marshall II (May 20, 1899–December 29, 1971)

Read law at Oxford University, England, as a Rhodes Scholar, and earned his law degree from New York Law School in 1924. He entered private practice. In 1925, when his mentor Emory Buckner became the U.S. attorney for the Southern District of New York, Harlan became his chief assistant. He also worked in the firm of Root, Clark, Buckner and Howland. He served in the Army Air Corps during World II, and returned to a highly successful private practice after the war. In 1953, he accepted an appointment to the Second Circuit of the U.S. Court of Appeals. President Dwight D. Eisenhower appointed him to the U.S. Supreme Court in 1954.

Hicklin Test

Chief Justice Sir Alexander James Edmund Cockburn's judicial definition of obscenity, from the 1868 case *Regina v. Benjamin Hicklin*. He held that the test of obscenity was "whether the tendency of the matter charged as obscenity is to deprave and corrupt those whose minds are open to such immoral influences, and into whose hands a publication of this sort might fall."

Holmes, Oliver Wendell, Jr.
(March 8, 1841–March 6, 1932)

Attended the Harvard Law School after service in the Union Army during the U.S. Civil War, served a clerkship, and was admitted to the bar in 1867. Worked as an independent scholar for a short time, supporting himself by writing articles and treatises. In 1881, he published *The Common Law,* one of the most influential books on the subject. He taught briefly at the Harvard Law School, and in 1882 he accepted an appointment to the Supreme Judicial Court of Massachusetts, where he served for twenty years. In 1899, he became that court's chief judge. Because of Holmes's reputation and stature in the legal community, President Theodore Roosevelt appointed him to the U.S. Supreme Court in 1902. He served on the Court for the next thirty years, writing 873 opinions—the greatest number authored by any justice in the Court's history.

Houston, Paula (1960–)

Earned her law degree from Brigham Young University and spent fifteen years as a state prosecutor in Salt Lake City. In 2001, she became Obscenity and Pornography Complaints Ombudsman in the Mormon-dominated state of Utah. Her charge is to advise local governments of the law on obscenity, to suggest approaches to controlling obscenity, and if necessary, to prosecute obscenity on behalf of the state of Utah.

Incorporation of the Bill of Rights

The process of applying the federal Bill of Rights against the states and against individuals in states through the due process clause of the Fourteenth Amendment.

Kennedy, Anthony McLeod (July 23, 1936–)

Earned his law degree from the Harvard Law School in 1960. He entered private practice and became a professor of law at the McGeorge School of Law, University of the Pacific. In 1975, he was appointed to the Ninth Circuit of the U.S. Court of Appeals. He also served on a wide variety of panels and commissions in the 1970s and

1980s. In 1988, President Ronald Reagan nominated him to the U.S. Supreme Court.

Local Community Standards

As established in the 1973 case *Miller v. California,* this rule assists judges and legislators in deciding what is and what is not "obscene" in any particular locale.

Lord Campbell's Act

An informal name for Parliament's Obscene Publications Act of 1857, after the bill's sponsor.

Manton, Martin T.
(August 2, 1880–November 17, 1946)

Earned his law degree from Columbia University Law School in 1901 and worked in private practice until 1916. Nominated to the U.S. Federal District Court for the Southern District of New York in 1916 by President Woodrow Wilson. Resigned from that bench in 1918 to assume appointment to the U.S. Court of Appeals, Second Circuit. Resigned his seat on the Second Circuit in 1939, after being impeached for "selling justice."

Marshall, Thurgood
(July 2, 1908–January 24, 1993)

Earned his law degree from the Howard University School of Law in 1933. He then joined the legal division of the National Association for the Advancement of Colored People, where he proved a tireless worker on behalf of the rights of African Americans. He helped win twenty-nine victories in civil rights cases heard by the U.S. Supreme Court, including *Brown v. Board of Education of Topeka* (1954). In 1961, President John F. Kennedy nominated him to the Second Circuit of the U.S. Court of Appeals. In 1965, President Lyndon B. Johnson appointed him solicitor general of the United States, and in 1967, nominated him to the U.S. Supreme Court. Marshall was the Court's first African American justice.

Miller Test

Obscenity test established by the U.S. Supreme Court in *Miller v. California* (1973), which overturned a long line of previous Court decisions. It became the new standard guiding legislative and judicial decisionmaking.

Miller v. California, 413 U.S. 15 (1973)

Landmark 5–4 case that established a three-part standard to assist judges and legislators in identifying obscenity. It also reaffirmed the importance of "local community standards" in establishing obscenity.

Murphy, Frank (April 13, 1890–July 19, 1949)

Earned his law degree from the University of Michigan Law School, and served in the Army in World War I. After the war, he entered private practice in Detroit, Michigan. He served as an assistant U.S. district attorney in 1921–1922, then on the Recorders' Court from 1924 to 1930, and as mayor of Detroit from 1930 to 1933. President Franklin D. Roosevelt appointed him to serve as governor general and high commissioner of the Philippine Islands from 1933 to 1936. He was elected governor of Michigan in 1937. In 1939, after being defeated in a bid for reelection, he served briefly as U.S. attorney general. That same year, President Roosevelt appointed him to the U.S. Supreme Court. He took his seat on the Court in 1940.

Obscene Publications Act

A 1857 statute (20 and 21 Vict., c. 83) passed by Parliament in response to a perception of increased obscenity circulating in mid-nineteenth-century England. The first statutory restriction on obscenity.

Obscenity

The legal term for pornography—a contested area of jurisprudence in U.S. law and constitutionalism.

O'Connor, Sandra Day (March 26, 1930–)

Earned her law degree from Stanford University School of Law. She served as deputy county attorney of San Mateo County, California, from 1952 to 1953, and worked as a civilian attorney for the Quartermaster Market Center, Frankfurt, Germany, from 1954 to 1957. She then entered private practice in Arizona. In 1965, she became assistant attorney general of Arizona before being elected to the Arizona Senate, where she served two consecutive terms. In 1975, she was elected to the Maricopa County Superior Court. She served on that court until 1979, when she was appointed to the Arizona Court of Appeals. President Ronald Reagan appointed her to the U.S. Supreme Court in 1981.

Pornography

The depiction of erotic behavior (in words, images, film, or any other medium), intended to cause sexual excitement or offense.

Powell, Lewis Franklin, Jr.
(September 19, 1907–August 25, 1998)

Earned his law degree from the Harvard Law School in 1932. He entered private practice in Virginia and served in the Army Air Force during World War II. He became one of the most respected and admired lawyers of the 1950s and 1960s. Because of his reputation and his moderate stance on race relations, President Richard M. Nixon appointed him to the U.S. Supreme Court in 1971. Powell took his seat on the Court in 1972, and served until his retirement in 1987.

Regina v. Benjamin Hicklin, L.R. 3 Q.B. 360 (1868)

Landmark case that established the famous judicial standard known as the "*Hicklin* test," for determining what was and what was not obscene. The *Hicklin* test became the guiding rule in both Great Britain and the United States in the nineteenth century.

Rehnquist, William Hubbs (October 1, 1924–)

Earned his law degree from Stanford University School of Law. He worked as a law clerk to Associate Justice Robert H. Jackson during the 1951 and 1952 terms of the U.S. Supreme Court. He pursued private practice until 1969, when he became assistant attorney general in the Office of Legal Counsel. In late 1971, President Richard M. Nixon nominated him to the U.S. Supreme Court. Rehnquist took his seat on the Court in early 1972. In 1986, President Ronald Reagan nominated him as chief justice of the Supreme Court.

Roth Test

The 1957 test established by the U.S. Supreme Court in *Roth v. United States* to determine obscenity. This test was devised as a replacement for the discredited 1868 *Hicklin* test.

Roth v. United States, 354 U.S. 476 (1957)

Landmark case that marked the start of Associate Justice William J. Brennan's efforts to better define obscenity and to establish a single, national standard for doing so.

Sanford, Edward Terry (July 23, 1865–March 8, 1930)

Earned his law degree from the Harvard Law School and entered private practice in Tennessee. While practicing law, he also taught law at the University of Tennessee Law School until 1907. In 1906, he was appointed special assistant to the attorney general of the United States, and the following year, assistant attorney general. In 1908, he was appointed federal district judge for eastern and middle Tennessee, a post he held until 1923. President Warren G. Harding appointed him to the U.S. Supreme Court in 1923.

Scalia, Antonin (March 11, 1936–)

Earned his law degree from the Harvard Law School and was a Sheldon Fellow at Harvard in 1960–1961. He entered private practice. He was appointed a professor of law, first at the University of Virginia Law School and then at the University of Chicago Law School. He served in numerous administrative agencies, and from 1974 to 1977 acted as assistant attorney general for the Office of Legal Counsel. In 1982, he was appointed to the U.S. Court of Appeals, District of Columbia Circuit, where he served until President Ronald Reagan appointed him to the U.S. Supreme Court in 1986.

Shiras, George, Jr. (January 26, 1832–August 2, 1924)

Educated at Yale College, where he attended law school, Shiras entered private practice in Pennsylvania. He did not enter military service during the U.S. Civil War but instead remained with his growing law practice. His reputation for political independence and his friendship with President Benjamin Harrison led to his appointment as a justice of the U.S. Supreme Court in 1892, although he had no prior legislative or judicial experience. He retired in 1903.

Souter, David (September 17, 1939–)

After completing two years as a Rhodes Scholar at Magdalen College, Oxford University, he earned his law degree from the Harvard Law School. He entered private practice, and in 1966 became assistant attorney general of New Hampshire. In 1971, he became deputy attorney general of New Hampshire, and in 1976, attorney general of that state. In 1978, he became an associate justice of the Superior Court of New Hampshire, and in 1983, he was raised to the Supreme Court of New Hampshire. In 1990, he became a federal judge, joining the First Circuit of the U.S. Court of Appeals. In 1988, President Ronald Reagan nominated him as associate justice of the U.S. Supreme Court, and he was duly appointed to the post that same year.

Stevens, John Paul (April 20, 1920–)

Earned his law degree from Northwestern School of Law. After serving in the Navy during World War II, he served as a law clerk to Associate Justice Wiley Rutledge during the 1947 term. He entered private practice in Illinois, during which time he served on a variety of legal commissions. In 1970, he became a judge on the Seventh Circuit, U.S. Court of Appeals. In 1975, President Gerald Ford nominated him as associate justice of the U.S. Supreme Court.

Stewart, Potter (January 23, 1915–December 7, 1985)

Earned his law degree from Yale University School of Law in 1941. He had planned to enter private practice, but the attack on Pearl Harbor altered those plans, and instead he joined the Navy, where he remained for the duration of the war. After the war, he settled in Cincinnati, Ohio, where he built a thriving private practice. In 1954, President Dwight D. Eisenhower appointed him to the Sixth Circuit of the U.S. Court of Appeals. Four years later, President Eisenhower appointed him to the U.S. Supreme Court. He retired in 1981.

Telecommunications Act of 1996

The congressional statute establishing guidelines for the transmission of "obscenity" and "adult" materials over cable television systems, and under Title V (the Communications Decency Act), over the Internet.

Thomas, Clarence (June 23, 1948–)

Earned his law degree from Yale University School of Law in 1974 and became an assistant attorney of Missouri until 1977. He worked as an attorney with the Monsanto Company from 1977 to 1979, and then served as a legislative assistant to Senator John Danforth from 1979 to 1981. He was appointed assistant secretary for civil rights in the U.S. Department of Education, and from 1982 to 1990, chaired the U.S. Equal Employment Opportunity Commission. In 1990, he became a judge on the District of Columbia Circuit of the U.S. Court of Appeals. In 1991, he was nominated by President Ronald Reagan as associate justice of the U.S. Supreme Court, a post to which he was appointed that same year.

Ulysses Test

The obscenity test proposed by the Second Circuit of the U.S. Court of Appeals in *United States v. One Book Entitled* Ulysses *by James Joyce* (1934) as a replacement for the inadequate 1868 *Hicklin* test.

United States v. One Book Entitled Ulysses *by James Joyce,* 72 F.2d 705 (1934)

Landmark case that largely overturned the *Hicklin* test for obscenity in U.S. law and established a "whole work" standard for judging obscenity.

Warren, Earl (March 19, 1891–July 9, 1974)

Earned his law degree from the University of California, Berkeley. After serving briefly in the Army during World War I, he joined the prosecutor's office in Alameda County, California, where he served thirteen years as district attorney. In 1938, he was elected attorney general of California, and in 1942, he was elected governor of California. He ran as the Republican candidate for U.S. vice president in 1948, with Governor Thomas Dewey of New York. President Dwight D. Eisenhower nominated him as chief justice of the U.S. Supreme Court in 1953. He became the most important chief justice of the twentieth century, overseeing and encouraging enormous legal and constitutional changes. He resigned in 1969.

White, Byron Raymond (June 8, 1917–April 15, 2002)

After earning All-American honors in football at the University of Colorado in 1938 and completing a term as a Rhodes Scholar at Oxford University, he was hired to play professional football. He served in the U.S. Navy during World War II. He earned his law degree from Yale University School of Law in 1946, and then clerked for Associate Justice Fred M. Vincent during the 1946–1947 term. He then entered private practice. President John F. Kennedy appointed him assistant attorney general in 1961, and in 1962, nominated him for a seat on the U.S. Supreme Court. He retired from the Court in 1993.

Whole Work Standard

As established in the 1934 case of *United States v. One Book Entitled* Ulysses *by James Joyce,* this rule proposed that any work named in obscenity litigation should be considered in its entirety: No part of a work should be scrutinized for obscenity in isolation from the author's overall purpose and the total effect of the work.

Woolsey, John M. (January 3, 1877–May 4, 1945)

Earned his law degree from Columbia University Law School in 1901. He was the founder and first secretary of the *Columbia Law Review.* He entered private practice and established himself as an expert in Admiralty law. In 1929, President Herbert Hoover appointed him to the Federal District Court for the Southern District of New York. He retired from the bench in December 1943.

Chronology

1815	*Commonwealth v. Sharpless:* common-law procedures and rules.

1815   *Commonwealth v. Sharpless:* common-law procedures and rules.

1821   *Commonwealth v. Holmes:* common-law prosecution for publication and dissemination of a book.

1868   *Regina v. Hicklin:* establishment of the *Hicklin* rule for obscenity.

1877   *Ex parte Jackson:* use of the mail service to deliver obscenity.

1879   *United States v. Bennett:* adoption of the *Hicklin* rule in U.S. law.

1896   *Rosen v. United States:* upholds *Hicklin* rule and Comstock Act.

       Swearingen v. United States: political opinion cannot be prosecuted as obscenity.

1913   *United States v. Kennerley:* first questioning of legitimacy of the *Hicklin* rule.

1919   *Schenck v. United States; Abrams v. United States:* World War I restrictions on speech and press reviewed by the Supreme Court.

1925   *Gitlow v. New York:* announcement of the "*Gitlow* assumption" and the start of the incorporation of speech and press rights against both the states and the federal government.

1933   *United States v. One Book Called "Ulysses":* federal district court Judge John M. Woolsey challenges the *Hicklin* rule as a threat to the freedom of expression.

1934   *United States v. One Book Entitled* Ulysses *by James Joyce:* "whole work" rule stated by Judge Augustus Hand.

1936   *United States v. Levine:* application of the "whole work" rule.

1954   Justice Earl Warren becomes chief justice of the U.S. Supreme Court.

       Brown v. Board of Education handed down, the start of judicial liberalism.

1957   *Butler v. Michigan:* U.S. Supreme Court rejects the *Hicklin* rule.

       Kingsley Books v. Brown: state civil procedure to identify obscenity upheld.

       Roth v. United States: establishment of the "*Roth* rule" for defining obscenity.

1962   *Manual Enterprises v. Day:* discussion of the controversial *Roth* rule.

1964   *Jacobellis v. Ohio:* reversal of state obscenity conviction on the *Roth* rule.

1966   *Memoirs v. Massachusetts:* reversal of state obscenity conviction on the *Roth* rule.

1968   *Ginsberg v. New York:* state obscenity prosecution valid to prohibit such materials reaching children.

1969   *Stanley v. Georgia:* mere possession of obscenity is not a crime.

       Justice Warren retires and Warren Burger becomes chief justice; new directions for the Supreme Court.

1971   *United States v. Reidel: Stanley* ruling did not imply a right to send obscenity through the mail.

       United States v. Thirty-Seven Photographs: importation of obscenity constitutionally prohibited.

1973   *Miller v. California* ends use of the *Roth* rule and establishes the tripartite *Miller* rule for determining obscenity.

       Paris Adult Theatre I v. Slaton: application of the *Miller* rule.

1974   *Jenkins v. Georgia:* film not obscene under the *Miller* rule.

1976   *Young v. American Mini Theatres:* municipal ordinance aimed to scatter "adult" theatres upheld as constitutional.

1978   *Federal Communications Commission v. Pacifica Foundation:* FCC regulation can prohibit obscene speech from the radio to protect children and nonconsenting adults.

1985   *American Booksellers Association v. Hudnut:* an attempt to define obscenity as a violation of women's civil rights struck down as a violation of the freedom of expression.

1986   *City of Renton v. Playtime Theatres:* municipal ordinance to limit "adult" movie theaters within a certain distance of schools and churches upheld.

1989   *Sable Communications of California v. Federal Communications Commission:* prohibition of indecent telephone businesses such as the "dial-a-porn" telephone numbers struck down, but reasonable regulations upheld.

1996   *Denver Area Educational Telecommunications Consortium v. Federal Communications Commission:* aspects of a 1992 congressional regulation of cable television programming upheld in part and struck down in part.

1997   *Reno v. American Civil Liberties Union:* sections of the 1996 Communications Decency Act dealing with the Internet are struck down as abridging free speech.

2000   *United States v. Playboy Entertainment Group:* section of the Telecommunications Act of 1996 held to violate the First Amendment.

Table of Cases

Gitlow v. New York, 268 U.S. 652 (1925)

Gray v. Sanders, 372 U.S. 368 (1963)

Green v. County School Board of New Kent County, 391 U.S. 430 (1968)

Griswold v. Connecticut, 381 U.S. 479 (1965)

Jacobellis v. Ohio, 378 U.S. 184 (1964)

Jenkins v. Georgia, 418 U.S. 153 (1974)

Kingsley Books, Inc., et al. v. Brown, Corporation Counsel, 354 U.S. 436 (1957)

Kingsley International Pictures Corporation v. Regents of the University of New York, 360 U.S. 684 (1959)

Manual Enterprises, Inc., et al. v. J. Edward Day, Postmaster General, 370 U.S. 478 (1962)

Marcus v. Search Warrant, 367 U.S. 717 (1968)

Miller v. California, 413 U.S. 15 (1973)

Milliken v. Bradley, 418 U.S. 717 (1974)

Miranda v. Arizona, 384 U.S. 436 (1966)

Paris Adult Theatre I et al. v. Slaton, District Attorney, et al., 413 U.S. 49 (1973)

Regina v. Benjamin Hicklin, Law Reporter 3 Q.B. 360 (1868)

Reno v. American Civil Liberties Union, 521 U.S. 844 (1997)

Reynolds v. Sims, 377 U.S. 533 (1964)

Roe v. Wade, 410 U.S. 113 (1973)

Rosen v. United States, 161 U.S. 29 (1896)

Roth v. United States and *Alberts v. California*, 354 U.S. 476 (1957)

Sable Communications of California, Inc. v. Federal Communications Commission et al., 492 U.S. 115 (1989)

Schenck v. United States, 249 U.S. 47 (1919)

Smith v. California, 361 U.S. 147 (1959)

Stanley v. Georgia, 394 U.S. 557 (1969)

Stromberg v. California, 283 U.S. 359 (1931)

Swann v. Charlotte-Mecklenberg County Board of Education, 402 U.S. 1 (1970)

Swearingen v. United States, 161 U.S. 446 (1896)

Teitel Film Corporation v. Cusack, 390 U.S. 139 (1968)

Times Film Corporation v. Chicago, 365 U.S. 43 (1961)

United States v. Bennett, 24 F.Cas. 1093 (1879)

United States v. Kennerley, 209 F. 119 (1913)

United States v. Levine, 83 F.2d 156 (1936)

United States v. One Book Called "Ulysses," 5 F.Supp. 182 (1933)

Annotated Bibliography

Alexander, Donald. *The Politics of Pornography.* Chicago: University of Chicago Press, 1989.

    Assesses how the justices of the U.S. Supreme Court, judges of the state courts and lower federal judiciary, federal and state legislators, and the wide variety of interest groups concerned about obscenity have interacted and helped to shape public policies regarding obscenity.

Bates, Anna Louise. *Weeder in the Garden of the Lord: Anthony Comstock's Life and Career.* Lanham, MD: University Press of America, 1995.

    A solid biography of the most important nineteenth-century reformer concerned with social morality.

Beisel, Nicola Kay. *Imperiled Innocents: Anthony Comstock and Family Reproduction in Victorian America.* Princeton: Princeton University Press, 1997.

    The most complete assessment of Anthony Comstock and his self-appointed mission to maintain traditional moral standards in the United States.

Boyer, Paul S. *Purity in Print: The Vice-Society Movement and Book Censorship in America.* New York: Charles Scribner's Sons, 1968.

    A classic but aging examination of moral purity movements and their concerns about obscenity in American culture. Reviews the actions of Anthony Comstock and describes the motivations of anti-vice reformers and book censors through the 1960s.

Broun, Heywood. *Anthony Comstock: Roundsman of the Lord.* New York: Literary Guild of America, 1927.

    The oldest biography of Anthony Comstock. Although more recent accounts have give vastly different interpretations of the man and his mission, this book remains good background reading.

Burnham, John C. *Bad Habits: Drinking, Smoking, Taking Drugs, Gambling, Sexual Misbehavior, and Swearing in American History.* New York: New York University Press, 1993.

A highly original interpretation of the cultural changes that swept across the United States in the course of the twentieth century. Burnham argues that as the century wore on, an inversion of values occurred—that is, what had been considered immoral (e.g., smoking and other so-called minor vices) became normal.

Clor, Harry. *Obscenity and Public Morality*. Chicago: University of Chicago Press, 1969.

One of the best-known and most influential examinations of obscenity and liberty. Clor fully supports the loosening of restrictions on obscenity in the era of the Warren Court.

The Committee of Fifteen. *The Social Evil, with Special Reference to Conditions Existing in the City of New York*. New York: G. P. Putnam's Sons, 1902; reprint ed., New York: Garland, 1979.

One of the classic municipal vice reports of the early twentieth century. Argues that society's only real choice for the control of immorality is the repression of prostitution and other vices.

Copp, David, and Susan Wendell, eds. *Pornography and Censorship*. Buffalo, NY: Prometheus Books, 1983.

A collection of in-depth scholarly articles investigating various aspects of the obscenity issue.

Cray, Ed. *Chief Justice: A Biography of Earl Warren*. New York: Simon & Schuster, 1997.

An important biography, the most recent on the twentieth century's most important and controversial chief justice of the U.S. Supreme Court.

Curtis, Michael Kent. *Free Speech, "The People's Darling Privilege": Struggles for Freedom of Expression in American History*. New York: Oxford University Press, 2000.

Best modern survey of the origins of free speech and press in the United States. Traces the concept of freedom of expression from colonial times through the middle of the nineteenth century.

Downs, Donald Alexander. *The New Politics of Pornography*. Chicago: University of Chicago Press, 1989.

Examines how the issue of pornography has been debated and how the debates have shaped the varied public policies on pornography.

Easton, Susan M. *The Problem of Pornography: Regulation and the Right to Free Speech*. London: Routledge, 1994.

Provides an interpretation of the tensions between regulating pornography in a culture and the threat to free speech that such regulation necessarily entails.

Ernst, Morris L., and Alan U. Schwartz. *Censorship: The Search for the Obscene*. New York: Macmillan, 1964.

An older but still useful examination of the problem of obscenity. Assesses the Supreme Court's *Roth* decision, and supports the actions of the Warren Court to ease the restrictions on obscenity.

Griffith, Kathryn. *Judge Learned Hand and the Role of the Judiciary*. Norman: University of Oklahoma Press, 1973.

An able examination of one of the most important lower federal judges of the twentieth century.

Gunther, Gerald. *Learned Hand: The Man and the Judge*. New York: Knopf, 1994.

The most modern and best treatment of this most important federal judge in the lower federal courts during the twentieth century.

Hixson, Richard F. *Pornography and the Justices: The Supreme Court and the Intractable Obscenity Problem*. Carbondale: Southern Illinois University Press, 1996.

An important and subtle examination of the problem of obscenity and the jurisprudence of obscenity. Provides the most thorough legal and philosophical examination of the issue and argues for a less restrictive public policy on pornography.

Hunt, Lynn, ed. *The Invention of Pornography: Obscenity and the Origins of Modernity, 1500–1800*. New York: Zone Books, 1993.

A collection of interpretive articles that examine in depth the development of the concept of pornography in early modern Western Europe.

Hunter, Ian, David Sauders, and Dugald Williamson. *On Pornography: Literature, Sexuality and Obscenity Law*. New York: St. Martin's Press, 1993.

Surveys and examines the problems that pornography regulations present for belles lettres, especially for the literary exploration and portrayal of sexuality.

Kelly, Alfred H., et al. *The American Constitution: Its Origins and Development*. 7th ed. New York: W. W. Norton, 1991.

Best textbook survey of U.S. constitutional history. Examines the gamut of constitutional and legal issues that have confronted policymakers.

Kendrick, Walter. *The Secret Museum: Pornography in Modern Culture*. Berkeley: University of California Press, 1996.

An analysis of the concept of "pornography" and the development of pornography in England and the United States over time.

Kobylka, Joseph F. *The Politics of Obscenity: Group Litigation in a Time of Legal Change*. Westport, CT: Greenwood Press, 1991.

A creative analysis of small interest group behavior, the obscenity issue, and the resort to the state and federal courts to provide rules and guidelines for dealing with this volatile social issue.

Lamb, Charles M., and Stephen H. Halpern, eds. *The Burger Court: Political and Judicial Profiles.* Champaign: University of Illinois Press, 1991.

   One of the best treatments of the obscenity jurisprudence of the U.S. Supreme Court under Chief Justice Warren Burger.

Latham, Robert, and William Matthews, eds. *The Diary of Samuel Pepys, IX, 1668–1669.* Berkeley: University of California Press, 1976.

   The definitive reprint edition of this important seventeenth-century diary, offering innumerable insights into early modern English history.

Leuchtenburg, William E. *A Troubled Feast: American Society since 1945.* Boston: Little, Brown, 1979.

   An insightful overview of the history of the United States since World War II, written by one of the twentieth century's most important historians.

MacKinnon, Catharine A., and Andrea Dworkin, eds. *In Harm's Way: The Pornography Civil Rights Hearings.* Cambridge, MA: Harvard University Press, 1997.

   Collected transcripts of testimonies by feminists in various U.S. cities, arguing that pornography is a threat to the civil rights and civil liberties of all women and therefore should be eliminated.

Matusow, Alan J. *The Unraveling of America.* New York: Harper & Row, 1984.

   A subtle and interesting critical examination of the tumultuous events of the 1960s in the United States and their long-term significance for American society and culture.

Moulton, Ian Frederick. *Before Pornography: Erotic Writing in Early Modern England.* New York: Oxford University Press, 2000.

   Interprets some of the earliest and most controversial writings and literature dealing with sexual themes and issues in English culture.

Murphy, Paul L. *World War I and the Origins of Civil Liberties in the United States.* New York: W. W. Norton, 1979.

   The best examination of the origins of speech and press liberties as a Supreme Court concern from 1919 forward. Traces this concern as a reaction to the policies of the Woodrow Wilson administration during World War I, such as the Sedition Act of 1917.

Nelson, Marcia. *The Remarkable Hands: An Affectionate Portrait.* New York: Foundation of the Federal Bar Council, 1983.

   A dual biography of cousins Augustus and Learned Hand, two of the most important lower federal judges in the twentieth-century United States.

Polenberg, Richard. *Fighting Faiths: The Abrams Case, the Supreme Court, and Free Speech.* New York: Penguin, 1987.

   An outstanding analysis of one of the earliest U.S. Supreme Court free speech and press cases, *Abrams v. United States* (1919).

Powe, Lucas A., Jr. *The Warren Court and American Politics.* Cambridge, MA: Belknap Press at Harvard University, 2000.

An even-handed treatment of the Supreme Court of Chief Justice Earl Warren and its innovations in legal and constitutional interpretation.

Rembar, Charles. *The End of Obscenity: The Trials of Lady Chatterly, Tropic of Cancer, and Fanny Hill.* New York: Random House, 1968.

An interesting first-person account of the obscenity cases of the 1960s, written by a leading lawyer and challenger of state and federal restrictions on obscenity.

Schauer, Frederick F. *The Law of Obscenity.* Washington, DC: Bureau of National Affairs, 1976.

A general reference that provides a comprehensive overview of obscenity as a legal and social problem.

Schwartz, Bernard. *The Ascent of Pragmatism: The Burger Court in Action.* Reading, MA: Addison-Wesley, 1990.

A useful interpretation of the Supreme Court of Chief Justice Warren Burger, detailing how the Supreme Court changed direction after the controversial Warren Court era of the 1950s and 1960s.

———, ed. *The Warren Court: A Retrospective.* New York: Oxford University Press, 1993.

A useful and even-handed interpretation of the motives, achievements, and shortcomings of this most controversial Supreme Court in U.S. history.

Schwartz, Joel. *Fighting Poverty with Virtue: Moral Reform and America's Urban Poor, 1825–2000.* Bloomington: Indiana University Press, 2000.

Examines various public policy approaches for dealing with the urban poor in the United States. Argues that efforts to instill values commonly regarded as virtuous in the poor have not been as effective as some social reformers have claimed.

Urofsky, Melvin I. *The Continuity of Change: The Supreme Court and Individual Liberties, 1953–1986.* Belmont, CA: Wadsworth, 1991.

A friendly examination of the Warren Court and the changes it fostered in American culture through its approach to criminal law and obscenity.

Urofsky, Melvin I., and Paul Finkelman. *A March of Liberty: A Constitutional History of the United States.* 2nd ed. New York: Oxford University Press, 2002.

A textbook surveying the range of constitutional and legal problems that have confronted U.S. policymakers at various periods.

White, G. Edward. *Earl Warren: A Public Life.* New York: Oxford University Press, 1982.

A highly accessible and laudatory biography of U.S. Supreme Court Chief Justice Earl Warren. Credits Warren and his Court with helping create a more just and open society.

Index

About the Author

Thomas C. Mackey is an associate professor and chair of the History Department at the University of Louisville.